MOBS, MESSIAHS, AND MARKETS

Surviving the Public Spectacle in Finance and Politics

WILLIAM BONNER
LILA RAJIVA

BICENTENNIAL
1807
WILEY
2007
BICENTENNIAL

John Wiley & Sons, Inc.

Published by John Wiley & Sons, Inc., Hoboken, New Jersey.
Published simultaneously in Canada.

Wiley Bicentennial Logo: Richard J. Pacifico.

For general information on our other products and services or for technical support, please contact our Customer Care Department within the United States at (800) 762-2974, outside the United States at (317) 572-3993 or fax (317) 572-4002.

Wiley also publishes its books in a variety of electronic formats. Some content that appears in print may not be available in electronic formats. For more information about Wiley products, visit our Web site at www.wiley.com.

Library of Congress Cataloging-in-Publication Data:

Bonner, William, 1948–
  Mobs, messiahs, and markets : surviving the public spectacle in finance and politics / William Bonner and Lila Rajiva.
    p. cm.
  ISBN 978-0-470-11232-8 (cloth)
   1. Finance—Corrupt practices.   2. Political corruption.   3. Collective behavior.
4. Delusions.   5. Right and wrong.   I. Rajiva, Lila.   II. Title.   III. Title: Surviving the public spectacle in finance and politics.
  HG173.B64 2007
  658.4'73—dc22
                                                                              2007012349

Printed in the United States of America.

10 9 8 7 6 5 4 3 2 1

FOREWORD

Mobs, Messiahs, and Markets by Bill Bonner and Lila Rajiva will never earn a Nobel Prize in economics. Why? Because this book is highly readable, makes sense, and does not contain the usual incomprehensible mumbo jumbo one finds in other financial and economic books. *Mobs, Messiahs, and Markets* makes very complex economic, social, and geopolitical issues understandable to normal people like you and me. What Barbara Tuchman did by writing informative and absorbing history books, Bonner and Rajiva do with this highly entertaining book written for the general public to help people understand politics and finance.

But who would have the time to read this close-to 400 page book? These days, most people are happy to gain knowledge and become informed about everything everywhere in the world from 30-second shots on TV news channels! Still, in my opinion they would be making a grave error if they did not find the time to read *Mobs, Messiahs, and Markets.*

Here is why. Books should be read for one or both of two reasons. Since reading is physically and mentally rather demanding, I obviously want to read a book that is informative, increases my knowledge, and is thought provoking. Otherwise, why bother? The other reason I would want to read a book is for pure enjoyment. Either the authors capture my attention through the complex plot of a thriller or a tragic drama or they do it through their superb command of the English language and their ability to make me laugh.

Well, I read the manuscript of this book on flights from Bangkok to Ho Chi Minh City, from Ho Chi Minh City to Singapore, from Singapore to Shanghai, and from Shanghai to Dubai, and I read it on China Beach in Vietnam. On each of those flights, people were staring at me, because I would repeatedly burst out laughing. *Mobs, Messiahs, and Markets* is one of the funniest and most entertaining books I have ever read. But, besides that, Bonner and Rajiva are also accomplished and honest historians who expose the dangerous conspiracy engineered with lies and deception by American elites, politicians, Wall Street, and the U.S. Federal Reserve, whose effect is to shift wealth from the middle and working classes to the elites and their cronies.

Referring to the eroding purchasing power of the U.S. dollar, Bonner and Rajiva note that even as the Federal Reserve increased the quantity of banknotes, the quality of the notes declined. The problem, they argue, is that while political power is in Washington and financial power lies in New York, the real power is where the two come together in the Federal Reserve system. And while the Fed may have been chartered to protect the currency, its new job is only to get the politicians reelected and keep the money flowing in order to give people the impression that they are economically better off. Not surprisingly, Bonner and Rajiva have a low opinion of central bankers. Modern central banking, like bank robbing, is a nefarious métier, they write. But while Bonnie and Clyde's crimes were obvious and deplorable, a central banker is often confused with an honest man.

In the world of finance, there are thousands of books on how to value stocks and on technical analysis, currencies, commodities, bonds, and macroeconomics; but there are hardly any books that capture the zeitgeist of gigantic financial excesses. Edwin Lefèvre's *Reminiscences of a Stock Operator*, based on the life of the legendary Jesse Livermore, was an enormously popular book that became a classic about the investment mania of the late 1920s. I predict that *Mobs, Messiahs, and Markets* will in time become as much a classic for the student of the current period in history, because it combines so many interesting aspects of psychology, politics, and finance into a captivating narrative. I am confident that the first edition of this book will command a high price among collectors of rare books in the future and that your children will one day shake their heads and wonder how today's generation could have been so badly deceived by blatant lies, would-be reformers, military messiahs, and world improvers.

In fact, *Mobs, Messiahs, and Markets* is such an excellent book that if I had to name just one book investors should read, this is the one I would select.

MARC FABER

ACKNOWLEDGMENTS

Writing a book is hard enough. Writing a book with someone else is even harder. And it ought not to be possible at all when one of the authors is running a multimillion-dollar publishing business from London and Paris and the other is wandering the globe with her laptop.

As it turned out, it was not only possible but a lot of fun. Despite time zones often a day apart, treacherous Net connections, and plenty of friendly tussling over everything from financial flows in India to Latin American politicians, we found enough common ground to write a book that takes on the "public spectacle" in politics and the market today. Ours is the home inspector's report on the wormy wreck of government policies and prescriptions that experts and ideologues are selling us.

The book is put together from joint and individual writing we did over the past year or two. Some of it has appeared online; some has not. John Mauldin speaks for many fans in calling Bill the best pure writer in the financial business. In some sections—such as the ones on finance—it's more of Bill; in others—such as the ones on globalization and propaganda—it's more of Lila. Everywhere else, we are equally culpable.

As with any book, there are people whose help we want to acknowledge. On Bill's side, there was Claire Lamotte from the Agora office in Paris, who helped with proofing. On Lila's end, as always, she owes everything to her parents, Adolf and Sylvia Walter, and to her brothers, Noel and David, for their endless support and encouragement.

Finally, both of us want to acknowledge Addison Wiggin, Mike Ward, and Danielle Morino at Agora for the marketing of this book, Jean Hanke for logistical help, our agent Theron Raines for his advice, and the team at John Wiley & Sons—Debra Englander, Mary Daniello, Greg Friedman, and Stacey Small—for their work putting together the manuscript.

Do we have any prescription at the end of it all? No—if that means suggesting what we ought to do. Yes—if it means suggesting what we ought *not* to do. And what we ought *not* to do—as the Good Book tells us—is clear: We ought not to put our faith in princes and powers; we ought not to be taken in by the "public spectacle."

WILLIAM BONNER
LILA RAJIVA

CONTENTS

PART FIVE: THE BUBBLE KINGS

PART SIX: FAR FROM THE MADDING MOB

Part One

A Critique of Impure Reason

CHAPTER 1

DO-GOODERS
GONE BAD

All reformers are bachelors.
—**George Moore**

It is a shame that the world improvers don't set off some signal before they go bad, like a fire alarm that is running out of juice. Maybe some adjustment could be made. Instead, the most successful of them—such as Benito Mussolini and Adolf Hitler—actually gain market share as they get worse. Their delusions are self-reinforcing, like the delusions of a stock market bubble; the higher prices go, the more people come to believe they make sense.

The do-gooders who never catch on, of course, are hopeless from the get-go. Take poor Armin Meiwes. The man thought he had a solution to the problems of poverty and overpopulation. He was, no doubt, discussing his program with Bernard Brandes just before the two cut off Brandes' most private part and ate it. Then, wouldn't you know it, Brandes died, either as a result of blood loss from the butchering or as a consequence of Meiwes slitting his throat. And then the press made a big stink about it, branding Meiwes the "Cannibal of Rotenburg." But Meiwes was not merely a pervert; he was an activist.

"We could solve the problem of overpopulation and famine at a stroke," said he, according to testimony in the *Times of London*. "The third world is really ripe for eating." But wait, a fellow omnivore thought he saw a flaw in Meiwes' utopia: "If we make cannibalism into the norm, then everyone will start eating each other and there will be nobody left." "That's why I'm not keen on eating women," replied Meiwes.[1]

It seems never to have occurred to either of them that just *perhaps* not everyone would want to be eaten. Or that maybe people would find being eaten even less desirable than having to stand in line or drive around looking for a parking space or the other symptoms of what they took to be planetary overcrowding. Still, anthropophagy might have solved the problems of overpopulation and undernourishment in a single slice. And if his recipe for planetary improvement had not been interrupted by the *polizei*, who knows what might have happened?

But now the poor fellow is in the hoosegow making do with hamburger. The same thing happened to another of the world's do-gooders gone bad, Saddam Hussein. We don't know much about the Butcher of Baghdad, but his defense was little different from that of all ex-dictators—he thought he was building a better world. Iraq is, after all, a wild and wacky place, with different tribes and religious groups ready to cut each other's throats. At least that was Saddam's story. Without his firm leadership, he claimed, the country would have been a mess. We think of another great world improver, Il Duce, a clown who thrashed around in typical do-gooder claptrap, looking for a theme that would bring him to power. When he finally got into office, he found a new program better suited to his ambitions: Put on silly uniforms. Strut around telling the masses that you're recreating the glory of ancient Rome. Spend a lot of money. So many people came to admire the man that he began to think himself admirable and to believe that his program might actually work as advertised. Then, he invaded Abyssinia ... and the bull market in Benito Mussolini was over.

BLUE BLOODS IN BLACK SHIRTS

But while Mussolini's star was on the rise, it claimed some strange followers. One of the strangest was carried away, with thousands of other old people, in the unusually long, hot summer of 2003—Diana Mitford. She was the woman who married Oswald Mosley, and at their wedding in 1936 were some of the most important people of the age, notably Adolf Hitler and Joseph Goebbels.[2]

Of all the stupidities into which a man can fall, the stupidity that Oswald Mosley launched headlong into was one that was especially vile. With money supplied by Mussolini, he organized Britain's "Blackshirts," an organization much like the Nazis in Germany. National Socialism was supposed to be the wave of the future, but Mosley's group couldn't seem to come up with anything more original than going into London's East End and beating up Jews. Most Englishmen were appalled. When World War II broke out, the Mosleys were interned as security risks. Though they were set free after the war was over, they were told to get out of town. They then joined their best friends, the Duke and Duchess of Edinburgh, in France, where they lived out their remaining days. Diana herself lasted into her 90s.

Diana was not only smart; she was among the world's great beauties. She was said to be the prettiest of the Mitford sisters, which was tough competition, and even in her 90s, she posed for *Vogue* magazine and she still looked good. She was "the most divine adolescent I have ever beheld: a goddess, more immaculate, more perfect, more celestial than Botticelli's sea-borne Venus," wrote a friend.[3]

Really, it is almost too bad she wasn't dumb. She might have glided through life and been a joy to all who saw her. Instead, she married badly . . . which is to say, she fell in love with Mosley, who was an idiot, and threw her lot in with him. Later, British counterespionage agents came to see her as the greater threat. "The real public danger is her," said a report. "She is much more intelligent and more dangerous than her husband."[4]

Of course, she was not the only one of the Mitford sisters to go bad. They were almost all too smart for their own good. Their synapses fired right, left, and overtime . . . and took them in strange directions. Sister Unity, like Diana, took up with the Nazis. Sister Jessica took an equally radical course, but in a different direction; she became a Marxist. It seems as though a smart person will go along with almost anything, no matter how preposterous. "I don't understand," said Lord Redesdale, father of the Mitford girls. "I am normal, my wife is normal, but my daughters are each more foolish than the other."[5]

While Hitler was praising Diana and Unity as "perfect specimens of Aryan womanhood," the other sister, Jessica, known in the family as Decca, was plotting to buy a handgun with which to kill the Führer. But it was Unity who actually used a pistol—on herself. She shot herself in the head and died in 1948. What had become of the sweet little girls raised in Swinbrook? How could normal people produce such extraordinary characters? How could such divine little angels turn mad?

We have no ready answer. But a friend tells us of a book by Riccardo Orizio, an Italian journalist, who hunted down and interviewed former dictators. Dead ones, of course, did no talking, but a surprising number seem to remain among the quick. His book, *Talk of the Devil: Encounters with Seven Dictators*, includes conversations with Idi Amin; Jean Bedel Bokassa; Wojciech Jaruzelski; Nexhmije Hoxha (who, with her husband Enver, ruled Albania for nearly 50 years until his death); Jean-Claude (Baby Doc) Duvalier; and Mengitsu Haile Mariam, the Marxist-Leninist dictator of Ethiopia.[6]

What is clear from the conversations is that they are all as mad as Diana and Oswald Mosley. Yet they all insist that whatever evil they may have done—mass murder, starvation, grand larceny—they were only making the world a better place. And none of them regretted or repented anything, except for the tactical "mistakes" that got them booted out of their countries eventually.

At least Diana Mitford Mosley had no blood on her hands. And, after four decades of peer pressure, she did finally admit that her wedding guests were not the nicest folks you could have to a party. "We all know he was a monster, that he was very cruel and did terrible things," she said of Hitler in 1994. "But that doesn't alter the fact that he was obviously an interesting figure. No torture on Earth would get me to say anything different."[7]

Diana Mitford Mosley—may she Rest In Peace . . .

WORLD IMPROVERS

The trouble with the big wide world is that it is never quite good enough for some people. They keep trying to improve it. No harm in that; you should always try to make your world a better place. Wink at a homely girl, perhaps, or curse a bad driver. But the world improvers are rarely content with private acts of kindness. Instead, they want gas chambers and Social Security—vast changes almost always brought about at the point of a gun. Thus it was that central banks were set up and given the power to control what doesn't belong to them—your money. Thus it came to be that we got regularly felt up by strangers at airports—and thought it normal.

Today's newspapers ooze world improvements. A single day's issue of the *New York Times*—an especially earnest journal—brings forth a plague of them. On the editorial page one day is "A Proposal to End Poverty." The proposal is made by world-class world improver, Jeffrey Sachs, who urges rich nations to rob their own citizens so that the money might be turned over to poor nations.[8]

While the *New York Times* merely dreams of ending poverty, our favorite columnist, Thomas L. Friedman, joins our president in wanting to "rid the world of evildoers." We are not making this up; this was George W. Bush's own line. Bush, Tony Blair, and Friedman are hoping that the forced conversion of the Iraqis—to democracy—will squeeze out a little more evil from the planet.[9]

When it comes to resisting the temptations of world improvement, married men, especially those with teenage children, have a great advantage. They are too busy trying to earn a living to pose much of a threat to anyone. And when they are not actually working, they have family tensions to arbitrate, tempers to calm, lightbulbs to change, and doorknobs to fix. There is something about domestic life that tames a man . . . brings him down to earth . . . and keeps him tethered and modest. If he is ever tempted to think he knows something, he has his wife and children to remind him how wrong he is.

The single man, on the other hand, is a desperado. Adolf Hitler and Joseph Stalin were, effectively, single. So was Alexander the

Great. They had no private lives; they had perforce to make public spectacles of themselves. The single man still feels the need to be a conqueror—of women or of men—by seduction or by brute force. That is why the public generally elects family men to high office; they don't trust the lone wolf. That may be one reason why George W. Bush—a married man—is likely to be denied the success that more notorious, and single, world improvers have had.

Take Alexander the Great, for instance. The American public learned all it needed to know about Alexander in 2004, when the Oliver Stone film first hit the screen. The scenery is fabulous—mountains, deserts, the Hanging Gardens of Babylon. There are extravagant battle scenes, Persian war chariots running through the Greeks' battle squares, elephant charges in the Indus valley.... Oliver Stone has done what we thought almost impossible. Using all of this and all the tricks of the filmmaker's art, he has produced a boring film. Not that it is a bad flick. Not at all. It would take a new script, a new cast, and a whole new shooting to get the level up to "bad." As it stands, it is merely pathetic. The only thing impressive about it is the ability of two of the leading actors to say the most absurd things without smiling. Alexander, for example, looks up toward the heavens and dreamily explains that he is conquering the whole Middle East in the name of "liberty." Readers will remark that George W. Bush does and says similar things. Neoconservatives even think they see a bit of Alexander in the American president—perhaps the curl of his hair, the cut of his jaw, or the humbug of his palaver. Maybe so. But we had hoped for more. Art should never be as dull and dim-witted as real life.

Invading Afghanistan and Iraq, Americans are following in the Macedonian's footprints. In fact, it is hard to go anywhere in the Middle East without tramping on one of Alexander's trails. In the spring of 334 B.C., for instance, Alexander's army crossed the Hellespont into what is today Turkey. What an adventure! Battles, jewels, women, strong drink, new and exotic places—what man could ask for more? The route was long—all the way to Libya and then over to the Indus river. But the poor man died less than 10 years after leaving

Greece, brought down not by the Iraqis or the Afghanis of the time, but by fever. Alexander had won every major battle, but he was a dead man at 33.

In the scene that is most memorable—because it is so bad—this ersatz Alexander turns his face to the sky and dreams of a better world . . . while his friend dies on the bed next to him. Like all world improvers ever since, the only better world Alexander could see was the reflection of his own face.

Just as Alexander wanted to remake Babylon into a Greek city, the new conquerors, two millennia later, try to turn Baghdad into an Anglo-American one. They want the Iraqis to "reform" their government. What the do-gooders mean is they want it made more like theirs. Private acts of charity or innovation that might actually make the world better are of little interest to the world improvers. They propose a ban on world hunger—without planting a single turnip. They take up the cause of "freedom" in other countries—and force the liquor store next door to close on Sunday. They insist so strongly on better treatment for women in the Islamic world, they forget to kiss their own wives.

Another *New York Times* columnist, David Brooks, is not content with poverty eradication and forced conversion to democracy. From this day forward, said Brooks, just after a State of the Union address in which George W. Bush had announced his aim of "ending tyranny in our world," the American president "will not be able to have warm relations" with dictators.[10]

We don't know what air Mr. Brooks breathes, but we suggest he open a window. He may be in need of oxygen. Already the U.S. president has sworn off drinks; if he swears off dictators as well, he will be as worthless, indeed as positively dangerous, in foreign affairs as Woodrow Wilson was. As for ending tyranny, Mr. Bush might just as well have pledged to ban bad taste . . . or ugliness . . . or death itself. In the contest between tyranny and George W. Bush, we have seen no odds. But we wouldn't put our money on the president. Mr. Bush has had only seven years of practice in high office. Tyranny has been rehearsing for centuries.

But while the President and his merry band of freedom fighters may claim they are jousting on behalf of democracy, it is not really the vote that they want to spread so much as their own favorite vision. After all, Hitler won elections. So did Mussolini. And Genghis Khan . . . and even Montezuma. No, what the world improvers want is a globe as familiar as their own boudoirs. If other people have other tastes and other ideas, well, they must be uneducated . . . or evil. Brooks claims, "It's the ideals that matter." He means *his own* ideals, of course. What he objects to are other people's ideals . . . and, as long as he has more firepower on his side, he doesn't mind forcing the issue.

Of course, ideals *do* matter. Honesty, integrity, honor, love, service, dignity, frugality, industry, self-discipline, charity—these are the qualities that make the world a better place. Brooks' ideals, on the other hand, are merely excuses for vain meddling. If an election is held in Iraq, will the world be a better place? No one knows. What really moves the world improvers is vanity; and what makes them odious is that they give in to it so readily.

STILL TRYING TO HUSTLE THE EAST

But, even in a whole nation of hallucinators, the grandeur of *New York Times* editorialist Thomas L. Friedman's follies stand out. Take that column in which he complained about "America's Failure of Imagination." In it, Friedman imagined Osama bin Laden as "a combination of Charles Manson and Jack Welch"—an evil personality, but with organizational skills. "We Americans can't imagine such evil," said Friedman. "We keep reverting to our natural, naively optimistic selves."[11]

Actually, at the time he wrote it, Americans were showing signs not of a lack of imagination, but of imagination run wild. Nuns and Girl Scouts were being patted down in airports all across the country. Penny loafers were being x-rayed. Tech stocks were selling at 60 times earnings . . . and U.S. Treasury bonds, at par. Americans had come to believe the most extraordinary things—not only that their soldiers could create American-style democracy in ancient Mesopotamia, but that they themselves could borrow and spend as much as they wanted, as long as they wanted, without ever having to pay anyone anything back. And Friedman himself seemed to have a full tank of imagination.

Still, according to our gassed-up columnist, the 39,000 employees of the National Security Agency and the hundreds of thousands of Central Intelligence Agency (CIA) employees, police, Homeland Security staff, and soldiers were not enough for America's imagining needs. "We need an 'Office of Evil,'" he urged, "whose job would be to constantly sift all intelligence data and imagine what the most twisted mind might be up to."[12]

Friedman went on to blame the Bush administration for "squandering all the positive feeling in America after September 11, particularly among Americans who wanted to be drafted for a great project."

What great project?

How about "a Manhattan project for energy independence . . . to wean us gradually off oil imports"?

Not only is there a shortage of imagination among America's security forces, but money is short, too. A billion dollars a week was the cost of the Iraq adventure at the time. But even that was not enough for Friedman. "Building a nation on the cheap," said he, wouldn't work. How he had come to know what it cost to build a nation is anyone's guess. No bids had been let, nor had any nation ever actually been put together by another. What did it cost to build China, or France, or Canada? In every case, the job was done by the people of the country themselves, stumbling toward it over the course of many, many years.

But Friedman was in a hot sweat of war fever. As one of the biggest backers of war against Iraq, he urged the Bush administration every week to plunge in deeper. One of his columns even began with the shocking announcement that "The U.S. and France Are Now At War."[13] What stirred his delirium in this instance was French president Jacques Chirac's plan for straightening out the Iraq situation.

Chirac's was an absurd plan, perhaps, but compared to Friedman's suggestions, it was almost reasonable. We were in Paris at the time and noticed that the French took the war news calmly. Women walked down the street in light, filmy dresses, admiring the new fall fashions in the shop windows . . . businessmen and saloon keepers went about their daily chores. They seemed unaware that Friedman was urging an attack.

The problem with real war, you see, is that people get killed. Friedman was ready to send the troops off to do his errands, but when the boys came back flat, the columnist could not bear to open the bags and look the poor dead grunts in the face. He would rather imagine his soldiers as they have never been and as no serious man would ever want to see them—dressed up in black turtlenecks with Birkenstocks on their feet and glasses of chardonnay in their hands.

American soldiers are not in Iraq as conquerors or warriors, writes Friedman. Instead, they're idealists sent, alas, by a "non-healing administration" on the "most important liberal, revolutionary U.S. democracy-building project since the Marshall Plan." "Nurturing," says the cuddly Friedman, "that is our real goal in Iraq."[14]

Readers must have gasped for air. The largest, most sophisticated and most lethal military force ever assembled—at a cost of, what, a quarter of a trillion dollars—was sent to "nurture" the desert tribes?

Hardly a week went by in the early years of the third millennium in which Friedman did not come up with yet another mind-boggling idea. In February 2005, for instance, he told readers of a scheme that had originated with his wife, Ann: "Free parking anywhere in America for anyone driving a hybrid car."[15] The specifics of this diktat were, as usual, not spelled out. We doubt that he would like us to park our old pickup in his garage free of charge, or on the White House lawn at any price.

Nor do we yet know what he meant by "hybrid car." A cross between a Volvo and a hyena? The fruit of the union of an SUV with a Greyhound bus? We presume he was talking about a mixture of gasoline and electric power . . .

So many humbugs, dear reader, and so little time.

We would not normally waste our time explaining why a columnist's proposal is lame and preposterous. It seems enough to hold it up to the light to see how threadbare it is. But in this case, we are compelled to undertake a bit of surgery, not to save it, for it never really had a chance of life, but to see how it was put together in the first place.

Let us say that we were to take Friedman's proposal seriously and that, tomorrow, Congressmen were to eat a foul breakfast ... and, with a kind of grave indigestion disturbing their thoughts and gas pains choking their laughter ... were to make it the law of the land. Henceforth, a fellow with a hybrid car would be able to park free, wherever he wanted. We will have to pass over the practical innards of the plan—how the owners of the parking spaces would be compensated, the paperwork, the enforcement, and so forth—and move at once to its theoretical pangs. Readers will quickly see that in order to improve the world in this manner, millions of private arrangements would first have to be *dis*improved. Someone must make up the lost parking revenue. Instead of buying an extra beer or upgrading his flight to Jamaica, the taxpayer must divert some of his spending power to pay for someone else's parking space. And those who get the free spaces then find that they have a little extra cash in their pockets to buy things they could not previously afford. And so the whole world is tilted, and everyone stands a little at an angle. Central planning will have created a world closer to Mr. Friedman's liking, but everyone else's planet will have been disturbed.

But maybe it is all still worthwhile. Who knows? Certainly not Thomas Friedman. Consider that this exercise in mass inconvenience is supposed to reduce America's use of oil ... in order to reduce oil revenues to Iran and Saudi Arabia ... which would in turn require these oil producers to "reform." But if there's many a slip twixt the cup and the lip, as the ancient proverb put it, here—the cup and lip might as well be on different planets. Americans who agree with Friedman are already free to buy hybrid cars, or they can simply drive their existing gas-guzzlers less often. His proposal is not needed for either. What it is really designed to do is discomfort those who don't agree with him; it is merely another way of bossing other people around, under cover of a "good purpose."

Do hybrid cars really reduce energy consumption? We don't know. They may use less energy per mile, but they may take more to make. Or to service . . . or drivers may be encouraged to drive more. Besides, in order for the free parking bribe to have any impact, it would have to be widely taken up. In other words, the world's auto factories would have to switch over to producing millions of hybrid cars. Whether this would actually reduce energy consumption we don't know, but the changeover itself would require massive new capital investment and retooling—which, itself, would mean the consumption of much more energy. Then, of course, the cities would be stuffed with cars parking for free and there would arise a whole new energy-guzzling bureaucracy to enforce and regulate the new system.

Meanwhile, regardless of whether even a smear of oil were actually saved, the price of petroleum might still rise to $100 a barrel in a few years, since world over, the easy oil has already been pumped out. And even then, Asia has three trillion people who are getting richer every day and are beginning to lick at the world's oil supplies like lost kittens at a bowl of milk. Americans might feel vaguely superior driving around in hybrid cars and parking in spaces provided at someone else's expense, but they are not likely to have much effect on the oil price.

But so what? Why does Friedman think that a high oil price stifles reform, or that the reforms that might be coming are the ones he would want? What if Iran and Saudi Arabia have world improvers of their own, with proposals even more absurd (if conceivable), and more lethal, than Friedman's? But no, Friedman thinks he can see not only his own future but, apparently, everyone else's.

But that is the indiscreet charm of the man—like all world improvers, he is a dreamy jackass. Ignorance increases by the square of the distance from a given event, so the odds that things won't work out the way you expect must be multiplied by the squares of all the intervening events. Between a proclamation of free parking for hybrid car drivers and the kind of "reform" in Iran that Friedman wants to see are a number of potential obstacles: People have to drive a lot of hybrid cars (enough to slacken oil sales); demand for oil actually has to go down (someone has to tell the rising middle classes in the rest of the world to turn down the air-conditioning); the price of oil actually has to fall (note to the feds: stop undermining the dollar; note to oil producers: keep pumping more oil, even if demand falls); Iran actually has to make less money from its oil exports (another note to Iran—pump more, but make sure you don't make more money from it); then, Iran actually has to be pressured to do something because of the lower oil revenues; and last of all, Iran must undertake a program of "reform" that would suit Mr. Friedman (we do not even consider here whether it would suit anyone else or whether it would increase the sum of human happiness in the world). Each of these events is at best a 50/50 proposition. Actually, we rate the likelihood of a fall in oil prices as a consequence of free parking for hybrids at zero, but for the purpose of this little exercise, we will spot the columnist a few points and simplify the math. Even if the odds of each event were one in two, the odds of the whole chain of events working out as expected could be expressed as $.5 \times .5 \times .5 \times .5 \times .5 \times .5$. We're not even going to bother with the math. What it amounts to is this: Icebergs will float in hell before free parking spaces for hybrids bring desirable "reform" to Iran.

"Well," you may say, "of course free parking won't do the job alone, but at least it's a step in the right direction." But who knows what direction the world is going . . . and whether it is right or wrong? If high oil revenues lead to wicked government, why is Texas no less wicked today than it was in its peak oil exporting era 40 years ago? The United Kingdom realized huge revenues from its North Sea rigs during the Margaret Thatcher years. We do not recall any outcry that the country was in need of regime change as a result. On the other hand, an oil exporter that *is* being widely tagged for regime change is Venezuela . . . whose government was duly elected and is thus under the heel of the majority . . . just as Friedman would want it.

However, just as high oil revenues don't always lead to wickedness, the lack of them doesn't guarantee virtue. Germany in the 1940s was not known for oil revenues or enlightened government. Nor was Italy. And if you go back more than a century, you won't find a single example of a people who were corrupted by oil profits or redeemed by cheap oil. It was not an oil bonanza that led Caesar to cross the Rubicon or drove the Huns to terrorize Europe or lured the Mongols into India. More recently, we don't recall newsworthy reforms in Iran, even when oil revenues declined sharply in the 1980s. As we remember it, the price of oil dropped 75 percent. If falling oil revenues led directly to "reform," you'd think that every oil exporter in the world would have reformed itself under that kind of pressure. Of course, if they had, Friedman would see nothing to reform now. Sin and wickedness have been with us for much longer than the internal combustion engine. We doubt that they will disappear, even if the price of oil were to drop to zero.

And yet, to give him his due, who today can say without doubt that Friedman is wrong? Who can say for sure that parking a hybrid for free in a downtown lot in Des Moines won't be the "tipping point" that causes a collapse in oil prices ... the little butterfly that flaps its wings and sets in motion a whole chain of airy events ... leading to a tornado in downtown Tehran? Finally, suddenly, a new wind could blow through the Persian capital ... and the mullahs would see their turbans take flight!

CALIPHS AND CRUSADERS

Nor is it the first time that people have tried to do good in the Near East. At the end of the eleventh century, Europeans decided to bring the blessings of Christian governance to the desert tribes. The Crusades of the eleventh, twelfth, and thirteenth centuries were doomed from the beginning. The Crusaders had the will and the weapons to kick Arab butts; what they lacked was a real reason for doing so, for Christianity was already firmly rooted in the Holy Lands, as it had been for more than 1,000 years, even though

Jerusalem had fallen to the caliph Umar Ibn al-Khattab in February of 638.

Amin Maalouf, in a delightful little book, *The Crusades from the Arab Point of View*, tells us how it happened:

> Umar had entered Jerusalem astride his famous white camel, and the Greek patriarch of the holy city came forward to meet him. The caliph first assured him that the lives and property of the city's inhabitants would be respected, and then asked the patriarch to take him to visit the Christian holy places. The time of Muslim prayer arrived while they were in the church of Qiyama, the Holy Sepulchre, and Umar asked his host if he could unroll his prayer mat. The patriarch invited Umar to do so right where he stood but the caliph answered: "If I do, the Muslims will want to appropriate this site, saying 'Umar prayed here.'" Then, carrying his prayer mat, he went and knelt outside.[16]

Jerusalem was taken again, in July 1099, by the Crusaders. This time Christians were the victors and the handover much less gracious.

> The population of the holy city was put to the sword, and the Franj [Franks] spent a week massacring Muslims. They killed more than seventy thousand people in al-Aqsa mosque. Ibn al-Qalanisi, who never reported figures he could not verify, says only: Many people were killed. The Jews had gathered in their synagogue and the Franj burned them alive.[17]

Not even their coreligionists were spared, adds Maalouf.

> . . . They arrested the priests who had been entrusted with custody of the Cross and tortured them to make them reveal the secret.[18]

This was only the beginning. Soon, the Franks were drawn into the internecine killings and intramural murders that afflicted the area.

Crusaders would make an alliance with the Eastern Orthodox emperor one day to fight one of the various Muslim warlords, viziers, caliphs, pashas, or Seljuks in the region. The next day, they would side with the Muslims and turn on the Eastern Empire. A particularly blockheaded Crusader was Reynald de Chatillon, known as "brins Arnat" (Prince Arnat) by the Arab chroniclers, to whom the Arabs refer whenever they want to prove that the Crusaders were wicked barbarians.

Reynald launched a punitive raid against Cyprus—a Christian island under the rule of the Eastern Empire—and demanded money from the patriarch of the Eastern Orthodox Church of Antioch to pay for the expedition. Naturally, the patriarch resisted. But Reynald had ways of getting people to cooperate; he tortured the priest and covered his wounds with honey. He then chained him down and left him in the sun for a whole day while insects feasted on him.

Even a good man yields to the proper persuasion. Reynald got his money, and the campaign against Cyprus was on. Amin Maalouf describes what happened next:

> Before setting off loaded with booty, Reynald ordered all the Greek priests and monks assembled; he then had their noses cut off before sending them, thus mutilated, to Constantinople.[19]

Hassan-i-Sabbah was born in 1048, not far from the present city of Tehran. Like Osama bin Laden many years later, Hassan had an ax to grind. And like Osama, he ground it on the whetstone provided by his Western allies. What stuck in Hassan's craw was the remarkable change that took place in the Arab world in the eleventh century. Shiism had dominated the region at the time of his birth. But the victory of the Seljuk Turks pushed the Shia to the back of the bus. The Seljuks were Sunnites and defenders of Sunni orthodoxy. Hassan fell in with Muslim fundamentalists and was soon active in a resistance movement centered in Cairo. In

1090, he made a sudden and successful assault on the eagle's-nest fortress at Alamout, near the Caspian Sea, giving him a base of operations—like Osama's mountain redoubts—that was inaccessible and impregnable. There, he recruited an army and trained them in terror.

The terrorists of the eleventh century had no fertilizer bombs and no commercial airplanes. All they had was the equivalent of box cutters—knives. Their technique was to infiltrate an enemy's city, pretending to be merchants or religious ascetics. Circulating around town, they got to know their target's movements while making themselves unremarkable. Then, they would spring on him suddenly and stick a knife between his ribs. So single-minded and unflappable were Hassan's agents that witnesses thought they must be drugged with hashish. Thus did they come to be known as the *haschaschin*, which evolved into the word we know, assassin. The Crusaders saw the assassins not as a threat, but as an opportunity. Like the Reagan administration in the twentieth century, the Franks of the twelfth century decided to make common cause with the assassins against their common enemy—Seljuk Shiite Muslims. Thus, the initial intentions, premises, and causes of the whole business were lost. *Quo fata ferunt.*

When the Crusaders arrived in the Holy Land, they found a place of general religious tolerance—there were churches next to synagogues, down the street from mosques. They also found a region that was divided into hundreds of political units, where loyalties and alliances were as unreliable as a discount airline is today. The Muslim world posed no threat to the Christian West; it was too disorganized, and it was unable to protect itself and incapable of projecting much in the way of military power.

But the Crusades changed that. Gradually, under Noureddin and then Saladin, the Islamic world came together to drive out the Franks. At the decisive battle of Hittin, Saladin brought together troops from all over the Near East and faced none other than Reynald de

Chatillon. Al–Malik al–Afdal, Saladin's son, then just 17 years old, described the battle:

> "When the king of the Franj found himself on the hill, he and his men launched a fierce attack that drove our own troops back to the place where my father was standing. I looked at him. He was saddened; he frowned and pulled nervously at his beard. Then he advanced, shouting 'Satan must not win!' "[20]

Saladin once again forced the enemy to retire to the hill, but when his son called out in triumph, he silenced him. Victory, he said, would not be won until a nearby tent collapsed. He had not yet finished the sentence when the tent did collapse. Saladin then dismounted, knelt, and thanked God, crying for joy.

Saladin had a reputation for mercy and evenhandedness. But it was a rough place and a rough time, and the Franks, especially, had a reputation for butchery. When Richard the Lionhearted took the city of Acre, for example, he massacred 2,700 soldiers he had taken prisoner, plus an additional 300 women and children found in the city. Under similar conditions, Saladin usually let his captives go free. But so great was his disgust with Reynald that the great caliph vowed to kill him with his own hands. When the prisoner was brought before him, he made good his promise.

Back in the homeland, A.D. 2005, most Americans persuaded themselves that, like the Crusaders, their troops were doing God's work in the land of the ancient Mesopotamians. But every action in a public spectacle is clownish or murderous. Every idea is buffoonish. Every outcome is perverse. And the fool who gets the thing going usually ends up with a monument in granite and an eternity in hell.

CHAPTER 2

LOVE IN THE
TIME OF VIAGRA

Love is the self-delusion we manufacture to justify the trouble we take
to have sex.

—Daniel S. Greenberg

But now we look at our subject from a different angle. We
wonder—how unique, after all, are mass political upheavals or financial manias? They may not be very different from a much more
everyday phenomenon we all know. When we fall—the word *fall* is
instructive—in love, don't we also take leave of our senses?

Rational men, philosophers say, always pursue their greatest good.
And they find their greatest good in life, liberty, and happiness, three
things as inextricably linked as Curly, Moe, and Larry. We need life
first, of course. But then, according to the preeminent theorist of
liberty, the Englishman John Locke, we need liberty to pursue our
happiness. And since our happiness is bound up most of all with those
whom we love, we cannot have real happiness until we are free to
choose the ones we love. The more choices we have, the freer we are,
and therefore, the more capable we are of choosing who and what
will bring us the greatest happiness. Locke wrote:

God Almighty himself is under the necessity of being happy; and the
more any intelligent being is so, the nearer is its approach to infinite
perfection and happiness. . . . Therefore the highest perfection of
intellectual nature lies in a careful and constant pursuit of true
and solid happiness; so the care of ourselves, that we mistake not

imaginary for real happiness, is the necessary foundation of our liberty.[1]

FLATTERING FRAUDS

Poor Locke. We see the problem right away in that one sentence. He flatters himself and his species. Man may build bridges with a "careful and constant pursuit" of the best choices. But in his pursuit of happiness, he is rarely either careful or constant.

"A great fallacy has marred Western thinking since Aristotle and most acutely since the Enlightenment," explains our friend Nassim Nicholas Taleb. "That is to say, that as much as we think of ourselves as rational animals, risk avoidance is not governed by reason, cognition or intellect. Rather, it comes chiefly from our emotional system."[2]

Taleb was referring to the reactions to the terrorist bombings. Reading the newspaper headlines, you might come to believe that terrorism was an enormous risk, whereas statistically it is actually rather insignificant. Following September 11, for example, many decided to drive rather than to fly; the result was that more people died in traffic accidents than died in airplanes. In 2005, when bombs went off in London, a cursory reading of the press reports revealed that the bombers were the rankest amateurs. Some didn't know how to detonate their bombs. And when they contacted their "mastermind," they did so on cell phones—which they then took with them on their bombing missions. All you have to do is watch a few spy movies and you know better than that—call from a pay phone; at least it's not registered in your name, and there's no record of the call. In America, anyway, you'd think terrorists with their wits about them would strike at the electricity grid during a heat wave. You'd think they'd know that without air-conditioning Americans could be made hot and bothered enough to do something really foolish.

But terrorists are not what we like to think they are. Nor are the other political and financial windmills against which Homo saps love to tilt. The truth is—popular politics and bubbles are almost always frauds that flatter our sense of vanity. Terrorists believe they are fighting in some great, heroic struggle against the West, rather than merely blowing themselves up on a fool's errand. Westerners, for their part, believe Muslim billionaires are plotting against them because they are jealous.

Of course, some things *are* too important to leave to the rational part of the brain. Faced with a postal worker in full battle armor or a fashion model stark naked, a smart man doesn't think at all. Not that he wouldn't like to; it's just that he hasn't the time for it. The thinking can come later. Along the same lines, romantic love may be a flattering fraud, too. A man never feels more noble, handsome, or worthy as when he sees himself reflected in the eyes of his admiring lover. All rational thought ceases immediately.

Unless he is a seasoned cynic with a pre-nup in his hand, he believes it will last forever, or at least as long as a bubble in the housing market. He looks at his lover and sees no faults or flaws. If she is fat, he finds her pleasingly plump. If she is stupid, he finds her admirably unpretentious. And she returns the favor, looking upon him as uncritically as a Wall Street analyst upon a balance sheet. To the rest of the world, he may be an oaf and a dimwit; to her he is an oaf and a dimwit, too, but an adorable one. She can't imagine anyone better suited to her—until he comes along next month.

All frauds have their price. A man who invests his dollars in a bubble or gives his life to a high-minded swindle pays dearly. And there is a price to pay for *l'amour*, too. If he were a Lockean man, he might avoid it altogether, just as he would stay away from overpriced stocks. Why waste caresses? Why wear out the heart? But nobody ever got rich or happy by storing up kisses. And even an ironicist looks upon a couple in love with a little envy; they are fools, he says to himself, and wishes he could be one, too.

LOVE IN THE TIME OF VIAGRA

Indeed, love, as a subject of analysis, is so profound that a man risks sinking in it. Before he knows it, his head has disappeared below the surface. Love is so profound, we suspect, it deserves to be treated only in the most superficial and flippant way.

We recall a recent case in England that makes our point. A couple had come to despise each other so greatly that they partitioned off the house—right up to the front door. One half was his, the other hers. Thus did they live for many years, until, grown old, the poor woman had had enough. She committed suicide. Only two weeks later, the man—freed of the terrible demonic witch to whom he had hitched himself—also killed himself.

There was a time when respectable marriages were based on more serious concerns—money, property, position, and so forth. Samuel Johnson even suggested that all marriages should be arranged by the Lord Chancellor. And the history books are chockablock with young maidens—often only 12 or 14 years old—who were put on a ship to wed some faraway rascal with a kingdom or a fortune. Some of these marriages ended badly, of course. But many, probably, were as happy as the typical marriage today. In some benighted parts of the world, notably the Islamic, arranged marriages are still common. A man may never have seen more of his bride than her eyes—and scarcely have spoken to her—before he is expected to agree to keep her as long as both shall live. A friend of ours, from Pakistan, was given the choice of three men—all of them distant cousins or family friends. She chose one of them. As near as we can tell, she is as happily married as anyone we know. And the divorce rate in Pakistan is very low. But in the modern Western world, arranged marriages have given way to deranged ones. People are expected to fall in love with each other—that is, they are expected to take leave of their senses, and while in this addled state, they are not only allowed, but encouraged, to sign a contract that is meant to last a lifetime. It is no wonder that half of them end up wanting out of the deal. What is amazing is that the other half stick with it.

THE DOWNFALL OF MARRIAGE: THE PURSUIT OF HAPPINESS

Another friend, recently remarried, offers this reflection: "Anecdotally, one gets the impression that many married men are not happy. In today's culture, where images of delectably beautiful women are being sent your way 400 times a day, it is hard to be satisfied with a fat, dumpy wife. Then, of course, there is Hollywood playing fast and loose with your expectations. Be that as it may, the man who has broken up more marriages than anyone else is not some pretty boy like Clark Gable or Brad Pitt, but a homely Oxford don and medical researcher, John Locke, who insisted in *An Essay Concerning Human Understanding* that the pursuit of happiness was the highest goal of life.

"This insight not only made it into the Declaration of Independence," our friend continues, "in the famous trilogy with Life and Liberty, it also informed a major shift in the way life is experienced. Locke became the godfather of romantic love. Hallmark Cards should have a portrait of John Locke in the lobby. By drawing attention to happiness and self-fulfillment as the central focuses of life, Locke gave the Valentine card, the soap opera, and the divorce lawyer their start. Romantic love was the undoing of marriage as it had been known. Romantic love set people yearning for more than obedience and social support—property accumulation—from marriage. You may think this is piffle. Or brilliant. In either case, this isn't my idea. It is a copyrighted insight of Stephanie Coontz."[3]

THE DOWNFALL OF MARRIAGE: BRAZIL

Our friend goes on, "Having just wed for the second time and spent the last few days in Brazil meeting my new wife's extended family, I've been thinking again about marriage, intimacy, and associated ramifications. Brazilian consumers increasingly believe they can find happiness purchasing various branded products, from McDonald's hamburgers to Louis Vuitton bags. The characters in Brazilian soap operas divorce and engage in all manner of sexual affairs. But notwithstanding the incitement, the divorce rate in Brazil is still minimal, approximately one-twentieth the rate in the U.S. In fact, today's divorce rate in Brazil is lower than it was a century ago in the U.S. As Princeton historian Hendrik Hartog put it, 'Though marriage continues to offer the fantasy of continuity and permanence (till death do us part), all sane people who enter into it know that it represents a choice to marry this person at this time and that if living with this person at a later time no longer suggests the possibility of happiness, that you are entitled (have a right) to leave and to try again.' "

Our friend may be right. Still, we wonder if you can really pursue happiness as if it were a getaway car. Locke acts as if happiness had held up a local bank. If you could just catch up with it, you could put it away for life. But it's a funny old world. Just when you think you've got your hands on the s.o.b., he vanishes. As near as we can determine, people are happy by accident, not by intention. They are born happy. Or they are lucky enough to make a happy marriage, rather than an unhappy one. It doesn't seem to matter whether they choose it or it is set up for them. Happiness finds them; they don't find it. Economists pull levers and turn knobs to make people more prosperous. Psychologists have their own buttons to push to make people happy. Investors, too, think they can get rich by making the kind of choices Locke describes. But what do any of them know? Do people really get what they want in life? Or do they get what they deserve? Is private passion, like public folly, a rational choice or a type of mania? Maybe Shakespeare had it right:

"The lunatic, the lover, and the poet
Are of imagination all compact . . ."

Some nights, at our country place, we walk out into the garden and wonder. When the moon is full down there, it lights up the clouds and the trees in so remarkable a way that you can see, but can see nothing distinctly . . . nothing clearly . . . and then—we have a thought. Romance may be all moonshine. We may go blind and limp from drinking it. Still, it may be worth it . . .

THE MATING GAME

You see, romance, like a market bubble or a war, seems to come from deep down in the more primitive part of a man's brain. For, while the brain may have two centers of decision making, one seems to be more important. The other is merely a lackey and a stooge; it does what it is told. The advanced part of the brain, the lateral prefrontal cortex, is where Locke's rational man debates how to pursue happiness. The limbic system, on the other hand, is where he pursues it. The limbic system is what tells him what he likes and doesn't like. It's what drives his reactions.

And what drives the limbic system? Under all the advanced, logical thinking, what is it that makes people happy?

We thought about that recently when we were back in the U.S. after an absence of several months. Suddenly, the roads were crowded with Hummers. Would anyone—if he were using his lateral prefrontal cortex—want to drive around in a big, awkward, ugly, expensive car when a small, cheap one would get him where he was going just as well? No. Then why do they do it? Because their limbic system tells them to "maximize their inclusive fitness," say scientists. Big cars help the owners get noticed. Hummers are like long, bright tail feathers on a bird or a big rack of antlers on a deer. From a utilitarian point of view, they are worthless. Worse than worthless, as a matter of fact. They increase the risk that the animal will be noticed by rivals and predators. They take energy to carry around. And they slow the animal down, making it hard for him to maneuver in a fight or to get away.

Why do people buy Hummers, for instance? For a simple reason. It's all about superiority. Why would you want to feel superior at all? Why would you want to feel one up on the other guy? Again, it's simple: because you want to impress some woman. Why do you want to impress her? Because you want as many of your genes floating around the gene pool as possible. Just look around.

"All progress is based on a universal innate desire on the part of every organism to live beyond its income," said Samuel Butler,[4] but he didn't explain why; so we will.

Why is there a $700 billion trade deficit? Because Americans want to buy things they can't afford. Why do they want to buy things they can't afford? To pretend to be richer than they are. Why do they want to appear richer than they are? Because it gives them higher social status. Why do they want higher social status? So they will have better access to the opposite sex.

There it is, dear reader. When it comes down to it, it's all sex and lies. Everything: Romance. Cars. Jobs. The debt bubble. The real estate bubble. The trade deficit bubble. The American Empire. They are useful only as evidence of conspicuous consumption; they wink to the opposite sex that the animal is fit for procreation and game for a little hanky-panky. If he can carry around all that extra baggage and still survive, he must be tough. So, too, if a person can live in a McMansion and drive a Hummer without going bankrupt, he must be a good prospect for a date.

But it's all relative. If everybody on the block buys a Hummer and puts in a swimming pool, the man who has those things already loses his edge. An arms race in consumption begins. He has to spend even more—bringing himself even closer to bankruptcy—in order to show off. What can he do? Write poetry and put a feminist bumper sticker on his old Hummer? No, he must carry around the biggest, gaudiest, most implausible rack of lies he can carry; he must make a public spectacle of himself.

"Yeah," said a divorced friend who has been studying dating strategies, "you have to be 'the man with the plan.' You signal to the woman that you've got it figured out and that, if she wants to hook up with you, she can, but only on *your* terms. You have to show that you have a lot of money, but you don't want to give her the impression that she'll be in charge of how it is spent. That would start the relationship off on the wrong foot."

"Women prefer men who are sure of themselves, even if they have no real reason to be," added another friend, a man of vast experience on the subject. "A man comes into a room. He looks at the women. If he sees one who catches his eye, he wants to have her. If the woman is with a dorky man, he is even more interested, because he thinks it increases his chances. And he'll take even the slightest nod or smile as encouragement.

"But when a woman comes into the room, she looks at the women, too. The man she wants is the one who is strong and capable—who knows what he is doing. But these aren't obvious characteristics, so she has to look for clues elsewhere: clothes, jewelry, tans—anything that signals social status. That is why men are so vain; genetically speaking, it pays. But most of all, she looks to see which men are surrounded by attractive females. The presence of other attractive females confirms that the man must be attractive.

"The woman has to be conscious of the subtle clues. But for the man, it's better to be an aggressive blockhead. The woman may signal, for example, that she's not interested. But he just pushes ahead anyway; he figures he might overcome her reluctance. At the margin, this is the guy who gets the girl—and who leaves the most offspring. And it's his genes—passed along and spread out over hundreds and hundreds of generations—that make us what we are today."

Women aren't stupid, of course. They know you can move into a McMansion with no money down and no money anywhere else. They know you can lease a Hummer and buy an Armani suit with credit cards. They try to find out whether the man really has money. It is the beginning of the battle between the sexes. The man tries to deceive the woman about his fitness for procreation, and the woman tries to detect the deception, while also deceiving him—with makeup and various artifices—about her own attractiveness. The poor man has to show more and more evidence that he's really the one with the large rack and the bright feathers. He has to take on more and more expensive burdens ... second and third houses ... European vacations ... a home theater ... cosmetic surgery. The schmuck needs to spend, spend, spend—or he's going to be spending his nights alone.

You might say that a smart woman would see her way through the foolishness of it all and prefer a man with no desire to show off—maybe a good, solid schoolteacher who cares about the environment and drives an old Pinto. But if she mates with such a man, she dooms her offspring, say the scientists, for the man is likely to father sons much like himself—men who are attractive only to smart women. And how many of those are there? And even so, the smart woman's own genes will find fewer opportunities for reproductive success—and what's so smart about that?

In order to spread her genes as widely as possible, a woman needs offspring, particularly males, who are high-ranking—that is, those who can carry around gaudy expenses without going broke. Her best strategy is to mate with a high-ranking male. Her good fortune would be to have many high-ranking sons with him, who would find many mates of their own. And for that she must spend much of her time and money as though she were a candidate for public office—that is, deceiving people about what she really is. She must appear high-ranking by wearing expensive clothes instead of cheap ones, by driving an expensive car, by living at an expensive address, and by sporting expensive jewelry. She must also appear as physically attractive as possible. Remember, it's all about sex.

CORPORATE HEIGHTS

And there you have the explanation for one of the many sordid features of the early twenty-first-century public spectacle ... outsize CEO salaries. They are the bright feathers of the high-ranking male. Top business leaders have become like sports heroes, but without the talent. You need not have any real knowledge of the business you are getting into, or, as Bernie Ebbers demonstrated, any real knowledge about business of any sort. What will get you a job as a leader in the corporate world is the same thing that will get you a woman in the mating game—outsize confidence.

Human life—apart from the obvious physical aspects—is largely about what scientists call "impression management." A man with a good line of talk and a confident air about him gets almost anything he wants, and that includes the CEO job at a major U.S. corporation. Psychologists have done studies to that effect. A man who is confident beyond his merits is much more likely to succeed than one with a modest assessment of his abilities. The modest man will, of course, usually be the better choice—his modesty is usually based on a reasonably accurate view of his skills and the challenges he faces. The immodest bluffer, on the other hand, is almost certainly a fool and likely a menace as well. He misjudges the situation in front of him and imagines himself the master of it. But shareholders—as well as voters—have no real way of knowing who will make the best leader, so they actually tend to prefer the tall, confident, incompetent one. But if you are not tall, dear reader, do not worry. Sometimes they will take a short, confident, incompetent manager, if they have to.

Then you may worry—what if the company doesn't do well? Well, what if? Again, recent history shows us that you can fail miserably in corporate America and still leave with a lot of money.

In 2005, after being ousted as CEO, Carly Fiorina got $42 million from Hewlett-Packard. Scott Livengood got $46,000 per month consulting for Krispy Kreme, the doughnut company he glazed with losses. Franklin Raines got booted out of Fannie Mae, but still gets $114,000 per month in pension benefits. Harry Stonecipher fooled around on the job and gets $600,000 a year in retirement benefits. In 2003, General Motors' Rick Wagoner got a pay hike, to $2.2 million, while guiding the company to its biggest loss in a decade. No matter what you do, apparently, the money keeps on coming. The *Washington Post* reports that executive bonuses alone at 100 big companies rose by more than 46 percent in 2004, to an average of more than $1.14 million, according to a study by Mercer Human Resource Consulting.[5]

Or take another study, by professors at Harvard and Cornell, that found that CEO pay at companies in the Standard & Poor's 500 index rose almost three times over 10 years, to an average of $10.3 million in 2002. Between 1998 and 2002, executive pay accounted for 10 percent of total corporate profit. Although average executive pay fell slightly in 2005, it is still up from 1990 by 300 percent, rising faster than the stock market or corporate profits.[6]

But perhaps that was just the market rewarding CEOs for superior performance? Well—consider this: According to one study, if you had put $10,000 into the stocks of companies with the highest-paid CEOs of the previous year from January 1991 to December 2004, you would have ended up with only $8,079, while the same money

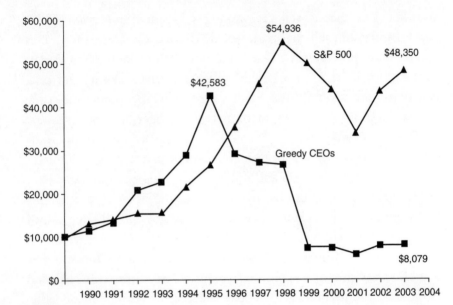

FIGURE 2.1   Highest-Paid CEOs' Stock Returns versus S&P Returns 1990–2004.
Source: Executive Excess 2005: Defense Contractors Get More Bucks for the Bang—12th Annual CEO Compensation Survey; Sarah Anderson and John Cavanagh, Institute for Policy Studies; Scott Klinger and Liz Stanton, United for Peace and Justice, August 30, 2005, p. 20. http://www.faireconomy.org/press/2005/EE2005.pdf. Accessed June 23, 2007.

invested in the S&P 500 would have returned you $48,350—that is, *six* times as much.[7] (See Figure 2.1.)

And one group of CEOs is making out even better than the rest. In the first four years after 9/11, the CEOs of the top 34 defense companies have made a total of $984 million (an average of $7.7 million a year each), their pay rising 108 percent in that period, compared to 6 percent for other CEOs. Responsibility for the war, you say? Would they be *44 times* more responsible than a general with 20 years of experience (paid $174,452 in 2005) or *308 times* more than an enlisted soldier (paid $25,085) or *19 times* more than even the commander-in-chief (over $400,000) himself? (See Figure 2.2.)

Anyway, being responsible for the war effort doesn't seem to be much on anyone's mind. Take George David of United Technologies

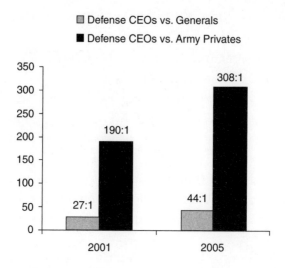

FIGURE 2.2 Defense CEOs' Pay versus Pay of Generals and Privates—Changes in Ratio from 2001 to 2005.
Data Source: Department of Defense, Defense Finance and Accounting Service, 2001 and 2005 Military Pay Rates for E-2 (second-lowest-rank enlisted personnel) and O-10 (generals). Includes: base pay, housing allowance, and imminent danger/hostile fire pay. Some military personnel qualify for additional assistance, such as a $250 allowance for family separation.
Source: Executive Excess 2006: Defense and Oil Executives Cash In on Conflict—13th Annual CEO Compensation Survey; Sarah Anderson and John Cavanagh, Institute for Policy Studies; Chuck Collins and Eric Benjamin, United for a Fair Economy, edited by Sam Pizzigati, August 30, 2006, p. 6. http://www.faireconomy.org/reports/2006/ExecutiveExcess2006.pdf. Acessed June 23, 2007.

Corporation (UTC), the highest paid of them all (more than $200 million between 2002 and 2005, with a peak total pay of $88.3 million in 2004). Right now, his main concern seems to be suing the Pentagon to keep information about alleged difficulties with his Black Hawk helicopters out of the public eye.[8]

At this point, we have to ask a simple question. Why would you pay a man $90 million to be a corporate bureaucrat? Couldn't you find others to do the work for less? Only a reckless madman would throw money around like that. The country must be full of them. Why so many? Why is there a blockhead on every corner?

PORTRAIT OF THE ARTIST AS A SCALAWAG

One corner full of them is the art world. Take *Heatwave*.

Heatwave is a Barbie doll inside a rotisserie oven, lit with an orange glow, so that Barbie is basking and baking. Another favorite is *Sunbeams*, where the doll is draped over a Sunbeam mixer with her posterior jutting into the air and the whisks of the Sunbeam whirring closely.

Defending his art in the *The Telegraph*,[9] Forsythe reminded us of another thing that grubbing for money is better than. Gimmicky and foolish, *Heatwave* is the sort of thing you would expect from today's culture today.

"When I hear the word *culture*, I reach for my gun," said Hermann Göring once.[10] The German aviator was roasting in hell before Forsythe was even born, so he never had a chance to see *Heatwave*. But had he seen it—and had you been present at the show—you probably would have wanted to duck.

The artist in Europe today has a special status, somewhere between a Grand Dragon in the Ku Klux Klan and a carny for Barnum and Bailey. The artist is a rebel who gets invited to all the best parties. He is a bit actor on the margins, taken seriously by the rich and the powerful. He is an icon buster, peddling his own shoddy image for worship and glorification. And he is a born genius, with no visible talent, except for self-promotion.

In short, the artist is a humbug.

Artists have always been critics of the conventions of the day. When Dante drew his picture of Hell, he made sure to put into it the leading citizens of his day, and Shakespeare made most of his Englishmen either pathetic or comic. But cometh the twentieth century—and now the twenty-first—and the artist takes on a new role. He has greased himself into the job of Arbiter of Cool. This humbug has a whole platoon of partakers—museum curators, critics, and, most important, art promoters. It is, after all, they who make the crucial decisions. And they are all in cahoots. One stumbles across some no-account brush wielder and promotes him to his friends in the museums. The friends bring in the critics early, so that the shysters can then claim to have discovered the great one before he became great. And at the end of the assembly line, weak-minded collectors and greedy investors are lured into forking over enormous prices for the tripe that is produced.

Meanwhile, the whole concatenation of grand larceny and petty indecency creates such a buzz that it convinces the rest of the world that it has a real talent on its hands. What else does the rest of the world have to go on? The artwork itself may be as empty and meaningless as a State of the Union address, but it is hanging in an important gallery! Van Der Loon said it was "original." Some chump paid big money for it!

We marvel at the elegant symmetry of it all: Things with no value are bought by people with no sense. Money flows from weaker hands to stronger ones. Make-believe art flows from scalawags and hustlers to dimwits and social climbers . . . and life goes on.

Andy Warhol was not a great artist, but he was no fool. When he died, it was discovered that with his own money he had bought traditional, representational paintings. But he was a great promoter. His *Portrait of Nelson A. Rockefeller #3* sold for $401,750 just six years ago. In the spring of 2006, it brought $1,136,000. Mark Rothko's *White, Orange, and Yellow* brought about $300,000 from some investor 12 years ago. In 2006, it was expected to go for as much as $3 million. Instead, a much greater fool came along and paid $4,160,000. And the big winner was Roy Lichtenstein's *Sinking Sun*, which brought $15,696,000—about 150 times more than it sold for in 1974.[11]

Why the high prices? A study published in the February 10, 2006, issue of *Science* magazine helps to explain it. The authors, Matthew J. Salganik and Peter Sheridan Dodds of Columbia University and Duncan J. Watts of the Santa Fe Institute, compared people's judgments of music on their own with their reactions when they knew how popular the music was among their peers. The results were hardly surprising. People appreciated songs in a fairly random way when they were left to their own devices, but as soon as they had "social influence" to guide them, they tended to focus on just one or two popular songs, while ignoring those that were judged by the group to be unpopular.[12]

A few decades ago, a man who made some money would buy his way into high society by getting Gainsborough to paint his wife or by buying a Chippendale dining room set. Now, it is cool that counts, and a man desperate for social status has to hang framed trash on his walls. Or put pickled sheep on his mantelpiece.

In 1997, a show of contemporary art in London called "Sensation" broke all records for attendance and bad taste. It was so lewd and repulsive the papers couldn't stop talking about it, which, of course, only brought in bigger mobs of gawkers. But there were also howls of complaint, too, for included in it was a giant painting of one Myra Hindley, composed from a child's handprints. Myra Hindley is infamous, and behind bars, for murdering children and recording their screams as she tortured them. Outraged viewers—including the parents of the murdered children—begged the Royal Academy not to exhibit the painting. When officials refused, protesters attacked the painting with eggs and ink. Thereafter, it had to be restored and protected by plastic. One of the mysteries of contemporary art is why anyone even bothered to restore it; the painting was no less attractive—and no less shocking—after its amending by the protestors. "Sensation" was sensational. It gave a boost to contemporary "art" that was felt across the pond. The show went on ... and the prices went on to rise.[13]

Since then, "art" has gotten even more repulsive and ridiculous. Ex-stripper Stella Vine, promoted by Charles Saatchi, pandered to celebrity culture with a painting of Princess Diana that had blood dripping from her lips.[14] "Artists" are already fornicating on stage. We wait for the day when they will be shooting each other, drenching the bodies in antifreeze and putting them on display. Then, perhaps a bout of mass murder, nun raping, and, even worse, cigarette smoking!

Even a dumbbell can see that this doctrine leads nowhere. Sooner or later, artists will run smack into the residual decency of the public, if there is any left. And then, of course, their oeuvre will really soar in value!

Mind you, earnest critics of contemporary art take the whole thing much too seriously. They miss the elegant comedy, the neat symmetry with which no sooner do people get their hands on money, than nature comes up with absurd ways to take it from them.

In their indignation they forget to chuckle, worrying over how the whole vulgar fraud undermines high taste and presses down on popular culture, like a container full of Che T-shirts. Of course, they are right to criticize, but wrong to find no fun in doing so. Who, after all, would have believed that anyone declared compos mentis—able to drive a car or serve on a jury—would pay $95 million for an opus of Pablo Picasso from his "I hate my girlfriend" period? Who would pay $553,600 for Elizabeth Peyton's wretched painting of Spencer Sweeney? Who would pay $3.38 million for Damien Hirst's sliced lamb in formaldehyde?[15]

But didn't Damien Hirst also entitle one of his paintings *Kiss My F**king A**?* What could be cooler than that? And isn't the whole idea of art to break taboos? No one held a gun to the buyers' heads. No court order required them to do it. They just did it, driven by some natural urge to part with their wealth.

And then what do you suppose happened? Even greater fools came and paid even more. If a bull market can turn a numskull into a genius, the art market deserves federal funding. It has done for the elite what the housing boom has done for the lumpen proletariat. They all think they deserve Nobel Prizes.

Recently, Chinese artist Zhou Tiehai decided to test the art establishment's pretensions. At first, he tried various combinations of avant-garde collages. At one point, so to speak, he even stuck fellow performance artists with a needle, prefiguring his later jabs at the art community. When none of that took off, he came up with a brain wave. Art itself—of course! The *idea* of the artist busting through the icons of bourgeois society ... liberating the masses from their subservience to the money gods and the sanctions of everyday convention. What better icon to smash with a sledgehammer? In short, Mr. Zhou decided to pull the art world's leg.

What, he must have asked himself, could be more commercial, more artistically shallow, more intellectually démodé and more culturally *mal vue* than that symbol of cigarette advertising—Joe Camel? He hired some local hacks (he saw no reason to get his own hands dirty), drew out a few images—putting Joe Camel's head into well-known, classic European paintings—and let his crew turn them into works of art. Perfect, he thought. An icon of modern predatory commercialism grafted onto the work of a great master. They will see that I am mocking the whole idea of icon-busting art.

"It's really not that hard to create art," he announced.[16]

Not the way Mr. Zhou does it, certainly. But, instead of being shunned by the elite art collectors, critics, and buyers whose legs he had pulled, he was embraced—warmly—by them. Instead of slipping his paintings into their closets and admitting that they'd been had, they proudly put them on their walls after shelling out as much as $100,000 each for them.[17]

But despite Zhou, contemporary art is still going up in price. *Vox populi, vox dei.* Collectors and investors are making money—lots of it. And now there are funds that trade canvases using the 2-and-20 terms of hedge funds (2 percent management fees and 20 percent of the profit) and indexes that track art sales. The Mei Moses semiannual all art index rose a record 22 percent in 2005–2006, a rate lower only than that in the bubble period in the late 1980s. The postwar and contemporary art index grew even faster, apparently beating many traditional asset classes.

Naysayers warn that the return is inflated because the index excluded transaction costs and works that failed to sell at auction. "You can't commodify art like corn or soybeans," points out a New York art dealer. What about differences in quality?[18]

Try telling that to the fellow who bought a Gustav Klimt for a record $135 million. No one before had ever paid that much for a painting. And only a few months later in the year, along came someone with even more money to spend. He laid out $140 million for a Jackson Pollock.[19]

And here, we have to sit down and compose ourselves. Our pulse races at the thought of it. The buyer chose to remain anonymous. What a shame. Anyone who would spend $140 million on a dreadful painting deserves notoriety. In fact, more than that, he deserves clinical study. That quantity of money would produce about $7 million in income each year, if invested at 5 percent. What kind of person could get $7 million worth of pleasure from looking at a Jackson Pollock painting? We need to know more. Is he allowed out in public?

If the owner cannot get $7 million in annual satisfaction from the painting, perhaps it can be rented out. Let's see, the daily rate should be something like $20,000. Surely you'd pay $20,000 to have one of Jackson Pollack's oeuvres on your wall for 24 hours. Who wouldn't?

Unless the owner can get a return of $7 million, he must be counting on something other than yield: capital gains! He must be counting on an even higher price and an even greater record! He's probably betting that there is an even greater fool. And maybe there is.

But pity them anyway. Their art may be worth a fortune, but they have to live with it. No sum of money could be worth that.

MONKEY BUSINESS

The explanation for all these absurdities of behavior comes to us from people who speculate about the evolution of mating strategies and genetic selection. It is very simple, they say. Our modest, clear-headed monkey ancestors got less sex than their overconfident rivals. The blusterer can find his way to the top spot of a major corporation or even the nation itself. The bigger a fool he is, the more he seems to be able to get other fools to fall in behind him—so long as he is confident enough ... and has convinced himself enough.

And the reason for this is that while all public spectacles may found themselves on a humbug, yet it is a humbug with no malice aforethought. The perpetrators of the humbug are often the most humbugged of all. They actually believe what they are doing is for the betterment of the world—no matter how disagreeable it may be to the people being bettered. Their thoughts contain such a tangle of deception and misconception that there is never the slightest hope they will extricate themselves from their assumption of unadulterated virtue. The words wrap around their feet, the ideas clutch their throats, and their own selfish emotions wriggle around their chests and squeeze their hearts, but the humbuggers are convinced that their humbuggery is as natural and as beautiful as ivy; it is for the public good.

How comes this to be? What primal instinct is so well served by humbug that the thing flourishes like bindweed in an orchard? Again, we look to evolution and instinct rather than to conscious purpose for an answer. Why? Because, too often, we forget that man is an animal little different from others. He shares almost all the same genes with apes and tree frogs. He, too, is the product of millions of years of evolutionary development. Suppose, as Desmond Morris did, we view man not as a fallen angel but as a risen ape?[20]

Yet, we notice that when scientists study man's behavior, they see it as entirely different from that of other animals. They assume that man is uniquely smart . . . uniquely purposeful. If he does something particularly stupid, they assume that he must have made some form of mistake, that he was misinformed. And making the same blunder as the scientists, we look at public spectacles and take the solemn promises and proposals of the actors at their face value; we assume they know what they are doing and intend it. But, suppose that it isn't true? Suppose, instead, that the swindlers and the con men are themselves swindled and conned?

Consider how little of animal behavior is the result of conscious intent. What marvels of organization and action are the result of pure instinctual drives: Emperor penguins find their way unerringly to breeding spots over 70 miles away in the worst weather in the world and pick out their mates from among thousands of other penguins. Lemmings, we know, throw themselves off cliffs and drown themselves, lured by the gravity of instinct. Yet, no one suggests that the lemmings were misinformed or that they miscalculated. It is simply assumed that when lemmings act, they do so on instinct, whereas when Homo sapiens act, we take it for granted that they do so rationally, with brainpower. Scientists assume that man is always a naive scientist himself. They assume he is learning about the world around him and gradually coming to know it better and better. That he is adapting his institutions to the world as if they were furnishings for a house he just bought and from time to time redecorates when he finds something better in the stores.

But what if man is neither as wholly rational, nor other animals as wholly irrational, as we have assumed? What if *all simply act according to various prefigured survival strategies, the purpose of which—as far as we know—is nothing more than genetic replication?* Wouldn't that explain Hummers and tall CEOs? That is to say, taller people make more money and are more likely to be put in leadership roles not because of some kind of prejudice, as Malcolm Gladwell assumes in *Blink*, but because height is part of an evolutionary game plan: "There's plenty of evidence to suggest that height—particularly in men—does trigger a certain set of very positive unconscious associations . . . We see a tall person and we swoon."[21]

But there's no reason tall men *shouldn't* earn more, except that it transgresses Gladwell's own prejudice in favor of equal distribution of earnings. How does he know who should earn what? He doesn't. The tall man, for his part, figures there is something inherent in his tallness that gives him the ability to earn more money. The short man, for his, figures he is the victim of a prejudice or mistake. Neither imagines that they are both creatures of nature, no more responsible for the collective biases of the race than a leopard is to blame for his spots.

But does genetic survival also explain do-gooding?

After all, Darwin's theory of evolution by natural selection maintains that traits are retained or discarded insofar as they influence reproductive viability. On its face, therefore, the theory seemed to leave no room for selfless acts of kindness or mercy, for, properly understood, altruism refers to actions that give the actor no reproductive advantage.

A man in a crowded lifeboat, for example, goes overboard so that others may live, entirely unselfishly—in evolutionary terms—unless the boat contains his offspring. How to explain this?

Could it be, and here we move tentatively, that a man may feel he *has* to jump over the gunwale or he will be shunned as a coward—in which case, his reproductive opportunities are likely to be few? Or could it be that he may operate under some sort of reciprocity code, in effect willingly giving up his life so that another man's offspring could survive—in the belief that the other fellow would do the same for his own children? That might make sense, except that in some primitive tribes, men *kill* the male children of a fallen comrade, presumably so that his widow will be liberated to bear their children. Even in ancient Rome, newly installed emperors would kill the families of their predecessors and anyone who might be a source of competition.

Reproductive advantage, thus, turns out to be a two-edged sword—capable of explaining the most viciously competitive behavior as well as the most altruistic. There is no clear answer.

All of which merely goes to show how variable and complicated human life can be. If the world improvers hope to mold or improve a species whose most basic instincts are expressed in such opposite ways, they would have to walk among the gods. Unfortunately, most of them think they do.

The truth is, when it comes down to it, human beings are hopeless jellyfish, taking the shape of almost any container you force them into. And then, let them out—they are smelly blobs again. That is the conclusion of psychologists who have spent the past half century examining the curiosities of the human race. What they have found is what any alert observer could have told them from the get-go. Study after study has shown people to be stupid, insipid, unfaithful, unreliable, illogical, selfish, unfathomable, mean, absurd, and often insane. That is not to say there is no good in them.

Nor does it mean that there is no sense in what they do. But even if there is a sense to it, they are themselves usually unaware of the real sense, and would deny it if you pointed it out to them. Human beings are neither good nor bad; they are merely subject to influence.

THE TIES THAT BIND

And why should they not be? Humans have lived in structured groups, under the influence of others, for at least 50,000 years. Group living gave them obvious advantages; they could hunt together and protect themselves more easily. One could become expert at hunting, another at making fires, and yet another at making weapons. But living together required a new level of complexity—and complicity—including communication, hierarchical organization, and that impression management we mentioned earlier. And now, at last, we may have come to a workable rationale for our do-gooders. Now we may be able to begin understanding the spectacles of modern life, from five-year plans and poverty programs to financial manias and wars to end all wars.

You see, one of the drawbacks of group living was that group identity made humans rivals of each other. They could now band together to exterminate a rival tribe—to gain themselves reproductive advantage. The cost of losing this kind of struggle—death—was so great that they had to evolve social systems and bigger brains to encourage solidarity and punish freethinking. (According to some scientists, larger brains evolved merely to handle the increased data-processing needs of large, sophisticated group structures.)

And here seems to be the explanation for why groups take their politics, sports, and cultures so seriously. Without that unifying glue, a group might not be able to survive the lethal struggles with other groups. A rival group could kill it or take over scarce resources.

And here, too, we find the source of group prejudices. A man would not particularly care to pay the ultimate price—giving up his life—to protect his own group, unless he thought it worth protecting. It had to be superior in some way, or he might just as well transfer his loyalty to the competing group. So, he came to detest other religions, other polities, other cultures, and other races for a perfectly honest and logical reason—they endangered his survival.

This is the real source of personal and group vanity.

On the surface of it, all groups on earth have evolved exactly the same number of years. That they have evolved different social structures provides no reasonable basis for thinking one is better than another ... or that the world itself would be better if one group were to prevail over another. As to fitness—the sole standard of the evolutionists' creed—all surviving genes are created equal. So, too, are all religions, cultures, and languages. And yet, since most religions claim to be the only true one, it must be that most of mankind lives in error. Likewise, since most cultures think of themselves as superior, they must all be wrong, since they cannot all be correct. Most races, too, feel (whether or not they will admit it) that they are somehow better than all others. They, too, must be making a mistake—but a rational one. For, we now see why, in an evolutionary sense, such bamboozles are rational; without them, the group might soon be annihilated.

But necessary or not, they do end up turning our whole extended tribe into a breed of criminal idiots, who mostly believe things that can't possibly be true. And are ready to undertake nearly any kind of skulduggery one can imagine in earnest pursuit of ideals that are nothing more than evolutionary flimflam.

BRIGHT SHINING LIES

Everywhere we look, nature tells us the same story. That deceit is nothing new. Humans didn't invent it. There are butterflies whose tails look like their heads. No one would say that the butterfly intends to mislead predators, but that is the effect of it. Other animals look like wasps but actually have no power to sting. Still others take the form of inedible species, when they are actually tasty. Some fireflies light up as though they were the females of another species, in order to prey on the males. Birds will pretend to be injured in order to distract predators from the nest. Dogs will sometimes pretend to be injured, too—merely to get petted. The only difference is that having bigger brains, human beings can lie better. "The dog ate my homework." "Honey, I had to stay late at the office." "The check is in the mail."

Ethnologists believe that in the animal kingdom staged battles are, in fact, more common than the fight to the death variety.[22]

Bluff, bluster, humbug, fraud—we live in it every day. And yet, who would be willing to admit it? Instead, we all take the lies even further—we lie about lying! We lie with body language. We lie with words. We tell each other we appreciate the truth, but in fact the truth is often the last thing we want to hear. Imagine the husband who says: "You look awful tonight, honey." "Boy, I sure had a good time last night at the strip joint." Imagine the politician who says: "You voters spend too much money . . . you eat too much. You're a bunch of self-indulgent slobs."

Who would appreciate such candor? No one. None of us really likes honesty. We prefer deception—but only when it is unabashedly flattering or artfully camouflaged. Groups seem to need to believe that they are superior to others and that they have a purpose greater than just passing along their genes to the next generation. Individuals seem to need similar delusions—about who they are and why they do what they do. They need heroes, however fraudulent. People ask actors who play doctors on television what they should do for their ailments, although they know perfectly well that the actors are just playing a role. Studies show that people are more likely to accept the opinion of a confident con man than the cautious view of someone who actually knows what he is talking about. And professionals who form overconfident opinions on the basis of incorrect readings of the facts are more likely to succeed than their more competent peers who display greater doubt.

What's more, deception works best, according to studies by psychologists, when the person doing the deceiving is fool enough to be deceived, too; that is, when he believes his own lies. That is why incompetent leaders—who are naive enough to fall for their own guff—are such a danger to civilized life. If they are modern leaders, they must also delude themselves into thinking they know how to make the world a better place. Invariably, the answers they propose to problems are ones that bubble up from their own vanity, the essence of which is to make the rest of the world look just like them! If they are Catholic, then the whole world must become Catholic. If they are democratic, then that is what the world must be. If they are hip-hop artists, then the rest of the world must hop with them.

CHAPTER 3

THE TRANSIT
OF VENUS

But man, proud man,
Drest in a little brief authority
Plays such fantastic tricks before high heaven
As make the angels weep.

—William Shakespeare, *Measure for Measure*

In Chapter 1, we attempted only to show that the world improvers were nitwits. It was light work, we admit, but it had to be done. In this chapter, our burden is equally modest: to show what the world improver has to work with—the soft mush and muscle that is man as he actually is.

We recall the week of June 5, 2004. It was a good one in which to die; you would have been in such good company. Ronald Reagan, Ray Charles, Robert Kephart . . .

Ronald Wilson Reagan was the nation's old friend; Robert Wilson Kephart was ours. Bob had waged war against cancer for two years. Even when all hope of victory seemed lost—he could not even hope for a draw—he refused to surrender. If God were going to take him, He'd have to fight for him. But the fight was rigged; Bob had no chance.

That week, too, Venus made a rare promenade directly between the Earth and the Sun—a transit of Venus, astrologers call it.

Why did it matter, we asked a friend.

"Serotonin" was her answer.

"It's why the transit of Venus makes a difference to stock prices," said the editor of London's *MoneyWeek* magazine, our colleague, Merryn Somerset-Webb.

"It's a proven fact," she went on, "that the sun, the moon, and other heavenly bodies affect the amount of serotonin in your brain. Serotonin affects your mood. That's why astrology really *is* a useful tool for predicting stock market trends."

Some people are eternal optimists. Others see clouds wrapped around every silver lining. Some will hold losing positions to the bitter end. Others will always give up without a fight and move on. But most people are open to suggestion. They can be swayed by the news, the weather, the stars . . . even campaign advertising.

"The transit of Venus across the sun on Tuesday," Merryn explained, "is a very bad omen. I read it in *Barron's*.

"Henry Weingarten has one of the best forecasting records on Wall Street," she continued. "He runs something called Astrologer's Fund. I guess he bases his selections on the stars. Whatever he's doing, it must work, because he's famous. He forecast almost to the day not only the collapse of the Nikkei after the bubble of the 1980s, but also the Hong Kong crash in 1997 and the bursting of the technology bubble in 2000.

"Weingarten says the position of the planets at the moment raises 'the specter of violence.' "

By the twentieth century, scientists could send men to the moon; little did they seem to realize that men had had the moon within them all along.

On June 8, a shriveled little heart in a crystal jar finally ended its long transit. A chunk of it had been cut out and subjected to the latest DNA testing. Using a strand of Marie Antoinette's hair, scientists found that the heart was truly that of Louis XVII, the lost dauphin, who died in a rank prison cell at the tender age of 10 after his mother and father had had their heads chopped off. Again, science enlightened us. Now, we know more of the how, but still not the why. The poor little boy was innocent. He had not lived long enough to commit a capital crime . . . or even to make a fool of himself. Why would anyone want him to die? In his final months, he sat in his cell, wheezing and coughing from tuberculosis, staring black-eyed, and shuffling a deck of cards. History tells us he died in the arms of the one and only guard who had the heart to comfort him, for he was a son of a hated king.

"What is the meaning of it all?" Bob wondered on his deathbed. "I don't know. I've spent a lot of time thinking about it, as I've been fighting this thing. And now I'm beat.

"I hope to see you on the other side. We'll meet again in a great assembly of the saints . . . a lot of platitudes . . . I don't have any idea what's coming. But I'm ready for it."

The fight was over. But Bob still would not wave the white flag. Drugged and weak, he gave a report, sounding more like a German field marshal briefing headquarters from the Eastern front than a cancer patient:

"The cancer is advancing along the liver line," he told us. "Pockets have been found in the lungs. The incursions into the brain and backbone are growing larger; we have ceased all treatment."

With that, he blew up the ammunition and spiked the cannon.

Venus made her transit . . . and God had his man.

What makes the world go round, dear reader? Is it love? Or money? Does it all work in some reasonable, logical way that we just have to decipher? What makes it better . . . or worse?

Is it the noisy world improvers with their "isms," their headlines and their wars? Or does the world improve only by the quiet efforts of ordinary people going about their business without ever making the news? You will recall that Hillary Clinton once explained that she could have stayed home and baked cookies. Instead, she chose to get her name in the paper. But which might have actually made the world better: her cookies . . . or her task force on health care reform?

TWO KINDS OF WORLD IMPROVERS

Can you really improve the world by telling it what to do? Or does it have to follow its own course to its own destination in its own good time?

We saw the two approaches to world improvement standing almost side by side one weekend in early 2005. The one on the silver screen wore a Nazi uniform. The other, in rural Normandy, wore the simple frock of a priest.

"I have devoted my entire life to making the world a better place," said Adolf Hitler, or words to that effect.

"But, mein Führer," explained one of his generals, "Berlin is nearly surrounded. We have no more ammunition. We must try to negotiate."

"You, too? I am surrounded by incompetents and traitors," came the reply. "We can never surrender. I'd rather put a bullet into my head. We have done all we could, so far. We must go all the way—to the end, if that is what is coming."

"But, mein Führer, think of the suffering of the German people."

"You want me to have compassion? My work was too important to let compassion or any personal motives interfere. So, don't expect me to be compassionate now. And besides, the German people deserve to die, too; they let me down. They aren't worthy of the great new world we were offering them."

It was on a Friday evening that we went to see the new German film, *Downfall*. It was everything that *Alexander the Great* was not. While Alexander was made to look absurd and laughable, Adolf Hitler looked very real—and pathetic. In *Downfall*, we see the Thousand-Year Reich coming to an end 990 years ahead of schedule. We see mature, battle-hardened generals who cannot bring themselves to disobey. There will be hell to pay, but they soldier on anyway. Many blow their brains out rather than try to come up with Plan B.

The Sunday after we saw *Downfall*, we went to the little church in Normandy. We introduced ourselves and the priest apologized for the small turnout and the humble circumstances. Looking around at the handful of the gray-haired faithful, it appeared that death was not only inevitable but imminent. There was hardly a person under the age of 70.

Later, in his sermon, the priest commented on Christ's beatitudes. "We Christians are urged to be a 'light unto the world.' But what does that mean? Does it mean we have to change the government? Or that we have to change the way people worship or the way they act? No, it means we have to change ourselves."

This type of world improver hardly even dares to think about improving *the* world. He is much more modest. The best he can do is to make small private gestures in his own world.

"We are called to be a 'light unto the world,'" continued the priest, "by lighting up our own little world. By visiting the sick. By welcoming strangers and newcomers to the community. By caring for the poor. By comforting those who suffer from sickness of the body or the spirit. We light up the world simply by being the decent people that Christ showed us how to be: by showing compassion, in other words . . . and by loving our neighbors as ourselves."

AMERICA'S REVOLT AGAINST THE GODS

But, in the autumn of 2005 Americans had come to believe not in being a light, but in packing heat. They believed in something they thought more dependable than traditions or gods—themselves.

The whole nation seemed to have become a giant O. J. Simpson jury, unable to imagine that its homeland boys could be doing anything but good. Pictures were exhibited on national television, clearly showing a U.S. marine gunning down a wounded prisoner. "This one's faking he's dead," said the marine. Then, after a clatter of gunfire, "He's dead now." A poll taken the next day revealed that the crowd back home was fully behind its troops—three out of four people thought the Iraqi had it coming.[1]

Americans believe themselves to be good people. How this special state of grace was accorded to them they do not know. How they might remain in such grace they do not ask. But they are sure they will get into heaven, even if they have to climb a pile of dead Iraqis to get there. Americans know they are good because their enemies are bad people. Can good people do bad things? Can bad people do good things? The questions are rarely raised and more rarely answered; one might as well ask a parrot to decline an irregular Latin verb. The few who take up the question at all quickly shut down their frontal lobes to avoid overheating and refer the matter back to more primitive parts of the brain for judgment.

On instinct and intuition alone the matter is resolved. This is a Public Spectacle, after all. The war in Iraq is a team sport; the hometown crowd will stand and do the wave right to the bitter end. There is no place for ambiguity, subtlety, or irony. Or arrière-pensées. On his own, you see, a man might be haunted by killing. He might see a murderer each time he looked into the mirror. He might feel guilt and the need to punish himself. Maybe he would begin to stutter, stand barefoot in the snow, or step in front of a bus.

On his own he might do all these things, but not in a mass. In a mass, men feel no guilt, no shame. The blood of a hundred thousand innocents might drip from their hands as from a leaky faucet, but the mass of Americans lined up in favor of war against Iraq asks no questions and feels neither guilt nor shame. It sees no need to apologize and senses no danger of retribution, neither from man nor from God himself. Such is always the nature of a public spectacle; the crowd can no more fear for its soul than a pebble can yearn for the beach.

"Fifty million people in Afghanistan and Iraq have been liberated from tyranny, and our homeland has been made more secure," said George Bush in his year-end message in 2003. "Our tax cuts returned money to people who earned it. They have put it to work in our economy, which is growing again and beginning to generate new jobs, but we won't rest until everybody who wants to work can find a stable, productive job."

Thus, Americans at the beginning of anno Domini 2007 were a fat, happy, and contented race—in revolt against fate. They had come to believe that things that couldn't be true even in one instance could be true forever.

Indeed, their self-contentment had reached such clinical levels that it caught the eye of clinicians.

A Yale University assistant professor of psychiatry, Bandy Xenobia Lee, appeared before the World Economic Forum in Davos in early 2004 and read aloud the standard medical description of narcissistic personality disorder. The narcissist, he explained:

- Has a grandiose sense of self-importance (e.g., exaggerates achievements and talents, expects to be recognized as superior without the commensurate achievements).
- Is preoccupied with fantasies of unlimited success, power, brilliance.
- Requires excessive admiration.
- Has a sense of entitlement (i.e., unreasonable expectations of especially favorable treatment or automatic compliance with his or her expectations).
- Shows arrogant, haughty behaviors or attitudes.

It was time, noted Dr. Lee, to apply these diagnostic criteria not just to people, but to nations.[2]

The point was not lost on the audience at Davos. It was obvious to the world that in economics, Americans' delusions of grandeur were threatening to ruin them. And in politics, it was worse; Americans were risking their very souls with murderous wars.

In 2004, when Dr. Lee made his statement, few nations could have afforded to live in the style to which Americans had become accustomed—not even Americans themselves. Their paper money—unbacked by anything more than the eager promises of the world's biggest debtor—was destined to go bad; all paper money always does. Their economy was doomed to slow down—debtors cannot increase spending forever. Their stocks were bound for a fall, victims of an excess of enthusiasm and a shortage of capital investment. Their bonds were living on borrowed time, too—for it was nothing more than a matter of amazement that foreign leaders should continue to buy bonds with 5 percent yields when the currency in which they were denominated was losing 20 percent of its value in a single year.

Yet, Americans had little doubt that they had liberated the desert tribes of Mesopotamia from "Tyranny," rather than imposed a new tyranny of their own. They managed to support—and applaud—the biggest growth in government spending, debt, and bureaucracy since Franklin Roosevelt, and applaud it, of all things, in the name of liberty.

After all, they told themselves, we are in a postmodern age, complete with the Internet, online trading, J-Lo, and Howard Stern. We no longer need to believe in gods or devils. We believe in psychologists and chronic fatigue syndrome. If the price of AOL discounts earnings to the year 2200, it must be right. The price is always right; the market is always perfectly rational; there is no room for human emotion, nor for folly, wishful thinking, chicanery, tomfoolery, or a severe case of seasonal affective disorder.

Success has transformed a modest people whose greatest virtue was once minding their own business into a vainglorious race, who mind everyone's business but their own. They cannot save a dime themselves, but now they offer to save the entire planet. There was a time when they admired the English for their literature ... the Germans for their organization ... the French for their intellect and style ... and the Japanese for their industrial discipline. Now they turn their heads to the heavens and see only their own reflection in the clouds. They revere themselves with double the adoration and thrice the fidelity. Old Europe is a museum, they complain. It is rigid, cowardly, and gummed up with social welfare regulation. And Japan? The so-called miracle economy has been stuck in an on-again, off-again recession for more than 16 years, they gibe, because the Japanese lack the guts to restructure their economy along American lines.

This disdain is not based in logic or reason, of course. Few attitudes are. Or as they say on Wall Street—"Markets make opinions." That is to say, when stocks have been rising for a long while, investors have opinions about why the bull market will last forever. If stocks arc falling, their feelings lead them to believe prices will continue to fall for all eternity.

But, of all attitudes, none is so irrationally conceived and so inveterately held as people's good opinions of themselves. And Americans' opinions of themselves are no exception. Since they have created their success themselves, surely they must be in charge of it, too, they think.

Discounted is the hard work of their fathers and grandfathers who went ahead of them. Dismissed are the virtues of thrift, sound money, limited government, and collective modesty. Flipping with boredom through the back pages of their history, Americans pay no attention to the dead. And the future ... the unborn? It is as if they think the book has no sequel ... as if it were the last opus ever ... the final word, the Omega Civilization.

We can almost hear the gods snickering.

One day, historians will look back at our era and marvel at how George Bush and Tony Blair determined to convert the Iraqis to democracy. To our descendants, it will look like a mad caprice; a quaint, religious gesture; an act of remarkable faith or delusion, like missionaries showing the heathen the correct posture for copulation.

THE AMERICAN BRAIN: THE FLAW IN THE DESIGN

A glimpse of that insanity was already available in the autumn of 2004, in what was billed as one of America's most important presidential races. Every election is to some extent an advance auction of stolen goods. In 2004, never before had so much been up for auction. But there was more than just money at stake. Both candidates—reading the temper of the times—made the center of their campaigns a promise to protect Americans from terrorism.

So enlivened by the campaigns of 2004—and so fearful of the terrorist threat—were American voters that they stood in line for up to five hours to cast their ballots.

Americans were afraid of terrorism, said the pollsters. Why wouldn't they be? The fear was incessantly jacked up by the media, politicians, and generals, to the point where the average man could practically see his house being fire-bombed, his children abducted, and his wife raped before his very eyes. "Terrorists threaten our way of life," said the president. "Terrorists put the U.S. Constitution at risk," added the chairman of the Joint Chiefs of Staff.[3]

But the actual risk of being a victim of terrorism is as remote as, say, the risk of being drowned in your bathtub. Even in Israel, a person is four times as likely to die in a traffic accident as in a terrorist attack. Indeed, since the State Department began counting terrorist deaths in the late 1960s, even including the deaths from the attack on the World Trade Center towers on September 11, 2001, the number of deaths from terrorism has been about the same as the number of people who have died from severe allergic reaction to peanut butter. Yet, since 2001, the U.S. government has spent billions in their effort to protect Americans from terrorism. As far as we know, it has spent none at all to protect us from peanut butter. For one of your authors, who is allergic to peanuts, Skippy, Jiffy, and Peter Pan represent a far bigger threat than Osama or Moktadar.

But the difference is this: Peanut butter, so far at least, is not part of a theater of mass passions. And it is this theater that draws the money and the headlines. Until peanut butter becomes part of a public spectacle, it will stay safely in obscurity.

Of course, people will counter that the real danger from terrorism comes from things the world has not yet seen. Terrorists might step up their operations, or they might get hold of weapons of mass destruction and *really* do some damage.

Well, let us suppose the terrorists *were* to bring down more airplanes. According to University of Michigan researchers, they'd have to crash as many planes as they did on September 11 every single month of the year in order for the risk of flying to equal the risk of driving a car.[4]

Or, suppose terrorists were to set off a dirty bomb? Yes, it would increase the radiation level. Enough to harm many people? Maybe, maybe not. No one really knows. That is the case with biological and chemical weapons, too; they are hard to control and deliver. That's why terrorists, as well as traditional military forces, usually stick to things that blow up the old-fashioned way. All the terrorism in the United States over the past 200 years has killed fewer people than the war George Bush launched against it in 2001.

Actually, the most effective response to terrorism is the one most likely to frustrate terrorists and least likely to become public policy—ignore it.

"Get on the damn elevator!" writes Senator John McCain. "Fly on the damn plane! Calculate the odds of being harmed by terrorists! It's still about as likely as being swept out to sea by a tidal wave."[5]

Instead, the attacks of September 11 produced exactly the results the terrorists desired—the Bush administration panicked, got out the duct tape, and created what Leif Wenar at the University of Sheffield cleverly calls "a false sense of insecurity."[6]

In short, they created panic—even terror—in the American people, which, of course, is precisely the aim of terrorists. In the language of the Marxist terrorists of the late 1960s, their real aim is to *radicalize* onlookers, moving them to join the cause. That is just what the Bush administration seems to have done. Rather than calmly and quietly proceeding to track down the perpetrators, it blundered right into Iraq and stirred up terrorist ambitions all over the Middle East. Where previously there had been only a handful of fanatics to worry about, now there are thousands of them.

Still, there were no terrorist attacks worth mentioning in the 50 states, neither in 2002, 2003, nor 2004. Homeland Security officials warned of attacks. Color-coded alarms were displayed, and General Richard Myers, chairman of the Joint Chiefs of Staff, even told television audiences that terrorists might kill 10,000 people and "do away with our way of life."[7]

Where were the terrorists, though? A reasonable voter might have decided that they didn't exist, or that if they did, they were not able to do much terrorizing. Still, voters told pollsters that they had made their choice for president based on this largely imaginary threat. Of course, they could not really know which candidate would do a better job against terrorism. Nonetheless, just as they had become caught up in the hysteria of terrorism, Americans had also come to be swept along by the mania of national elections.

But, what Americans think about voting is only what they are repeatedly told. Every man's vote counts, intone the well-meaning. In fact, almost none of the voters have any idea what they are voting for or against in any election; none have a realistic opinion on the threats that face the nation. In effect, if not in theory, elections have become a ritual of modern government. They serve roughly the same purpose as used to be served by crowning the king or bowing to the tyrant. They are all equally actions that are merely emblems of submission and adherence. Individually, none of them has any effect whatever on the outcome. Voters might as well be the home crowd at a ball game.

Indeed, the odds that your vote will actually matter are so slight as to not be worth thinking about. The race would have to be dead even without your vote for it to count. And then, of course, you would have to be voting in an electoral state where it mattered. The real odds that your vote will decide the outcome of an election are something on the order of 8 chances out of 10 raised to the 8,000th power. For comparison, the number of seconds since time began is something like 3 times 10 to the power of 17. In other words, you could be shipwrecked on an island with Paris Hilton and win the lottery every day before your one vote would be decisive.

But one might as well try to convince Americans that terrorists are not circling the shores of the Homeland. On both issues, people's convictions arise not from proofs supplied by the brain but prejudices amplified by the heart.

Which only goes to show that man is badly designed—not in every particular, but in a few. This insight comes to us not only as a theoretical point, but as a piece of practical information the older of your authors was offered recently. Sketching out a man's internal plumbing on a piece of prescription paper, Dr. Moreau of the emergency room of the American Hospital in Paris revealed a design flaw:

"As you can see," he explained with the impatience of a nuclear physicist explaining photons to an orangutan, "it's bound to cause trouble sooner or later."

What a strange thing. The same Father Creator or Mother Evolution who built such an exquisite universe seems to have lost interest when He or She got to mankind's entrails. For there, on the right side of the intestinal tract, is a little appendix—with no role except to create problems.

"And look at that," cried Dr. Moreau, holding up an X-ray as if it were an aerial photo of the Hindu Kush. "You're going to have trouble here." He was pointing to the range of lower vertebrae. "You must have lower back pain from time to time," he noted.

It is not our place to carp and criticize. But it would have been nice if the manufacturer had installed more durable cartilage in the 1948 models. And more flexible tubing.

"But that is the problem," said the French tutor from whom we take lessons. "Men are not as you want them to be; they are as they are." What had set Sylvie off was neither our plumbing nor our neglect of the subjunctive, but our thoughts on war and peace.

"Almost every war Americans have ever fought has turned out to be a mistake," we had told her, concluding a brief tour of American military history. Every war had its supposed reasons, but in retrospect they were all absurd. What good did the American Revolution accomplish, we wondered aloud, when all of Britain's other colonies negotiated their way to independence and were no worse off for it? What about the War Between the States? If it was fought to get rid of slavery, it was a poor way to do it. Slavery disappeared from the rest of the world with hardly a fatality. Or, if it was fought to Preserve the

Union, it was a fraud; the founders had declared it self-evident that Americans had a right to dissolve the Union.

"As for the First World War," we explained, "the average American was as ignorant of the Austro-Hungarian Empire as he or she was of the contents of Austrian sausages. Americans of sound mind and decent judgment would just as soon have seen the Archduke Ferdinand stuffed and used as a parlor ornament as avenged. But once stirred up by the big idea of 'making the world safe for democracy,' Americans were ready to enlist and get themselves blown up believing that they were protecting Western civilization from the invading Huns."

Sylvie had sat quietly through this rant, merely correcting our grammar as necessary. But now she calmly replied: "You're right. War doesn't make much sense. But so what? Who ever said it had to?"

Exactly so. Once a great collective enterprise is under way, it does not listen to reason; it rolls over anyone who gets in its way. What anyone thinks or says does not matter.

What they feel does matter, however. Mood matters. Before World War I, Europeans were practically delirious with confidence. People everywhere were becoming healthier, freer, richer, and better behaved, they believed. Property prices were at a peak that was not seen again, in real terms, until 2006—when again, people were supremely confident. As they are now. The S&P 500 index is selling at 30 times earnings. Lenders lend out money for 30 years at only 5 percent interest—this in a currency that loses at least 2 percent per year to inflation and one that has gone down 20 percent against gold in 2006 alone. The U.S. savings rate has fallen to its lowest level in history. Americans think, why save for a rainy day? It will never rain again.

And maybe it never will. Most often, it is true, nothing happens. Most often, things go on, day to day, with little change. The sun shines. The birds sing.

But occasionally, just occasionally, not only does it rain, it pours.

NO ROOM FOR NO

And when it pours, dissent becomes dangerous. It is only then that one can be sure one has a public spectacle on one's hands.

We recall that when one of us began writing daily market commentary at the end of the 1990s, it seemed obvious to us that stocks, especially tech stocks, were trading at absurd multiples—not of earnings, for they had no earnings, but of sales. But when we held them up to ridicule, we were soon the target of hateful e-mails explaining that we just didn't get it and were destined to remain poor while the rest of the world became fabulously rich.

Just so, in times of war, dissent can be fatal. More than 300 soldiers were shot by firing squads in World War I. These were men who either went off their heads ... or actually used them. In his private life, the poor soldier was needed elsewhere. There were crops to be harvested; children to be bounced on his knee; wives, mothers, and sisters to be helped and caressed. But what could he do? Perhaps he might have sent a letter to the British, French, and German high commanders during World War I: "Well, this is clearly not working out. Why don't we all go back to our original positions and forget the whole thing?"

But there was no going back. That is why, in war and speculation, it is often better to lose the first encounter than win it; it might make you reconsider. Otherwise, you're likely to go on until you are broke, exhausted, or dead.

Before we move on, therefore, we pause to honor the short sellers of the dot-com era; they were the only people with the courage to think for themselves ... or at least with the gall to defect.

BASIC INSTINCTS

The point is not that people do not think. It is that they cannot stop thinking. Only what they take for thought is most often delusion compounded by the contagion of others' opinions. Which is why most people would be better off not thinking at all but going on their instincts. Ask any really successful man and he will tell you his success comes as much from his intuition as from his brain.[8]

Yet, intuition is generally dismissed—as though it were no more than myth. This is remarkable to us, for, if you were to ask the average man for an intuition, it would almost invariably be reasonable, far more than anything produced by his reason. "The weather is turning bad," he would say. "That marriage is bound for trouble," he might guess. "There's a young man who will go places," he would venture.

Yet, were you to ask the same man to use his brain to produce a compound logical thought about a public matter, the result would likely be preposterous or simply incomprehensible: "The rich should pay more taxes because the poor need the money more than they do." "Stocks will go up because more people want them." "We have to defend ourselves against terrorists; therefore, we have no choice but to go to war."

Each of these statements is bundled up with a mass of ideas, prejudices, assumptions, metaphors, and delusions. And if you were to strip them off, you would find such a scrawny skeleton of a real idea underneath that if it were not propped up artificially, it would fall down straightaway in a heap.

That shows that it is mostly instinct, not intellect, that drives us. Before mankind even existed, protoman lived on his gut reactions, like the rest of the animals. He had no language and no words. He had to react quickly. In nanoseconds he made life-or-death decisions, without reference to any formal reasons, electoral polls, or newspaper headlines.

The approach of a lion, for example, had the same effect as a registered letter from the IRS today. It triggered an immediate response—flight. For all our monkey ancestor knew, the big cat was a vegetarian. Or only another monkey masquerading in a cat suit. He could not possibly know everything about it. So, he acted as modern humans still do—on the basis of instinct, intuition, and the limbic system. He evolved reactions, or, it is probably more correct to say, *they* evolved him. See a big catlike thing approaching? Get the heck out of here as soon as possible! Those without the quick response became lunch, not parents.

The development of words and language made a big difference, because it introduced a new kind of thinking. Words were not nearly as subtle and fluid as intuitions, but they were versatile in their own way, because they allowed humans to pass along more complex thoughts and sentiments: "Cat! Big cat! Hungry cat!"

Unlike sounds that conveyed only emotions—fear, opportunity, danger, sorrow, and the like—words contained ideas . . . and large, supercharged images and metaphors.

"Home," for example, triggers a happy flush in one person; in another, it smarts like a bee sting. It has a specific meaning—you can imagine your own ivy-covered cottage in the foothills of the Cotswolds. It has a general meaning, too; home is where people live. It is a financial asset for millions. A cost center for others. It is even a political term. Some extremists hate the word so much that, given the opportunity, they would abolish it and replace it with state-run crèches and drab worker housing for adults.

Just there, you have the disadvantage of man over animal. An animal will invariably follow its instincts. But man—especially thinking man—will convince himself that his instincts are wrong . . . outmoded . . . retrograde. Then, he will do the most remarkable things in the name of progress, such as substituting reformatories for family homes or hanging trendy abominations on his walls.

And, often, the smarter he is, the more absurd and idiotic he will be, for his intelligence helps him use clever words and arguments to persuade himself and others to do the most preposterous things! That is perhaps George Bush's one great advantage; he doesn't appear smart enough to be an idiot; voters took a look at him and sensed that he had an intuitive understanding of the world similar to their own. Bush may be a fool, they reasoned, but in his mug they saw their own *honnête* face—and they liked it.

WORD GAMES

That is to say, the instinctual, popular suspicion of the glib intellectual is not lacking merit, for today we humans are smothered with words. They tumble out of newspapers, books, reports, television, radio, and the Internet. Some are precise and useful—the formula for making bombs, the recipe for sponge cake, and so on. But most are nothing more than an invitation to rumble.

Take our commander-in-chief. When he learned that sovereignty had been passed back to the Iraqis, he sent a little note on his own to Condoleezza Rice. With no spinmeisters to smooth out his dyslexic syntax, he wrote, "Let freedom reign."

We have no idea what the president meant by this. If he meant that we should now back off and "let freedom reign," it was a strange thought for someone who had just killed several hundred thousand foreigners—who, as far as we know, never did anything to us.

But, maybe he meant that the Iraqis are now free—a situation he was applauding. But was that true, either? Left to their own devices—that is to say, free of foreign meddlers—Iraqis seemed quite content with their dictatorship. If getting rid of Saddam Hussein were so important to them, why would they not have done it themselves? Surely the Iraqis had their own Cromwell somewhere, ready to do the "cruel necessity." It is certainly a strange freedom that is available at the whim of foreign invaders.

And it is even more certainly one of the great conceits of Western civilization, circa 2007, that freedom or democracy makes people more peaceful and more prosperous. The evidence for this is blemished by the history of the twentieth century—in which nations that were free and democratic (at least at the beginning) fought the bloodiest wars in history.

In any case, given the choice between a dictator who left us alone and a democracy where everything we did required state approval—we would choose the dictator!

But how about prosperity? Perhaps voting makes people wealthier?

A study conducted by Professors Dani Rodrik of Harvard University and Romain Wacziarg of Stanford University was intended to examine just this point. The pair spent many pages explaining how democratic openness leads to market reforms, which then lead to greater output. But the actual evidence they supplied seems rather inconclusive. They compared growth rates in the 10 years before a country became democratic to rates of growth in the 10 years following. Looking down the list, we saw several marginal winners and only one big one—Chile, where gross domestic product (GDP) growth rose from 1.6 percent in the 10 years prior to democratization to 5.8 percent in the years after. However, what strikes our eye is a few big losers. Portugal's growth rate fell from 7 percent before democratization in 1974 to 1.2 percent after. Spain's growth rate dropped to 0.3 percent from 5.4 percent, and Ecuador practically went broke; its growth rate fell from 6.8 percent to minus 0.4 percent![9] (See Table 3.1.)

Democracy is widely thought to promote peace and prosperity. But we have always wondered about that assumption, and now we have a superb counterexample in a recent book by James Bartholomew, *The Welfare State We're In.*[10]

During most of the last fifty years of the twentieth century, the citizens of Hong Kong were ruled by a distant and almost uninterested bureaucracy, represented in the colony by John Cowperthwaite, a flinty Scot and a modest civil servant. He had been appointed financial secretary in charge of all that concerned Hong Kong's economy.

Cowperthwaite found himself in charge of an economy of millions of poor people—the output per capita was only one-fifth that of Great Britain—with millions more streaming in, seeking refuge from China. The colony had little arable land. It had no natural resources. It lacked even enough water. But it had one huge advantage—it had no democracy.

Back in England, explains James Bartholomew, the government was busy responding to the demands of voters. More and more social programs were added. Taxes were raised. Wars were financed. By the

TABLE 3.1   Average Growth 10 Years before and 10 Years after Democratization in 24 Countries

Country	Year of Democratization	Average Growth Before %	Average Growth After %	Growth Difference %
Ecuador	1979	6.764	−0.425	−7.189
Romania	1989	4.174	−2.424	−6.598
Portugal	1974	7.022	1.222	−5.800
Spain	1975	5.430	0.313	−5.117
El Salvador	1979	1.809	−3.112	−4.920
Bolivia	1982	1.694	−1.969	−3.664
Hungary	1988	2.354	−0.668	−3.022
Dominican Republic	1978	4.364	1.628	−2.736
Honduras	1980	2.256	−0.080	−2.336
Peru	1978	1.685	−0.107	−1.792
Brazil	1985	1.441	1.199	−0.242
Paraguay	1989	1.424	1.204	−0.220
Bangladesh	1991	2.725	2.757	0.032
Nicaragua	1990	−3.738	−3.091	0.646
Nepal	1990	1.559	2.568	1.009
Rep. of Korea	1987	5.841	6.857	1.016
Philippines	1986	−0.126	0.931	1.057
Panama	1989	0.886	1.952	1.066
Madagascar	1991	−1.871	−0.754	1.117
Benin	1990	0.277	1.449	1.172
Poland	1989	−0.795	1.783	2.578
Uruguay	1985	−0.022	3.739	3.761
Chile	1985	1.589	5.797	4.208
Mali	1991	−2.243	2.504	4.746

Source: Dani Rodrik and Romain Wacziarg, "Do Democratic Transitions Produce Bad Economic Outcomes?" *American Economic Review Papers and Proceedings* 95, no. 2, May 2005, p. 53, http://www.stanford.edu/~wacziarg/downloads/democratictransitions.pdf.

1970s, Britain was nearly bankrupt and had to beg money from the International Monetary Fund (IMF).

In Hong Kong, meanwhile, Cowperthwaite resisted all entreaties to follow Britain's example. Taxes were left at 15 percent and were levied only on salaries. The rich paid no higher rate than the middle classes. Regulations were few. If the middle classes wanted housing, they could pay for it themselves, said the financial secretary. If businessmen thought a cross-harbor tunnel was such a good idea, he added, let them build it with their own money. As a result, Hong Kong boomed. Its annual growth rates during the entire period were typically two to three times those of Britain. By 1992, Hong Kong's output per person passed Britain's—the old colony now was richer than the mother country. Undemocratically, dictatorially, Hong Kong had become one of the most peaceful and prosperous places on the entire planet. And one of the most free.

The truth is one could ask a million questions about freedom or democracy and still know nothing. The exchange would make as much sense as an argument between a lunatic and a U.S. senator: half incomprehensible, half soothing lie. The words would not confront each other; instead they would pass like busloads of tourists in front of a philosopher's grave. Who was he? What did he say? What does it mean? No one knows or cares.

Words may be inescapable, but they are also indefinable. In the name of freedom and democracy, for instance, Americans have rushed into their own enslavement. The world has never seen greater recklessness. Eight trillion dollars' worth of government debt—what Evel Knievel of state finance would attempt to jump over it? Democracy in Iraq? Even woolly Woodrow Wilson would have been shocked by the idea. But that's the charm of the frontal lobe; it sets up thoughts as casually as drinks at an Irish wedding. Before long, the guests can barely find their car keys, let alone their way home.

THE INTUITIVE MIND

So how smart is intelligence, really?

A recent Dutch study has shown that when decisions are very complicated, people are better off "sleeping on it," a piece of folk wisdom that until recently was scoffed at.[11]

"People can only focus on a limited amount of information," says the study which is cited in the journal *Science*. "The conscious brain should be reserved for simple choices like picking between towels and shampoos."

Especially when it came to more complicated decisions involving 12 or more criteria, conscious deciders were at a loss; they succeeded only 23 percent of the time, while the unconscious decision makers succeeded 60 percent of the time.

Lead researcher Dr. Ap Dijksterhuis suggests that when you have to make a complex decision, you should gather all the information you can and consciously reflect on it; but then, he says, you should sleep on the information, letting your unconscious mind make the decision for you.

In short, there is another kind of intelligence, too. It is the more ancient variety—the intelligence of animals, the intelligence that distills experience and instinct into an intuition about things. It is the intelligence it takes to read people and to have a feeling about a situation. It is the intelligence that draws not only from words and symbols, but from the weather, the way people smile, and the way they talk. You might call it "social intelligence," as opposed to the other sort, which is "techno intelligence" or "literary intelligence."

The modern world of universities, business, talk shows, and books cares only about techno intelligence. But it is actually social intelligence—deeper, more refined, more subtle, more instinctive, and more intuitive—that guides our actions. Most of the world's people barely attempt to use techno intelligence. Instead, they make their decisions on the basis of custom, ritual, and tradition, and with the gut and the heart. What sensible man, for instance, chooses his wife by analysis? Who adds up the qualities and assigns them numbers? Which woman would marry a man who chose her using his frontal lobe only? A man who selects his wife logically makes a fool for a husband.

The real trouble is that we tend to think of our reasoning power as if it is cordoned off from the rowdy world of the emotions like a football star from a mob of crazy fans. But the truth may be that thinking—whether it is making choices or choosing between right and wrong—involves far more than logic and verbal dexterity.

University of Virginia psychologist Jonathan Haidt argues that moral thinking is actually highly intuitive and emotional. It only *appears* to be a product of careful reasoning because of people's after-the-fact rationalizations of their preferences. Most of the time, he says, people don't even know why they feel revolted by something. When pressed, they may give reasons, but if the reasons are taken away, few of them—unless they are graduate students in analytical philosophy—change their minds. They may try to come up with other reasons or want more time to think about it, but they are unlikely to switch their opinions just because they can't find good explanations for them. According to Haidt, even if eating your dead pet dog or having sex with a chicken does not harm anyone, most people will tend to find it "just wrong."[12]   But here Haidt himself sounds a bit confused, for how does he know what is harmed or not harmed by what someone does? As for eating your pet dog, outside the world of Armin Meiwes there are few people who nurse any desire to make a three-course meal out of their loved ones, even four-footed.

But once we leave the clinically logical world of moral philosophers and cannibals, we begin to see the virtues of our emotional and intuitive minds. We recognize that while the judgments we make conceal emotions, our emotions, too, conceal hidden judgments. The distinction between our emotional mind and our reasoning mind is simply not as clean-cut as we like to think.

Women, of course, have always known that, for they often seem to have a keener social intelligence than men—sharper intuitions about people and places. Theirs is the intelligence of Venus and the moon and a billion years of evolution. From our own personal experience, we know that if a woman says, "This guy gives me the creeps," it pays to listen—she is drawing on not just worthless superstition but a well of distilled experience and instinct that is a thousand generations deep. In the same way, when someone refuses to go along with the crowd, it is often because they are drawing from an intuition deep down inside them. They are relying on something more than what the world praises as intelligence. It is that "something" which makes real heroes.

REAL HEROES

"Crucify him! Crucify him!"

"The mob in front of Pontius Pilate wanted blood," explained the visiting priest at St. Marcel. "Not just any blood. It wanted the blood of Jesus of Nazareth, the 'King of the Jews.'"

"What crime has he committed?" Pilate asked. But the crowd cared little for legal procedure. "Let the deed be on our heads," they said, giving Pilate a way out.

Any one of the group might have killed Jesus himself. The man walked among them, unarmed.

A man's sense of fair play and his common decency usually prevent him from making a real beast or fool of himself. For that, he needs a mob. It is mob thinking that makes attitudes toward war such a puzzle of contradictions. The mob is happy when a war begins, but usually happier when it ends. It claims to hate war, but it reveres war heroes and war leaders. Of course, most of the time the difference between a war hero and a war criminal is determined less by the actual events than by the outcome.

But still, there are also real heroes who have done their duty in war time and deserve our respect. Usually, these are the war heroes who had sense enough not to follow orders, but instead, listened to their own moral intuition.

Here, we recall an incident from France's war in Algeria. It was after World War II that an independent movement in Algeria took hold. France sent its brave young men to put down the uprising, but after fighting for a few years, the French had had enough. They could win the battles, but they could never win "hearts and minds" by killing Algerians. Only when the French had withdrawn did the real killing begin and the real heroes appear.

Hundreds of thousands of local Algerian soldiers had fought next to the French. These Harkis had been loyal to the French for many years. But when the time came for the French to leave, the Harkis were to be left behind. What awaited them was vengeance.

An article in *Le Point* from February 2002 noted that there were 200,000 Muslim Harkis who had fought with the French. And after the French left, approximately 50,000 of them—including entire families as well as civilian leaders who had cooperated with the French—were murdered. Whether the French saw it coming or not, we don't know. But a few *officiers* realized that their men—if they were left behind—would be massacred.

The killing was often barbaric. People were crucified. Their limbs were torn off. They were butchered, mutilated ... tortured in ways that plumb the darkness of the human spirit. A mayor was buried up to his neck; honey was smeared on his head. He suffered five hours of agony, being eaten by flies and ants, before finally passing out and dying.

Some of the French military officers were outraged that they had been ordered to abandon their men under these circumstances. Brave men, they say, follow orders. But braver ones, we think, have the courage to disobey.

We recall our neighbor, François, who fought in Algeria, telling us:

"One colonel didn't want to abandon his men. He marched them up to Oran where the ships were taking the French back to France. He went up to the ship's captain and demanded that he load on his troops—who were not French, but local Harkis—you know, Arabs. The captain of the ship said he was not authorized to take the Harkis. The colonel pulled out his pistol and put it up to the captain's head. 'Take them all, or I'll blow your brains out,' he said. The colonel got them back to France, but I think he was arrested. And the Harkis were sent back."

Still, a few officers—such as Daniel Abolivier—were able to organize an underground railway to get the Harkis to France. A few survived. The others were lucky if their throats were cut.

There is a time for thought ... and a time for action. For a married man who has fallen in love with his secretary, for example, it is already too late. He should have thought about it earlier. And when George W. Bush decided to invade Iraq, too, the opportunity for reflection was missed. Now, he has to wonder what will happen to his own Harkis when he leaves.

In his private world, you see, a man is often an oaf but rarely a beast. But give him a big idea—a New Era, a Master Race, a Domino Theory—then put a throng of morons at his back, and he'll do almost anything. You can put bullets, ballots, or a day-trading terminal in his hands; there is practically no way to anticipate the mischief he'll get up to.

What a world we live in! And what extraordinarily bad things ordinary people do—when they think they have a good reason.

Yet, sometimes it is also true that ordinary people can do extraordinarily good things, like Sophie Scholl. The young woman was a student at the University of Munich when she began to discuss a forbidden topic—how individuals ought to conduct themselves when the rest of the world has gone mad. One thought led to another, and then the thoughts led her to join a passive resistance group called the White Rose Society. The group handed out leaflets opposing the Nazi regime. Within weeks they were picked up by the Gestapo. What was their crime? They had quoted the Bible, Lao-tsu, Aristotle, Goethe, and Schiller. They had suggested that Germany might be better off sticking to Christian charity and forgiveness. They had dared to point out that the Führer was a monster. Sophie Scholl, her brother Hans, and their friend Christoph Probst were put on trial on February 22, 1943, found guilty of treason, and executed that same day—by guillotine. Their lives were by far their most precious assets. What rational economic model would predict that they would take such a risk? And yet, they did—and we salute them for it.

The Scholls lost their heads. But unlike thousands in Germany, they did not lose their souls.

Part Two

Witch Hunts and War Drums

CHAPTER 4

THE DEVIL MADE THEM DO IT

A single sentence will suffice for modern man: he fornicated and read the papers.

—Albert Camus, *The Fall*

EXTRAORDINARY POPULAR HEADLINES

We turn our inquiry now to one of the principal organs of mob sentiment—the press. In London, expecially, the newspapers are robust and shameless. We recall the greatest headline ever written in the tabloid press, after a minor figure in the Tory Party, Boris Johnson, was caught in a lurid peccadillo. The headline—over a photo of the woman—ran:

"Bonking Boris Made Me Pregnant"

Bonking Boris is still around. Still around, too, are the newspaper headlines that shout the latest news as though they were announcing the next match at a World Wide Wrasslin' match. We look through the newspaper headlines at random to share them with you:

"NHS [National Health System] Cuts Put Your Children in Danger," says the front page of the *Daily Express*.

"Why, why, why does Sir [Sex Bomb] Tom [Jones] have darker hair than his son?" readers apparently want to know on page 3.

Turn the page—and read about the "Bully chef [who] ran around the kitchen in his underpants." Accompanying the headline is not only a photo of the chef with his pants on, but the waitress who got £124,000 in a sexual harassment settlement.

The *Sun*, meanwhile, takes the high road, with its lead:

"No Peace: Child killers Ian Huntley and Roy Whiting were quizzed in jail yesterday after sick "sorry" notes and roses were left on their victims' graves. The stunt brought new torment to the families. . . ."

We turn the page and . . . whoa! Nicola, 22, from Croydon, seems to have lost her shirt—and her mind. She likes to go to Madame Tussaud's new wax museum, we are told, because there's a statue of Prince Harry there "and now I can go and see him whenever I like," she says. Lucky Prince Harry.

Further on in the paper, we find this jewel: "I Shot Hubby Dead in Sexy Shania Dance."

The *Sun* felt it was important to tell readers about the bully chef, too, but took a different angle: "124,000 Pounds for Bar Girl's Sex Hell."

Then, on page 7, is timely and important news: "Victoria [formerly Posh Spice] to reveal her fashion secrets in glossy beauty bible."

Of course, you say, this is just the scurrilous tabloid press. What about the serious papers? So, we pick up the *Times* and find bigger words, true, but also the front page story, "Betrayal of Justice . . . Hundreds of rapists are escaping justice because of the continuing confusion over the issue of consent and a court environment hostile to victims."

And on page 11, the venerable *Times* takes up the same sorry story of the bully cook. The *Times* thinks the important detail is not that he ran around in his underwear, but the nature of the clientele for whom he baked his soufflés: "Chef to stars unmasked as sex-obsessed bully."[1]

Even in the responsible English press, the reader gets a heavy wallop of sex, class envy, celebrities, and murder. "It's show business," says an English journalist friend.

But, if you think about it, the word *newspaper* is itself a conceit. It pretends that the news industry is a clean pane of glass through which we look out at the spectacle of public events. But it is not a pane of glass at all; it is a microscope in which particular events are magnified and distorted. News that neither encourages journalistic prejudices nor inflates the journal's profits is invisible. The press lords must think their typical readers are louts. And, if not before, soon after they begin reading the newspapers, they will be.

In the United States, France, and Spain, journalists take themselves more seriously. They believe themselves to be heirs to Jonathan Swift—informing people on the crucial matters that affect their lives. Never mind that they are also inflating and protecting their own status. Self-awareness is not a trait taught in journalism school. And, to give them their due, people these days do feel the need—indeed the right—to be informed. They read the paper as if it were a kind of daily hygiene—like brushing their teeth or dumping out the ashtray.

Every headline is written by a hack with his own dog in the fight. It is not news that sells papers, but papers that sell news. And sometimes the papers sell news that is so far removed from the actual events that even they are eventually embarrassed.

"Network of pedophiles: Searchers at Outreau look for the body of a little girl," was the headline in *Le Monde*. "The police began searching, Thursday, the 10th of January [2002] in the gardens of the working class section of Outreau, near Boulogne-sur-Mer, for the body of a young victim of a Franco-Belgian pedophile network."[2]

At least *Le Monde* was fairly reserved about it. The rest of the press was howling in all capital letters about the gruesome details. Not only was the poor little girl tortured, raped, and murdered, it seemed like half the town was in on it.

Sexual orgies, bizarre rituals, confessions, breakdowns—first there were a couple of adults charged, and then the papers and the local prosecutor got their blood up. Soon, a taxi driver, a baker and his wife, a priest! Boy, have we got a story now. Five, ten—the list of pedophiles was beginning to look like the phone book. And why not? The child shrinks were on the case, too. They couldn't believe the kids didn't know or wouldn't say what was really going on. They encouraged them to rat out their parents, their neighbors, their priests, and their guardians. They cajoled them. They pressured them. They wanted them to remember—to think hard. "Is it possible that someone put his hand on you? Wouldn't you like to tell us something? No? Try harder. . . ."

Finally, the kids played along.

"You say a tall [*grand*] man did something to you?" Believe it or not, the investigators went to the phone book, found a man whose name was "LeGrand," and had him arrested.

The prosecutor was a fool. But behind him was such a strong, foul wind from the news media, he could barely keep his feet on the ground. Every day brought fresh gusts: "Pedophile Films Found in Belgium," "Pedophile Ring Arrested," "New Arrests of Leading Citizens." The headlines alone practically had the accused dangling from the gallows, even before any formal charges were filed.

The media wallowed on with new, dazzling details: "18 children . . . now it is certain . . . have been the victims of sexual abuse, by their parents, by their neighbors, and by their friends. . . . The children's testimony was sufficiently precise and detailed as to sweep away all doubt and eliminate any possibility of manipulation." Prominent figures were "recognized in the photos," averred the scribes confidently.

Over and over again, the press referred to the "pedophile ring," as if it were a fact as established as gravity. Pretty soon, people began to believe that not only was it true, it was ubiquitous.

"Things like that, they happen all the time," said a lawyer to the TV cameras, gravely.

In fact, it never happened.

That didn't stop the criminal justice system. Someone—anyone—had to go to jail for such a crime. In this case, 18 people did. Many of them served years in jail; three of them attempted suicide; one succeeded.

And then, the entire *affaire Outreau* imploded; the main accusers recanted. They admitted that they had made the whole thing up. There was no pedophile ring. There was no little girl who had been murdered. There was no orgy of rape and murder. It was all a lie. The accused were innocent.

The government opened the cells, apologized, and gave each of the wrongly accused inmates over $1 million in indemnity.

But the hacks? From them, hardly a word of contrition or regret was heard. As far as their own role was concerned, they seemed to have been afflicted suddenly with a case of collective amnesia. Instead, out came new headlines: "Judicial Scandal," announced *Le Monde*. "Lives Ruined," pronounced another. And then, *Le Monde* deigned to bend its head: "A Media Tempest Turns into a Judicial Shipwreck," it noted.

The gusts keep coming. . . .

WITCHY WOMEN

Newspapers, you see, do not simply give you the news, as they are said to, in the way that you are given a bunch of apples at the grocer's or fresh fish at the market. You would recognize a Granny Smith or a slab of hake no matter where you found it. But how do you tell news from anything else? News is simply what the newspapers tell you it is.

On its front pages, the *Times* could as well serve up Icelandic folk dancing or the Pope's views on Vatican II, for all it really matters to you.

Once something shows up in the papers, it immediately becomes of the greatest importance to every literate adult in the area—and most of the illiterates. They forget their own private affairs and give themselves over to earnest cogitation on the great world. Before you know it, there is a full-blown panic, with all the good citizens looking for demons under their beds.

Such was the case with witchcraft in seventeenth-century Europe. All told, the European witch hunts killed between 40,000 and 100,000 accused witches, the Salem witch trials in 1692 in Colonial America being the best known today. The Great Burning, as it is now called, had all the hallmarks of an episode of mass mania. There was popular hysteria and there were unpopular victims; there were sensational pamphlets, misbegotten theories, sex, lies, and . . . devilry.[3] It could have been mistaken for a session of Congress.

In his studies of the witch hunts, historian Norman Cohn thinks he sees a single persistent theme of paranoia centering around the idea of the infiltration and destruction of a larger group by a small, well-organized, and secret subgroup given to diabolical practices.[4]

Elaine Pagels, a professor of religion at Princeton University, reaches a similar conclusion in *The Origin of Satan*. First the Jews demonized Christ; then, the Romans persecuted his followers; finally, it was the turn of Christians to harass Jews and heretics—by accusing them of being in league with Satan.[5]

Such mass persecutions are, after all, useful to society. Getting everyone in a group to point and cackle at the odd fellows outside seems guaranteed to make them feel superior. The more they feel one up on the outsider, the more they confirm their own standing in the group. It almost seems as if aggression against other people might be a survival strategy as deeply coded into our genes as the desire to reproduce with the fittest specimens we can attract or the urge to protect our offspring.

If so, a realist might ask with a shrug, why bother? After all, we've been around for thousands of years and haven't wiped ourselves out yet. Perhaps regular bouts of bloodshed are a way of keeping our numbers down and forging closer ties with our own groups. War and persecution seem to be part of our genes.

"War is the health of the state," wrote Randolph Bourne. Maybe it is also the health of humanity. A periodic bloodletting might be as good for the social body as it was once thought necessary for the human body. But then, we have to ask, if aggression is hardwired in us, why is it we seem to be able to go long stretches without it? If war is part of human nature, you would expect to find every age equally drenched in blood. But that doesn't seem to be so. In the nineteenth century there was a long bout of peace in Europe after the defeat of Napoleon in 1815. In 265 B.C., during the classical period of India, the emperor Ashoka was so appalled by his own slaughter of over 100,000 people at the battle of Kalinga that he laid down his sword and never took it up again. Except for two wars in the seventeenth century, the Edo Period (1603–1868 A.D.) in Japan, under the Tokugawa Shogunate, was a remarkable age of peace, prosperity, and scientific achievement. And witches seem to have been coexisting with Christians during the Middle Ages, if not lovingly, at least with less bloodshed than during the Great Burning. Then, after those years of persecution, witches once again went back to coexisting with society in relative peace.

That tells us something. Even if our genes do flex their muscles automatically, like Popeye on spinach, it seems to take a lot more than just genetic predisposition to bring about actual carnage in the world.

What undid the witches seems to have been not one thing but a combination of several things. First, there was a series of stressful events in Europe around the time of the witch hunts: the Black Death, the breakup of Christendom into Catholics and Protestants, and the religious wars that followed. This was a time when different groups were at each other's throats over a number of things, including power and land. The fighting displaced increasing numbers of outsiders—unmarried old women, especially—who did not fit easily into local communities. And, critically, there was also a set of big ideas—bad ideas—percolating down to the masses and infecting them with fear. Once it got going, the panic was made even worse by the invention, earlier in the Renaissance, of printing. So, again it was words—and wordmongers—at the root of the trouble.

But the neocortex made a mess of things in another way, too. Not only did it get the witch hunts going in the first place, it also stirred up things long after the fact—by rewriting what happened.

Thumbing through the accounts of the witch trials, we find that those who write the history of yesteryear have no more of a grip on truth than those who keep us up to date with today's gossip. If it is a fib that newspapers deliver the news as immaculately as the virgin birth, it is also a fib that history brings back the past as accurately as a truth serum.

So, too, with the witch hunts. They soon sprouted a rain forest of explanations and theories, and, as always in a public spectacle, these were the most entertaining part of the whole business.

One popular theory was that the Great Burning was a kind of Catholic Final Solution directed against heretics and pagans, the sort of thing we could expect from bigoted old fogies in drag. But the closer historians have looked at what happened, the more this fraud—so flattering to modern minds—has fallen apart. In fact, politics, rather than religion, was what drove most prosecutions. Almost all the witchcraft trials took place in areas where there were frequent border disputes and where Protestant-Catholic tensions were high. It was the secular courts that dealt the most extreme punishments to those who were convicted, not the church courts. The witch trials were often only a convenient pretext to haul people into court and strip them of their land.

It is true that witches were fined and penalized even earlier, under the barbarians. And that when Europe was Christianized, the stakes—in a manner of speaking—got higher. Even so, in the Middle Ages, actual trials of witches were not that widespread; execution was only for the most hardened sinners. The Church *did* forbid the practice of magic*k*, but it usually assigned relatively mild penalties to it. The witches were seen as deluded more than wicked.

The result was that large-scale witch hunts really became common only later, during the Renaissance. The very fiercest hunts took place in the 1620s and 1630s, in German-speaking areas, not in the strongholds of the Inquisition, in Italy and Spain, as you would otherwise think. Where does that leave us? Instead of a neat fable about progress, modernity, and the spread of reason and light, we get an unsettling paradox: The worst of the witch-hunting took place not in the Dark Ages, in a murky fog of superstition and irrationality, but in the clear dawn of the Enlightenment, in the century of genius, in the days of Descartes, Locke, and Pascal.[6]

Then there is the idea that the witch trials were an attack on women healers by a male hierarchy threatened by their skills. We are inclined to think that that theory, too, can be put to rest. Actually, the record seems to show that whenever suspected witches were found to have been healers or midwives, they were actually *less* likely to have been brought to trial. And although most witches were older women, we also now know that some were males. And some of the accusers were also females.[7]

A bigger reason for what went on was that there were all too many witches eager to blame their rivals for whatever calamities visited their community. In short, there was professional rivalry, even some catfighting.

How can one be sure? Well, of course, one can't. One can hardly be sure what happened a day ago under one's own roof, much less 500 years ago in rural Europe. But the problem is that everyone else seems to be sure. And that is what creates public spectacles in the first place—the delightful certainty with which ordinary people read history or the front pages of their newspapers, convinced they know about fifteenth-century Würzberg what no one could possibly know about twenty-first-century Washington.

Was there a gender holocaust in the early modern period?[8] The truth—if one can ever come up with truth in such matters—is that a significant number of witches killed may actually have been *men*—up to 95 percent in one country, Iceland. And there never was a time or a place where the majority of witches killed were healers or midwives. In most places, only around 20 percent of accused witches were. And, often, it seems to have been the presence of the church that checked the persecution.

Still, we have no dog in this fight and no particular reason to believe that the churchmen were any better than they have been painted. They might even have been worse. But if we are unwilling to take the church in the seventeenth century at its face value, we wonder why we should be expected to take feminist historians in the twentieth at theirs.

WITNESS FOR THE PERSECUTION

But, if the witchcraft trials of early modern Europe were not really a purge of moon-worshipping midwives by patriarchal Catholic inquisitors, how did they ever come about?

In *Extraordinary Popular Delusions and the Madness of Crowds*, Charles Mackay describes a typical manifestation of witches in the South of France:

> All the witches confessed that they had been present at the great Domdaniel, or Sabbath. At these Saturnalia, the devil sat upon a large gilded throne, sometimes in the form of a goat; sometimes as a gentleman, dressed all in black, with boots, spurs, and sword; and very often as a shapeless mass, resembling the trunk of a blasted tree, seen indistinctly among the darkness. They generally proceeded to the Domdaniel, riding on spits, pitchforks, or broomsticks, and on their arrival indulged with the fiends in every species of debauchery.[9]

But how could all the witches have concurred in such extraordinary detail? Why, at a traffic accident, one can hardly get three witnesses to agree to what happened. One swears he saw nothing, while the other two will tell you tales as far apart as the innards of their wrecked cars are scattered. But here, the witches all see the same things, down to the finest detail.

Our instincts tell us they could not have. And, indeed, they did not. What the witches are repeating, Mackay tells us, was simply what the pundits of the time were reading.

Mackay goes on:

Grave and learned doctors of divinity openly sustained the possibility of these transformations, relying mainly upon the history of Nebuchadnazzar. They could not understand why, if he had been an ox, modern man could not become wolves by Divine permission and the power of the devil.

There you have it. The gullible minds of the masses picked up the theories of the experts and repeated them ad nauseum until the craze spread like a typhus epidemic through the breadth and length of the Continent. No evidence was needed. So powerfully had the old stories about the devil put down roots in the minds of the mob that confessions alone were enough to convict, even if they came only after a session of torture.

Which only goes to show that the mob is never the sole reason for moral panics or manias. It takes much more than a credulous peasant to set off an avalanche that careens down the slope to general panic. What you really need is a half-baked pedant armed with damp formulas and moldy sayings out of a dog-eared textbook; you need catchy phrases that spray around and lodge themselves like bird shot in the fuzzy neocortexes of the masses.

In fact, Jenny Gibbons, a revisionist historian of the Great Hunt, has shown how the interplay of learned ideas about witchcraft with the actual practice of heresy turned things lethal.[10]

It was not illiterate fools who drove the persecution of the witches. It was the bigger semi-literate fools. It was not what people did not know that proved their undoing; it was what they *thought* they knew that wasn't so. And what the devil did was one of those things that wasn't so.

And, as with all public spectacles, the details of what people imagined the devil to be up to increased in inverse proportion to their actual encounters with him. Precisely because no one had actually run into Satan, he proved to be a convenient nail on which to hang every twisted fantasy, repressed desire, and foul imagining that ever swirled in anemic heads.

THE HAMMER OF WITCHES

But there was one other way in which words played into the mob's madness. And that was through the book that came to symbolize the Great Hunt, *The Malleus Maleficorum* (*The Hammer of the Witches*).

"Women are by nature instruments of Satan," says this gem. "They are by nature carnal, a structural defect rooted in the original creation."[11]

The Malleus Maleficorum was largely written by Heinrich Kramer, an inquisitor whose fascination with the sex life of the witches had already led one bishop to shut down a trial, claiming that the only devil around was inside Kramer. The man apparently suffered from the delusion that his private parts were capable of wandering around at midnight, and he devoted seven chapters of his opus to the grotesque things he thought witches were liable to do to them. Nonetheless, he somehow managed to forge a recommendation from the Inquisition's theologians—who had actually condemned the book. It was enough to fool the civil courts. They took up *The Malleus* with so much glee that when witch burning hit full stride in the middle of the sixteenth century, it was the manual that witch hunters automatically reached for, becoming one of the hottest items off the new presses and skewing the views of generations of historians.

The Malleus was so drenched with Kramer's sexual obsessions that it made readers believe the trials were run by perverts. And it fed the imaginations of prosecutors and witches, many of whom regurgitated its obscene drivel in their forced confessions.

But there's another sense in which the witch trials turn out to be about sex, after all. You could see them as a variation of the reproductive game, only this time not centering around the winners but centering around the losers—the kind of people it would be easy to blame if anything did go wrong somewhere.

Most witches were alienated from ordinary family life; they were seen as different by their neighbors; they were disliked and feared. It was easy for a housewife to imagine that the childless old woman in the shack outside her home was eaten up inside with envy and ready to do her in. Even more important, the outsiders often had land that could be grabbed if they were convicted.[12]

Especially after the horrible ravages of the Black Death (1347–1349), rumors of this sort multiplied. Stories about malign outsiders conspiring against the Christian kingdom quickly become popular, growing in intensity especially toward pariah groups like Jews, lepers, Moslems, and witches. Witches were feared as plague spreaders, as poisoners, and as workers of black magic on the community. They were the losers in the reproductive game. Then at the height of the Reformation, when Catholics and Protestants were already at each other's throats, it was natural that the rumors would grow thicker, spread, and burst into wild, cyclical panics.[13]

And that is the problem with the neocortex. It can always find plausible reasons ... cunning justifications ... and impeccable logic to do what it means to do anyway, and means to do for the most senseless of reasons. The neocortex found its justification with the publication of *The Malleus Maleficorum*. Until then, diabolism—the belief that the devil was behind every evil thing that happened—was fashionable mainly among the educated. Now the mob, too, got a heavy dose of it. Not surprisingly, when a match was put to the tinderbox, Europe exploded. The image of the devil preying on innocent children was enough to start an avalanche of revulsion and hatred in the mob. The devil was the trigger, as animal behaviorists would say.

HOW TO MAKE A TURKEY STEW

Indeed, animal behavior provides many cases of how such triggers work. Take the mother turkey and its natural enemy, the polecat. When a mother turkey sees a polecat, she automatically starts squawking, pecking, and clawing in anger. Even a stuffed polecat elicits the same rage from the turkey. However, what animal behaviorist M. W. Fox found was that if you put a tiny tape recorder inside the faux cat and let it play the *cheep-cheep* sound characteristic of baby turkeys, mama turkey not only welcomes the polecat but even gathers it underneath her. Turning off the tape recorder, however, sends her back into a frenzy of rage.[14]

The mother turkey is exhibiting what animal behaviorists call a fixed-action pattern—a sequence of intricate behaviors of the type involved in a mating ritual, for instance. Fixed-action patterns always run the same way and in the same order, as though they have been preprogrammed into the animal's behavior. What is especially interesting, for our purposes, is that they are triggered by specific parts or attributes of the enemy, not by the enemy as a whole. For instance, a male robin's territorial instincts are provoked by nothing more than the clump of red breast feathers belonging to its rival. Sans red fluff, another male robin can sail through without a challenge. But the threatened male will pounce on red feathers even if they are just lying around on the ground or even if they are attached to another species of bird. The red fluff—not the bird—is the trigger.[15]

As Homo sapiens, we smugly believe that we are above such robotic behavior. When men go off their collective rockers or act in a frenzy, we assume they have more complicated reasons. They must, we imagine, be suffering from some deep-seated maladjustment. Scholars charge off to the archives to look for structural defects in society, for failures in the economy, or even for anomalies in weather conditions. They are sure that some kind of tectonic shift underground must have produced World War I, that it was a change in ocean currents that set off the industrial revolution, and that a virus threat lurked behind the rise of the Pharaohs. Not many of them want to consider so simple a mechanism as an automatic animal response. And fewer of them consider what sorts of ideas or events or figures might trigger such automatic responses.

But, it turns out that, indeed, there are enduring patterns in history. Dr. Pagels finds one in the myth of a diabolical conspiracy that recurs in Western culture, "especially," she says, "when we are thinking politically and socially." The myth appears first during the second century, when it is directed against the early Christians. It shows up again in the persecution of Jews in Nazi Germany. And then, with a leap and a bound, it comes calling in the Satanic child abuse cases in America in the 1980s and 1990s.

There is a difference, though. The child abuse panic had two elements, not just one: fear of child abuse and fear of Satanism. For that reason, it was doubly poisonous—and doubly useful.

OLD McMARTIN HAD A CRÈCHE

The McMartin Satanic child abuse trials, which cost taxpayers more than $13 million, were the most expensive trials in U.S. history, far ahead of the O. J. Simpson trial at $8 million. The preliminary hearing took 18 months; the whole case took 7 years, 6 judges, 17 attorneys, and hundreds of witnesses, including 9 of the 11 children alleged to have been molested. One of the defendants was retried after the first jury deadlocked, but the second jury also deadlocked and a mistrial was declared. Hundreds of Manhattan Beach, California, children grew up thinking they had once been grotesquely abused. The seven adults charged—some elderly women—were bankrupted and turned into social pariahs. McMartin preschool itself was closed and razed, and the other eight schools involved were closed down forever. The pastor of the St. Cross church was the target of harassment and death threats. "He had to close his church and move to another part of the country." Copycat trials erupted all across North America.[16]

What provoked the hue and cry was a police complaint on August 12, 1983, by a woman called Judy Johnson. She claimed her son had been molested by Ray Buckey of the McMartin preschool. Ms. Johnson, it turns out, had also accused her ex-husband of child abuse, and her claims against the McMartins were—on their face, at least—delusional. She charged that people had flown through windows, killed lions, and had sexual encounters with giraffes. Buckey, she alleged, had beaten a giraffe to death with a baseball bat. This was a woman, mind you, who had been diagnosed with acute paranoid schizophrenia by the University of California–Irvine Medical Center at the time she first made her allegation that "satanic sex rituals" had been practiced on her child.

You'd think the poor creature would have been hauled off to the nearest psychiatric clinic or at least given a stiff dose of Haldol. Instead, 97 percent of adults polled about the case, who had an opinion on it, believed that Buckey was guilty, while 93 percent believed that Peggy McMartin—then a grandmother—was a Satanic child molester.

A year later, 208 counts of child abuse involving about 40 children were handed down against seven adults: the McMartins, Ray Buckey, and four schoolteachers.

Thus began a modern public spectacle.

It took more than two decades before it wound down. That was in 2005, when the *Los Angeles Times* finally got around to publishing the first retraction from one of the student victims. Kyle Zirpolo (then known as Kyle Sapp) confessed that he had made up his accusations at the age of eight because of pressure from his family and the social workers who interviewed him.

"Anytime I would give them an answer that they didn't like," Kyle said, "they would ask again and encourage me to give them the answer they were looking for. It was really obvious what they wanted. I know the types of language they used on me: things like I was smart, or I could help the other kids who were scared."

Kyle also revealed where the nasty details of the supposed crimes came from:

"I think I got the satanic details by picturing our church," he said. "We went to American Martyrs, which was a huge Catholic church. . . . What I would do was picture the altar, pews, and stained-glass windows, and if [investigators] said, 'Describe an altar,' I would describe the one in our church. Or instead of, 'There was a priest in a green suit'—someone who was real—I would say, 'A man dressed in red as a cult member.' From going to church you know that God is good, and the devil is bad and has horns and is about evil and red and blood. I'd just throw a twist in there with Satan and devil-worshipping."[17]

We understand why a rambunctious eight-year-old with a precocious imagination might be so fascinated with Satan that he mixes him up with the fellow on the corner. But how do you account for the way adults all over the land gobbled up the story?

Was there something going on in society then, as with the witchcraft hysteria, that made people more vulnerable to a moral panic? In fact, there was.

The 1970s had been a particularly difficult time for Americans. There was an oil crisis and stagflation on the economic front. New social movements in feminism and environmentalism were threatening traditional attitudes. The numbers of immigrants were increasing. And in politics, there was escalating conflict in the cold war, the growth of the black power movement, and the rise of third world nationalism, especially in the Middle East. The country was in need of a bogeyman on which it could pin all its anxieties.

Along came the McMartin story. It was the first of what police were soon calling multi-victim multi-offender (MVMO) child abuse cases in North America. In essence, these were cases where accusations were sprayed around as wildly as paint on a Jackson Pollock canvas. In both instances, the result was a mess. Other cases followed—in Bakersfield and Kern County, California, where two couples were given centuries-long jail sentences. Only after they had spent 14 years in prison in isolation, separated from each other, were their convictions overturned.

Alexander Cockburn, writing in the *Nation*, gives a brief survey of the national hysteria:

Children in more than a hundred cities, from Fort Bragg, California, to Grenada, Mississippi, came forward. In June 1984 children in Sacramento told of witnessing orgies, cannibalism and snuff films. Two months later in Miami children reported being made to drink urine and eat feces. In Wilkes-Barre, Pennsylvania, in March 1985 two children said adults had forced them into having oral sex with a goat and eating a dismembered deer's raw heart . . . In April 1986 children in a preschool in Sequim, Washington, charged they had been taken to graveyards and forced to witness animal sacrifice. In Chicago children said they had been made to eat a boiled baby.[18]

The madness that began with Bakersfield and Manhattan Beach in 1983 was to end only 10 years later with the Wenatchee, Washington, case in 1994–1995, in which:

> 43 adults were falsely arrested on 29,726 fabricated charges of child sex abuse involving 60 children. Parents, Sunday school teachers and a local pastor were indicted and many were convicted of raping their own children and the children of other members of a sex-ring.[19]

HISTORY OF A HYSTERIA

What on earth had gone haywire in the United States? What allergen could have set off such a rash of insanity? And was there some convenient theory behind it that evoked deep-rooted archetypes in twentieth-century minds, much in the way the *The Malleus Maleficorum* had stirred up the nightmares of sixteenth-century minds?

There was.

It seems that in 1980, just three years before Judy Johnson made her zoological accusations, a Canadian psychiatrist, Lawrence Pazder, published the book *Michelle Remembers*. In it, he and his wife, Michelle Smith, charged that she had been abused by Satanists when she was a child. There were the usual sordid experiences but, in this case, the victim had been so traumatized that she had repressed her memory of them until she had had sessions with Pazder's therapy. Pazder was called in as an expert in the McMartin case, and the story was at once taken up by the popular press. Here was the trigger: a pretty 20-year-old victimized by horrors too horrible to tell, and a therapist-cum-lover who awakens her from her trauma and heals her. There was a princess. Finding the dragon wasn't too hard. Before *Michelle Remembers*, there had never been a satanic child abuse case in the United

States at all. After it, there were to be two decades of nothing but. The entire sordid hysteria was set off by nothing more than a colorful yarn from the modern equivalent of the magic flying carpet—the therapist's couch.

Michelle Smith's story soon began to fray like a cheap rug, too. In 1990, London's *Mail on Sunday* newspaper exposed the book as a fraud. There was an extensive investigation, including interviews with her father, an alcoholic who had abandoned his family. The reporters found that it was only after a miscarriage in 1976 that Smith had begun the psychiatric treatment during which she first recalled her abuse. There was no record of the car crash she described and her father and sisters all denied her claims. And it was also found that her descriptions of what went on, including visits from no less than Satan himself, were nothing like actual Satanic rituals, at least according to the experts.

By then, of course, the book had already done its damage, spawning a whole cottage industry of yammering anti-abuse advocates, recovered memory mavens, and victims advocates. Other books had joined it on the talk circuits, notably one by Lauren Stratford. Stratford's opus, *Satan's Underground*, published in 1988, claimed that its author had been used to breed sacrificial victims for Satan. This, too, was later exposed as a fraud, but not before noted fundamentalist apocalypse-monger Hal Lindsey—the best-selling author of *The Late Great Planet Earth* and a close friend of President Reagan—had given it a blurb. Other evangelists and professional recovered satanists jumped onto the gravy train, only to be shown up for frauds as well. Defrocked physicians, raunchy talk show hosts, a mother who blamed the popular game "Dungeons and Dragons" for her son's suicide, and even the ubiquitous Lyndon LaRouche joined in. The whole business was soon reeking like a Cantonese fish stew.

Cockburn describes how cases were prosecuted:

> infants as young as 2 and 3, permitted in fifty states to testify without corroboration from adults or physical evidence; without

cross-examination in many states . . . interrogated as many as thirty times by social workers or other investigators, told they would remain separated from their parents if they retracted their charges, held in sterile environments during questioning, to a degree that one critic described as kindred to "brainwashing" in the Korean War . . .[20]

Social workers would use anatomically correct dolls sometimes named after the defendants and repeatedly subject the children to leading questions that were often suggestive, and, at times, so explicit and ugly that asking them could only constitute abuse of its own. Children who gave the answers the social workers wanted were rewarded. Those who didn't were scolded or warned darkly that they were hurting their friends and families. No physical evidence showed up, but that, too, was fine.

One California doctor of the mind claimed to have identified symptoms in children abused by satanic cults—said symptoms including "fear of monsters," making farting noises, and laughing when other children farted.[21]

The hysteria was bipartisan. The right contributed Christian fundamentalists, who were eager to use the scandals to discredit recent New Age religions like Wicca and the Church of Satan and to push homeschooling. The left did its part with feminists like Gloria Steinem, Catherine McKinnon, and Bill Clinton's new attorney general, Janet Reno, who found in child protection the perfect racket to increase bureaucratic budgets and make herself a name.

In fact, Reno shot up to the national stage because of her prosecutions of alleged child abusers. Her most famous case took place in an upscale suburban Miami development and was notable for the extreme brutality with which her office went after a confession from a 17-year-old Honduran immigrant. The girl, pretty black-haired Ileana Fuster, was held 11 months in an isolation cell, often drugged and nude in front of everyone. She was subjected to so much stress that she "came to look as if she were 50, her skin covered with sores and infections." She finally cracked and confessed to the usual farrago of bizarre crimes, but her husband Frank never did. He got six life sentences plus 165 years and remains in jail today.[22] The perps at the witchcraft trials usually got off lighter than poor Frank and Ileana.

But the satanic abuse cases were only a dry run for Reno. Her real moment came when she authorized the government's face-down against the Branch Davidian cult at Waco in 1993, where the authorities demonstrated the perfect way to rescue abused children—incinerate them.[23]

We are not suggesting that child abuse is not a problem in America. It is. But the real cases, say the experts, usually don't involve a predatory stranger—they involve the family. Maybe it was because people couldn't quite come to terms with that fact that they latched onto the figure of a child molester hovering around the schoolyard, a figure that quickly morphed into Satan. Soon Satanic cult killings were said to be disposing of some 50,000 to 2 million American children a year without the knowledge of law enforcement.[24]

The higher figure would mean about 10 million deaths in five years, which is a little under the number of people that Hitler killed during World War II, and for which he needed half a dozen major concentration camps like Buchenwald and Auschwitz as well as hundreds of minor camps. And the Nazis had to employ over 150,000 people to do their dirty work. Since the total number of Satanists in the country is not more than a thousand or so, one might have thought that would have effectively put a crimp in the ritual crime business. If we take the lower number, remember that the Vietnam War that killed around 50,000 Americans (and at least 2 million Vietnamese) was one of the most traumatic events in American history. Think about how severely that loss was felt throughout the population and then also figure the logistics involved in carrying out such an operation openly, let alone in secret.

What's more, how could such hordes of people be vanishing off the face of the nation, unknown to the police (as some claimed), when the entire murder rate in America around the time was only about 20,000 a year? And when, according to figures given by the

Child Safety Council (a branch of the Department of Justice), the number of children who were kidnapped *by strangers* in 1990 was lower than 100 a year? How could otherwise sane people have come to believe that Satanists were killing hundreds of thousands, if not millions a year?[25]

But they did. They were perfectly able to believe that a small group of self-styled occultists (most Satanic churches numbered no more than a few hundred members) were capable of feats of evacuation and extermination that would have turned the SS pea-green with envy. Actually, between 1985 and 1990, fewer than 100 credible reports of *ritual* child abuse were filed nationally. None of those accused were members of any Satanic church or identified devil-worshipping cult. Cardinal O'Connor himself stated publicly that there were only two exorcisms in the whole of the New York archdiocese in 1989, a poor showing, one might be forgiven for thinking, for such a monumental conspiracy.[26]

It didn't matter to people that most Wiccans (modern witches) and many Satanists do not even believe in Satan and follow a rather innocuous form of paganism that differs very little from Christianity in ethics and expressly forbids criminal acts. It didn't matter to people that the founder of the main Satanic church, Anton LaVey, was more of a public relations man, a former circus trainer who once kept a lion on the back porch of his home in San Francisco, and that, while he may have liked to shave his head, call himself "the Black Pope," and dress the part to the nines, his Satanic Bible explicitly rejects the Christian versions both of God and of the devil.[27]

It didn't matter to them that if you added up the numbers, far more human beings—several orders of magnitude more—have been murdered by people acting in the name of mainstream religions like Christianity and Islam than have ever been killed in the name of Satan.

And, it didn't matter that only four months before the McMartin trial started in 1987, police found the woman who started it all lying naked facedown in her son's bedroom, dead of alcoholism-related liver disease. Journalists had found a crusade that allowed them to keep a straight face while wallowing like pigs in obscene pornography.

At the height of the frenzy, even the original "cult cop," who first started the whole carnival by selling lectures and tapes about the abuse, came out with the admission that Satanism and neopaganism might not, after all, be the criminal organizations she'd depicted them as. But that didn't stop the Prince of Darkness from continuing to show up, like Elvis, on the program bills of every hick gathering of oddball educators and law enforcement misfits. Seminars on the occult were money-spinners, especially among those fundamentalists who thought the Antichrist was about to show up momentarily and set off a nuclear showdown.

But then, as suddenly as it began, the Satanic child abuse craze died down, leaving a trail of devastation. Innocent people had been carted off to jail, careers and reputations flushed down the toilet; thousands of children had grown up traumatized by the interrogations, believing wrongly that unspeakable things had been done to them. Suddenly, statements started being retracted, conclusions hurriedly withdrawn or contradicted. The interrogation techniques were discredited. The show was over.

Then they sent in the clowns. Even after the fraud had been uncovered, there were people who argued that, yes, it might all have been a pack of nonsense, but it could not have been that bad because it had been for a worthy cause. Who could object to their children being protected from abuse, after all? Why bother waiting for petty details like physical evidence or witnesses? Anyone who criticized the spectacle could have only one reason for doing so—they, too, were pedophiles!

CHAPTER 5

WORDS OF WAR

"No, no!" said the Queen. "Sentence first—verdict afterwards."
"Stuff and nonsense!" said Alice loudly....
"Off with her head!" the Queen shouted at the top of her voice.
—**Lewis Carroll,** *Alice's Adventures in Wonderland*

ON THE SELF-IMPORTANCE OF SCRIBBLERS

And there you have the typical do-gooder. From the protection of children to the jailing of grandmothers is a smooth and natural step for him. Children, he thinks, are innocent. From that he infers that children can do no wrong. Which means that if they say their teachers are molesting them, then in fact their teachers must be molesting them. And since an adult who molests children is prima facie a monster of the most monstrous sort, hanging would be too good for him and a proper hearing quite out of the question.

Thus does the neocortex sputter in fits and starts from dubious assumptions to preposterous conclusions with nary a whisper of doubt in between. And only a man capable of committing logic is liable to commit such an absurdity.

Of course, even as logic the thing does not hold together. The innocence of children is more in the nature of a statement of dogma than an assertion that can be falsified. Innocent of what? Innocent compared to what? The demagogues can give no answer between their rants. Nor can they tell us when childhood ends. Are eight-year-olds as innocent as two-year-olds? And when does the age of innocence end? At 14? 16? 18? And what is it that signifies that adulthood has arrived? Is it the driver's license or the marriage license? Is it making love or making war?

And even if children were as pure as the seraphim and cherubim, how does that make a crime against them any more or less heinous than a crime against, say, an old woman or a cripple? But we have yet to have a public panic about paraplegics. You might begin to wonder whether the child abuse hysteria had as much to do with moral palpitations as it had to do with sexual titillation. And you would be right.

Sex, after all, not only drives the human race, it also drives newspaper headlines.

Given the option between a compelling story about the fall of interest rates on the one hand and the rise of Jenna Jamieson on the other, the pulchritudinous Ms. Jamieson wins hands down. Sex sells—even when it is perverse and ugly... even if it is a 50-year-old senator with an eye for buff young pages. A sex story will still bump war with Iraq off the front pages, seven days a week.

Next to sex, even death is not always a very interesting business to the average pillar of the fourth estate. Take one leading cause of fatalities in the United States. Nationwide there are probably 5,000 deaths a year from asthma.[1] That makes it two and a half times deadlier than the murder of children by their parents—which is the most common and deadly form of child abuse around—and 50 times more prevalent than the kidnapping of children by strangers. But asthma is not something many reporters are very interested in. There is no pizzazz in the thing. You merely either have it or you don't. And the remedy is available for you to purchase or not. There is no program, world historical project, or second international involved in tackling it. A year's supply of medicine for all 5,000 victims of asthma every year would probably not put a dent in the child protection budget of one state.

But child abuse comes with so many perks and angles attached to it, it is hard for the average scribbler, with his eye cocked to a Pulitzer, to take a levelheaded approach.

First, there is the sex angle. Then, as if that were not enough, the reporter gets to preen in self-congratulation as a defender of the defenseless. Even if no abuse is found, no one is likely to remember the luckless day care worker in jail. He is a mere adult, after all. Then, even more satisfying, our scribe gets to hold forth on any number of Burning Issues of the Day: Is Day Care A Good Thing or A Bad Thing? Should women work outside the home or in? How much Satanism turns you into a pedophile? How much pedophilia turns you into Satan?

He does not know any more than you do, but that does not prevent him from puffing up like a swamp toad before he delivers his bit on each subject. He gets to save the family—or is it the child? He becomes a guardian of public morality ... a defender of the American way of life! It matters little which it is. He is cast in the role of savior—St. George rolled into Sonny Bono. Sex, self-importance, salvation—all in one. What more could any do-gooder want?

THE POTOMAC MILITERATI

But for every Eros, there is a Thanatos.

Sex may sell newspapers, but it is War that buys newsmen and publishers.

The do-gooder who until now was agonizing over what might possibly have happened to two four-year-olds in the lunch-room of their preschool is suddenly breezily indifferent to the starvation, burning, and bombing of hundreds of thousands of children.

For, now he is off on another tack. He has become a steely-eyed pupil of Machiavelli. He talks casually about Realpolitik and Geostrategy, as though he had found them on sale at the local supermarket. He narrows his eyes keenly when he hears the words "national interest"; he can point out Kandahar on a map. He knows the difference between Ayman al-Zawahiri and Abu Musab al-Zarqawi without googling.

Now, he is no longer a part of the fourth estate; he is no longer interested in being a watchdog of the people. He has a better-paying job. He is an attack dog for the politicians.

Here is an MIT security studies maven, writing in a column in the Outlook section of the *Washington Post*, that the new U.S. strategy of paying Iraqi journalists to place stories favorable to the U.S. in the media is perfectly kosher.[2] A reporter, says Michael Schrage, should be helping the military along, not just chattering about it. Even Christopher Hitchens, the latest unlikely adornment to the Potomac militerati, has condemned "storyboarding" as a breach of journalistic faith. But Schrage isn't having any.

"Enough already," he writes in his piece. "Securing positive coverage for our troops in Iraq can be as important to their safety as 'up-armoring' vehicles and providing state-of-the-art body armor. The failure to wage the media war is a failure to command."

Ah—the media war. Until now we thought the war meant those cluster bombs going off in Baghdad. But we realize we were mistaken. It must have been the blood that got us confused! The real war, we now see, is on the front pages. Take cover!

The pen pushers are no longer making obscure marks on paper as before. No, they have joined Rommel and Patton. Left and right, they load up their cannons with dangling modifiers and prepositional phrases and go in like gangbusters. With every well-turned phrase and pithy bon mot, the borders of the empire are pushed further along. In the old days, you at least had to have an arm shot off or a leg shot out from under you to corner such glory. But no more.

That is the monumental conceit of it all. The fact is the average reporter today knows less than ever before about what happens on the battlefield. He knows only what he is told by some gasbag general or what he reads in some other fellow's article. His stories are vetted, his questions at press conferences are scripted, his private e-mails get him censored and thrown off his assignment. That's what happened to Farnaz Fassihi, a reporter for the *Wall Street Journal* who happened to voice her opinions about the war to friends.[3]

We even read of a fellow, Jeff Gannon, who managed to join the White House Press Corps on the strength of having been a male escort. That is the sort of experience that really counts these days, we imagine.[4]

But resigning himself to being as much in the dark as anyone else would puncture the self-importance of the modern journalist. It simply won't do. So what does he do? He lets you know that yes, he is simply parroting the military's line, but so what? That's what he is *supposed* to do. If he can't beat them, he will join them. True, he has been turned into a "presstitute," as one wag remarked. But he is a willing one. He revels in it. He is waging war, you see. And so, off he goes, squirting black ink in every direction like a wounded octopus. And the sorry fact is he probably will do more damage this way than at the head of a battalion of Abrams tanks.

Now, if the pundits would only stick to arguing that massaging the news is not a recent development for the military and leave it at that, they would be on strong ground. Fake news is not new. It has been part of military offensives since Neanderthal man first tricked his neighbor and clubbed him over the head.

The classics are full of such swindles. In the Indian epic *Mahabharatha*, Yudhishthira—the eldest of the five Pandava brothers—is a legend for always telling the truth. Then, things come to a head during the battle between the Pandavas and their cousins, the Kauravas, who want to usurp their kingdom. The Kauravas have an invincible warrior-guru, Drona. But the Pandavas get the bright idea of demoralizing Drona by spreading the lie that his son, Ashvathama, is dead. Ashvathama, it happens, is also the name of an elephant—which really *is* dead. Until then Yudhishthira had always been so truthful that his chariot wheels never touched the ground; they hovered just above it. Now, he succumbs and allows himself to whisper, "Ashvathama, *the elephant* [sotto voce], is dead." Drona believes the rumor and dies of a broken heart. The tide turns for the Pandavas, but Yudhishthira's wheels start hitting the ground like everyone else's.

SWINDLING THE HOME CROWD

So, fake news is not new at all. It's old news. Storyboarding does to the news what waterboarding does to prisoners—it persuades it to say what you want to hear. Hoodwinking the enemy on a classical battlefield—which follows its own rules of engagement—is one thing. Bamboozling civilians in modern total warfare is rather different. And swindling the crowd cheering at home is something else altogether.

By that standard, American chariot wheels have not just hit the ground. They have gone through it and are burrowing down into Hades. Storyboarding was directed not at the population in Iraq, which is supposed to be a born-again democracy now, anyway. It was aimed at the population back home in America. Journalists who faked news stories were firing on this pathetic home crowd, making it impossible for the lumps to get even the tiniest scrap of real information about the war, even though they were being asked to give up their children for it. They thought they were volunteering to fight for the republic; they didn't know they were signing up for Aztec child sacrifice.

Of course, there are always people who will say that you need to put out spin to counter the other fellow. *They did it first*, is their argument. This is a bit thick. The U.S., after all, went jackbooting into Iraq. Iraqis can hardly be expected to keep still about it. If a quarter of a million Arabs flooded Washington, D.C., and set up camp in the White House, we expect Americans would not remain mute, either. And the Iraqi insurgents, by definition, did not come into existence until *after* the second Gulf War in 2003. The U.S. government, by contrast, has been brewing disinformation in Iraq since well before the first Gulf War.

Still, there's no denying that the press can do damage—lots of it. Back in 1990, the fellows in charge of the PR game came from a D.C. firm, Hill & Knowlton, which hatched the first of many fables that took the country down the road to war. Iraqi soldiers in Kuwait were tossing babies out of incubators, they claimed, taking the line from old fibs about the Germans from World War I. Then they roped in the Kuwaiti ambassador's daughter, Nayira, who at the time was nowhere in the vicinity. It was her tear-jerking I-was-there account on the floor of the U.S. Congress that got the war started. The psyop was directed not against Iraqis but mainly against the American public and Congress. And as atrocity stories go, it is the gold standard of them all.

Another firm, Rendon, was hired by the CIA in 1990 to help "create the conditions for the removal of Hussein from power." Rendon went on to earn a hundred million dollars in government contracts in just the five years following. It got together a rabble of militants, gave them a brand as though they were homemade potpies—the Iraqi National Congress—and advised them on PR strategy. It also handpicked Ahmad Chalabi, an ex-bank con turned peddler of prowar propaganda, and primed a fly-specked assortment of defectors in the fine art of bluffing polygraph tests. All for a five-year plan for "creative destruction" in the Middle East that a bunch of hacks and apparatchiks in D.C. had dreamed up.[5]

Even bungled lie-detector tests didn't stop Rendon. They planted fake stories about where exactly Saddam had stashed his Weapons of Mass Destruction. They used a paid operative, who masqueraded as a freelancer for the Australian Broadcasting Corporation. What made them pick Australia? Because, under U.S. law, the government is not supposed to be directing its propaganda at the American public. That's supposed to be the job of American journalists!

And how well they did it. There was Ms. Miller—the Madame Roland of the *New York Times*—giving heads-up to the Iraq flimflam right on the front pages of the gray lady. Liberty itself was at stake, she assured us. A mushroom cloud was going to pop up over Manhattan like a Japanese umbrella if we didn't get rid of Saddam. From there the faux news spread like avian flu to every chicken hawk in the West.

But wait; maybe this extravaganza was performed outside the decorous sight of the military? Wrong again. Rendon was patted down, sniffed, and approved by the military. "We've worked in ninety-one countries," boasted the firm's boss, John Rendon.

"Going all the way back to Panama, we've been involved in every war, with the exception of Somalia."[6]

Rendon didn't work alone, either. It coordinated its work with a whole bevy of wholesalers of disinformation. In 2001, the Office of Strategic Information (OSI) was created, with its very own express line for junk news. Even the military is supposed to have found the OSI "scary." Then there was the Office of Global Communications (OGC), run out of the White House Information War Room. The OGC monitored breaking news reports all over the globe—English and Arabic Internet chat rooms, web sites in at least four more languages, and e-mail lists, and planted false stories abroad. The OGC was tasked with punishing journalists who broke ranks all over the world—in Jakarta, Islamabad, Riyadh, Cairo, Ankara, and Tashkent. Propaganda, psy-ops, and espionage—they were all part of the imperial carnival.[7]

Private contractors like Rendon—that now perform much of the CIA's work—run half the nation's most secret military operations, and they don't have to say a word about what they do to the people who foot the bill and face the fire. So, there you have your free and fair press. As one wag remarked, freedom of the press is limited to those who own one.

SLIMED BY THE LIMEYS: BRITISH PROPAGANDA IN WORLD WAR I

Why do intelligent Americans continue to believe that their lives depend on which tin-pot dictator straddles the Tigris and Euphrates? Why do they believe that a government they think too incompetent to deliver the mail on time can be trusted with delivering freedom to foreigners who don't want it?

The short answer is that they are brainwashed. Without government propaganda—and a lot of it—people might come to their senses and most wars would blow over fairly quickly. But here we stumble across one of those astonishing facts that make the study of the human biped so entertaining.

It may be true that the lumps are brainwashed by incessant government propaganda. But at least when they find out they've been lied
to, they can reach for their pitchforks or for the tar and feathers. They
will probably get the wrong person and get him too late, but they
will have seen the light. Not so for the hacks and apparatchiks who
run the circus. Nobody ends up as brainwashed as the brainwashers.

Sheldon Rampton, who has been studying American propaganda
for decades, writes:

> ... The Washington opinion-makers in their think tanks, lobby
> shops and bureaucracies are the people who have come to believe
> in their own propaganda with the greatest passion and the least
> ability to absorb nuance and criticism.[8]

What that means, of course, is that once a public spectacle gets
going, it is next to impossible to stop. Not because the lumps gawking
at the show have bought into it, but because the Florenz Ziegfelds
who run it have. Propaganda does not deceive people; it merely helps
them to deceive themselves, as Eric Hoffer said. *Mundus vulp decipi.*

Take World War I, one of the greatest public spectacles of all
time in terms of money, destruction, and death. Everyone knows
the Great War had as many causes as cancer. Militarism, nationalism,
interlocking alliances, and imperialism—there was no end to the
reasons. Every step of the way to utopia seemed to need paving with
lies. And the ones laying down the paving were the first to trip down
it on the royal road to hell.

It was in the one country that had no apparent reason to be
involved at all that the lies piled up. Until April of 1917, the
United States of America had largely heeded the words of its founding fathers. On the advice of Washington, it had avoided "foreign
entanglements." On the advice of Adams, it did "not go forth looking for monsters to slay." On the advice of Monroe, it restricted
its meddling to the weak nations south of the Rio Grande, where
Yanquis could still throw their weight around without too much loss
of life or money.

The United States of America had reelected Woodrow Wilson because the man had kept U.S. troops at home. The Princeton professor then used his second term to keep the troops from staying at home. He saw something in the Great War that beckoned to him like the Sirens to Ulysses. Rather than stuff wax in his ears and tie himself to the mast, he simply turned the tiller and headed straight for the rocks.

The negative consequences at the end of an effort at world improvement are roughly equal and opposite to the positive aspirations at the beginning. In his campaign to make the world safe for democracy, Wilson imagined not just a little tiddling at the edges but a wholesale revamping of the globe. In order to make his bid for calamity, Wilson & Co. had to overcome the native good sense of the American people by resorting to public disinformation on an industrial scale.

August 6, 1914—two years before the United States entered the war—the *New York Times* reported on a little-remarked incident that occurred on the seas north of Emden, Germany. The British ship *Telconia* had lowered its grappling hooks and pulled up the under-sea cables that connected Germany to the outside world. These lines—one of which ran right to New York—were cut and tossed back into the water. From that moment forward, almost no news could leave Germany and reach the U.S. without first passing through the British propaganda mill in London, at Wellington House.[9]

Contrary to popular myth, Germany did not start the war. But being afraid of a war on two fronts, the Germans were prepared for it. The Schlieffen Plan called for German troops to attack France across the lowlands of Belgium before turning east to knock out the Russians. And it was here that control of the news really began to pay off for Britain and France.

WAFFLING ABOUT BELGIUM

The first lie was that poor, innocent Belgium—practically a virgin in matters of foreign policy—was a neutral country. But, although

Belgium had no public alliances with France or Britain, privately she had a deal with them that put her squarely in the Anglo-French camp. So, when Germany asked for safe passage for her troops through Belgium and the latter refused, the London thought police saw their chance. Belgium was no more democratic than Germany was. Both had kings and elected assemblies jockeying for power. In the Belgian parliament, the wealthy had three times the voting power of other parts of the population, almost as they did in Prussia. Yet, British propaganda succeeded in branding the Germans as autocratic militarists and the Belgians as democratic peaceniks.

For the British to be calling anyone a militarist was an exercise in breathtaking chutzpah. The British Empire controlled more of the world through force of arms than any other government. Its navy ruled the seas. Its armies—including various colonial forces such as the famous Gurkhas—were garrisoned all over the planet. As for democracy, even at home many low-class British subjects did not have the right to vote.

The second lie was that poor little Belgium was being "raped" by the evil Huns. Here, too, the propagandists had their work cut out for them since Belgium had a rap sheet of her own. Leopold II, former king of Belgium, was perhaps the worst of the colonialists in Africa. In the Congo, his agents had treated the local blacks worse than slaves; they were rounded up, starved, beaten, and worked to death in forced labor camps. An estimated 10 million died.

Now, 10 years later, the Belgians' hands were said to be as clean as a brain surgeon's. And the Germans were said to be doing them dirty on a scale not seen since the Hundred Years War.

If the Belgians were not innocent, even less were they defenseless. They had 340,000 troops—a large force for a nation of only seven million inhabitants. Many formed a kind of home guard that wore no uniforms apart from a shoulder ribbon, giving the German soldiers the impression that they were being fired on by civilians. The krauts reacted as you might expect.

But soon the press—especially in America, which got all its news from British sources—was full of atrocity stories. Eyewitnesses said

they had seen German troops marching and singing while spear-
ing Belgian babies on their bayonets. Another report said that 20
women were dragged from their homes and stretched out on tables in the public square, where each one was raped by at least 20
Huns. Other reports circulated of the Germans amputating the breasts
of Belgian women. In still others, young boys had their hands cut
off—supposedly to prevent them from using guns.[10]

But the Germans had let eight American reporters accompany
their troops through Belgium, and on September 3, 1914, the reporters sent out a joint telegram to the Associated Press:

> In spirit fairness we unite in declaring German atrocities groundless
> as far as we are able to observe. After spending two weeks with Ger-
> man army accompanying troops upward hundred miles we unable
> report single incident unprovoked reprisal.[11]

Still, the British weren't about to give up. They pulled Viscount
James Bryce into their propaganda headquarters and gave him the
assignment of "investigating" the reports. Bryce was a famous historian and a man of recognized integrity. But his team of seven
commissioners did not travel to the war zone. They did not actually
interrogate witnesses—or even identify a single witness by name. Instead, they merely "analyzed" the statements coming from Belgian
refugees and returning English soldiers. The result was a landmark
in the history of public opinion management: the Bryce Report of
May 13, 1915.

When it was released, the British propaganda machinery went
into high gear, making sure that every newspaper in America got a
copy. Soon the sulfurous headlines began to bubble up:

"Young and Old Mutilated"

"Wanton Firing on Red Cross and White Flag: Prisoners and
Wounded Shot"

"Civilians Used as Shields"

Wellington House was by now functioning as perhaps the most efficient lie factory ever built. Charles Masterman, who ran the place, had gotten almost all leading British authors—including H. G. Wells, Rudyard Kipling, Arthur Conan Doyle, and John Galsworthy—behind the war effort. He had even gotten a group of 53 leading writers to back a statement calling on the English to "defend the rights of small nations against the rule of blood and iron." A group of distinguished Englishmen was also dispatched to America to argue that Britain and France were fighting to protect peaceful nations against German militarism—a line that the Americans took up like a telegram from St. Paul.

England was, at the time, the world's biggest imperial power—actively denying the vote to millions of people all over the planet and with a subject population of 444 million. Even in nearby Ireland, England ruled with an iron fist over people of her own color, race, and language. In the slums of Dublin in 1911, death rates were as high as in the slums of Calcutta.

Later, after the public spectacle was long over, historians pored over the Bryce Report and the whole phenomenon. They were unable to find any evidence of mass rapes or, indeed, of any rapes. Nor were any women's breasts cut off. Nor were the hands of boys or men amputated. What they found is what you'd expect; fired upon by hidden snipers, the Germans fired back—and sometimes hit women and children. And, as in the town of Dinant, they sometimes executed civilians in reprisal for attacks or in an effort to stop them.

The truth about German atrocities had actually been revealed as early as 1915 by none other than Clarence Darrow, the lawyer made famous by the Scopes Trial. Journeying to France to find out for himself, he came up with nothing. He then announced that he would pay $1,000—about $17,000 in today's money—to anyone whose hands had been amputated by a German soldier. No one stepped forward.

Part Three

Militant Messiahs

CHAPTER 6

WAR AND REMEMBRANCE

Dulce et decorum est pro patria mori.
War is hell.
—William T. Sherman, before burning down Atlanta, September 1864

POPPYCOCK

What we are saying is that man is an imposter. He is not the naive scientist he passes for. Instead, he is a slobbering sentimentalist. He pretends to square his view of the world to new facts and experiences. But what he really does is pry the facts into whatever self-delusion is popular. Like a fat woman trying on a new pair of jeans, he forces the flesh into the space fashion allows and holds his breath to make it fit.

For instance, is there anyone in London who does not wear a red poppy on November 11? The paper flowers are everywhere. They are seen in boardrooms and in supermarkets. Television presenters wear them. The Queen wears one. Ministers show them off on pulpits. A lapel without one seems naked, as if it just stepped out of the shower.

The flowers that bloom in the week of Remembrance Day mark someone as a patriot, as a person of compassion. . . and as a sentimental fool. London goes silent, commemorating with all its heart the day the guns fell silent on the Western front. But it is not the heart we are worried about here.

What is it really that the English remember in those silent seconds of Remembrance Day? The practical ones focus on shopping lists. A few romantics think of lovers. But pity the Brits with a sense of history or a photo of the Queen in their living room. They search for pride and meaning and find only poppycock. People can't seem to honor fallen soldiers without wanting to wrap the corpses in a lie. Everywhere, the dead Tommies are praised for "helping to preserve Britain's independence . . . and its freedom." The editorialists at the *Daily Express* propose that they were "instrumental in saving the British way of life."

"What people seem to have forgotten," said an old veteran a couple of years ago, "is that so many people fought and died to keep Britain independent so we can be British. I mean English. Well, *I'm* English, anyway."

The old man was one of Britain's last living relics of the Great War, whose thoughts were recorded on a BBC special in 2005 while he still had wit to express them. After four score and 10 years you'd expect the man would have had time to think; to wonder about what it was he had been a part of, why he had done it, and what good it had done. In a single day on the Somme, 20,000 of his comrades were killed in an eight-hour period. You'd think he might have focused his mind on a thing like that.

But his thoughts made no more sense than the Great War itself.

England's independence hasn't really been at risk for nearly 1,000 years. And when it was, in 1066, the one and only time when the island was invaded by an organized army between the departure of the Romans and the arrival of Tony Blair, the English defenders suffered a defeat and ran away. A tiny force of Normans was able to take over the whole place.

Nor was Britain's way of life in danger in World War I or World War II or in any of the hundreds of wars in which English troops have participated over the last 929 years. Instead, every one of them was fought to interfere with someone else's way of life, not to protect Britain's own.

In World War I, the United Kingdom and its colonial subjects lost nearly a million (942,135) troops, not including over a hundred thousand (116,516) Americans.[1] But even if nary a single armed English speaker had set foot on French soil, the English would still be

English, sitting on their dreary little island, driving on the wrong side of the road, speaking to each other in their strange versions of the mother tongue and eating their bangers and mash. The French lost or were badly beaten up in every war since Waterloo. They are still far too French to suit most visitors. And the Germans? The krauts lost the two biggest wars of all time, and yet . . . do they not still speak German? Do they not still eat sauerkraut?

Still, even the rector of St. Mary's Anglican church had a problem remembering Remembrance Day honestly. It was not enough to say the dead veterans fought for Britain's independence; political independence has no particular value in a house of God. Nor was it useful to say they had fought to "preserve our British way of life." Even if it were true, Christ was famously indifferent; He said to follow Him and Him alone.

Barred from the convenient lies of the secular world, the minister at St. Mary's cautiously resorted to the convenient humbug of the clergy. She preached a sermon against hatred. But if hatred played any role at all in the Great War, it was merely a cameo appearance late in the performance. English soldiers hardly hated their enemies; they merely killed them. The Germans did no less. It was just war. At the beginning of the war at least, if the British hated anyone at all, it was their historical enemies, the French. By contrast, they respected the Germans and generally got on well with them when they had a chance. The only country in which hatred played a major role was the United States, where the masses had been whipped up to hate Germans by politicians eager to get the nation into the war, and by members of the press who had been fed outrageous lies by Britain's propaganda machine.

At least Colonel Mike Dewar, formerly of the Royal Green Jackets, knew what British forces had been up to. "Let us also be aware," wrote he, "that our soldiers, sailors, and airmen are still striving to make the world a better place." By God, they're not a bunch of hard-hearted grunts after all; they're soft-headed do-gooders!

And thus, though the history of warfare is a history of appalling public spectacles, though in every chapter of it the bodies are pressed like flies between the pages, almost *nowhere* will you find any explanation for *why* they are there. Who can find a *single* reason for World War I that justifies the inconvenience of even a single person, let alone the deaths of nine million of them?

Still, the dead men were no less dead for want of a good reason.

Any fight that isn't forced upon you is a sucker's game. Yet the English soldier—and American—plays the unsuspecting mark, time after time. The Crusades, the War of the Roses, the Scottish war of independence, the war with the Spanish, the Anglo-French wars, the American Revolution, the Napoleonic wars, the Crimean War—each time, the bowmen, infantry, cavalry, and their stiff-upper-lipped officers answered the call to protect crown and country. And each time, they were swindled good and hard. Nearly every one of these was a war the combatants wished upon themselves—wars of choice—and most were merely greasy attempts to push out the frontiers of the great Anglo-Saxon empire. America and Britain even fought each other more than once. And what came out of it that really matters to anyone? A different flag? A different national anthem? Neither Canada, nor Australia, nor New Zealand bothered to fight. Each got its independence in a civilized manner and was none the worse for it.

And yet, each year we sit in solemn humbug, honoring the veterans of these conflicts as national heroes. If we were reasonable, we might better hang our heads and pin yellow daisies on our lapels, remembering the shirkers, cowards, malingerers, and artful dodgers who stayed home. At least they delivered the mail and fed the pigs.

IN PRAISE OF BLOCKHEADS

Indeed, as a profession, soldiering must be nearly as hopeless as psychology or marriage counseling. We can think of scarcely a single war that was not begun in treachery and fraud. Nor can we think of any that wasn't carried out with wooden-headed imbecility. Troops never seem to get *where* they are supposed to get ... *when* they are supposed to get there. Armies walk into obvious traps with their eyes wide open. Orders are mixed up ... or lost ... or handed to the enemy. When a victory is gained, it is as much a result of luck as of skill. Most of mankind's wars—far from being stories of valiant heroism—are absurd farces that even the cavalry horses must have laughed at ... until they starved to death.

If World War I had been a movie rather than an actual event, the actors would have turned up their noses at the script and refused to have anything to do with it. But put the actors in uniform and they are ready to play any part—no matter how preposterous. Told to go over the top and advance across a no-man's-land with the enemy shooting at them, the soldiers acted like dumb mules—that is, they did as they were told. It was a case of "lions led by donkeys," said the popular press. And yet, looked at with an unsentimental eye, nearly all of them look like jackasses.

Take the so-called "Great War." On the Eastern front, the Russian army was commanded largely by German-speaking officers. As often as not, their orders would fall into the hands of the enemy—meaning the Germans—who could read them without translation. If they fell into the hands of their own Russian troops, meanwhile, the orders were unintelligible.

Then, 26 years later, in World War II, another Russian army faced yet another German army. In the intervening years, Stalin had had most of the decent officers shot. You'd think the officer class might have seen what was coming and revolted again. Instead, those in charge of the guns let themselves be shot. It has been estimated that in the first months of the war, half of all Soviet casualties were caused by the Soviets themselves. Their planes were so badly made that as many fell from the air because of construction defects as enemy fire. And their officers showed as little mercy to their own infantry as to the Wehrmacht.

A thoughtful soldier might begin to wonder what the point was. He might spend his moments on guard duty reflecting on the why of it. Why in hell would I want to do something so stupid?, he would eventually ask himself. At that point, he'd be useless for further military service.

But the real military man—even one of great genius—is a martinet and a numskull who never asks questions, not even the questions that are critical to his survival. The legendary "fog of war" seems to seep into the brains of commanders and soldiers alike. Alexander, perhaps the greatest general of all time, marched his troops through the desert, where tens of thousands of them perished from thirst and hunger. He hadn't bothered to ask directions. The Romans, supposedly among the greatest military geniuses of history, were taken completely by surprise when Hannibal came down from the Alps. And then the Carthaginian wandered around Italy for the next 10 years before the Roman troops could finally get rid of him. Napoleon attacked Russia, and later, so did Hitler—both of them apparently unaware of the Russian weather. Neither had thought to properly outfit his troops for the cold winter. Yet, German generals even carried copies of Caulaincourt's history of Napoleon's bitter experience in their pockets!

In the Crimean War, Lord Cardigan was told to attack a Russian gun emplacement with his light brigade of cavalry. But inasmuch as his lordship had barely visited front lines—he preferred the lodging of his own private yacht, anchored offshore in the Black Sea, and the cuisine of his own private French chef—he was unfamiliar with the battlefield. Naturally, he charged off in the wrong direction, getting almost all of his men annihilated. He returned to England a national hero.[2]

And in the Great War, when critics complained about "generals fighting the last war"—this judgment was nothing but flattery to the top brass; they were fighting wars that hadn't been fought in generations. Early in the U.S. War Between the States, General Thomas Jackson noticed that a good defensive position was practically impossible to take. "Remember the stone wall," Jackson used to remind his fellow officers, urging them to let the Yankees do the attacking. But "Stonewall" Jackson got his arm shot off—by his own men, predictably—and barely had his body reached room temperature when General Robert E. Lee forgot the advice and ordered a fatal Napoleonic charge against Union positions at Gettysburg. It was obvious even then, a half a century before Passchendaele, that being the attacker was a losing proposition. Still, the French colonel Grandmaison founded what was almost a cult based on the mad cavalry charge.[3]

But what altered the course of warfare was not the gay cavalryman but the dour mechanic. The introduction of the tank made it possible to advance against an entrenched enemy without getting your derriere shot off. Naturally, none of the leading generals and strategists wanted anything to do with it. The French were particularly loath to get involved with the infernal machines. Instead, at a cost of millions of dollars—up and down the Rhine Valley, over a period of many years—they poured concrete bunkers and laid up stone ramparts. The Maginot Line was obsolete before it was built, but the French realized it only when the whole line was sidestepped by a blitzkrieg of tanks. Then, in a matter of hours the French defensive line was behind the Germans' line! General Gamelin, arriving at the front a bit after the fact and much behind the times, is actually said to have wanted to send a warning message back to Paris—by carrier pigeon, though it wasn't as if the blitzkrieg was a secret. The Wehrmacht had just given French military leaders a preview eight and a half months before, when they invaded Poland. Practically the entire Polish army was wiped out. Those officers who managed to escape to the east were rounded up later by the Russians and systematically murdered.

But so it is. Even when the officer class is painfully close to the facts, it often cannot see them. The same officers who had ordered the deaths of millions, in more than four years of warfare, in prison camps, and before Hitler's firing squads, could not seem to summon up the gumption to put a bullet into one especially vile and addled head.

And there you have the glory of a public spectacle. What any of them died for we don't know. For, of the many ways of understanding the Great War, the standard ones are like bright-colored balloons;

you have to hold on to them or they blow away. Never were Britain or America in danger. Never was there any question of preserving freedom, independence, or democracy. The war was just another imperial fight between Britain and Germany over who would be cock-of-the-walk. While the Anglo-Saxon empire, founded on the profits of factories in Manchester, was in decline at the beginning of the twentieth century, German factories were newer and more efficient. The German economy surpassed Britain's in 1910. And whereas the British still bore the cost of maintaining order, their competitors used Pax Britannica to increase their own market share.

But that, ultimately, is the trouble with running an empire. It ends up running you. Before you know it, you are doing suicidal things for no other reason than that is what empires do.

In World War I, the British goose probably would have been cooked had it not been for the ganders in America. But by 1900, the Yankees' output, too, exceeded that of their English cousins and it was they who came to the aid of the Brits, helped kick Teuton butts, and moved the capital of the Anglo-Saxon empire from the banks of the Thames to the mosquito coast of the Potomac.

But now it is factories in Taipei and Guangdong that are the world's newest and most productive, and the gross domestic product (GDP) of Asia is already greater than that of all the Anglo-Saxon countries combined.[4] And America must borrow to hold its empire together, just as the British once did. Only, instead of borrowing from friendly former colonies in the West, she must borrow from her future rivals in the East.

Somewhere, there must be a wall with handwriting on it, announcing the end of this great empire, too, and someone ready to sell red paper flowers to help people remember what never was.

THE LONDON BLITZ

Such is the delightful quality of man himself. He is a sentimentalist, not a scientist. He honors the dead—even when they were imbeciles.

Gutless ... witless ... fighting today's pointless wars with yesterday's senseless tactics—nonetheless, the dead Tommies were human beings exactly like us. And it is the heart that remembers them; the brain is appalled.

So, although we have never killed anyone ourselves, we like to read the obituaries of those who have with keen interest and satisfaction. First, of course, we are pleased not to find ourselves listed among the day's casualties. Second, even if they baffle our minds—the old goners always leave behind a little trace of unwitting humor or unintended enlightenment for anyone who takes the trouble to pick it up.

Just read the London papers. Hardly a day goes by that some antique from the Great War or World War II doesn't finally bite the dust. Many of them, we find, had lived through the Blitz of London in 1940–1941 and had then gone on to fight in romantic places—Malaya, Katmandu, El Alamein—all the distant outposts of what was then the world's greatest power and its dominant empire. They came back home dazed and glad to be alive. Then, the homeland pinned medals on their chests and sent them out to take up jobs selling insurance or elaborating plans for milk distribution.

Compared to what they had been through, it must have been boring. Maybe that is why so many people retain a fond memory for the war years.

It is not ideas that rule the world, though, but the world that rules our ideas. When Britain was at war, the English believed it was their duty to fight and die if that was what it came to. When the war was over, they saw their duties otherwise; now was the time to put on suits and fight the good fight in boardrooms and factories. Each was satisfying in its own way, we suppose.

People did what they did not because they had decided in their own minds that it was satisfying, but because that was what was expected of them. It was the world around them that directed their ideas and told them where their duties lay, not their own hearts and minds. Malleable as soldiers, they were also malleable as citizens. In the beginning, soldiers might be bamboozled into fighting by the bosh and humbug printed in the newspapers. But it takes something much stronger to keep them going. What could it be? We turn to students of war to tell us:

> A hero will not court death—indeed it in no way increases his honor to be killed. He will not fight for his country, nor for his leader; but he will die rather than lose face.[5]

In Greek society, for example, a warrior's self-esteem depended on what his peers thought of him; and what they thought of him depended on how bravely he fought. The real coercion came from the fear of being despised by fellow fighters and of losing one's "reputation as a man among other men."[6]

It is not hard to see why. In earlier societies, when men banded together in small groups to hunt or forage for food, the life of each man depended to an extraordinary degree on his mates. For instance, when one member found food, the group's survival depended on his sharing it with the others, instead of going off alone to gobble it.[7]

Being part of group life meant not only eating together, but fighting and dying together. The group protected each clansman from being killed by rival tribes or torn to pieces by wild animals. He had to depend on the willingness of his fellows to fight for his life, as well as their own, and in turn he had to be prepared to fight for theirs as well as his.

Anything less than fierce fighting might be seen as reneging on the code of reciprocity. And, if the code failed, then the group failed, too, and with it, each of its members.

But just as turkeys and red-breasted robins will react to a code representing a threat, even in the absence of a real threat, human beings also act out fixed-action patterns when something triggers them, even when there is no real threat around. In other words, a fake threat is just as good as a real one when it comes to setting off a crowd reaction.

We were given an illustration of this recently. After the terrorist bombings in London in July 2005, people began reminding themselves of the city's "finest hour." They remembered, too, how they had prevailed without much help from outside.

But, we wonder if this is a comparison that makes any sense at all. How could people not have seen that there is a world of difference between the London terrorist bombings of 2005 and the Blitz of World War II?

Recall for a moment what happened during the Blitz.

The Brits had declared war on Germany in September 1939 and were expecting a German attack. In preparation, air raid systems were set up. But nothing happened. Everything seemed normal, so much so that Londoners even started coming back into town. Then, suddenly, France capitulated and Germany now began sending over waves of planes to bomb strategic targets in Britain. Britain had few experienced pilots, but it had a remarkable airplane, the Spitfire. Together, they managed to hold off the Luftwaffe, inspiring Winston Churchill's famous words: "Never in the field of human conflict was so much owed by so many to so few."

London Blitz: Beginning the Bombing

Eventually, however, Britain's air defenses were in danger of collapsing. Then, at the last moment, a retaliatory British air strike made the Führer lose his wits—and the war; he began bombing English cities instead of military targets, giving the RAF time to recover from the damage inflicted on it.

The raids came almost every night, leaving hundreds of casualties and billions in property damage. London's infrastructure—roads, railways, water, sewage, power—was blown up repeatedly and was under constant repair. But remarkably—and here we make our first point—the longer the raids went on, the more people took them for granted and went about their business. People stopped going into air raid shelters (only about 4 percent of the population ever went into them). Instead, they went to movie theaters and enjoyed the shows.

The threat from outside demolished London's buildings and infrastructure, but it rebuilt her spirit. The more they came under attack, the more people felt their solidarity as Londoners.

Finally, in November 1940, the raids began to tail off, although they remained no less deadly. A huge raid in May of the following year, for instance, brought 550 German bombers over London, dropping 700 tons of bombs and thousands of incendiaries. This was probably the worst raid of the entire war, killing nearly 1,500 people in addition to destroying much of the House of Commons. The House of Lords, Westminster Abbey, Westminster Hall, St James's Palace, and Lambeth Palace were all blasted. So were 14 hospitals, the British Museum, and the Old Bailey.

By the time the Blitz ended, more than a quarter of a million people were homeless. Thousands were dead; many thousands more were injured. The only good was that Britain's island fortress was still under British management. As to whether that was a good thing, under subsequent Labor governments even the British had their doubts.

The London Bombings: What the Wehrmacht Never Was

And then in 2005 when terrorist bombs went off again, more than half a century later, Brits with long teeth and poor memories—and Americans with rich imaginations—thought they heard the boom of the Blitz. They thought they saw Panzer troops rolling across the drumlins of Yorkshire and U-boats crashing through Cardiff Bay. They thought the bombings confirmed the importance of the new threat they faced.

But Muslim terrorists were everything the Wehrmacht never was, and so much less!

What the bombings really confirmed was how insignificant a threat the terrorists were and how unlike the Luftwaffe. Because—while we have never tried it personally—we have to believe that blowing up one or two trains in London must be easy; after all, there are thousands of them running over hundreds of miles all over the place. And since it happens so rarely, we also have to believe that what terrorists there are must be few and feeble. The Luftwaffe, on the other hand, was neither. The first major German raid on London saw as many as 350 bombers attacking the city. In comparison, in military terms, the terrorist attack on London in the summer of 2005 was pathetic and piddling—nothing whatsoever like the Blitz.

But as times change, ideas and beliefs change to suit them. People come to believe *what* they must believe *when* they must believe it. You don't run an empire. Instead, you are run by it, and by the beliefs that go along with it.

There was another difference between the Blitz and the 2005 terrorist bombings. When the Luftwaffe attacked, the Brits looked around and found themselves completely alone. Americans, still new to the empire business, watched from across the broad Atlantic and waited by their phones for orders for more war matériel. Nobody had to tell the Brits then that they had an enemy—it was staring them in the face.

In 2005 Britain was not alone. The United States was fully engaged, from the get-go, in the war against terror. Indeed, it was the United States that was calling the shots this time around. And it was the United States that was telling the British that they have an enemy on par with the *boches*. It was the imperial delusions of Uncle Sam that had got Britons looking for terrorists under their beds.

The difference lies in the fact that, by the twenty-first century, the United States had already reached an advanced stage of empire—and an aging empire needs a little more than banal reality. It needs delusion to keep it going. It desperately needs an enemy to justify defense budgets and military meddling. What else can you expect? Americans need to believe that they are confronted by a vast army of terrorists ready to "destroy our civilization."

You see, finally, it is all about biology. The bigger the threat can be made out to be, the braver the warriors will seem in comparison, and the braver the warriors are, the more solid the group, and the longer it is likely to live. In other words, when it comes to the survival of their genes, human beings are not above lying, exaggerating, and even hallucinating.

When the Luftwaffe's bombs fell in the early 1940s, the British needed calm nerves and resolute action more than anything else. The Anglo-Saxon empire was faced with a real and formidable enemy it had to defeat, and courage was in order. But when bombs go off now the cries for calm or courage are only a charade. You don't need calm at all. What you really need is panic. Without a good and proper panic, people might forget the scare and go about their business as usual.

When you have an enemy so hopelessly ill equipped and feeble as the terrorists today, you are faced with an entirely different sort of challenge. Your task is no longer to defeat an enemy ... but to create one.

IVAN'S WAR

The Brits are not the only ones prone to misrecollection.

Russkie vets seem to remember World War II in their own peculiar way, too—in a sentimental haze of vodka and pierogies.

Was ever there a group of people so hapless, so luckless ... so witless? There they were, up to 30 million of them in the heartland of Eurasia, some 6,000 years after civilization began, 20 centuries after the birth of Christ, 200 years after the industrial revolution began, and during the living memory of many people reading this reflection. They listened to Debussy and Chopin on record players. They tuned into the radio, ate food that came in tins, used condoms, and enjoyed nearly painless dentistry, at least in Moscow. How did these poor Soviet grunts get themselves into such a fix?

And here we add an aggravating detail. They thought themselves not backward, but in the very vanguard of human progress. They were men who had chosen to follow the prophets, Vladimir and Josef, into the land of scientific socialism. Gone were the old traditions. Gone were the old rules. Now, the Soviets had a new religion of collectivism, new rules shaped by the Communist Party, and new traditions enforced by the Narodnyi Komissariat Vnutrennikh Del (NKVD) or the People's Commissariat for Internal Affairs.

Readers may have relaxed by now, like parishioners at a sermon who see the preacher's accusing finger pass them by. But not so fast. While the victims in this story are the Soviets, the protagonists—the dramatis personae—of our theme include us all. We may not be communists, or Russians, or soldiers, but we, too, are spellbound by our own delusions.

When war with Germany began, the Soviet soldier found himself in a no-man's-land. In front of him was the Wehrmacht, the best attack force ever put into the field. The German army would most likely kill him or take him prisoner. If he were taken prisoner, he would almost certainly die, because prisoners were often left out in the open, surrounded with barbed wire and used for target practice until they finally collapsed from hunger and exposure. In back of him, his prospects were not much better. Stalin's police had put up so-called blocking battalions behind him who were meant to shoot their own comrades if they tried to retreat. "Not a step back," Stalin had said in his secret order number 227. Elsewhere, he noted grimly that in the Soviet army it took more courage to retreat than advance. Between the Germans and the blocking battalions, there was almost certain death.

"The rates of loss were ... extravagant," writes Catherine Merridale in *Ivan's War*:

> By December 1941, six months into the conflict, the Red Army had lost 4.5 million men. The carnage was beyond imagination. Eyewitnesses described the battlefields as landscapes of charred steel and ash. The round shapes of lifeless heads caught the late summer light like potatoes turned up from new-broken soil. The prisoners were marched off in their multitudes. Even the Germans did not have the guards, let alone enough barbed wire, to contain the 2.5 million Red Army troops they captured in the first five months. One single campaign, the defense of Kiev, cost the Soviets nearly 700,000 killed or missing in a matter of weeks. Almost the entire

army of the pre-war years ... was dead or captured by the end of 1941.[8]

Behind these amazing figures is a long story. The Bolsheviks believed they had the secret recipe for a better world. It required destroying the old institutions, relationships, customs, attitudes, traditions, and religion. Naturally, not everyone was cooperative. Well, said Lenin, "you can't make an omelet without breaking some eggs." So, the shells were cracked with rifle butts.

> The seven years after 1914 were a time of unrelenting crisis: the civil war between 1918 and 1921 alone would bring cruel fighting, desperate shortages of everything from heating fuel to bread and blankets, epidemic disease, and a new scourge that Lenin chose to call class war.[9]

The famine that came in its wake was terrible by any standards, but a decade later, in 1932–1933, when starvation claimed more than seven million lives, the great hunger of 1921 would come to seem, as one witness put it, "like child's play." By then, too, Soviet society had torn itself apart in the upheaval of the first of many five-year plans for economic growth, driving the peasants into collectives, destroying political opponents, and forcing some citizens to work like slaves. The men and women who were called upon to fight in 1941 were the survivors of an era of turmoil that had cost well over 15 million lives in little more than two decades.[10]

This campaign to improve the world included getting rid of experienced military officers who were from the wrong class—as most were.

You'd think that even a government employee could figure out that soldiers needed rifles, but many went to war without them. Nor did they have proper food, shelter, sanitation, or clothing. Fortunately, from a central planner's point of view, without weapons or training they were usually killed before they starved to death. Little things were missing, too. The soldiers were ordered to go places, but there were no maps to show them how to get there. Only the Germans had maps. Soviet tanks were equipped with radios, but without an adequate code system, Germans could listen in on their tactical discussions.

By February 1942, three million Soviet soldiers had been captured. The Red Army had also lost 2,663,000 who were killed in action. The math was bad, even for a country as large as Russia; for every German who was killed, 20 Soviet soldiers died.

And here, we pause and we wonder. There were more than five million armed men at any given time in the Red Army. They could have turned on their incompetent and merciless leaders if they had wanted to. Instead, they lined up and marched to their own slaughter, many of them, perhaps the majority, believing that it would help make the world a better place.

Like the Anglo-Saxon survivors of the first and second world wars, even now the old Russkies sit around shabby old soldiers' homes and congratulate themselves. They beat the fascists! They saved the proletarian revolution! Thus, they live out almost their entire lives under the heel of an even more delusional and murderous regime than the one they fought, but they don't seem to notice. It is enough that their delusions give them grandeur.

Here, too, people don't seem to notice that much of what they take for granted future generations will see as absurd. Whatever allows them to puff up in importance they believe . . . even if it kills them.

PERICLES: "I SHALL BEGIN WITH OUR ANCESTORS"

So the swindle goes on: one generation outdoing itself to undo the work of the others. Even the classics are full of the high-sounding humbug.

"I shall begin with our ancestors," said Pericles, in his speech for the dead soldiers of Athens.[11] This was after the first battles of the Peloponnesian War in 431–430 B.C. The custom was to give a public eulogy—a kind of Thanksgiving and Veterans Day rolled into one—each year.

"And if our remote ancestors deserve praise, much more do our own fathers, who added to their inheritance the empire which we now possess, and spared no pains to be able to leave their acquisitions to the present generation."

Pericles began as George W. Bush might, honoring the achievements of the nation's fighting men. An unsentimental historian might wonder what those achievements were worth. Athens, like other city-states, seemed prone to go to war with its neighbors for no particular reason and no particular advantage. Finally, it was brought low by plague, treachery, and other empire builders; all the Sturm und Drang seemed to get it nowhere.

Then, in his speech, Pericles made equally dubious remarks about Athens itself. These, too, might have come from the mouth of America's current president, if someone would write them out for him in short words. This little insight should put to rest forever the idea of Athens as a center of serious thinking. Pericles was a better humbugger than Bush, but the flatteries were the same. Athens' government was better than those of its rivals, he said. Its people were more courageous and better organized. Even artists flourished in Athens as nowhere else.

Pericles may have urged Athenians to war, but the war itself did not go well. Twice, the Spartans invaded and laid waste Athenian lands. A year later, the same people who praised Pericles were at his throat. The great orator held them off—urging them to stay the course. Yes, he pointed out, your lands and houses might have been ruined, but this is a fight for something much more—liberty! "You cannot decline the burdens of empire and still expect to share its honors," he said.

The Athenians did stay the course; it led them to total disaster, and Pericles died of plague.

We know what thanks Pericles' generation owed its predecessors. But what thanks did the next generation of Athenians owe to them?

Athens was destroyed. Their parents' empire building had cost them dearly: their wealth, their independence, even the empire itself.

The blessings that one generation enjoys are passed on to the next generation as a curse. A child born in the United States in 1900 came into the world naked and free of debt. Today, American children pop into the world and are immediately swaddled in the chains of empire and imperial debt. All their lives they will have to be paying them off—debts from bonuses paid to government employees in 1986, from bombs dropped in 2003, from boondoggles built in 1995, from checks written in 1974, from promises made to old people in 2002, from the expenses of hurricanes in 2005, and so on. The poor children will have to drag around with them the entire pathetic history of America's financial decline.

"Stay the course," says Bush. "We cannot stop now."

"Damned b★★tards," the next generation is likely to grumble.

CHAPTER 7

—————

EMPIRE OF DELUSION

Our enemies never stop thinking about new ways to harm our country
and our people, and neither do we.

—**George W. Bush**

On March 15, 2,051 years ago, Julius Caesar was assassinated by
his friend Brutus and other conspirators. Caesar had it coming, of
course. He had crossed the Rubicon with his army—something that
was forbidden under Roman law—and had seized power by force.
But when Caesar fell to the "unkindest cut of all," it set off a power
struggle in Rome that soon had armies on the march all around the
Mediterranean. Among other things, it put an end to Ptolemaic rule
of Egypt with the death of Mark Antony's lover, Cleopatra.

What a marvelous story—full of power, war, deceit, backstabbing,
jealousy, sex . . . even animals! No wonder people love politics; it is
so much like real life.

We turn to Julius only to render unto Caesar what is his.

That is to say, we turn to him simply to find out what is happening
in the war against terror.

> Fierce fiery warriors fought upon the clouds,
> In ranks and squadrons and right form of war,
> Which drizzled blood upon the Capitol.[1]

Caesar's wife, Calpurnia, might have been describing Baghdad.
Instead, she was recalling a nightmare and giving her husband a
warning: Beware the Ides of March.

But what husband listens to his wife's bad dreams? And who con-
sults the headlines—except as the Romans consulted augurs—looking

for things that might cause trouble? Is something happening in the world that might trump the normal patterns of boom and bust or overrule a financial trend, as World War II is said to have brought an end to the Great Depression? Is there some sign or wonder that tells us that this empire is not going to go the way of every empire before it?

We ask, because the current American ideology has one more layer of deception running through it than the usual imperial fraud. Americans expect their empire to keep running not on tribute as the old empires did, but on debt. It is as if you expected to keep your car going by letting out a little fuel from your tank each time you stopped at the gas station.

According to the theory of it, at any rate, the imperial power, like the Mafia, maintains order so that under the protection of the imperial *pax dollarum* trade and commerce can flourish and people can get rich. And of course, the imperial power must charge for the service; otherwise, what would be the point?

But the United States has so cleverly deceived itself that it believes it gets its tribute from globalized commerce itself and from the loans given to it by its tributary states and trading partners.

"The United States, even more than any other economically and militarily dominant powers in the recent past, has acquired an empire," writes Deepak Lal, "but is reluctant to face up to the resulting imperial responsibilities."[2]

Au contraire, Mr. Lal. Americans have taken to the imperial purple on their backs like a gorilla to a tutu. The spectacle is more exhilarating than any we've seen before. We see the mighty falling for some mighty foolish ideas. It makes the whole thing doubly comic.

Little noticed in the celebration of its victories is the fact that the U.S. military has gotten so far ahead of the competition that it represents a threat to everyone—including itself. And with no enemy capable of delivering a decisive strike, it may have to blow itself up.

Even in Caesar's day, Rome did not enjoy the margin of power that the United States does today.

Paul Kennedy writes, "It is simply staggering to learn that this single country—a democratic republic that claims to despise large government—now spends more each year on the military than the next nine largest national defense budgets combined."[3]

What does this mean? Just as the U.S. economy is now thought to be too indebted to fail, has the U.S. military become too big to fail?

STAGE ONE OF A PUBLIC SPECTACLE—LIES

The answer lies in the nature of mass delusions. Like all public spectacles, the delusion of empire has its roots in a deception. In this case, it is the belief that America is virtuous above all other nations.

Rainbow Warriors: The *Chosin* People

"I never sleep well on warships," begins one column we read recently.[4] From the very first line, we are thrown off stride. Our head tilts to the left. What is *New York Times* opinion-monger Thomas L. Friedman doing on a warship?, we wonder.

Apparently he is a frequent guest of the U.S. fleet.

We don't begrudge Friedman his celebrity. Still, we can't think of anyone who holds himself up to ridicule the way he does; unwittingly—the only way possible for Friedman—he has become a traveling minstrel, singing the praises of the new delusion. His books are best sellers. His column is wisely admired and widely distributed. His sugary views have become ubiquitous; they have done for American intellectual life what Krispy Kreme has done to its diet.

Writing from the USS *Chosin*, the imperial hallucinator thinks he has discovered yet more evidence of the empire's superiority:

> When the Iraqi Navy drops you off on the *Chosin*, a guided missile cruiser, two things just hit you in the face. One is the diversity of the U.S. Navy—blacks, whites, Hispanics, Christians, Jews, atheists,

Muslims, all working together, bound by a shared idea, not by an iron fist.[5]

Not only is the U.S. Navy generous in offering bed and board to *New York Times* journalists, it apparently does so to a wide variety of humans, and all on the same condition: They agree to promote and protect the empire.

Sailors Designed by Benetton

Friedman finds this astonishingly virtuous; we are the *Chosin* people, he seems to say, because we have a fighting force designed by Lucian Benetton.

What the man is applauding, though, is not the American but the Anglo-Saxon empire—filled with debt and delusion. A multicultural fighting force is just one of the many features of imperial rule. A humble nation-state can stay within its borders and leave its citizens alone to run their own lives. An empire is a comedy on a much larger scale; it absorbs other races, nations, and religious groups as it grows.

By the time they fought the battle of Gaugamela, the Macedonians had a rainbow army composed of many races and nationalities, from Greeks to Egyptians and Indians. Likewise, the Romans soon found themselves with legions recruited from dozens of Italian tribes, and then from all over the empire—Scythians, Slavs, Celts, Gauls, Germans, Persians, Armenians, and so on.

The British levied up not just Englishmen from imperial outposts in Canada and Australia, but subject peoples in India and Egypt, such as the tough Gurkhas who fought in World War II.

Hitler's rainbow army—including large units from Italy and the Balkans—carried his campaign into the Soviet Union.

Showing the Heathen How to Live

But America's rainbow outdoes them all, says Friedman. It has brighter shades of pink!

"In trying to bring some democracy to Iraq," the writer continues, "America is not just challenging the dictatorial-tribal political order here, but the male-dominated culture as well."

For the Navy has broken the taboo of thousands of years of fighting at sea. It has put women on its warships: "The U.S. Coast Guard cutter *Monomoy*, alongside the *Chosin*, has a female executive officer, who often leads the landing parties that inspect boats in the Gulf; one of the U.S. Navy's fast patrol boats, also alongside the *Chosin*, had a female captain."

If only the Iraqis could be more like us, says the world improver.

We swoon at the thought of it. We are feeding so many good things to the Iraqis all at once: democracy, diversity, feminism. It is no wonder the poor Iraqis choke.

STAGE TWO OF A PUBLIC SPECTACLE—FARCE

As with any public spectacle, deceit and deception are quickly followed by farce. Day after day now, we hear of imperial pratfalls in Baghdad.

Clueless in Baghdad

Of course, you can't really fault the Bush team for wanting to take Baghdad. Every serious empire does. The Assyrians, Greeks, Romans, Persians, Arabs, Mongols, Turks, even the English got their hands on it. In terms of killing, the most recent imperial grab ranks somewhere between those of Tamerlane and George V. The English killed about 10,000 insurgents in the 1920s. Tamerlane is reputed to have butchered millions in the fourteenth century.

But in terms of humbug, the Bush administration outdoes them both. If it weren't for the deaths, watching the Bush gang stumble along the banks of the Tigris and Euphrates would be amusing. The U.S. forces bring the usual mayhem and single-source contracts.

But using the language of Thomas Jefferson, they preach "liberty." Borrowing the words of the Tory jurist Blackstone, they offer their victims a "fair trial."

But that is where they wash up. In the words of Saddam Hussein, if the United States, Britain, and every other imperial ruler who ever cut off a head or blew up an outhouse can kill insurgents, why couldn't I?

Mind you, no one doubts that the noose was too good for Saddam. But compared to the present, his rule is beginning to look like the good old days.

"People are doing the same as [in] Saddam's time and worse," says Ayad Allawi, former prime minister and foe of Saddam. "We are hearing about secret police, secret bunkers, where people are being interrogated. A lot of Iraqis are being tortured or killed in the course of interrogations. We are even witnessing Sharia courts based on Islamic law that are trying people and executing them."[6]

Saddam may have been a ruthless dictator, but at least he was honest. What Iraq has now are social workers with automatic rifles. That is all very well for the lumpenvoters in the United States. They can imagine whatever they want. But it is a dangerous swindle in Baghdad.

They say that those who do not study history are doomed to repeat it. But generations of empire builders have read Thucydides' history of Athens' empire; it didn't seem to have helped them. And the Bush administration seems almost uniquely benighted. Not since the Hapsburgs has any empire been so incompetent. Never has any been taken in so completely by its own claptrap.

When General Mark C. Clark took control of Naples in World War II, he had the good sense to bring over New York mobster Lucky Luciano to keep order. The Bush team sent over cronies with MBAs and Texas driver's licenses.

After the fall of the Soviet Union, the United States had no enemies worthy of the name; now it is creating them faster than dollar bills. It has the finest attack force ever created; now it is used to patrol gas stations. It bears the immense costs single-handedly—with no way of paying them, save by borrowing from its foremost rivals, the communist Chinese.

Our imperialists look in the mirror and see only good things—democracy, freedom, negative amortization mortgages, reality TV. Surely they should play the leading men on the world's stage! And so they take up the imperial role like a child playing with a rattlesnake: They are fascinated . . . until it bites them.

And thus they got their mitts on a man who had nothing left to lose—a former CIA asset and then a U.S. liability—Saddam Hussein. Instead of strangling him when they pulled him from his hole, they put him on television. From there he rallied the desert tribes against the one thing they hate more than each other—the foreign invader. Then they hanged him. Now he is a martyr and Muslim lads all over the world live only to avenge him.

Every day, it seems, is brand-spanking-new to the Bush boys, with no trace of yesterday in it and no hint of tomorrow. It is not as if they were born yesterday; it is as if they had never been born at all.

Offshore Assets

And now comes news that the Americans have done one better even than the Butcher of Baghdad himself. The "CIA holds terror suspects in secret prisons," writes Dana Priest in the *Washington Post*.[7]

The article talks about some 30 of the highest-value suspects being held in "black sites" dotting nameless Eastern European democracies. "The Eastern European countries that the CIA has persuaded to hide Al Qaeda captives are democracies that have embraced the rule of law and individual rights after decades of Soviet domination."

Oh, good. It's always reassuring to know that hired torturers believe in the Bill of Rights.

Remember those?

- Citizens are guaranteed inviolability of the person. No one may be arrested except by a court decision or on the warrant of a procurator.

- Citizens are guaranteed inviolability of the home. No one may, without lawful grounds, enter a home against the will of those residing in it.

But did we imply the U.S. Constitution? We correct ourselves—we meant the *Soviet* Constitution. Those seem to be Articles 54 and 55 of the Constitution of the old *Soviet* Union, which was in full force all through show trials, Siberian gulags, and the disappearing of inconvenient dissidents in the bad old days of the Evil Empire. Readers will know which one, we are sure.

Senior officials (here we mean the U.S., not the Soviet) are coy about outing their new buddies. Still, we can always take an educated guess. Poland, maybe? Readers may remember news reports detailing complaints that Iraqi prisoners at Abu Ghraib were being abused by Polish troops.[8] Or wait, now we find an old *New York Times* article that claims the Pentagon is "smitten with Romania. And Poland. And Bulgaria, too."[9] It is so smitten it seems that Pentagon officials were thinking of transferring five army brigades from Germany to the east.

The author of the article, Lawrence Korb, a former assistant secretary of defense, pooh-poohs the notion that the move to Eastern Europe has anything to do with costs; upgrading crumbling Soviet-era bases and transportation networks, he says, would easily outweigh cheaper living costs. Besides, these nouveau capitalists are piss-poor; they can't possibly pay for their own protection like the elitist pinko Huns. Korb believes the obsession with the New Europe is only to punish Old Europe for not getting with the imperial program in Iraq. It is only another case of the Bush boys cutting off their own noses to spite their faces, says he.

With their Pinocchio-like tendencies, a nose job might be just what the Bush gang needs. But we have to ask if they really are that dumb or are only playing dumb. If the U.S. army has been offshoring its barracks to Eastern Europe despite the costs, maybe costs are just what it wants. You see, it all depends on how you look at things. Every crumbling facility in need of upgrading is also a reconstruction contract for a building contractor. And if torture is relocating east, it may be because every new prison brings in a new prison contract.

But there's nary a word about the new economics in the *Post* article. It's all round-eyed innocence and nobody here but us chickens. If the CIA does wrong, it's only a dumb mistake to be fixed by better laws passed by Democrats. "We'd probably shoot ourselves," says an ex–CIA officer quoted in the *Post* piece when questioned about a plan floated in days of yore for hit squads to take out foreign targets.

On the one hand, no kidding. Violence is the last refuge of the incompetent, as Asimov once said. This is the gang that came up with plans to kill Fidel Castro by spraying a television studio where he was going to appear with LSD. Another brain wave was to poison him with thallium in his shoes in the hope his beard would fall out. But on the other hand, dumb and deadly not only are not mutually exclusive, they tend to stumble around together like contestants in a three-legged race. And dumb is often pretty good cover for deadly.

Take, for instance, the KUBARK counterintelligence manual. It taught no-touch torture throughout Central America as early as 1963. But, to read the *Post* article, you'd think that until now, except for a few honest-to-goodness blunders, it was all sweetness, light, and the rule of law down at Langley:

"We never sat down, as far as I know, and came up with a grand strategy," says one official. Cross our hearts.

But, CIA confessions are like cooking with onions. They make you weep, and when you're done peeling through all the layers, you're usually left with nothing. And you'll get plenty of nothing trying to get the CIA to admit what it's been up to.

Rewind, for a moment, to the Gildered 1990s. The stock market was soaring. Al Gore was busy inventing the Internet, when not starring in *Love Story*. Kremlinologists were beating down the doors of D.C. soup kitchens. Enron was not yet a verb and Monica's dress hung neatly in her closet. With the Cold War defunct, the CIA was in limbo.

Then came the Clinton-Gore Partnership for Reinventing Government in 1993; streamlining the government became the order of the day, and hundreds of intelligence jobs were cut. Information technology firms like CACI International Inc. and Titan Corporation moved into the gap, hiring retired spooks and then contracting them back to the government.

In September 1999, the CIA created In-Q-It (later renamed In-Q-Tel), a venture capital firm that contracted out a huge range of services and adopted the business model wholesale.[10] And it adopted business jargon. The president and defense secretary became "old customers." Homeland Security was a new one. Of course, even before, the CIA had always been known as the "Company." Its operatives had always been called "assets" and its operations, "accounts." But the old gobbledygook was only meant to sanitize the dirty business of spy versus spy. Now it was taken literally. The new director, George Tenet, boasted like a CEO that he had "turned the business around."[11]

The spy trade was shuffled off to private contractors, who didn't have to stick to any legal standards set by Congress. Of course, neither does Congress—but invisible spooks tend to be even more unaccountable than visible Congresspersons.

A private intelligence contractor paid half a million a year needs a lot of intelligence to justify its existence. Torture produces information. Mostly unreliable, of course, but who cares, as long as the money comes in. Long before Mr. Rumsfeld got his new model army, the new model CIA of the Clinton era had figured out that filthy lucre gushes like a geyser from a trade in torture.

It was under Clinton that the kinder, gentler doctrine of "war without blood" was developed. That and cuddly "no-touch torture" have been in the works ever since World War II. The logic was faultless: Make war and torture legal, invisible, and acceptable—and fatten defense budgets as well. Pork with principle! How could any self-respecting Congressman resist?

Private interrogators driven to produce information at any cost snatched up a random bunch of Ahmeds and Mohammeds, who—with a little suasion—coughed up whatever was needed. Now

Americans could do unto Iraqis what they had done unto American prisoners for years.

Thus did the spy business become infested with a network of lobbyists and government connections as thick as anything in the defense business—with one difference. Defense contractors are at least monitored. Intelligence contractors, in contrast, have budgets that are classified; they work in secret, without a soul to check on them.

Half the board members of the leading trade association of the intelligence business are current government officials.[12]

Today's assets are MBAs who think the CIA makes a better employer than Apple. They want the industry deregulated, and they accept hit squads, assassinations, and "torture lite" as sound business practices. Now the CIA takes to renditions like a Louisiana governor to strippers.[13]

The headquarters of the spy business isn't Langley anymore; it's Wall Street. And the root of the problem is not the law but the brand-new, shiny, bubble economy with the scum on top—bid rigging, inflated billing, questionable accountancy, preferential treatment. Why would American laws stop a business that can hide its assets offshore?

STAGE THREE OF A PUBLIC SPECTACLE—DISASTER

So it is that even with catastrophe staring plainly in front of it, the Bush gang doesn't hesitate. It is as if they already know that the last stage of a public spectacle is a disaster. "Bring it on!" they cry, as though the stars had foretold it.

Signs of the Times

Indeed, we wondered recently if they had. We were enjoying one of the most beautiful nights we had ever seen in the south of France. After dinner—followed by a concert performed by the family band—we wandered outside. The earth looked like it had been covered with a shimmering gauze. And then there was a strange apparition in the southern skies: a shooting star that would not stop shooting. A comet? What could it herald?

At dinner earlier, a French historian had wondered why Americans had supported the Bush administration's military adventures in Iraq and Afghanistan. "You are wasting your most precious resources," she told us, "your military strength and your money, on nothing. Why?"

We tried to explain. "Because our experience with war has been rather positive for the last 100 years," we began. "The military is the one institution that people seem to trust."

Americans' faith in the righteousness of their military is an old one, only paralleled by their faith in the solidity of land and houses as investments. "You can't go wrong with real estate," is a stock phrase. But, of course, it's simply not true. When our office in Baltimore was sold during the early 1900s, it brought a price that—in real terms—was not matched for another 70 years. Our point is that really big moves in the market or in the military are driven by sentiment, which follows very long patterns, like the orbit of a distant comet that makes its appearance in the southern skies only once in a lifetime.

Right now, people have begun to talk about recession, about bear markets, about war. But they don't really feel the misery of these things; they are only abstractions now.

But, if there is one thing we know about the sentiments of crowds, it is that they change. Today it is greed. Tomorrow it is fear. But rarely is it doubt. So, when mass sentiment goes negative, it goes completely negative. People stop worrying about the return *on* their money and begin to be concerned about the return *of* their money.

It has been a long time since that sort of fiery comet has come around and people have forgotten the sense of awe and dread it inspires, as if it announced the end of a world. They can't quite imagine what that might be like. They will have to see it again for themselves. It's only a matter of time.

Creating Terrorists with Grudges

Here is Zbigniew Brzezinski, a former U.S. national security adviser. Quoting Arnold Toynbee, he accuses the Bush administration of "suicidal statecraft . . . the ultimate cause of imperial collapse."[14]

What the man doesn't seem to realize is that "suicidal statecraft" is just what the situation calls for. And Bush is perfectly up to the task. The great Anglo-Saxon empire has reached its "sell by" date. But while its homeland citizens groan under the burden of debt, many of its military and political leaders still talk tough.

"You got terrorists with a grudge against the United States?" asked the commander-in-chief. Well, "bring 'em on." He might as well have put a gun to his head. Now, with the curiosity of a reporter watching a hanging, we wait to see if he pulls the trigger, for Iraq is full of potential terrorists with grudges. Had the Anglo-Americans bothered to look before they leaped, they would have seen a country that is a mix of tribes, clans, families, and religious groups—all of whom take it as an inherited obligation to avenge any wrong done to any of their own group by any member of any other group going back five generations. We cannot kill terrorists as fast as the State Department can create them, say some.

Patrick Cockburn, writing in the *Independent*, reminds us of the insights of a British civil servant, Arnold Wilson, in 1919, two years after the British took Baghdad from the Turks: "Wilson . . . warned that the creation of a new state out of Iraq was a recipe for disaster. He said it was impossible to weld together Shia, Sunni, and Kurd, three groups of people who detested each other. . . . The Kurds in the north, whom it was intended to include in Iraq, 'will never accept Arab rule.' "[15]

But what they would accept even less was rule by the British. The whole country soon rose up against British forces; there were more than 10,000 dead before it was over. Still, every great empire—from the Assyrians to the Mongols to the British—has taken Baghdad.

America has to do it, too. It is the imperial script and America is right on cue.

We doubt that even comets and signs in the skies could change her course.

FULL SPECTRUM DUMBBELLS

That is why every public spectacle makes the headlines at least twice: first, in pleasant expectation; later, in miserable regret. The war in Iraq is no exception. The *Independent* ran a photograph of George W. Bush and Tony Blair on its cover in 2006. "Are these the only two men in the world who think the Iraq War is a success?" asked the headline.

In the public spectacle, blame, responsibility, truth, and consequences are usually extremely remote; the spectacle proceeds by separating cause from effect, reward from punishment, and truth from consequences. In private, the punishment usually fits the crime, not only perfectly but poetically. The fool is separated from his money. The reckless driver wrecks his car. The heavy drinker falls down heavily.

Still, eventually, even in a spectacle, there are consequences. Researchers recently tried to guess how much of a debacle the war in Iraq really is. They focused on the number of people who had died since the government of Saddam Hussein was run out of Baghdad. Various estimates came in, from a low of 300,000 or so to nearly a million. Estimates of the costs are similarly wide—from a couple of hundred billion dollars to more than $1 trillion—and projected into the future, as high as $2 trillion. Where does a nation already $65 trillion short get that kind of money? And how could the damage to its diplomatic prestige ever be repaired—at any cost?

We recall when the news of 9/11 spread around the globe. "We all feel like Americans now," said French friends. In Britain, the Queen ordered the band to play "The Star-Spangled Banner." Guardsmen at

Buckingham Palace wept upon hearing it. Even Yasser Arafat rolled up his sleeve and gave blood.

But five years later, the whole world had backed away. In the intervening years, the Bush administration did nothing to stop the so-called Axis of Evil; instead, it greased its moving parts. North Korea managed to get a nuclear bomb under the watchful gaze of the United States, while the American military actually helped Iran achieve all of its most important foreign policy objectives. It eliminated Iran's biggest rival in the region—Saddam Hussein—and neutralized its biggest enemy—Iraq. Mission accomplished!

Then came the election results on November 7, 2006. The Republicans were punished. By midnight on election day, they had lost the House of Representatives. By sunset the next day, the Senate had been lost, too. "The vote was a vote against the war," said the press reports. Then, the following day, Donald Rumsfeld resigned. He didn't "do quagmires," he had once told the nation. And now, he was being punished for getting the nation into its biggest foreign policy quagmire ever.

But losing a job hardly seems a suitable chastisement for an epic blunder like the war in Iraq. Saddam Hussein was hanged for killing only 148 people during his career as dictator of the country. By the close of 2006, that many people were being killed in Iraq every day. Roman bridge builders used to stand under their arches as the scaffolding was removed. If they made a mistake, the whole thing would come down on their heads. At Iwo Jima, the Japanese commander committed ritual seppuku, opening up his own belly to remove his intestines and dying in agony. Donald Rumsfeld got off easy.

But it is a strange, strange world we live in. Can you really measure success or failure in terms of lives and treasure? The Bush team aims for "full spectrum dominance." Who's to say the occupation of Iraq didn't help them get it?

Suppose, for example, the gods intended the Muslims to triumph over the West. Suppose they considered Western civilization irredeemably decadent and intended to cleanse it. It wouldn't be the first time. And suppose this time the gods decided to use the sword of Mohammed to do the job. If this were the case, the man who resisted it wouldn't be combating evil; he would be Canute fighting the tides. Who can know the mind of God? Or who can know what the lesser gods intend—or how they plan to accomplish it? "Oh, but there are no gods," you will say. "We are all alone in the universe, and only we can determine what is good and what is evil." Then explain something to us. How do you know President Bush's vision of good and evil is superior to, say, Osama bin Laden's?

In private, a man must find his own happiness—by calling on his own gods, his own reason, and his own madness for guidance. Sometimes he will find heaven, sometimes hell; we cannot know. Public man, on the other hand, undertakes not only to find his own way in the world, but to dictate to others where they must go; he substitutes his own preferences for those of the people he wants to boss around. He pretends to know things he cannot possibly know—heaven from hell, blue skies from pain, good from evil.

No one gets to read tomorrow's newspaper headlines today. Still, after six centuries of movable type, you'd think the basic template for public spectacles would at least be vaguely understood. Seeing one set of headlines—"Germany Invades Poland," "Dow Surges to All-Time High," "China Is the New 'Miracle Economy'"—a reader might expect to see another set, later, headed in the other direction.

Looking ahead to a long retreat, you'd think people would be tempted to stay home. Why bother?, they might ask themselves. The troops might as well stay in their barracks. Investors could just as soon put their money in the bank. But they don't. All of them follow the same hiker's trail—up the mountain on one side and down it on the other. The great historical achievement of the Bush team was only to step on the gas.

We turn to logic—not for an answer, but for a culprit. Any man who has had teenage children will tell you to be suspicious of logic, for as soon as a teenager gets the hang of it, his sense of reason seems to leave him—and doesn't return for at least five or six years. Or, if he takes up politics, law, or economics, it may never return. "If there really were a God," says the teenager triumphantly, "He wouldn't let there be people starving, He wouldn't allow Bush to kill people, and He wouldn't make me do homework on Friday night." But we've been around long enough to believe that God can do any damned thing He wants, even if it makes no sense to a 15-year-old.

The poor creatures that walk on four legs can't pick up a screwdriver, so they can't take a clock apart to look at how the pieces go together. Humans, however, can't seem to stop doing it. And as their knowledge of the material world advances, by fits and starts, they are gradually able to enjoy a kind of full spectrum dominance over the natural world. Except for tiny viruses, no living thing seriously challenges them.

But, out on the penumbras and umbras of the spectrum of life where the public spectacles occur, the light is either so white you are blinded by it or so black you cannot see a thing. Yet, even there, the logical mind looks at politics, social order, economics, and finance as though they were as simple as a rudimentary cuckoo clock. The naive scientist imagines that here, too, he can take the pieces apart and study them. Standing on two legs, with all the natural world at his feet, he cannot help but think he can master this social world, also.

It is here that he runs into trouble. He picks up the pieces, but he immediately sees that they are unlike the sprockets, wheels, and gears of a clock. Instead, they are full of body fluids, bile, and air—hearts and guts—and facts as vague as a cloud and as elusive as a bead of mercury.

Small things can have huge, unforeseeable consequences. When the Germans put Lenin on a train and sent him to Russia ... or when Ho Chi Minh decided not to become a pastry chef ... the results were incalculable. But our naive scientist, finding the parts impossible to grasp, reduces complex ideas and contradictory information to harebrained slogans that the masses can understand as reasons. Then, he strings the reasons together with the artful finesse of a rail-yard worker putting together boxcars. One rusty simplification is connected to the next until they get him where he wants to go. He becomes thoroughly logical ... and completely unreasonable.

"The terrorists are out to get us," he says, as if it were a fact. After that, his next fact sounds almost sensible—"We have to defend ourselves." "Better to do so in the streets of Baghdad than in the streets of Baltimore," comes the next heavy hulk. Does Baghdad have anything to do with terrorism? No, but it's close enough for government work, as they say. And so, he eventually reaches Baghdad and gets himself into such a mess even the English papers are laughing at him.

Meanwhile, back in the financial markets, so great is the uncertainly and unpredictability of things that professors of finance have tied themselves up with a formula called the Efficient Market Hypothesis (EMH), according to which prices set by the market are so perfect you're wasting your time trying to outsmart them. The hypothesis is nonsense, of course. Prices are not perfect at all, but wrong most of the time, shifting constantly from being too expensive to being too cheap.

But EMH is a useful fraud, reminding investors how hard it is to beat the broad market—or even understand it—and we believe that something similar should be developed for politics. The world is not perfect. But it is the reflection of the judgment of the world's people—developed, elaborated, and evolved over thousands of years of experience. If a country like Iraq has a dictator of whom we do not approve, it may make sense to refer to the Perfect World Hypothesis, just to remind ourselves that What Is is for a reason—one we cannot necessarily know. We might want to replace What Is with What Should Be (In Our Opinion)—but, at least, we ought to think twice about it.

CHAPTER 8

HEROES OF THE REVOLUTION

Every revolution evaporates and leaves behind only the slime of a new bureaucracy.

—**Franz Kafka**

Whether the War on Terror will prove beneficial either to the United States or to the human race we cannot say. But it certainly proves that every once in a while a man seems to feel the need to turn howling mad and swing his arms around. That is an aspect of war that is underappreciated—the apishness of it.

People are much too simpleminded about mass killing. They see it as either good or bad, right or wrong. Either you are for it or you are against it. A battle turns out to be either a magnificent triumph or an abysmal defeat. When they come up against a Korea or a Vietnam, people don't know what to make of it. It seems incomplete and unsatisfying—like a baseball game that got rained out. They yearn for a simple answer: yes, no; friend, foe. They want to know who wins and who loses.

But, judging from the historical record, most wars have no identifiable winners—especially wars on terror. Usually, such wars end neither in victory nor in defeat, but in humiliation. The fighters merely give up because they are exhausted, broke, and embarrassed. Even when there is an apparent victor, the winner is hardly any better off. Nor is the apparent loser always worse off! France lost the Franco-Prussian War after the battle of Sedan in 1870. After that came the Belle Epoch; the nation never had it so good. And a fat lot of good it did the "winners" after they "won" World War I. When the war was over, the loser, Germany, picked itself up and was soon the strongest, most confident, and most dynamic nation in Europe.

That wars for empire are a sorry spectacle is not in doubt, but the opponents they draw out of the woodwork are not much better. Claptrap about imperial destiny and the *mission civilisatrice* on one side seems to elicit humbug about the proletarian revolution and the dialectic of history on the other. When it comes down to it, every actor in a public spectacle has an eye cocked to the cameras and a mouth full of cant.

RADICAL CHE

Thus, we laughed when we read recently in the newspaper that Evo Morales, the new president of Bolivia, said he was "following in the footsteps of Che Guevara."[1] Either the fellow has a sense of humor or he does not know much about Che.

Like all world improvers, Che claimed a remarkable ability to look into the future and then improve it before it happened. Of course, we all try to peek ahead and try to avoid traffic collisions and bad restaurants, but only a chump thinks he knows best how to improve the entire planet.

Still, who are we to argue with success? Che has become one of the best-selling brands of all time. At the Sundance Film Festival, the audience gave a standing ovation to the film *Motorcycle Diaries*, which recounts the story of the young Che's goofball adventures.[2] That towering intellectual Mike Tyson has a picture of him tattooed on his abdomen. Even some of Evo Morales's Bolivian voters apparently pray to "Santo Che" in the hope that he will intervene with the heavens to make it rain.

But if ever there was anyone who got what he deserved, it was Che. On October 9, 1967, a Bolivian firing squad put Che against the wall of a schoolhouse in La Higuera. "Don't shoot!" he whimpered. "I'm Che! I'm worth more to you alive than dead!"[3]

But while the Russians had let their young revolutionaries escape a number of times and whereas the Cubans had opened the doors of the cell that held Fidel Castro and let him out years before his term was served, the Bolivians in the 1960s weren't fooling around. Che's associates had bought a tract of land in the country on which he was planning a revolutionary movement that would spread into all of South America. This was it, he had said; this is the struggle that will determine whether the world goes capitalist or Marxist. Of course, in a sense, he was right. After they shot him dead, the world did seem to give up on the Bolshevik swindle. Most of the governments in Latin America hardened against it.

That was typical of Che, too. Practically everything he tried to do went bad. He was in Bolivia for 11 months trying to stir up a popular uprising, but his projects were not popular even with the local commies, who denounced him to the police.

But here, we let Che prove it in his own writings:

The past makes itself felt not only in the individual consciousness—in which the residue of an education systematically oriented toward isolating the individual still weighs heavily—but also through the very character of this transition period in which commodity relations still persist, although this is still a subjective aspiration, not yet systematized.[4]

As bad as he was as a thinker, as a man of action Che was even worse. As a military strategist he made Custer look like Julius Caesar. As a central banker, he made Alan Greenspan look like—well—John Law. And as a guerrilla leader, he was an embarrassment to an embarrassing trade. Confronting the Bay of Pigs invasion in 1961, he mistakenly thought the landing was at another spot and went thither. When the fighting was over, he came back with a bullet wound to the face. How did he manage to get it when he was nowhere near the actual combat? Apparently, his pistol went off in his hands.

What launched Che on his road to T-shirt stardom was a meeting in Mexico with Fidel Castro. Che was, by then, a doctor by training—or so he claimed—and a Marxist by inclination. The Cuban Lenin and the Marxist sawbones spoke for 10 hours. Then, Che decided to cast his lot with Fidel's insurgency against the Batista government in Cuba.

The planned assault by sea got off to a rough start. The insurgents' yacht was sold by a turncoat, and they ended up crowded onto a smaller boat, retching on the deck all the way to Cuba. There, they were so pathetically unprepared that most of their group was killed straightaway. Che and only 11 others got away into the hills, where they began their war of terror, gnawing on sugarcane to keep themselves going. The whole preposterous campaign would have come to nothing at all had not the Batista government been even more incompetent than the insurgents were. When the United States decided not to poke its nose into the business, Batista thought he had better get out while the getting was good. And so, unlikely as it was, power was left in the hands of Fidel, his brother Raúl, Che, and a small group of megalomaniacs, imposters, and sociopaths. They promptly turned the island into a tropical version of Abu Ghraib.

Che executed as many as eight people himself—without trial, and often even without real cause. Then, the real killing began. He signed between 500 and 2,000 death warrants and presided over a whole system of torture, labor camps, and murder.

No surprise there. He was simply living out what he had written earlier in his *Motorcycle Diaries*:

> Crazy with fury I will stain my rifle red while slaughtering any enemy that falls in my hands! My nostrils dilate while savoring the acrid odor of gunpowder and blood. With the deaths of my enemies I prepare my being for the sacred fight and join the triumphant proletariat with a bestial howl![5]

When the blood dried, Che started howling in another direction: He was made head of Cuba's central bank.

Before the revolution, in the late 1950s, Cuba was no paradise, but it might have come close for some. American tourists—especially the rich—came by the boatloads. There, they could gamble, drink, swim in the warm sea, take drugs, smoke fine cigars, fish, and relax. Everything was cheap, sweet, and warm: the hotels ... the liquor ... the women ... The island was growing rich from tourism and exports to the United States.

According to one source, Cuba "ranked first in Latin America in national income invested in education, and its literacy rate was 80 percent. In 1958, Cuba had even more female college graduates (to scale) than the United States."[6]

In terms of literacy, daily nutrition, and access to mass media, Cuba was a leader in Latin America—though, admittedly, this was not always saying a lot—and was crowding the heels of some developed, Western countries.[7]

Of course, not everyone benefited equally. Doctors were aplenty, but not always where they were needed. The rural poor, especially sugar workers, had a hard life. Havana was the Latin Las Vegas, the destination of mobsters like Lucky Luciano and Vito Genovese, who converged on it while Frank Sinatra was making his singing debut. Fulgencio Batista, who had come to power through a coup, ruled without elections. Still, many countries in Latin America were to overcome such deficiencies without resorting to mass arrests, murder, and death squads. Whether Batista ruled well or ill we don't know, but when, in the last century, the world improvers grabbed many countries by the throat, Cuba didn't get away.

Under Che, it went from a playground to a penal colony.

Again, we wonder: what was he thinking? Or was he thinking at all?

We see it again today. The United States wants peace and prosperity in the Middle East, observes President Bush. Here in the West we have peace and prosperity, he notices. Our governments are democracies, he muses. In democracies, people vote. Ergo, let us force people to vote in the Middle East and they will be peaceful and prosperous.

The proposition sounds logical on the surface, but underneath it is laced with ambiguity and adulterated by fat layers of uncertainty and wishful thinking—as were Che's rationalizations.

Yet, Che is the man called by no less a thinker than Jean-Paul Sartre—and there is no other thinker we think less of—"this intellectual, this most complete human being of our time." Well, at least we can vouch that he was a complete failure.

It is true, of course, that we never met the man. We should probably be glad of it. We might have clamped onto the glamorous guerrilla like a calendar magnet to a refrigerator door; we might have followed him to Bolivia. We might have abandoned our family the way he did—leaving a wife and five children to the tender mercies of the Castro regime. We might have ended up in a dry Bolivian grave with holes in our chest, too.

We can only hope for the good fortune to have a gifted photographer take photos of us laid out on the table before we got dumped in a hole. Then, at least our family might get royalty payments from all the T-shirts and book sales. Che owes the Bolivian Guardia Civil a big thank-you. He was on the way to becoming a pathetic has-been. Actually, those who knew him well already thought he was a has-been. It's true that he still had those curls and that he would still have made a fairly decent-looking corpse, if you ignored the flabby chest and paunchy stomach. But his career as revolutionary jester and gonzo-guerrilla *jefe* was clearly in decline, and if they hadn't gunned him down when they did, people would have soon begun to laugh at him.

Che's career proves our point. Like other revolutionaries, he might have profited from some vocational counseling. Robespierre, for instance, was a decent lawyer. Stalin might have comforted souls as an Eastern Orthodox priest. In both cases, the world would have been better off. And was the world not impoverished once more when, in the mid-1950s, Ernesto "Che" Guevara, a young man from a good Argentine family, abandoned the practice of saving people through medicine and took up the technique of destroying them—through revolutionary politics? Wouldn't the world clearly be a better place now if Che had made a career treating the skin disorders of the people who came to him rather than botching the good health of the whole planet?

In 1960, Che took a trip around the world visiting sundry crack-pot regimes. It was a kind of Hellhole Tour for Revolutionaries. The country that impressed him the most, it is reported, was North Korea, where even 40 years later people are struggling to get enough to eat. According to one study, "crop failures" have caused such a drastic cut in daily rations in 2003 that North Korean "households have to rely on alternative ways of getting food, including rearing livestock, growing kitchen gardens and collecting wild foods like edible grasses, acorns, tree bark and sea algae."[8]

Of course, if Che liked North Korea so much, he might have considered staying on there and munching on the tree bark. But if you think that *that* was ever a possibility, you are missing the malignant stupidity that defines the world improver's mind. It is not enough for him to live in a stifling prison; he insists that you live in one, too. This is why Che chose Bolivia for his last campaign; the country lies in the heart of South America, bordered by Peru, Chile, Paraguay, Brazil, and Argentina, and from there he could export revolution to the entire continent and then the world. He considered Bolivia the final showdown between capitalism and communism.

But Che did not merely want a new world; he also insisted on a whole new race of human beings to put into it.

During the course of the guerrilla war against the Batista government, Che took over the town of Sancti Spiritus and immediately issued a series of edicts that sounded like Oliver Cromwell bossing the Irish around. He imposed regulations covering everything: sex, drinking, gambling.

But as soon as his back was turned, what did the ungrateful, fun-loving Cubans do? They went right back to pitching woo and getting drunk—just as they always had.

Thus, Che learned that edicts alone were not enough. Later, he would try to correct his heaving masses in a more familiar way—by sending them to concentration camps.

Guanahacabibes (set up in Western Cuba at the end of 1960) was the model for a whole gulag of labor camps intended to punish, confine, and eliminate people thought to be uncooperative. Besides

bohemians (Haight-Ashbury, Greenwich Village types) and homosexuals, these camps were crammed with *roqueros*, who qualified in
Che's and Fidel's eyes as useless "delinquents." Some inmates of these
camps were probably guilty only of the heinous crime of listening to
the Beatles or the Rolling Stones.

In the 1980s and 1990s, the camps were to confine dissidents,
homosexuals, AIDS victims, Catholics, Jehovah's Witnesses, Afro-
Cuban priests—some were tortured, some were worked to death,
some eventually returned. Some didn't.[9]

Yet, in 1959, newspapers like the *New York Times* and the *London
Observer*, newsmen like Walter Lippman, and writers like Norman
Mailer were applauding the theft and killing under Fidel Castro and
Che Guevara, as though they heralded a new golden age.[10]

The Soviets had been Che's backers and his inspiration for his
work camps, his kangaroo courts, and much of his appalling rhetoric.
But no matter how much support they gave, it wasn't enough. When
the Cuban missile crisis erupted, Moscow backed down. Che was
dreadfully disappointed.[11] Even the Russians had let him down. The
whole race had let him down.

No, this sorry species was not good enough for him. He began to
call for a "new socialist man" to populate his new world. He argued
that to build communism, you had to build a "new man" as well as
a new economic base.

Readers will recognize the New Man; he is not that much different in essentials, actually, from the old one: ready to believe almost anything and ready to go along with almost anything. He is a
good revolutionary, Che explained, because he hates the bourgeoisie,
"which pushes a human being beyond his natural limitations, making
him into an effective, violent, selective, and cold-blooded killing machine." One of his friends then asked how he could reconcile this line
of thinking with his oath as a doctor. "Look," he replied, sounding
more like an unreconstructed hit man than a new socialist man, "in
this thing you have to kill before they kill you."[12]

Actually, like his Bolshevik role models, Che did not hesitate to
kill peasants as well as factory owners when they became inconvenient

or recalcitrant. He also had an old-world way of lying, cheating, and stealing to get what he wanted. He murdered people on trumped-up charges, stole their property, redistributed choice property to Communist Party cronies, and set up forced labor camps on the Soviet model. After Batista fled the country, Che seized an immigrant's mansion for himself. Opponents were hauled in front of the military court, which set about cleansing Cuba of counterrevolutionary elements.

Javier Arzuaga, a Basque chaplain who succored the condemned men, gives this recollection of life in the old stone fortress of La Cubana with Che in command:

"There were about eight hundred prisoners in a space fit for no more than three hundred: former Batista military and police personnel, some journalists, a few businessmen and merchants. The revolutionary tribunal was made of militiamen. . . . I remember especially the case of Ariel Lima, a young boy. Che did not budge."[13]

Che's legal philosophy was admirably to the point:

To send men to the firing squad, judicial proof is unnecessary.. . .
These procedures are an archaic bourgeois detail. This is a revolution! And a revolutionary must become a cold killing machine motivated by pure hate![14]

Che-as-central-banker was just as bad as Che-as-judge-and-jury, but at least at least as central banker he didn't shoot anyone. He was only comic.

"[He] was ignorant of the most elementary economic principles," said his deputy, Ernesto Betancourt. Had Che understood anything about economics, he wouldn't have been in Fidel's little band of sweaty revolutionaries and would never have gotten the job running the Central Bank of Cuba. In his case, not knowing anything about economics was a job requirement.

So, what does a man who doesn't know a thing about economics do when he gets to be head of a central bank? Alvaro Vargas Llosa explains what happened:

> Guevara's powers of perception regarding the world economy were famously expressed in 1961, at a hemispheric conference in Uruguay, where he predicted a 10 percent rate of growth for Cuba "without the slightest fear," and, by 1980, a per capita income greater than that of "the U.S. today." In fact, by 1997, the thirtieth anniversary of his death, Cubans were dieting on a ration of five pounds of rice and one pound of beans per month; four ounces of meat twice a year; four ounces of soybean paste per week; and four eggs per month.[15]

Of course, all world improvers depend on central planning; they know their plans are absolutely central to improving you. But while planning was easy enough, getting a result was difficult, as Che began to realize:

"Today we can see clearly that the masses did not participate in the plan, and a plan that lacks the participation of the masses is a plan that is always threatened with defeat."[16]

Those masses! What a pain in the neck they were. You had to boss them around, but you had to get them on your side, too!"

How could there ever have been any doubt that the *Fidelistas* were mad? Anyway, there was concrete proof of it soon enough—within months, the sugarcane industry had collapsed, Soviet-style industrialization failed completely, and food had to be rationed.

After a few more months, Che gave up. The economy was a wreck and Che longed for the good old days when "it was all a lot of fun, what with the bombs, speeches, and other distractions to break the monotony I was living in."[17]

So, in 1965, the now-famous revolutionary went to Africa, where he backed Pierre Mulele in the Congo. Nobel Prize-winning novelist V. S. Naipaul described how Mulele spiffed up things in the heart of darkness: by killing everyone who could read and who wore a tie. Che's intervention may have helped Mulele lose to Mobutu, who crushed the insurgents and ruled like a brutal oaf for decades.[18]

When the Africans had failed him, Che went off to Bolivia and mounted another slapstick revolutionary movement. It ended when he was shot by a Bolivian firing squad.

That was when Che the blundering world improver died. It was not long after that he was resurrected as Che the romantic revolutionary and T-shirt symbol.

THE WAY OF ALL CASH

January 22, 1944, is a memorable date in the history of humbug. It marks the occasion on which Juan Perón met Evita in Luna Park in Buenos Aires, the capital of Argentina.[19]

At the opening of the twentieth century, Argentine farmers enjoyed a land of milk and honey—with rising farm prices. Argentines were getting rich shipping agricultural products to Europe. They built palaces out on their farms, complete with opera houses and polo fields. And in the capital, they put up some of the most handsome buildings in the world. They came to Europe as tourists and stayed in the best hotels. Argentines were wealthy, and everyone knew it. Between the turn of the century and the beginning of the Great War, capital accumulated at the rate of 9 percent per year, while population grew at only half that rate.

At least at first, it also seemed that Argentina was spared the cultural decline of Europe. European civilization had come to be dominated by vulgar bunkum. A cheap rot encrusted everything—art, manners, architecture, and politics. Interventionists, meddlers, and world improvers—that is to say, accomplished liars—had taken over at the world's major popular assemblies and hijacked most of its leading central banks. But Argentina seemed to have escaped unscathed. Its armies never got into either world war. It never suffered a great depression in the 1930s. Life in Buenos Aires was safe and civilized even while Europe's cities were being blown up and its peoples being exterminated.

But then, suddenly, the people of the pampas also caught the populist bug. And unlike Europeans or North Americans, they were never able to shake it off.

Juan Perón ruled Argentina tentatively before 1946 and then conclusively between 1946 and 1955. We like to look at a photo of him, decked out in a white cap like a ship's captain, garlanded with a blue-and-white sash, trimmed with enough gold filigree to support a central bank. In his prime, he would have made a splendid corpse. Had he been strung up like his hero, Benito Mussolini, he might have done less damage, too. Argentina might only have been occupied and reconstructed and then taken off in a burst of postwar dynamism, like Japan or Germany.

We once accompanied a group of investors and economists on a visit to the Casa Rosada in Argentina during a frenzied period of economic counseling in the 1980s and 1990s. There, we found President Carlos Menem looking friendly . . . but short. Argentina's many financial crises seemed to have taken the inches off of him. He had just done something even more remarkable than what our own Paul Volcker did. He had reduced the inflation rate from 200 percent per month to just 4 percent per year by pegging the peso to the dollar at a one-to-one ratio.

Our group was stone sober and barely interested in height; what we wanted to know was whether the gaucho would be able to maintain the peso equal to the dollar.

"Yes" was the answer we got from the president of the pampas. "No" was the fact of the matter. A few years later, the peso peg broke off like an airplane wing, and the Argentine currency suddenly crashed 60 percent.

That was not the end of our little chat. We got some advice and we gave some. The advice we got from Menem was that Argentina was safe for foreign investment; indeed, such investment was most welcome. The advice we gave was: "Dollarize." Our advice proved better than his.

Then as now, the United States of America was the world's dominant financial power. And the coin of the realm was then, as now, not coin at all, but paper. Converting to dollars would take Argentine monetary policy out of its own hands. Judging from the evidence, past and future, it surely would have been a good idea. Rather than let the Bank of Argentina manage the nation's money, we would have put it into the hands of Alan Greenspan.

Little did we know at the time, but Alan Greenspan had tango in his blood, too.

Still, it was good advice. Argentina should have followed it. Instead, its own people juiced up the money supply at an average rate of 60 percent per year between 1991 and 1994. In 1996 and 1997, money supply went up at 15 percent and 20 percent respectively. It didn't take long before prices were rising again and investors were beginning to call their banks in Miami. Even with very strong economic growth (Argentina grew at an 8 percent rate in the mid-1990s, second only to China), the government still could not balance the budget. Public-sector debt soared.[20]

By 1998, Argentina was in a slump; it needed to borrow more and more money to keep up with spending and make up for lost tax revenue. By late 2000, one out of every five bonds issued by an emerging-market country was Argentine. Investors began to wonder how the country could ever make good on so much debt. Speculators started dumping Argentine bonds and withdrawing capital from the country. Scarcely a year later, the whole jig was up. The peso collapsed, and along with it the Argentine economy. Unemployment soared. Banks were closed. Deposits were confiscated. And the Argentine middle class was practically wiped out.

Still, today, we cross the wide River Plata not to offer advice, but to seek it, for we sense a financial crisis coming here to the norte americanos. And who knows more about how to survive it than the gauchos down south?

So, let us back up to a more benign period in Argentine history when the country was so blessed by nature that people lived as happily as *Gott im Frankreich* until the 1930s. Before World War II, Argentina exported beef and farm products the way France now exports champagne and petits fours. By the war's end, Argentina was a substantial net creditor to the rest of the world with an annual current account surplus of more than $6 billion (in 1950 dollars, which is to say, when the dollar was worth about 10 times as much as it is today). Left alone, the country probably would have gradually diversified its economy, improved its brands, sharpened its marketing, and prospered at about the same rate as European nations. As we will see, the spirit was willing, but the cash was weak. In less than a decade, the surpluses were squandered and the nation was already suffering its first financial crisis of the postwar period. There would be many more.

Argentines have their own opinions about what went wrong. And, when the most recent crisis hit in 2001, they voiced them in the press.[21]

"People are dying because there is no food," wrote one. "People are dying and are going to die because of lack of treatment for common illnesses: asthma, heart attacks, malnutrition, etc. We owe that to corruption."

"You could buy anything from anywhere [before the crisis; now] not even Tylenol can be found on pharmacy shelves," added another eyewitness. "The price of the typical cereal has tripled, and even people with offshore accounts can't access them. Crime has increased exponentially, as has the number of poor people begging in the streets."

"The middle class, something we used to feel proud of, is now disappearing," wrote another.

But one citizen brought the hammer down squarely. "All our problems effectively started as far back as 1930," he wrote, "with the 'radical' revolution. World War II was a respite and at the end we were very rich compared to Europe. Then came Perón, who squandered it all. After that came the military, who borrowed heavily. This is the basis of our current debt. All governments, since the military was thrown out by Maggie Thatcher, have been crooks. And stealing is a way of life. Any Argentine who does not steal is mad at those who do … until he gets a chance at it himself. We are a nation of liars, cheats, bullies, and thieves. We deserve what we get."

On whether or not Argentines deserve what they get, we have no opinion. But we propose a theory for what went wrong in Argentina not too different from the writer's—Perónism. It was Juan Perón who brought National Socialism to Argentina in the war years. And at the close of World War II, when the other National Socialists were either hanging from hooks in Rome or being incinerated in Berlin, Perón refused to die. Italy and Germany were reconstructed after the war, but in Argentina, Perónism lived on.

"Perónism," said Perón himself, "is a new political doctrine." We follow him up to that point. Then we are lost:

> Perónism is not learned, nor just talked about: one feels it or else disagrees. Perónism is a question of the heart rather than of the head. I feel an intimate satisfaction when I see a workman who is well dressed or taking his family to the theatre. I feel just as satisfied as I would feel if I were that workman myself. That is Perónism.[22]

Perónism, it seems, was neither capitalistic nor communistic. Instead, it was advertised as a "third way." What it really did was to take the worst elements from each. It was central planning, without plans. It was price fixing, without fixed prices. It was higher wages, with lower real earnings. It was crackpot economics, with the cracks and minus the pots. It was huge new pork-barrel projects, without the pork. It was doggles without boons.

Perón's government followed in Mussolini's footsteps, encouraging higher levels of consumption, higher spending for government, more regulation, huge new doses of debt, nationalism, price controls, inflation, and special treatment for favored industries, particularly defense. This was a revolutionary new program for South America at the time, but a dead ringer for the U.S. Republic Party platform of 2004. Perón called it *Justicialismo*. It could as well be "compassionate conservativism." Perón even put forth the notion of a "Homeland," ranking it number one on his "scale of values."

Once the Perónists were in control, the surpluses disappeared. Overspending and overmeddling produced their inevitable result. The economy began to wobble. What could Perón do? He was no economist, not even a quack one. But a skillful politician can more easily wreck an economy than build one up, and if he can tell whoppers well enough, he'll be able to pin the blame on someone else. Perón looked around. There they were, the rich, the traitors! The conservative old families, the stick-in-the-muds! And the Catholic Church!

Perón's world-improvement ambitions went beyond finance and economics. He planned to legalize prostitution and legalize divorce. When the church opposed him, he sent out his trade-union goons to sack every major church in Buenos Aires. And when the old money squawked, he burned down the Jockey Club.

By now, the idealist was really getting wound up:

"From now on, the order for every *Perónista*, alone or in a group, is to respond to an act of violence with another act of violence. And whenever one of us falls, five of them will fall."[23]

Soon, he had gone too far. He was inciting his prole followers to mob violence—the very thing the military most feared. The army rose up against him. On September 16, 1955, the Cordoba garrison broke out in open revolt. Navy warships blockaded Buenos Aires and threatened to blow up the oil refineries on the Rio Plata. A cruiser began shelling the docks on September 18, 1955. General Pedro Aramburu declared himself against the regime in the Northeast. General Lonardi swept into Buenos Aires itself on the 23rd, greeted by cheering crowds.

Perón was finally gone, but when he left office he left, in the words of Argentine economist Raul Prebisch, a "crisis of unparalleled gravity." Instead of investing in industries that might have created jobs and profits, people had shifted to speculating and had taken their money offshore to protect against inflation and devaluations. On their own, the smart gauchos had learned how to dollarize themselves.

The economy slumped. Prices rose. Argentina experienced stagflation years before it hit the United States. The money supply exploded. Corruption became common. The middle class, too, tried to duck and dodge the Perónist economy. A large part of the economy went underground. Half of all eligible taxpayers didn't bother to file a return.

The generals quickly tried to undo the damage, but the whole rotten system was beginning to stink. Prices rose out of control. Debts increased. Taxes went unpaid. Still Perónism wouldn't die. New crises came: devaluations, inflation, strikes, coups d'état, defaults, revolutions. They continued for the next 35 years, right up until the early 1990s. Each of these crises had Perón's fingerprints all over it, for they were the products of the old *justicialismo*: too much spending, too much debt, too much currency, and too much meddling. Debts mounted up even higher. Banks tottered. Inflation rose to 600 percent and then to over 5,000 percent. It finally settled around 4,000 percent. Between 1991 and 2001, budget deficits rose to 13 percent of GDP. External debt-to-GDP ratio rose from 33 to 55 percent.

Then, Carlos Menem, a member of the Perónist party, linked the peso to the dollar on a one-to-one basis and began, again, to remove the Perón-era controls. Finally, with this new, more solid money, the economy breathed; it opened up; it prospered. Argentina was escaping the dead hands of Perón at last. Just to make sure, someone broke into Juan Perón's crypt in La Chacarita Cemetery and cut his hands off![24]

Even while Menem reformed, the old habits continued. Debt. Spending. Inflation. Finally, the government caved in, and the peso collapsed. Once again, from 2001 to 2002, Argentina was in crisis.

But the Argentines are resilient. The economy has been recovering for the past few years. In 2003, the economy grew at a rate even India would be proud of: 8.4 percent.[25] The cafes are filling up. Prices are rising. The country would probably prosper, if the *Perónistas* would just leave it alone.

DON'T CRY FOR EVITA

Of course, the strangest of all the *Perónistas* was the wife of Juan, Evita, as the *descamisados*—or shirtless ones—called her.

We went to visit her grave on our recent trip there. It is in the Recoleta cemetery, a short walk from our apartment near the French Embassy. There, you will find a whole city of the dead, laid out in tiny houses of marble or granite, often with statues on the roof, sometimes with glass domes and elaborate carvings. Most of the mausoleums have glass doors, some even open, through which you can look in at the cobwebs and caskets.

People wander around, down one street, up another—often looking for a family tomb, or if tourists, just looking. It is a huge place, with a thousand stories, some of them chiseled in stone. After roaming the streets in the *ciudad de los muertos* (city of the dead) for half an hour, we finally found the grave we were looking for, that of Eva Perón.

We had expected more: a fountain maybe, or a giant statue of the woman. Maybe even crowds of poor people, crossing themselves, vowing revenge on the rich and plotting revolution. But the tomb is like any other—plainer than you'd expect, just gray granite with no particular style or flourish. All that sets it apart from those around it are the flowers—there were several bouquets—along with candles and a few notes. The few other people visiting the monument were, like us, only casually curious.

Eva Perón was a favorite of the poor of Argentina. She had a warm heart, it was said. But like that other great champion of the masses, Che Guevara, Eva realized her greatest glories after she was stone-cold dead. That was when the common people really took to her. For that she can thank her embalmer, a man who worked on her corpse like Rembrandt on a canvas. You can check for yourself. Eva was pretty enough, but no great beauty, even when she was young, warm flesh. But after death, her looks became transcendent.

She must have had something going for her. She got a tango singer to take her to Buenos Aires when she was only 15, and if she gave herself to him in exchange, as her upper-class critics whispered, would that have been so bad? After that, she managed to make something of a career for herself and by 24 was already a popular radio actress. She did most of her real work in the bedroom, went the jealous rumors. But all we know is that she must have had talents that don't show in a public photograph. She managed to get one colonel to fall for her and then, at a charity event, she got her hands on another one, Juan Perón, and never let him go.

Juan Perón was at the time 48 years old. His first wife had died. He had spent his career in the army and greatly admired the way Mussolini had handled Italy, some of which he had seen firsthand during officer training in the 1930s. In 1943, when he met Eva, Perón wanted to do in Argentina what Mussolini had been able to do in Italy—line up the support of the working classes and take control of the government. But, he desperately lacked one thing Il Duce had—charisma . . . a powerful personality.

When he met Eva, he must have realized that she could supply what he lacked. Here was a woman with the gumption to elbow her way through a society crowd so she could sit down to dinner next to him, and then, yes, he hardly had to say a word—she was in his bedroom before his soup got cold. What a woman! And besides, she had the right credentials. She was born poor, and even illegitimate. She had had to make her own way in the world—we won't dwell on the details—and now could stand before the lumpen as one of their own. Publicly, she could be Evita, the Princess Di of the Argentine fascists . . . the people's princess of the pampas. Privately, she was more than that—she was a tough and determined *arriviste.*

In 1945, Perón was arrested. While he wobbled and even considered going into exile, Evita kept her nerve. She used the money she had embezzled from an earthquake relief fund and went directly to the unions to rally support. By October of that year, she could field 200,000 demonstrators, and forced the authorities to back down. A year later, she helped Perón win a landslide election victory; he was well on his way to realizing his ambition of becoming a Latin

American Mussolini. Later, after Il Duce—and his mistress—were strung up by fickle followers, Perón would amend his ambition, saying that what he really wanted was "a fascism that is careful to avoid all the errors of Mussolini."

If Evita was a humbug and a scalawag, it no longer showed. Bargain basement when she started out, her price skyrocketed with her ascent to power. By the time she flamed out, she was pure Tiffany's. Yet, this was a woman who looted the "charitable" foundations that were meant to serve the poor; a woman who helped hundreds of Nazi war criminals escape to the pampas. Perón himself made 1,000 blank passports available to the defeated Germans after the war—again, it was for a price. You see, Eva and Perón were world improvers, but of the better sort—they could be bought.[26]

On June 6, 1947, Evita began a triumphal tour of Europe. It was called a Rainbow Tour, anticipating the great celebrity promenades later in the century. She visited heads of state—even Pope Pius XII. She visited her Swiss bank. She made the cover of *Time* magazine. It was about that time that Argentina became a refuge for war criminals on the lam. Thus it was that Juan Perón won reelection in 1951 with money whose provenance was not quite certain, but may have come, many thought, from the grateful Nazis.

Argentina might still be a hard place to govern, but for such as they, it has always been a good place to disappear. Debtors, criminals, and political refugees were always running off to the pampas; a few Nazis could hardly make much difference one way or another. And the krauts turned out to have their uses. Later, when the Argentine generals needed to disappear others, it is said they turned to squads of professionals, trained and originally organized by those who had disappeared themselves after World War II.

The Peróns learned quickly that the masses could be manipulated with vulgar demagoguery. Evita gave away Christmas presents to the poor and brought in poor orphans so they could be photographed with her before they were tossed back onto the streets. But the masses needed to be controlled, too, and that was the hard part. The collapse of commodity prices in the 1930s had made them restless and had initially led them to support Perón. But Mussolini's economic meddling worked no better on the banks of the Rio Plata than it had on the banks of the Tiber. In 1949, the stock market collapsed and the mobs became restless again. The incomes of the working class fell 30 percent. And this time, Juan Perón could not pose as an outsider. This time, *he* was in power; the plebes held him responsible. At first, Evita tried grander gestures to appease them, but then the lace gloves came off. Troublemakers were arrested, and drawing on the talents and training of Argentina's new immigrants from the Third Reich, she had many of them tortured. "One cannot accomplish anything without fanaticism," said she.

Evita burned hot, but she burned fast. By 1952 she was burned out and burned up. She appeared at Juan Perón's side for his second inauguration in an open car, held up, like El Cid, by a plaster support under a long fur coat. Cancer had eaten away at her, as had the radiation with which doctors had burned her to try to kill the cancer. Between the doctors and the cancer, she was left with not much time. She died seven weeks later, weighing only 82 pounds and only 33 years old, younger than Elvis, the two Kennedys, and Che—but older than Joan of Arc.[27]

She may have died young, but she did not leave a good-looking corpse. The burnished looks that hundreds of thousands of mourners admired, sobbing into white handkerchiefs, touching her coffin, even kissing it, were not those given to her by God. No—they were the handiwork of the mysterious Spaniard who embalmed her.

Jesus Christ himself only managed to change water into wine, but Dr. Ara all but resurrected Eva's worn-out corpse. He laid on the waxes, the paint, and the rouge with a touch nearly divine, and somehow transformed the gutter girl into a veritable saint.

And then, when Evita's corpse had finally cooled and Juan was thrown out of the Casa Rosada, it was Evita herself who disappeared. The generals were afraid her dust might provide a rallying point for the mobs, so they shipped her casket to Germany ... then to Italy ... and didn't return it to Juan until 16 years later.

And what happened to Evita's Swiss bank account? That disappeared, too. After her death, her brother, who had rushed to Switzerland, died suddenly and mysteriously on his return in his apartment in Buenos Aires. Authorities were never able to figure out whether it was murder or suicide, but either way, the money never turned up.

After Evita's death, Perón took a 13-year-old mistress and dodged a military coup by running abroad, wherever his money and strongman credentials would take him.

And then, when the policies he began worked their way through to their inevitable conclusion—that is to say, when Argentina was all but broke—they called him back from Madrid to Buenos Aires in 1973 to do more damage. A pitched battle was even fought at Ezeiza Airport on his behalf. The populace couldn't seem to get enough of the man . . . or his women. His new wife, Isabel, was ambitious, too. When Evita's coffin was put in the living room, Isabel lay on top of it (some say she lay down inside of it) to draw power from the dried-up corpse.[28]

When he died in 1974, Perón left the country to Isabel to run. Naturally, she ran it into the ground until, at last in 1976, the military decided it had had enough.

It was only then that the Peróns were finished. The handsome general and his pushy wives were finally gone. But Perónism continued—and continues to this day.

THE LATE, GREAT HELMSMAN

The last time the world went really mad was in the 1930s. For some reason, never fully explained, people in that decade seemed to take leave of their senses. Of course, in light of what had happened in the Great War and the period just afterward, the two were barely on speaking terms already. World War I killed millions and toppled and bankrupted almost all the major governments of Europe. No one knows why, but the absurdity didn't end with the long, pointless war; it just seemed to pick up speed. And by the 1930s practically every major nation was caught up in it. The only important exceptions were France, Britain, and the United States, and in these countries, too, the institutions of relatively free societies were twisted into hideous new shapes. But the changes were far worse elsewhere. Germany was taken over by the Nazis, Italy by the Fascists, Japan by militarists, and China by Maoists, Nationalists, and the Japanese! And, of course, Russia was taken over by the Stalinists.

Monarchists, Republicans, Unionists, Troskyites, Stalinists, Fascists—when voting failed to get them what they wanted, they took to the streets, formed alliances, stormed the arsenals, stole weapons, commandeered trucks and artillery, murdered authorities and rivals . . . took revenge, and generally made a bloody mess of things.

When the pot gets stirred up, it is the most ruthless who rise to the surface. Why not? There is a time and a place for everything. Chastity is of no use to a prostitute. And the killer who declines to work on Sunday is at a disadvantage; someone less restrained is likely to put a bullet into his brain while he is on his way to Mass.

Spain was relatively lucky; it got Franco. Germany got Hitler. Russia got Stalin. China got Mao. Cambodia got Pol Pot.

What are we going to get next?

What bothers us is that there is no satisfactory explanation for these periods of madness. We don't know why black becomes white and day becomes night.

And we don't know how the farcical spectacles that play out in the financial markets affect the tragic episodes in political history. Many analysts trace Germany's collapse into the hands of the Nazis to the collapse of the deutsche mark 10 years before. After the financial collapse, people didn't know what to believe or what to expect next. Germany's role in the world and Germans' roles in their own country were undermined. When Adolf appeared on the scene—sure of himself, with a tough plan to put Germany back together and no scruples to hold him back—people found it appealing, say historians. Maybe so. But, then again, maybe not.

The problem is the more history you read, the less you learn from it. Not that it isn't entertaining; to the contrary, history is nothing if not diverting. The trouble is, it seems to be nothing more. In the end, all you take away is a gaping mouth and a mind pried so wide open it is ready to believe anything—and nothing.

At least that is how we felt reading an extraordinary biography of Mao Tse-tung, written by Jung Chang and Jon Halliday.[29] What is most extraordinary about it is that it shows how man—and here we speak of the species, not the gender—can get away with almost anything. And the people who commit the worst crimes often find themselves the subjects of popular adoration. Likenesses of them are chiseled out of granite and hoisted onto pedestals in public squares. Their quips and sayings are printed up in little books, distributed to the masses like Christmas candies, and studied by callow scholars as if they were gospel lessons.

In the 1960s, the older of your authors spent some time in a center of higher learning in Paris. We recall that the most difficult choice a young European intellectual faced then was whether to sign up with the Trotskyites, the Leninists, or the Maoists. Students stayed up late into the night arguing the fine points of one or the other, none of them with a single clue about who these men really were or what their bloody creeds really meant.

Now, with the opening of archives and the closing of the lives of most of the principals, we get to find out what these great revolutionary heroes were really like. And what a ghastly show it is! Hegel meets *Helter Skelter. Das Kapital* meets *Texas Chainsaw Massacre.*

The Chinese are a smart people; just look at the names that make it to advanced science programs at top U.S. universities. IQ aficionados tell us that the Chinese and Japanese have an edge over the rest of us. But read the story of Mao; it makes you wonder: How could so many smart people do something so moronic that it would be flattery to call them stupid?

Who would have thought that one of the planet's most ancient and refined civilizations would yield itself over to a lamebrained psuedo-intellectual whose principal preoccupations were creating havoc and making sure his own bowels moved?[30]

What could they have thought when the man who claimed to be a champion of the poor starved, robbed, and tortured them without mercy, so ruthlessly that any peasants with the strength to escape ran off to the other side?

Or, if they didn't flee, they hanged themselves or opened their veins. When Mao first got his hands on a little chunk of China, he immediately turned the place into a prison. Armed guards patrolled the streets and borders to prevent people from escaping. People were encouraged to denounce each other; barbaric torture was practiced; executions were everyday occurrences. Families were not allowed to visit each other, as the authorities worried that they might be up to something. A family found to have welcomed a visitor was to be killed.

Not surprisingly, people found this proto-Maoist workers' paradise rather depressing. Even top-ranking cadres began to take their own lives. "Suicides are the most shameful elements in the revolutionary ranks," came the slogan designed to halt the trend.

During his career, Mao Tse-tung was responsible for more deaths—by murder, starvation, or torture ... the usual ways of dying ... plus a few novelties he and his thugs added—than probably any other man in history. Seventy million is the sum given by Chang and Halliday.[31]

We don't know how accurate this number is. Some dispute it. But if it is true, the entire Mongol reign of Genghis Khan and his line—which brought down three civilizations (Muslim, Chinese, and Hindu) and threatened to conquer Christendom, too—didn't match Mao in killing people. You'd think one or other of the millions of Chinese who suffered at his hands would have done something about it. But maybe that's the trouble with the modern world; people don't take the obligation of revenge seriously enough. Mao died of natural causes, many decades later.

It is a relief to many that Mao was a Communist and that bolshevism no longer fires hearts and heavy artillery. But it is a counterfeit comfort, for Mao never cared about ideology. He murdered his keen Communist followers as readily as the capitalist roaders. He took money from Moscow, but turned his back on the Russians when-ever he could get away with it. He might just as well have been a Republican ... or a Lutheran.

In short, Mao Tse-tung seems to have been a humbug and a mountebank.

As a soldier, he was a disaster. He absented himself from the fight on every possible occasion, usually holing up in the biggest, safest, most luxurious house in the area, generally feasting and resting while his gang of killers did their work. Ordered by the Marxist hierarchy to join the battle, he would take his army in the opposite direction or just wait out the fight and then come in afterward.

To say that he was hard-hearted is a bit like saying that the Peking sewer is malodorous; it fails to capture the smell vividly enough. A text that he chose for his trainees described activists discussing ways to deal with victims who were "stubborn": "We'll split their ankle tendons and cut off their ears."[32]

Mao would take part in torture and keep photographs of the sessions for his private enjoyment.[33] He would waste his own soldiers in pointless battles and unnecessary suffering. Even on the famous Long March he did little marching himself. His skinny soldiers had to carry him on a litter!

Military men are often blockheads (at least the best of them are), but Mao was in a class by himself. The Long March was so long partly because Mao wasn't going anywhere. He marched his men uphill and down, hundreds of miles this way and that, with meager rations and almost no medical attention even for the wounded, just to avoid going to a rendezvous with another army boss, one just as ruthless as he was.

The Communists' main enemy at the time—almost everyone hated them—was Chiang Kai-shek. At Tucheng, for example, Mao put his own troops in about the worst possible position—with their backs to the Red River—and faced the best of Chiang's force. Natu-rally, the Communists were nearly wiped out—while Mao watched from a nearby mountain. Of those Red soldiers who weren't killed in the fighting itself, many soon died of cold and wounds or were killed by the local farmers, who were getting even for the way the Communists had treated them. Wherever he went, Mao handled the locals with such naked brutality that he caused revolts—against the revolutionaries!

The whole Long March is nothing but a recitation of one Mao-caused calamity after another. But the gods must have had a sour sense of humor in the 1930s; they let Mao, Adolf, and Joseph rise to power anyway.

While Mao was a dud of a general, he was a bad joke of a political philosopher. Early in his life, he might have been a follower of Ayn Rand. "People like me only have a duty to ourselves," he wrote. "We have no duty to other people."[34] Later, he dipped his fork into Marxism like a Western teenager sampling sushi. He was not too sure what was in it, and wasn't too eager to find out. Instead, he took Emperor Qin Shi Huangdi (221–206 B.C.), who founded imperial China, as his model. Qin's empire lasted nearly two thousand years. Not only did he build the Great Wall, he also killed Confucian scholars, burned classical books, and persecuted thousands—perhaps millions—of people.

Like Qin, it was his single-minded pursuit of power that made Mao so successful. His rivals were hampered by actually believing the Marxist dogmas. They took their orders from the party hierarchy and earnestly tried to implement many silly and impossible programs.

Mao operated under no such restriction. He eliminated enemies and friends—as it suited him. He listened to Moscow when he wanted to; when Moscow gave him directions he didn't like, he ignored them. He was not a "good Communist." He was hardly a Communist at all.

"Communism is not love," he said. "Communism is a hammer we use to crush the enemy."

But it is in his relations with the fair sex that the worst of Mao is visible. When it came to women, the Great Helmsman was more than a bungler or a butcher; he was a cad.

He married one woman, and then dismissed her. The next bore him two children. Scarcely 18 months later, he was conducting some atrocious campaign of murder and brought his army up near where she lived. Mao could have and should have immediately gotten his wife out of harm's way, but he didn't. His enemies seized the poor woman and put her to death, hoping to strike a blow at Mao's heart in that way. But the man seemed not even to notice. He had a new paramour by then and had forgotten spouse number two.

The new girlfriend, Gui-yuan, then became his third wife and had a baby during the Long March. Again, Mao was nearby but did not come to see her. Thinking to save her baby from the appalling conditions prevailing, she gave it to a local farmer, along with a sum of money to pay for its care. It soon died.

Then, Gui-yuan herself nearly died when she was struck by one of Chiang's bombs. Doctors said she only had a few hours to live and her pain was so great that she even begged her comrades to put her out of her misery. Once again, Mao, who was in a nearby village, said he was too "tired" to come see her.

But let us return to that famous episode, the Long March.

There our sordid protagonist was, being carried around China in a cushy sedan chair by scrawny porters with knees skinned up from trying to climb mountains and feet scabby from lack of proper footwear, bad diet, lack of medicine, and little rest.

What a sight it must have been! As many as 80,000 soldiers backed the Communists under Mao when the Long March began, a ragtag band walking along, feared and reviled almost everywhere they went. And in the midst of it all went the litters carrying the people's top honchos and the wives of the people's top honchos. By the time the wandering was over—Mao didn't especially want to arrive anywhere—he had managed to reduce his own ranks to only 10,000. The rest died along the way, were killed in pointless battles, or ran off as soon as they got the opportunity.

How was it possible that a nation of so many millions couldn't manage to figure out that their leader was an incompetent, self-interested charlatan? Or find one person who would put an end to him?

When, in Yenan province, he brought out his first torturers, his policies of mass starvation and working the peasants to death, his proto-purges, and his early assassinations, wasn't it clear then where he would take the nation? An earnest Communist from Sweden later visited this part of the country and wondered why it was so poor. It was such an important part of our Marxist traditions; what went wrong?, he wanted to know.

"Ah, traditions ... traditions ..." Mao laughed heartily. He couldn't believe the Swede was so naive.

Mao cared nothing for traditions—neither real Chinese traditions nor manufactured Communist ones. What he cared for was power. And he exercised it pitilessly, recklessly, and absurdly.

What is troubling about Mao's life is not Mao himself—for he was merely a talented cutthroat and a lucky slob—but the rest of us. What is wrong with us? Normal, decent human beings repeatedly buckled under to Mao; they let him get away or couldn't get organized to oppose him. When they were ordered to persecute each other, they took up the task readily, even knowing that their own necks could be next. When they were summoned to carry Mao on their shoulders or procure women for him or embark on some suicidal military campaign or build him another luxury villa, did any one of them raise a serious objection? Some did; but the rest went along, usually taking the objector out to execute him.

Mao worried about being murdered all his life. Cronies, henchmen, and servants were kept under surveillance and in a state of terror. Mao encouraged periodic purges, denunciations, and confessions. Even his most trusted and loyal bagmen—such as Chou En-lai—were required to humiliate themselves from time to time for Chairman Mao.

Still, only one person was known to have tried to assassinate Mao, Marshal Lin Biao's son, "Tiger," in 1971. The plot quickly thickened, then dissolved altogether. Tiger and his wife died in an airplane crash in Mongolia as they were making their getaway.

There must have been a hundred million people in China who would have liked to see Mao dead, and hundreds of millions more who would have if they had known what was going on. But Mao controlled the press. And he had created such an atmosphere of fear that people dared not talk, even to friends or relatives.

In the late 1930s and early 1940s, while Chiang Kai-shek's Nationalist forces fought the Japanese, Mao focused on killing and purging his own troops and supporting his strange kingdom by selling drugs. Even this Mao could not do well. Opium production soon expanded beyond what the market would take up. By the time the first American officials arrived on the scene, Mao had filled his coffers with cash and was ready to suppress the trade. (The Russians estimated his opium sales at $640 million in today's money.)

Mao also experimented with central banking during this period. He printed his own currency, the *bianbi*. This, too, went in the predictable way. Neither Communists nor capitalists seem able to resist the lure of easy money for long. By 1944, the Reds had printed so many *bianbi* that the price of matches was 25,000 times greater than the price in 1937.

During this whole time, Chiang had threatened to wipe out the Communists several times, but he relented each time; Chiang's only son was held captive in Moscow. Stalin had let him know that if he ever wanted to see his son again, he would have to let up on Mao's troops.

Then, after the Japanese were defeated, Mao found another protector—the United States. Once again, Chiang was going after Mao. By this time the Nationalist forces were seasoned fighters—they'd been engaged in serious fighting with the Japanese for years, while the Reds had been doing nothing more than preventing each other from escaping. When the two forces clashed, the outcome was inevitable; Mao's men were run off. Chiang was about to go after them and crush them completely when George Marshall intervened. With an apparently straight face, Chou told Marshall that Mao preferred the United States to Russia, and Mao let it be known that he was even considering dropping the word *Communist* from their party name! Marshall must have fallen for it, because Chiang was pulled off the chase, and the commies got away to Manchuria.

The mistake proved fatal to the Nationalists. Out in the northwest, the Reds linked up with the turncoat Chinese *Manchukuans* who had supported the Japanese during the war and who were also closer to their supply lines from Russia. With these supports, not to mention a clandestine campaign against poor Chiang, they were able to boot the Nationalists out of the country and turn the whole place into the largest Auschwitz in history. We say that not to exaggerate. In the famine Mao forced on China in the late 1950s and early 1960s, the average daily calorie intake was about 1,200. Mao meanwhile was given a "comprehensive set of European menus" that included seafood, duck, pork, lamb, beef, chicken, and soup—each with scores of dishes.[35] But, of course, he still thought the peasants had too much to eat. He was determined to squeeze the grain out of them so it could be shipped overseas to help pay for his crackpot modernization programs. His agents went about their work with the same zeal they had shown in his earlier famines and purges:

> Horrific punishments were widespread; some people were buried alive, others strangled with ropes, others had their noses cut off.[36]

Millions died of starvation during China's Great Leap Forward, reportedly the greatest famine of the twentieth century and one of the worst in all recorded history.[37] Yet, in the West, countless students and intellectuals were taken with Mao. Jean-Paul Sartre even called his revolutionary violence "profoundly moral."[38]

But, there are also funny parts to the Mao story. So eager were the Maoists to industrialize that they completely neglected quality control. Chinese planes couldn't fly. Tanks couldn't drive in a straight line (on one occasion, a Chinese-made tank swerved around and charged at a group of VIPs). Chinese ships were more of a danger to their crews than to the enemy. And when a Chinese helicopter was to be presented to Ho Chi Minh, the manufacturers detained it at the border because they were afraid it might crash.

And that is usually the case. The people who want to force their ideas on you are always the people whose ideas are the most idiotic. Mao had peasants digging up the soil by hand, down to a depth of half a meter. Next, he figured that crop yields could be enhanced by planting seeds closer together while actually reducing the amount of fertilizer applied. He had the whole country launched on a goofy program of making steel in backyard furnaces. And then, he decided that sparrows were eating too much of the nation's harvest, so he got the peasants to shoo away the birds and kill them. As the sparrows disappeared, along came the bugs and insects that they had kept under control, in such numbers that they soon threatened the entire harvest. Secretly, the Chinese government finally had to ask the Russians for aid: Please send sparrows, in the name of socialist internationalism!

And in at least one way, Mao was worse than both Hitler and Stalin, who had at least left most of the culture of their countries alone. Mao banned Chinese opera, the folk arts, and the fine arts on the grounds of their being feudal or capitalistic. He drove singers, poets, playrights, and writers out of the cities and threatened them with starvation during the Cultural Revolution. Old tombs, monuments, and temples were the next to go. Even ping-pong stars were on his hit list.[39]

And to top it all off, Mao was a humbug on sex, as on everything else. Not that there was a great deal of it going on. There was little privacy, and with people dressed in those tawdry, gray Mao outfits and crowded into tiny, charmless tenements, there was neither the time, the energy, nor the place for romance—or even sexual congress. Couples were often posted to different cities and allowed to see each other only 12 days per year. Even masturbation was outlawed.

Meanwhile, Mao himself lived it up in his luxurious villas— dozens of them spread all over the country—complete with indoor swimming pools. He ate like a pig and had his agents scour the countryside to find young women—imperial concubines for the Chairman. Singers, dancers, nurses, house staff—they were all available to Mao as he pleased.[40]

Still, the chairman himself was fat and repulsive. He hadn't bathed in 27 years, according to some reports, although he did swim regularly. And his teeth, which he never brushed, had gone black.[41] How did he get women to sleep with him?

Ah, dear reader, that is just another mystery of our race; people seem willing and able to do just about anything.

Part Four

Flattening the Globe

CHAPTER 9

THE NUMBER GAME

Nothing is so firmly believed as that which we least know.

—Michel de Montaigne

Imperialists, anti-imperialists, capitalists, communists—as soon as they get a grand scheme into their heads, a pet project for world improvement, they all seem to end up in the same place—bungling, botching, and butchering. It is not a matter of intelligence or ability. Napoleon Bonaparte, Julius Caesar, Ho Chi Minh, Mao Tse-tung—none of them were stupid men in the ordinary sense of the word. President Bill Clinton was a Rhodes scholar. Even our Texas Tiberius, George Bush, apparently possesses enough cunning to conduct his personal life with a modicum of success.

But put them at a head of a country or an army, then they are off on some fool mission—bringing civilization to the barbarians, making the world safe for democracy, or ushering in the proletarian revolution. Competent beings suddenly turn into cretins who wander from one disaster into the next with hardly a pause in between, never learning from any of them.

Why is the human brain so prone to error when it steps out of the charmed circle of things and people close to it?

THE MAGIC NUMBER

We get an insight from the field studies of anthropologists:

The figure of 150 seems to represent the maximum number of individuals with whom we can have a genuinely social relationship, the kind of relationship that goes with knowing who they are and how they relate to us. Putting it another way, it's the number of people you would not feel embarrassed about joining uninvited for a drink if you happened to bump into them in a bar.[1]

Here, a British anthropologist, Robin Dunbar, makes an interesting case for social capacity—that is, the maximum number of people and things with which the human brain can cope effectively. Primates like monkeys, chimpanzees, baboons, and human beings, he observes, have the largest brain capacities of all mammals. And the neocortex—the part of the brain that deals with complex reasoning—is a lot larger in primates than in other mammals. Of all primates, humans socialize in the biggest groups, because only the human neocortex is of the right size. That right size, however, turns out to be far smaller than the size of most modern organizations. Dunbar has got it down to a formula. He claims that in the human primate the ratio of the size of the neocortex to the brain as a whole can tell him the maximum size of the group with which the human primate can best network. In humans that number is 147.8 or, approximately, 150.

Dunbar says anthropology yields dozens of examples of this magic number. In 21 different hunter-gatherer cultures that he looked at—including the Australian Walbiri, the Tauade of New Guinea, the Ammassalik of Greenland, and the Ona of Tierra del Fuego—the average number of people in their villages was 148.4.[2]

And he notes that groups in modern societies also seem to have picked up on the number. The Hutterites, a fundamentalist group who live and farm communally in South Dakota and Manitoba, limit their groups to 150 individuals. In the military, cohesive fighting units, traditionally, have been limited to no more than 200 men. The classical Roman army, for instance, employed a basic unit, the maniple (or double century), made up of 120 to 130 men. And the modern army fields a company of 100 to 200 soldiers as the smallest independent unit. It's not that you can't have larger units, says Dunbar. You can, but it gets much harder. And you would also have to create a complex structure of rules and regulations to get the same level of cohesion. But if you stick with the limits prescribed by nature, cohesion results naturally.

Human beings, according to the sociobiologists, cannot understand much more than the things about which they are concerned for their daily existence. In other things—of which human beings don't have firsthand knowledge—their reasoning power tends to lead them astray.

Indeed, maverick economist Steven Levitt has written a whole book (*Freakonomics*, with Stephen Dubner) on the fallacies of popular reasoning on public matters.

For instance, take the popular conviction that money determines election outcomes. Examining 1,000 congressional races in 1972, where the same two candidates had run against each other in consecutive races, Levitt found that the winners could have halved their spending and lost only 1 percent of the vote, while the losers could have doubled their spending and gained only 1 percent. Who you are seems to have been more important than what you spend. But, what of the widespread conviction that much too much money is spent on elections in the United States? Well—what of it? It seems that Americans spend about a billion dollars on elections, all told, which is also what they spend annually . . . on chewing gum. The belief—like many beliefs we hold as a group—is simply not as well-founded as people think it is.[3]

In this, men are like the legendary czar who—on finding that the province with the most disease also had the greatest number of doctors—had the doctors shot.

People are just too quick to accept inadequate or wrong explanations for things in the world outside their immediate circle, and Dunbar's magic number helps to explain why. The human brain is just not big enough for the big world. In order to think, people are forced to start simplifying and eliminating a lot of the detail. They have to abstract . . . theorize . . . generalize. They turn to the cogito. And the problem with the cogito is that it is not as pure as it thinks it is. Cogitation on things we know nothing about personally is driven a lot by what others think, especially experts. If experts have a particular squint on a subject, we develop cross-eyes, too. The bee buzzing in their bonnet starts roaring like a sawmill in ours. If gun control is what the experts like, then we find gun control floating in our soup; if the flavor of the month is campaign reform, then we are apt to blame electoral results on evil money rather than dumb voters. It doesn't matter how untrue a thing is. If enough people (especially people we look up to) repeat it often enough, it soon becomes conventional wisdom.

A hundred years ago, Gustave Le Bon understood this when he wrote his classic work on crowds. He realized that the popular mind wanted most of all to simplify things.

Le Bon called the process—by which an idea gets simplified, repeated, imitated, and spread by the crowd—contagion.[4]

WHY MEN GO APE

What we are saying is that when people are dealing with things that are really too big for their brains, they tend to fall back on the irrational, for deep in the older part of their brains, deep in their hearts, under the spell of Venus, mankind still lives according to instincts as old and as savage as zebras and wildebeests. Instinctively, humans still despise anyone who endangers the integrity of the group or the effectiveness of group action by thinking for himself. Men are ready to die for the group and ready to kill anyone who resists its will.

Most likely a combination of cultural and genetic selection led to the elimination—at least in the West—of people unwilling to make the supreme sacrifice "for the country." Nothing was a bigger disgrace than cowardice. Spartan mothers told their sons to come back with their shields . . . or upon them. Socrates drank the cup of hemlock, Plato tells us, because he could not imagine himself in contravention of the group.

There is no greater disgrace than failing to do one's duty to the group, nor any greater glory than dying in the course of doing it.

And so, as a group's opinion changes from negative to positive . . . from bullish to bearish . . . from supporting a war to opposing it, individuals come under great pressure to conform; dissent is made illegal. Noncompliance in politics—such as refusing military service—is often fatal. Markets, in contrast, are more comic than tragic; nonconformance is punished first with losses and then . . . with great gains!

Of course, investment markets can behave like aggregated groups of individuals—each acting on his or her private judgment. But the nature of public markets and media practically guarantees that, occasionally, they become mobs.

Economists' theories don't account for this, for they are generally so simple-minded that they require a simple-minded individual to give them force. And so, they have invented the biggest simpleton who ever lived—economic man.

Economic man is presumed to act always in his self-interest, and always rationally. That is, if he can pick twice as many apples per hour with a long ladder as with a short one, and the two ladders are the same price and otherwise equal, the fellow is supposed to use the long ladder. It rarely bothers economists that real live man seldom does.

We have seen, for example, that he will try to "go over the top" in war—even where there is little chance of surviving and little reason to think the war makes a difference. Economists explain away these anomalies with a broader definition of self-interest. But then they end up with such distended reasoning that, like a taut bungee cord, it snaps back and hits them in the face. Human beings are always more complicated than the theories about them allow for.

Part of the problem is that the theorists fail to account adequately for the difference between two different realms of action. A man driving on the highway knows that if he pulls the wheel of the car further to the left, he will miss the road buttress, but will hit the cement truck coming at him. If he pulls it to the right, though, he will stay within the white lines and probably live. He makes the reasonable decision, based on a reasonable set of reasonably perceived facts and inferences.

In the public sphere the frontal lobe may be engaged, but his reasoning rests on nothing more solid than the shifting bog of group-think, which is not only completely different from private thinking but is an illusion, piled on top of a fraud, stacked on a foundation of humbug, built in the mud of misconception with the building blocks of lunacy.

Crowds cannot think. They can only feel and act. They can't think, because they have no set of facts solid enough on which to build. Are stocks really cheap? By what measure? Are we talking about real rates or nominal rates? Relative or absolute? Do the terrorists really pose a threat? To whom? Is the threat diminished or enlarged by attacking them? Each shovelful of answers takes you deeper and deeper into the bog, until you're so deep you can neither see over the top nor climb your way out. Investors may believe that stocks are headed higher. If so, they have a reason why—because they are bouncing off a low . . . because the boomers need to invest . . . because interest rates are low. Reasons are not scarce, and rational analysis is as plentiful as debris after a flood.

Before long you're spitting out bumper-sticker thoughts. Slogans replace reason. And the private world of right and wrong has been replaced by the public spectacle, which knows no moral authority beyond its own desires.

ALL MEN ARE DIFFERENT (AND DAMN WELL BETTER STAY THAT WAY)

"We hold these truths to be self-evident, that all men are created equal . . ." Thomas Jefferson wrote in 1776.

What made Jefferson think it was self-evident, we don't know. All the evidence we've seen tells us just the opposite—men are not born equal. One is rich; one is poor. One is fat; one is skinny. One has Viking blue eyes and pale skin; the other has eyes like burning coals and ebony skin. Maybe twins are born equal, but the rest of us are as variable as snowflakes. No two are alike. No two are equal.

When Americans celebrate the birth of their nation, it bothers no one that the founders' most important insights are palpably untrue. People are born different. It is only before the law that they are equal, and then only if they don't have enough money for a good lawyer.

The English legal philosopher Jeremy Bentham was probably thinking on those lines when he scoffed at the theory behind the American Revolution. "Natural rights," he growled, "is simple nonsense: natural and imprescriptible rights, rhetorical nonsense—nonsense upon stilts."[5]

People occasionally appreciate the truth in the same way they appreciate a good joke. It breaks the monotony. But it is to falsehood that they look to organize their lives. Myths stick to them like burrs to a sweater. Warren Buffett, for example, is giving away his fortune because he doesn't want to corrupt his own children with too much wealth. "I have given them enough so they can do anything," he says, "but not enough so they can do nothing." The Sage of the Plains also strongly supports death duties, because he believes it is better for babes to start out life like worker bees—each one an exact duplicate of the other.

But they don't ever start out equal, anyway. Warren Buffett was born into the most privileged ranks of American society—the son of a U.S. congressman. Few make as good as Buffett, but the man from Omaha can't exactly claim that he started life on an equal footing with the average man, most of whom never get close enough to a congressman to shoot him, let alone have dinner with him every night.

And the whole race of Americans seems to be especially favored. A baby born to a high-caste Goldman vice president in Connecticut clearly has an edge over one born to a low-caste street sweeper in Kerala. One born to a middle-class teacher in Silver City is almost surely in a better position than another born to a teacher in Sadr City. But, as for the child of a trashy drug addict in St. Paul, is he really starting off on a better footing than one born to a decent trash picker in São Paulo?

As things now stand, through no virtue or effort on their part, American babies on average can expect to earn 10 times as much per hour as babies born in most other places.

It's not equal, but it's not bad. Nor is it necessarily permanent. Foreigners still use the U.S. dollar as the world's reserve currency. And you can still usually sell a house for more than you paid for it. When those conditions end, the levelers should be happy; the advantage American babies have enjoyed for nearly a century will begin to disappear. We suspect, though, that even then, people will be very far from equal. They will still come in assorted shapes, sizes, flavors, and tastes—no two of them ever alike.

$\star$ $\star$ $\star$

Ultimately, it is largely a matter of scale. Once you get beyond what is usually known as the human scale, things lose their meaning.

The size of a New England town meeting lets the brain know which of the people it is dealing with is a hero and which is a hustler. But when it comes to national politics, the average voter is totally ill-equipped—like a mechanic who shows up with a pair of pruning shears or a veterinarian with a wrench in his hand.

What can the poor fellow do? The ideas he hears are too complex, too grand, too remote, too vague, too unknown, too hard to grab hold of. He has to try to simplify them. "All men are created equal," for example. He knows it contradicts the evidence of his own eyes. And what of the so-called level playing field of the investment markets? He's been told that he has as much chance to make money from his investments as Warren Buffett and George Soros. In the abstract, it sounds as though it might be true. But if he drove his car based on abstract principles, he'd soon be dead. For investing as well as driving, it's the precise details that matter. A turn of 45 percent might be fine, while one of 39 percent might be fatal. A cement company stock might be a good investment in November of 2006. By June of 2007, it could be a disaster.

And what of the government? "The voters decide on their own misgovernment" is the accepted formula. Majority rule is the essential math. There is some truth to it. But there is a bigger measure of falsehood. No president in modern times ever got a majority of Americans to come out and vote for him, and the president in office, as of this writing, didn't even get a majority of the votes cast. And even if the system of defining a majority were legitimate, there is still the question—so what? Whether they vote on it or not, by the time three wolves and one sheep sit down to decide what to have for dinner, the menu has already been drawn up. When voters go to the polls faced with, say, George W. Bush or John Kerry, the oven is already warmed. The voter is more likely to be served an iced daiquiri in hell than to cast the winning vote in a presidential race. In the one-in-a-billion chance that he did, what difference would it make? The voter might have cast his vote for George W. Bush, for example, because he had heard the man was a conservative. Then, he finds himself faced with the most activist administration since Franklin Roosevelt. Or, suppose he *does* cast the winning ballot. If he bore the responsibility for the actual government of the country, wouldn't the other 299 million Americans rightly ask: Why should we be ruled according to this man's desires and not our own?

What can the poor sap do but succumb to such *uber*-simplifications as take your breath away? Thus, "If we don't fight the commies in Vietnam," he said in 1965, "we'll have to fight them in California!" "If you want better-educated people, you have to spend more on public education," he said in 1975. "If we don't stand up to the Evil Empire, it will take over the world," he said in 1985. "If you invest in a balanced portfolio of stocks, you will always make money over the long run," he said in 1995. "If you want to become rich, you need to globalize," he proclaimed in 2005.

The precise figures and intricate calculations that people use on their own give way to statistics and averages. To the woodcutter in New Hampshire and the cowpuncher on the western plains, the world on TV becomes their world, too—a world where the color is washed out and replaced by caricatures and national averages. Standards are set according to the great wash of broadcasting and advertising in which local particularities are bleached out and local colors faded. Everything comes to be seen through the grayish-white light of the national media. Instead of speaking their regional dialect, the lumps are soon speaking the lingua franca of the evening news. Instead of wearing the clothes they like, they are dressed to suit The Gap or Brooks Brothers.

It no longer matters whether a man's home is comfortable and attractive on his own terms; now it has to be acceptable in national terms. Now, a good part of the population is said to be lodged in substandard housing. Of course, the whole idea makes no sense whatever without a standard based on averages, generalities, and public information. How many square feet per person? How much heating? Rules are imposed—building codes, zoning rules, materials standards. It is no longer "Is this house safe enough for me?" It is "Does this house meet modern safety standards?" By the new standards, even the Sun King, Louis XIV, probably lived in substandard housing.

And education. It is not enough to learn things now. Everyone has to learn the same thing, and learn it in the same way. In the national educational program, the details have to be knocked off—like the fine trim work from an old house—so that all that is left is standardized space, to be quantified and allocated by bureaucrats, who may have never met a single student in their entire lives. Are students not learning? Spend more money! The critical thing is that all students get the same claptrap pounded into their poor heads and leave the machinery of education with the same prejudices and illusions.

The woodchopper from New Hampshire may be perfectly happy with his lot in life. He may have no running water, no central heat, no money. But imagine him happily tending his garden, cooking on his woodstove, feeding his chickens, and fixing his tattered roof. Out in the woods, he may even have set up a home still for refining the fruits of the earth into even more pleasurable distillates. But as the scale of comparison grows, the details that make his life so agreeable to him disappear in a flush of statistics. He finds that he is "below the poverty line." He discovers that he is "disadvantaged" and "underprivileged." He may even realize that he has a "right" to "decent" housing and qualifies for food stamps.

Now that the spell is on him, it sits like a curse. Poverty seems like something he has to get out of, something that someone had better do something about! His new scaled-up consciousness has turned him into a malcontent. The poor man, who was happy in his naive particulars, is miserable in his role as a poverty-stricken hick.

And now it is the public view of himself that really matters. He might as well be a stock market investor. He sees himself on television as an unfortunate hillbilly. As the scale increases and the globalized market economy expands, people are homogenized, leveled, standardized. Regional variations hang on in vestigial, folkloric form, but whether you go to New Orleans, Nashville, or Vienna, you will hear about the same music, find the same fashions, and be able to eat the same McDonald's hamburgers. An investor in Bombay speaks the same language—balance sheets, price-earnings (P/E) ratios, cash flow—as one in New York. Yet, it is the particularities that make the difference between investment failure and investment success. But what investors get from the financial news is a public school education—they know nothing much and think they know everything. And since investors share the same illusions and take them for wisdom, the markets tend to reflect the popular fashions as if they were the season's latest blue jeans.

Even in matters as personal as health, people soon find themselves the victims of scale. The state of their own health scarcely matters anymore. What matters is statistics. Do they weigh too much? Do they get enough exercise? What do the papers tell them? They may have enjoyed a perfectly satisfactory sex life until they turn on their TVs. But now they are confronted with the statistical expectations of the national press. Are they doing it often enough? Are they doing it well enough? No longer do they know what really matters except by reference to the public spectacle, from how frequently people make love to what kind of misgovernment there is in Iraq. We are now all created equal. We live in the same houses, we eat the same food, and we suffer from the same universal flimflams.

Welcome to the flat world.

CHAPTER 10

THE FLAT EARTH
SOCIETY

He can't even find the earth on the globe.
—Doug Ferrari, comedian

Each time we look, our favorite columnist's favorite oeuvre is way ahead of our *Empire of Debt* in the rankings. We see people reading *The World Is Flat* numbly on airplanes. We see it stacked up like waffles at the entrances of B. Dalton's and Barnes & Noble. And what earnest business executive has failed to read at least enough of it so he can talk about globalization unintelligently? For a long time, we couldn't bring ourselves to read the book, but finally we did. As expected, it is suitable only for children . . . and only for them to sit on or club each other over the head with.

Thomas Friedman's opus claims that information technology and American-style capitalism (to say nothing of the protection racket run by the empire's military forces) have connected the world so much that the Renaissance discovery by Columbus that the world is round has given way to the postmodern discovery by Friedman that it is really flat.[1] Now we all play on the same level field of global commerce. We all wear the same clothes (business suits for adults, Che T-shirts for the young); talk the same language (English); share the same political ideology (humbug democracy); and worship the same God (mammon).

We are all one: one people, one world, with one idea—to get rich. And in this new flat earth, we can all get rich, too. It is as if the world had been flattened into a kind of United States of Earth, where people in Mississippi can live as well as those in New Guinea—competing for the same jobs, trading, cooperating, and schlepping their way toward a new world order that is better for everyone.

Globalization takes the wrinkles and creases out of the planet. You can buy the same clothes in Toronto as in Quangzshou. You can live in the same apartment, designed by the same architect and built of the same materials, in Buenos Aires as in Belfast. And of course, you can watch CNN everywhere.

The only thing threatening this brave, new, ironed-out world is that some people don't want to go along with it—losers, who think religion is more important than material progress; insurgents, who defy the empire; and protectionists, who want to push a stick into the wheels of history. If those were the only threats, Friedman might have a decent point, but Friedman is like a geologist who has just noticed the weather: Rain, wind, sun, storm—all of it seems to wash down and wear down the surface of the earth, he notices astutely. Aha, he concludes, the mountains will keep on eroding. Pretty soon, the whole world will be as flat as Kansas.

If he had any imagination or curiosity or even had remembered to look down at the ground under his feet, he would have wondered how it was possible that after so many millions of years of leveling, the earth was not flat already. And if he had bothered to look beneath the surface, he would have seen why: There are new volcanoes bubbling up all the time, new mountain ranges welling up, and eruptions waiting to explode.

Economist-cum-geologist Stephen Roach sees his seismograph twitching:

> First in manufacturing, now in services, the global labor arbitrage has been unrelenting in pushing U.S. pay rates down to international norms. . . .
>
> Courtesy of near-ubiquitous connectivity, the output of the knowledge worker can now be e-mailed to a desktop from anywhere in the world. That brings low-cost, well-trained, highly educated

workers in Bangalore, Shanghai, and Eastern and Central Europe into the global knowledge-worker pool. That's now true of software programmers, engineers, designers, as well as a broad array of professionals toiling in legal, accounting, medical, actuarial, consulting, and financial-analyst positions. . . . In short, the IT-enabled global labor arbitrage is a guaranteed recipe for mounting income inequality.[2]

Income inequality has been growing in the United States for the past 35 years, says Roach. Per capita income is $1,700 in China. It is $38,000 in America. As the Chinese (and others) compete with Americans, the low end of the wage scale in the United States is held down. Since the wage difference is still great, this process has a long way to go. The average American employee may not enjoy any real income growth for the next two decades. The rich, however, own the companies that benefit from lower wages and globalized markets.

Economists measure income equality with what they call a Gini index. At zero, people all earn the same thing. At 100, the rich get all the income. Currently, in Japan the Gini index is 25. In Europe, it is 32. In America, the index is at 41, and in China, it is at 45.[3]

In America, low-level earners can't get ahead, because they have no bargaining power. They are competing with a billion workers in Asia willing to do the same work for less than one-tenth the salary. And in China, there is also growing income inequality between those who have joined the global economy and those who have not. Some 500 million people live in coastal cities in China and participate in modern commerce, but there are another 700 million who still live in the countryside. While the cities grow richer, the poor in China are left behind, like America's industrial workers.

In short, the world is getting flatter in some areas, and steeper in others. There is less difference between China's industrial workers and those in America, but the difference between the globalized employees and the capitalists who employ them is growing. Beneath the surface of Friedman's flat earth, the pressure is growing. Sooner or later, it is bound to explode. (See Figure 10.1.)

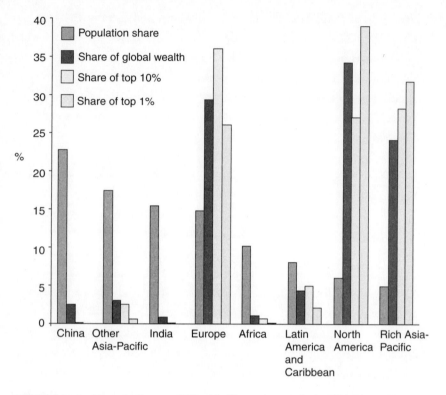

FIGURE 10.1   Population and Wealth Shares across the World by Region.

The richest 2 percent of adults owned more than 50 percent of global assets in the year 2000, and the richest 10 percent of adults accounted for 85 percent of the world total. In contrast, the bottom half of the world adult population owned barely 1 percent of global wealth. Assets of $2,200 per adult placed a household in the top 50 percent of world wealth distribution in 2000. The top 10 percent adults had $61,000 in assets, and the top 1 percent (37 million people) had more than $500,000.

Source: "The World Distribution of Household Wealth," James B. Davies of the University of Western Ontario, Anthony Shorrocks and Susanna Sandstrom of UNU-WIDER, and Edward Wolff of New York University, World Institute for Development Economics Research of the United Nations University (UNU-WIDER). Reprinted with the kind permission of UNU-WIDER from the study on "The World Distribution of Household Wealth." http://www.globalpolicy.org/socecon/inequal/income/2006/1206unupress.pdf.

The Flat Earth Society 201

THE MADNESS IN HIS METHODS—9/11 AND 7/11

It is not just that Thomas Friedman's metaphors clash with each other like mismatched furniture at a yard sale. What insults logic is that he tries to squeeze his theories into his metaphoric hand-me-downs.

Having latched onto "flatness" as his theme, he crams a whole swathe of technical, economic, and political developments into it, without hindrance of reason. He even employs kabbalistic numbering for the effort. There are *ten* flatteners . . . *four* steroids . . . *three* convergences—9/11 (the attack on the World Trade Center) is mystically born out of 11/9 (the fall of the Berlin Wall), but it's also connected to 8/9, the day Netscape released its initial public offering. Who would have thought? And why stop there? Why be so selective? Looked at properly, an almost *infinite* number of things are related to 9/11.

Let's see. The long stock market crash in 1973 began on 1/11. That was just about when the Organization of Petroleum Exporting Countries (OPEC) was tightening the screws on the West and reasserting the power of Arab nationalism. Undoubtedly, there's a direct connection to the attacks on the Twin Towers just there.

Or what about 9/11/1941, when the construction of the Pentagon began officially? How about that? Surely the fall of the Berlin Wall wasn't half as annoying to all those scowling young Saudi or Pakistani men as the rise of the Pentagon. Didn't one of those hijacked planes hit the Pentagon? We rest our case!

Or why not 11/9/1938, the Night of the Broken Glass (*Kristallnacht*), when enraged Germans turned on their Jewish compatriots? Didn't it eventually lead to the Holocaust? And didn't the Holocaust lead to the creation of a Jewish state, which displaced the Palestinian people? And isn't it the Palestinian cause that drives worldwide *jihad* today?

However, a glance at the Hebrew scriptures takes us in another direction. 9-11-1999 was the 6,000th anniversary of Adam's creation and year 1 on the Hebrew calendar. How about that? Can we be sure that it wasn't this that influenced those little anti-Semitic bigots when they picked the date for their kamikaze act?

In fact, if you dig around a bit, the coincidences begin to fly out and slap you in the face. Take 7-Eleven, the largest chain in the convenience retailing industry. It looks fairly innocuous until you realize that it licenses more than 23,600 stores abroad in 17 countries and U.S. territories, according to its web site. Come to think of it, it is also one of the nation's largest independent gasoline retailers. Altogether, a fairly ominous business from a Muslim viewpoint. Imagine all those Taylor pork rolls on Saudi soil . . . or the glossy copies of *Penthouse*. It makes you wonder—was it U.S. bases in the Gulf or that local 7-Eleven that finally got to Osama?

Mind you, it's not as if there is no sense at all in Friedman's squint on the world. On the contrary. Had he pointed out the connections between things, as one might trace the pout of a girl's mouth to a forgotten grandaunt, we might find them convincing. But they would be convincing not as explanations of the immutable logic by which events lead one to the other but as instances of the fascinating but obscure patterns thrown up by history.

But that is always the case with world improvers like Friedman. They are always smoothing out the past and gilding the future with the unctuous certainty of tea-leaf readers at a country fair. They are perpetually looking for numbers and formulas to convince their readers—and themselves—that they are onto something deep. Left to their own devices, the plebes might conclude that they, like everyone else, are in the dark about the workings of history. They might throw up their hands and abandon hope of bringing paradise to earth. They might even content themselves with merely improving the little parcel of earth they know firsthand. But string a couple of numbers together, line up statistics like blindfolded prisoners and fire away; even the most skeptical come around.

This is not to suggest that Friedman lards his books with statistical evidence, compelling or not. Far from it. What he does instead is to throw out a few figures, which in the midst of his commercials for globalization carry a force they would otherwise lack.

Take his defense of free trade in *The World Is Flat*. There's nothing wrong with his argument that jobs in big companies that are lost to outsourcing and free trade are replaced by jobs created by small companies that never make the headlines. Theoretically, that is the way David Ricardo's classical theory of comparative advantage works. But, is it the way things have been working in the United States in recent years? Yes, says Friedman, pointing to the U.S. unemployment rate of a bit over 5 percent, roughly half that of most developing countries. On this fragile thread dangles practically the entire weight of the chapter on free trade. But where does the 5 percent number come from? And what does it mean? Are we to assume from it that the other 95 percent of Americans are wiping the sweat off their brows after days packed with toil?

Obviously not. In any population at any time there is a whole segment that does not work and cannot be expected to. From toddlers to teens, the age group under 20 is likely almost entirely unemployed. The same goes for the age group over 60. Neither gets much room in calculations of the labor market. But in the 20-to-60 group, there are also whole populations whom we eliminate—stay-at-home wives and mothers (and sometimes fathers), those in hospital or homebound by illness, the insane, prisoners, gang members, and other criminals.

Beyond that, the picture is also skewed by language, because what economists mean by "full employment" is a slippery thing. For instance, if you work just one hour a day, you are considered employed for official purposes. And if you get discouraged looking for work and give up after just six months, you are not considered unemployed at all; you simply become marginal to the labor market—like the prison or hospital population. You disappear. If your work starts paying you less, taking up more of your time or yielding fewer benefits, or if you need to hold several jobs to meet the needs that used to be met by just one, that, too, is not factored into the unemployment figure most often used in public. Then there is the rise in the number of professional workers receiving disability payments from 1984 to 2005—up 148 percent, from 2.6 million to 6.5 million.[4] Those who receive disability don't count as unemployed. And workers who return to school, work for cash, or temp also fall into the black hole. What this means is that if you juggled all the variables that go into the production of the unemployment figure, you could come up with all sorts of results to suit every agenda.

And so it is. Critics on the left, for instance, argue that building more and more prisons and turning petty offenses into crimes masks rising unemployment. If all adults behind bars were counted, they argue, the unemployment rate would be about one percentage point higher, and the rate for black men would shoot up to almost 20 percent. The United States does have a government program for the unemployed, they quip—it's called prison.

But one doesn't have to sit left of center to notice the fraud on-stage. Just look at the figures for one month from when Thomas was laboring at his magnum opus: In July 2004 the official unemployment rate in the United States was 5.5 percent, exactly as he claims. But wait. The actual number of the unemployed at the time was 16,265,736, the highest in 20 years. The actual percentage of unemployed was thus really 9.7 percent, up 3 percent from 2002.[5]

And how about this: The percentage of employed adults in the United States reached a high of 64.8 percent in April 2000 at the peak of the stock market and then dropped to around 61 or 62 percent in September 2003, a low for 10 years. But even with this drop—which ought to mean a total unemployment rate of 8 percent—the unemployment rate supposedly still held around 6 percent under the Bush administration.[6]

So what gives? Where are these missing five million unemployed? Did they all make their fortunes selling the QQQs short and retire? Not so, alas. Labor Department (Bureau of Labor Statistics) reports from the same month show what happened: 300,000 workers left the labor pool and several million professionals lost their unemployment benefits, even though they found no new jobs. When all of that is taken into account, it turns out that employers created only 32,000 jobs in July 2004.[7]

Of course, that figure, too, is as much a piece of fiction as any other governmental statistic, but at least it doesn't cover up the number of unemployed workers. The *Washington Post* noted, "The unemployment rate fell to 5.7 percent in December 2003, a 14-month low, from 5.9 percent in November. But that reflected the decisions of 309,000 people to either stop working or stop looking for jobs, which means they are no longer counted as part of the labor force."[8]

In fact, although the recession in the United States lasted officially just eight months (March to November 2001), jobs continued to be cut thereafter in most major companies.[9] Companies became more productive during the wobbly recovery that followed, but only because they were using fewer workers. What jobs were added were added in real estate and finance, where they were the result of speculative and nonproductive activity; in health care, where they signaled inflated costs and an aging population; or in low-wage service jobs at all the Home Depots or Wal-Marts around.

But that's the fun of the flat world. Friedman can just flatten over statistical potholes with a shovelful of quotes. And where does he go for them? To the International Monetary Fund (IMF)—only one of the biggest players in the whole trade game—and to McKinsey, the most prominent outsourcing consultant.

One out of seven . . . 10.3 percent . . . the mob flocks to statistics, like the faithful to the altar. They must think they're eating the bread of the martyrs of science from Galileo onward. The less they understand the numbers, the more they are enamored of them. What they can't see clearly must—like veiled houris—have charms beyond what they do see.

Of course, no real statistician, mathematician, or scientist would accept the sort of numbers that pop social scientists like Friedman palm off as the real thing. There is no logical, mathematical, or linguistic structure that does not rest on a blind spot. There is no sense that does not have a foundation that is nonsense. The charm of real mathematics, in fact, is its absurd poetry. And great mathematicians have always had about them the fantastic air of magicians. The writer who created the Mad Hatter and the Red Queen and invented the nonsense language of Jabberwocky and the insane logic of the Looking Glass was also an Oxford don in mathematics, Charles Dodgson.

Math and science, at their core, nurse a kernel of irrationality. A straitjacket of logic can never fully tie them down. Gödel's theorem on incompleteness demonstrates this, and every systems analyst assumes it. But in Friedman's world, a few feeble economic statistics are Manifest Destiny. Numbers are immutable laws from Mount Sinai that require the tribes of the world to fall down and worship. And straitjackets are not only good things, they are *golden*. In *The Lexus and the Olive Tree*, he recommends that every nation put one on to get the best out of the global economy.[10] The Golden Straitjacket is pure Friedmanese, shorthand for the neoliberal economics of downsized government and deregulated commerce. Wages are held low, public assets are privatized or turned over to the international securities markets, and tariffs and quotas are eliminated. Financial speculators—the Electronic Herd, Friedman calls them—stampede in and paw up the turf in search of quick profits, bringing with them prosperity for some and joblessness, chaos, and uprooted lives for others.[11]

But no matter. It's all in a day's work for our columnist. Get with the program. Sit down at the table. Enter the cash economy or be condemned to the backward, antimodern, low-tech, unflat world.

Or, as Friedman writes about a Vietnamese woman whom he paid a dollar a day to be weighed (purely as his "contribution to the globalization of Vietnam"): "Whatever you've got, no matter how big or small—sell it, trade it, barter it, leverage it, rent it, but do something with it to turn a profit, improve your standard of living and get into the game."

Exactly. For the Friedmans of the world, globalization is a game. That's why they have to lace the thin gruel they serve us with a heady brew of pseudostatistics and jargon. It's the 80 percent proof with which they knock themselves and their readers out. Take it away, and all that remains is a feeble hash of platitudes. Friedman understands globalization like the pilot of a B-52 follows street signs—rarely and only remotely. On ground zero, a storm rages over large tracts of the globe. Its fallout is neither clear nor always hopeful. But you'd never know that from the well-fed weatherman flying high and dry above.

THE ANGELIC EMPIRE

Globalization gurus like Friedman are always quick to point out that the phenomenon is not new. Some leading pontificators on the subject think we are in the third wave of it, the first having begun in the Age of Exploration, with Columbus and Magellan. Others think globalization goes back only to the heyday of the British Empire, in the midnineteenth century. What all of them are united on, however, is that it is a good thing because it is free trade between free people. And it is an inevitable thing, they add, because it is a force of nature. A call of destiny. A historical imperative.

It is The Way Things Ought to Be.

When pushed further, the gurus will tell you why they think this. They will tell you that globalization is also The Way Things Have Been Before. They will point out to you the British Empire. *That*, they will say, is what globalization looked like once. That's how it worked once. And since what the Romans were to the Greeks, we are to the British, that's also where we should be heading. After all, wasn't the British Empire, indisputably, A Good Thing?

Was it?

Were the British the one (and only) angelic imperialists? We are not in a position to say one way or other, nor do we think we will ever be in such a position, but we offer a caveat to the argument itself: If what we had under the British Empire was globalization, then whatever globalization was, it was not free trade. And we also offer a corollary to the caveat: If what we are looking for is free trade, then the British Empire is not what we should be imitating, for whatever trade took place under the Empire was from the beginning not free but wrapped up in force and fraud—and plenty of it.

Take the way in which the Indian state of Bengal passed into the hands of the East India Company. The salient fact was that a clerk turned soldier-adventurer, Robert Clive, managed to defeat a vastly larger Bengali army. How? Was it by superior skill or advanced technology? Not at all. The Muslim ruler (the *nabob*) of Bengal had insulted a fabulously wealthy Hindu merchant who controlled the flow of goods to the ports of Bengal. In revenge, the merchant led a group of his fellow traders to talk the *nabob's* generals into negotiating with the English. A treacherous general threw away the Battle of Plassey in 1757 and received the right to rule Bengal in return. The East India Company then became the rent collector for the area. Within a few years, it acquired the right to collect revenue for the whole of northeast India.[12]

Plassey was the cornerstone of British imperial rule, and it made Clive one of the icons of the Empire. But it was simply a fraud—the outcome of Clive's treachery toward the local ruler whom he had first befriended.

As for the benevolence of the British Empire, consider this: In the first half of the nineteenth century, there were seven famines in India, leading to a million and a half deaths. After Victoria was crowned Empress of India (1876), there were 24 famines (18 between 1876 and 1900), causing over 20 million deaths according to official records, up to 40 million according to others, or between 12 and 29 million according to a recent scholar.[13]

As early as 1901, W. R. Digby noted in *Prosperous British India* that famines had been four times as numerous in the last thirty years of the 19th century as they were one hundred years earlier, and four times as widespread.

The British *mission civilisatrice* took perverse forms. During the famines of 1877 and 1878, the British viceroy, Lord Lytton, actually had merchants export millions of hundredweight of wheat to England. Lytton, whose father was the well-known novelist Edward Bulwer-Lytton, seems to have been certifiably insane. He passed the Anti-Charitable Contributions Act of 1877, which prohibited, at the pain of imprisonment, private relief donations that potentially interfered with the market fixing of grain prices. Those who worked in the labor camps were reportedly fed less than the inmates of Buchenwald. Women and children were "branded, tortured, had their noses cut off, and were sometimes killed"—a circumstance regarded with equanimity by the British governor, who subscribed to the Malthusian notion that famine was nature's way of keeping the Indians from overbreeding. Meanwhile, funds were available for extravagant celebrations of Victoria's investiture as Empress of India. And the viceroy even ran "a militarized campaign" to tax those who survived to raise funds for the Empire's ongoing war in Afghanistan. So finally, even in northwest India—which had crop *surpluses*—1.25 million people died.[14]

Yet, so powerful are myths that even the victims buy into them. Long after India became independent, the younger of your two authors recalls a granduncle reminiscing fondly about his days recruiting for the British army, although its history was marred even then with imbecilities.

Take the invasion of Kabul in 1842. The invasion is legendary now for the incompetence of its leader. It should be remembered equally for the incompetence of those who appointed him in the first place. The appointment casts some doubt about the *pukka*-ness of the *pukka* British administration. The hapless commander, Major-General William Elphinstone, actually tried to turn down the job, but it was no use. The governor-general of India—at the time, Lord Auckland—was determined he should go. He went, and it cost him his life.

"Elphy Bey" (*bey* is the Turkish term for commander) was a gentle, doddering old fool who was coming apart at the seams. Just 60, the ailments he suffered from could have filled a small hospital ward. He was mentally incompetent . . . and incontinent . . . flatulent . . . and gouty . . . and his rheumatism was so bad that he was crippled and had to be carried everywhere on a litter. And to top it off, his arm was in a sling. Afghanistan, with its ferocious climate and even more ferocious warriors, was no place for the soft, senile general who had been retired on half-pay since acquitting himself—creditably it seems—at Waterloo. But Lord Auckland was determined to take Afghanistan, and thus in 1839, the Afghan emir, Dost Mohammed, was driven into hiding. He was replaced by another incompetent, Shah Suja, and British garrisons were left at the capital, Kabul, as well as all along the route back to India.

Unfortunately, the new cantonment at Kabul provoked the suspicion of the Afghan rebels, led by the old emir's son. The British were there to stay for a while, he thought, and began to look for ways to strike at them.

He did not have to look for long. The cantonment was located in a low, swampy area, which presented an easy target to the rebels swarming in the hills and forts around it. The circumference of the place was too great to be defended, and all the supply stores were outside. The British might just as well have sent out an engraved invitation to the enemy to seize their supplies and starve the population inside—which is precisely what happened.

"You will have nothing to do here. All is peace," opined the outgoing commander when Elphy Bey and his main man, the brutal and belligerent Brigadier John Shelton, arrived. It was a singularly inaccurate prediction.

Not long thereafter, a brigade returning to India was besieged. Then, when Elphinstone's health took a turn for the worse and the governor-general had to send out a replacement for him, he, too, was attacked and forced to hole up in a fortress.

The Kabul cantonment seems to have turned into the nineteenth-century version of Baghdad's Green Zone. No one could go outside without drawing fire, and even inside, soldiers were constantly being gunned down. In short order, the British resident and his staff were polished off by the rebels. Then, the supply stores were pillaged, leaving those inside the cantonment with only about three days' worth of food.

Not content with a broken arm, poor Elphy tried mounting his horse and fell off. Then he hurt his leg when the beast decided—perhaps with some justification—to step on it. That may have sent the old man straight out of his mind, because he now started begging for more ammunition to be sent around, although there was actually enough left for a year. By then, all he knew about the military situation was what random civilians were telling him, for Shelton was keeping mum and treating him with unrelenting scorn. The old man had to make do with councils of war where almost anyone would wander in and say anything he wanted. Junior officers lectured their seniors. Civilians offered their unsolicited advice to the soldiers. In the midst of it all lay Shelton on his bedding, snoring, to show his contempt for the whole proceeding.

But Shelton was hardly a military genius himself. Once, he led his men to no more than 20 paces from the Afghans and fired. When not one enemy soldier, or even horse, was killed, the Brits were forced to turn and flee. Another time, he ordered his soldiers to fall into squares so concentrated and tidy that the Afghans, who were experts at hitting targets that were scattered and hidden, thought they were getting a Ramadan gift. Each of their bullets sent a small handful of the poor Englishmen tumbling like bowling pins. Shelton, who had compounded this criminal performance by taking with him only one cannon when British army regulations—with good reason—mandated two, soon found it too hot to operate. He had to fall back on muskets. But these were so poorly handled that the Afghans actually managed to get to point-blank range unscathed. By then Shelton's men were down to throwing stones, but their wretched leader still held on pigheadedly. Finding themselves being picked off one by one, the soldiers finally came to their senses and fled, pointedly ignoring even Elphy's attempts to rally them. The punch line of the whole business came when they learned that they had been driven back not by Afghanistan's notorious warriors but by a bunch of Kabul shopkeepers.

The farce degenerated further. Elphinstone got himself shot—of all places—in the buttocks. The British envoy, unable to stand things any longer, took it upon himself to make nice to the head of the rebels. For his pains, he was assassinated and his head and torso skewered like a kebab and paraded through Kabul. Elphy, a world-class ditherer, now made the worst decision yet of his life. In return for Afghan guarantees of safe conduct he agreed that the cantonment would return to Jalalabad in India. They would go through the Khyber Pass, the infamous point of entry of every foreign conqueror—in midwinter.

And so, 16,000 men, women, and children marched through snow a foot deep, on the orders of a senile general. Along the way, tribesmen from every neighboring village, including children, taunted, harassed, and picked them off like ripe plums. At the end of all the hacking and butchering, Elphinstone was dead and so was every European except the surgeon-general. But the British got their revenge in time. Elphinstone's replacement, General Nott, finally extricated himself from his corner, marched to Kabul, and burned down its famous bazaar.

Still, even then, the luckless Elphy could get no peace. On the way to Jalalabad, his coffin, decorously prepared by the new emir, was ambushed by tribesmen. They cracked it open, stripped the body, and pelted it with stones. The emir had to send out another expedition before the dimwitted general was allowed to go to his rest with full—and completely undeserved—military honors.[15]

The story of Elphy Bey was not unusual. Wherever the empire builders succeed, it is most often *in spite of* incompetence. It is from force and fraud ... some luck ... and not from genius. If there is a grand design in anything they did, it eludes us.

ERIN RISEN

Does it take an empire, we wonder, to bring civilization and prosperity to people?

"Ireland has arrived," writes David McWilliams in his book *The Pope's Children*.[16] Driving around the countryside, we saw many substantial houses and condominium developments under construction, along with shopping malls and fancy automobiles. Except for the hedgerows and the people driving on the wrong side of the road, it might have been a suburb of Cincinnati.

"We are richer than any of us imagined possible 10 years ago," continues McWilliams. "No Irish person has to emigrate, none of us need pay for education, and even our universities are free. Unemployment is the lowest in our history. We are at the top of foreigners' lists as places to live. Unlike many of our rich neighbors, in survey after survey, we claim to be very happy. We no longer need to beg from others in the EU; in fact, we are giving them cash. We are a success."[17]

"Yes, it's not like it used to be," said our cab driver. "You won't see any more houses with thatched roofs, for example. Nobody knows how to put on the thatch. And then you can't get insurance for them. Too bad, I liked to see a nice thatched roof—and it was so warm and cozy in winter. But nothing is like it used to be."

The River Liffey still flows through Dublin just as it always has. But it's not the same water—and not the same city, either. Nowadays, you're likely to enter a pub and be served not by a smiling publican with a round bog-trotters' face, a turned-up Paddy nose, and a lilting Irish voice, but by an immigrant from Slovakia or Serbia.

We attended a conference held in an old castle on a private 300-acre island near Waterford. The place had been converted to a resort, with tennis courts and a golf course. Soon, developers are planning to build high-end houses. Our cab driver filled us in.

"I remember when this place was for sale; 20 years ago it's been. Somebody came along and paid 300,000 Irish pounds for it, and people called him a silly fool for spending that much money. But now they're planning on selling each lot—just the empty building lot—for a million euros. I don't have to tell you, I wish I was the fool."

At lunch, we noticed that both of the serving staff were foreigners. One must have been Polish; the other, perhaps Greek or Bulgarian. For 500 years, boats on the Liffey carried out Ireland's biggest and most successful exports—the Irish themselves. Now they import people.

How did it happen? How did Ireland change? It was not the benevolence of the British Empire, we suspect. Indeed, for decades, the Irish had been fleeing their English masters. They left to find work; to get away from revolutions, uprisings, massacres, and suppression; to make their fortunes; or to avoid starving to death. They left for Baltimore, New York, Boston, Sydney, and Buenos Aires—a vast diaspora that helped to fill up the New World. "No Irish need apply," said the signs. The Irish were riffraff. They drank too much and had too many children. The Irish slums were dangerous, dirty, and desperate. Besides, they were papists.

When, in New Orleans, work began on the Pontchartrain canal in the early nineteenth century, the diggers were laid down by fever. They began with slave labor, but fever got them so often their owners refused to let them continue. So, Irish laborers were brought in. The micks could die as often as they wanted; who would care? Likewise, on the loading docks of the Old South, black laborers pitched bales of cotton into the cargo ships, but Irish laborers had to catch them. That end of the transaction was considered too dangerous for slaves. But on the River Liffey they had no choice. They had to leave the green and glorious island; the great river of history carried them away.

And what is history itself but a vast public spectacle? Some people—usually fools and knaves—make history. Others suffer it. Decent people, who mind their own business and do their best, seem to appear in history only as statistics. An Gorta Mor, the Irish potato famine of the mid-1800s, caused between 500,000 and a million deaths. Millions more avoided starvation only by emigrating. Ireland's population was cut in half—from eight million to only four million—during the famine years.

How many were killed in the Easter Rising?

A shadow of cloud on the stream
Changes minute by minute

wrote Ireland's greatest poet about that fateful moment in history.

And how many were massacred in Portadown?

The proximate cause of the Great Hunger was an act of nature, a fungus. Behind it were acts of parliament—centuries of man-made history. Catholics risked having their land taken away. Those who retained them saw their holdings grow smaller and smaller. The English had taken up much of the land in large plantations. What was left for the Irish was divided, and redivided, so that the typical farm was only a few acres—and much of that was marsh or swampland. The only thing that could be grown on such land that would produce enough calories to feed a family was potatoes. And done on such a small scale, there was no margin for error; there were no savings, no cushion on which the typical family could fall back in times of trouble. When trouble came with the spuds, they were in a jam.

Much is made of how the English authorities caused the problem, and then made it worse through various interventions. But Lord Russell just made history, like Cromwell and Henry VIII before him. The Irish bore it as best they could.

Your authors do not stoop to making history. Instead, we study it carefully—usually with amusement—so that we won't have to suffer it ourselves. We watch the waters flowing ... life ... the Liffey ... sometimes bringing good news, and sometimes bearing barges with trouble. We wonder where the clouds and currents come from. For example, what turned Ireland from one of Europe's poorest countries into one of its richest?

"The Irish economy has been booming at an annual growth rate of over 5.6% for 20 years now. In barely 18 years Ireland has made the unbelievable jump from 22nd to the 4th place in OECD prosperity ranking," write Martin De Vlieghere and Paul Vreymans of the Flemish think tank, *Work for All*.[18]

How did Ireland do it? By joining the European Union—and cutting taxes. "Ireland thanks its success to its clear-cut different tax policy," say the Flemish thinkers. "With 33%, the Irish overall tax burden is the most moderate of Europe. Ireland also has a unique fair flat-tax structure ... the key to Ireland's success."

But is anything ever so simple? We don't know. We just observe that the river of history now flows in Ireland's direction.

CHAPTER 11

WHAT THE
YONGHY-BONGHY-BO
DIDN'T KNOW

"On this Coast of Coromandel,
Shrimps and watercresses grow,
Prawns are plentiful and cheap,"
Said the Yonghy-Bonghy-Bo.
> **—Edward Lear, "The Courtship of the Yonghy-Bonghy-Bo"**

The Yonghy-Bonghy-Bo got only half the story right, it seems. Today, the Coromandel Coast of India is booming, and for the past decade, prawns have become both cheaper and more plentiful—at least for Western consumers. But, there is a downside. The new prawn farms set up on the east coast after Indian trade was liberalized in the 1990s may not quite be dark satanic mills, but they do look more and more like an overall loss to the local economy. They suck up water desperately needed for drinking, say activists. They also displace small fish farmers, who then trudge off to the cities and add to the jungle of slums there. Because the farms work by flooding the soil with seawater, whole tracts of once arable land have turned permanently salty and barren. And worst of all, the farms destroy the old mangrove forests that until now have held together the Indian coastline and protected it from floods and typhoons. All this, according to the critics, offsets any gains commercial prawn farms bring the economy in terms of foreign reserves and employment.[1]

216

Critics are not a pleasing lot, dear reader. They carp and they complain when we would prefer a little good cheer, a more Friedmanesque delight in the way things are.

Instead, the Gloomy Guses grumble tastelessly about dying fisherfolk and drying wells.

If people don't have water to drink, we might be tempted to wonder, why don't they just drink Coke?

Well—apparently, they tried that, too, on the opposite coast of India, in the little village of Plachimada. But it didn't take. The locals there, for some perverse reason, seemed to prefer their liquid intake in the venerable form of H_2O. So, the Coca-Cola bottling plant in Plachimada was shut down in 2004 and placed under a stop order (later reversed) in 2005, because it was bleeding an interesting mix of metals, including cadmium and lead, into the water in the surrounding ground. That seems to have troubled the backward denizens of Kerala state, who prefer to drink their water neat.[2]

Of course, Coke is a target as broad as the side of a double-decker bus. A fight between picturesque villagers who want to drink water where they've lived all their lives and a multinational that wants to buy it on the cheap, whip some corn syrup into it, and sell it back to them at irrationally exuberant prices is one into which even Tom Friedman might find it hard to fly B-52s. America's right to consume as much oil as it can lay its hands on may be god-given and defensible by thermonuclear warfare. But obesity from sugary water still sounds like a dubious privilege in a constitutional republic. That, briefly, is the quandary of the new globalized world. On the one hand—jobs, growth, and Nike. On the other—dislocation, waste, and pollution.

That issue was uppermost in the mind of the more earnest of your two authors as she recently disembarked at Chennai, the humid state capital that sits on one of the longer stretches of oceanfront in the world—the Marina beach. Madras is big, dirty, and crowded, but since it was November, the weather was pleasantly cool. Still, we managed to get ourselves a bit hot and bothered by the city's name even though it's been some time since a populist Tamil government rechristened it in its own likeness. Like a lot of people, we still prefer the old tag. Why? We have no explanation except that we see no need to improve something that was working just fine.

The name switch strikes us as a piece of bombast, a red rag waved at the populace. Linguistic chauvinists complained that Madras was of Portuguese origin. It was a corruption of *Madre de Sois*, so they said. But now they think Chennai might not be *echt Tamil*, either. It reminds one of the old story of the archaeologist who came across a gold coin in his backyard and got into a heated debate about its classification. It was Byzantine, he argued; no, no, it was older than that—it was Roman, a late Caesar. Maybe it was even from the Persian empire. Then he rubbed it with his sleeve, and lo—it was an old coat button.

That tells you how misbegotten these searches for the real, real *desi* (indigenous) identity are. After all, whatever you might think about the British, Madras city was their brainchild—and the capital of one of the main administrative divisions of the British Empire. No need to rewrite history.

But now Madras is no longer just rewriting history in its own image. Instead it is busy making it.

The Coast of Coromandel has come to be identified by a Harvard University study as a potential "regional gateway to Asia." And *fDi*, the specialist global investment magazine, dubs it the Asian Region of the Future 2005/06. It even leads other Indian states in the Economic Freedom Index of 2005.[3]

In India, state governments change as quickly as song-and-dance routines on a Bollywood set, but the support for foreign investment in the southern state has held steady.

How did this happen?, we wonder. When did this patch of land in the Deccan decide to forget the claptrap of politics and let its subjects pursue their own happiness in their own way? And does it really work?

We got some tangible sense of the answer on the way back home from Chennai airport, which compares favorably to other airports in the country. At least, it is fairly well organized and clean. The 140-kilometer to the town of Vellore, which usually takes about three and a half hours, had suddenly been shortened by a third because of a new national highway system—the Golden Quadrilateral—5,846 kilometers of four- and six-lane expressways connecting Delhi, Mumbai, Calcutta, and Chennai in a rough quadrilateral. The last time we were here, in 2003, work had just begun, but now the segment we were using was complete. The result was quite impressive. Cars were moving along much faster; there was more traffic and the old decrepit buses with their extravagant tilts had disappeared—hauled off to the scrap yard, we guessed. We remembered hanging precariously out of them on the bottommost step, one hand clutching our book bag and the other the edge of the door, our braids flying madly in the wind on our way to school . . . or an early death.

Now, bougainvillea and oleander splash stretches of the road with magenta, white, and green, and in between peep acres of gleaming factories, housing developments, refurbished temples and mosques, new colleges and schools. By now we can rattle off the names—Hyundai, Nokia, Saint Gobain, Cognizant . . . Saint Gobain is a French glass manufacturer that has invested about 800 crore rupees (a crore is 10 million) in its latest project and employs about 2 lakhs of people (a lakh is 100,000).[4]

THE MARKET COMES TO MADRAS

What would make the French abandon their elegant cities and lush countryside to make glass outside a hot, dusty city in the south of India? We can safely assume it is not a sudden liking for *idli-dosai* or a yen for the fancy footwork of an Indian dancer. French glass manufacturers, we venture to guess, are not in the business of philanthropy. It is not a soft heart for the Indian populace but a hard head for French profits that has the frogs serenading the lily pads in this Asian pond.

But therein lies the beauty of the market. Even our vices and our warts are turned into virtues in spite of themselves. Only commerce and the hope of a dollar could force us into the company of people so dissimilar from ourselves that we might not otherwise have chosen to know them.

To the French and the rest of the global brigade making good, what goods do the Indians have to make and offer? That's easily reckoned. Billion-dollar firms like Infosys, Wipro, Sathyam, and Cognizant, as well as even second-string information technology players, have most of their people located in the south of India for one reason. The four southern states of Tamil Nadu, Karnataka, Kerala, and Andhra Pradesh (home to India's "cybercity," Hyderabad) together account for about 64 percent of Indian software exports. Tamil Nadu state alone churns out 22,000 engineers every year. And the software industry's national association in India has rated Chennai as the best place for software development in the country.[5]

It's really no surprise. World-class technical and mathematical knowledge is not hard to find around here. Madras city, after all, was once the home of Sreenivas Ramanujan, a name that doesn't easily trip off the lips of people in the West but which every Indian knows. Ramanujan was a savant who rivaled Leibniz or Einstein in his abilities—with an eerie difference. While the European mathematicians had the best libraries and trained minds to work with, Ramanujan scribbled down his ideas after hours working as an accounts clerk in Madras. A high school dropout often on the verge of starving, he had no formal training worth the name, yet he managed to catch up with centuries of mathematical development on his own. On the way, he created theorems of such dazzling brilliance that a world-famous don to whom he wrote brought him to Cambridge immediately. G. H. Hardy, the don, concluded that Ramanujan's results had to be true because "if they were not true, no one would have had the imagination to invent them."[6]

Something in the spices in Madras curry must be good for numbers, for Tamil Brahmins for centuries have nurtured a talent for them. Today, the Madras branch of the Indian Institute for Technology (IIT) is the prime breeding ground for the engineers and scientists who make up almost half the engineering departments at American corporations.

This observation is bound to irk those who think that policy pronouncements and fiats from bureaucrats are the only way the world progresses. We, however, observe that the world moves at its own pace and government diktats that get too far ahead of that pace seldom do any lasting good. But, while it did not take a core knowledge program to produce great mathematicians in the south of India, the IIT branches themselves were founded and funded by no less than the Indian government. We would have been the last people to guess that a socialist government would successfully tap the talent that peoples the most capitalist of capitalist worlds—Silicon Valley—or that it would become worthwhile one day for Madrassis to exchange their talents for goods and services from the west coast of California. But so it is. It goes to show how limited our neocortexes are when it comes to predicting how things will work out in the real world.

Still, that has never stopped politicians, who can't seem to juggle more than two variables at a time, from acting on their simplistic assumptions. Now, the experts—and here we mean economists—are often almost as simple-minded as the politicians, but at least they do have some inkling, however dim, that if a moth flutters its wings in Uganda, the polar ice caps might shrink. Stir up a breeze in Moscow and a typhoon could hit the Philippines. Thus, economists who have been around a while have learned to have a skeptical view of policies that tout one-for-one benefits. They know there's something fishy, something amiss in the calculation. Recycling programs, they point out, often only worsen the problem of garbage, and using cloth napkins might actually hit the environment harder than simply using paper ones. There is all that water that goes into washing them ... and the detergent ... and the factories that make the detergent ... and the plastic packages the detergents come in.

That is why classical economists generally look on free trade and pronounce it good. They know from experience that the law of unintended consequences nips at the heels of government *pronunciamentos* like an irate guard dog at a prisoner in one of Mr. Rumsfeld's facilities. Leave people to exchange goods and services as they see fit, and they do the least damage to each other. Thus, free trade is the theory that underpins—or ought to underpin—the process of globalization.

But between theory and practice is a chasm so large, dear reader, that a posse of economists might fall into it and never be missed. The practice of globalization is far stranger and far more contradictory than its theory. Indeed, it is so prone to anomalies that we should consider talking about plural globalizations rather than a single homogeneous one.

Who, for instance, could have ever foreseen that automotive work, the gold standard of all blue-collar American jobs, would someday take flight from the sturdy manufacturing hubs of the North? And that steel work would join it? That Pittsburgh would end up motheaten with dying boroughs and Detroit houses would fall to bargain basement levels in the middle of the greatest housing bubble in history? And most of all, who would have ever foreseen that there would be beneficiaries to the whole sad business and that, worse yet, one would lie at the other end of the world, on the Coromandel coast?

But that, in fact, is the case. The advent, for the first time in years, of travel sans potholes in South India has meant more interest in driving, which in turn means that the Western automotive industry has headed off in the direction of India. Chennai seems to have turned into a rough-and-ready version of Detroit—in South Asia—and other towns altogether unknown in the West now have auto ancillary units.

What makes the state attractive to the automakers? A number of things—research and development capacity, an extensive vendor base, the long history of the auto component sector in South India. Ford, Hyundai, Leyland, and TVS all have major presences in Tamil Nadu, and they mean to be there for the long haul.[7]

That means that not only is globalization in Tamil Nadu crossing over industries, from software to cars, it is also spreading out geographically. What growth has taken place in India so far has been concentrated in the larger cities, but there are over a billion people in India. And most of them don't live in the cities at all, but in the countryside (in villages and small towns), that could be where the potential now lies.

And here again we bumble into the sticky trap of language, like a myopic fly butting against a spiderweb. Small is a very relative term. A small town in the United States might have a thousand people; a small town in India can have 500,000 people or a million. And while East Elvis, Mississippi, may be small, it will usually have sleek four-lane highways and 24-hour electricity, whereas a small town in India is liable to have neither.

You see the problem, dear reader? As soon as we start talking to someone outside our immediate circle, we find ourselves in the business of bamboozling others, albeit unknowingly. The words we use might sound similar, but they refer to quite different things. So, when hacks and demagogues tell the poor in the United States that their jobs have been taken away by the middle class in India, they don't let on to them that poverty in America would not only *not* be recognized as poverty in about 99 percent of the world, it would be considered a swell way of life. Many Indians—like many other Asians and Africans—have been yearning to be poor in America for years.

JEKYLL AND HYDE

What all this means for the global game is that a small town in India can have wayward dirt roads and power shortages at the very same time that it has cutting-edge computer technology. It can have malarial mosquitos and biomedical engineering. So, if you are gung-ho for globalization, it is a simple thing to point out the improvements and call for more of the same.

But if you are one of the thousands of new social organizations that have sprung up in the past few years whose job it is to turn over the rocks and look underneath, you might spot a few not-so-fancy ants squirming there.

Who is right? We don't claim to know, but we believe that where you stand might depend on where you sit. Seated in the taxi going home, leaving behind the Golden Quadrilateral, we noticed that globalization seems to have entirely passed by whole sections of the state. The little dirt road home to our parents' house was death by a thousand bumps. It was so twisted you could have uncorked a bottle of *feni* (rice alcohol) with it. And the most obvious accomplishment of the new factories that have sprung up like pesky Congress weed all over the place is that they've sucked the wells for miles around as dry as a rattlesnake's tongue. There were people who relied on their wells for drinking and washing who were forced to spend the 20,000 rupees needed to dig another. The lucky ones found water. But that is not always the case in the south, which can be parched and arid, and where a failed monsoon can mean empty taps for months. Bottled water is not a yuppie whim here, but a matter of survival.

Globalization, in other words, has its downside, although how extensive and how deep is another question. There's the Yonghy-Bonghy-Bo's prawns, for instance—which have become the subject of popular agitation and a raft of government regulations. They're Exhibit A for a lot of people for why globalization hurts nature. Greedy developers and commercial farming are ruining the coastlines, the critics say. Were it not for the damage to the mangrove forests, far fewer people would have been killed by the great Asian tsunami of late 2004 is the complaint.

We are not immune to the power of such arguments. We can see with our own befuddled eyes that economic growth is a very selective thing, and that behind the GDP and the per capita numbers lie pockets of immense affluence muddled together with large swathes of misery.

The statistics—if they can be trusted—tell a Jekyll and Hyde story about the new world of globalization: On the Jekyll side, India has almost 100,000 dollar millionaires and ranks eighth in the world in the number of billionaires it has. And the net worth of these Indian billionaires is second only to those in the United States. Meanwhile, on the Hyde side, Indian per capita GDP, according to the UN, is below that of Nicaragua or Indonesia. The country might have been the 15th largest donor to the World Food Program in 2005, but over the past decade it has also added more hungry people to its population than anywhere else in the world. Hunger increased in India, when it was falling even in Ethiopia. And while India exports grain to Europe, it is to feed Europe's cattle at prices lower than Indians at home get.[8]

One used to hear that trade liberalization would bring $500 billion worth of benefits to the developing world.[9] Nowadays, more modest figures of $100 million, or less, are cited. And people are beginning to admit that as trade increased in the 1990s, most of the gains were concentrated in the advanced economies or newly industrialized ones. Almost half of the more mixed agricultural economies actually contracted. Along with the growth of the GDP went the growth of poverty for some, and for others—notably China—growth came from policies that defied the neoliberal prescription.[10]

Still, other things being equal, freeing up trade is usually more often a good thing than a bad. Studies of trade liberalization proposed under the Uruguay round of multilateral trade negotiations, for instance, showed that it would move agricultural production from costly pesticide-intensive European farms to cheaper manure-intensive farms in the third world.[11]

And trade *restrictions* aren't always as benign as they're said to be. They can hurt communities and the environment just as often as liberalization can. In the early 1980s, for instance, the Japanese agreed to restrain the export of their cars to the United States. The object was to prevent their compact models from competing with American cars. The restrictions drove up the imports of gas-guzzlers because the bigger cars gave the manufacturers a bigger profit margin. The prescription turned out to be worse than the problem.[12]

THE TAO OF JONES

Of course, we doubt if many public prescriptions are really intended to solve problems. People certainly believe they are when they propose them. But, like so much of what goes on in a public spectacle, its favorite slogans, too, are delusional—more in the nature of placebos than propositions. People repeat them like Hail Marys because it makes them feel better.

We hear from followers of Maharishi's Transcendental Meditation that muttering "OM" raises our brain potential. And other groups have still other ways of confronting the great unknown. Confucians call it the Tao or Dao—the Way—and tell us that we should treat it reverently. Wall Street also treats the Dao reverently—the Dao Jones. And it, too, has a mantra it likes to repeat—Dow 12,000 . . . Dow 24,000 . . . Dow 36,000. . . .

Most of our beliefs about the economy—and everything else—are of this nature. They are forms of self-medication, superstitious lip service we pay to the powers of the dark, like touching wood . . . or throwing salt over your shoulder. "Stocks for the long run," "Globalization is good." We repeat slogans to ourselves, because everyone else does. It is not so much bad luck we want to avoid as being on our own. How flattering to say you "lost a bundle in semiconductors"! It makes you feel—momentarily—like a Goldman banker about to spring for a fetching blob by Robert Motherwell. We might not know a pixel from a byte and our last acquaintance with a chip might have been at Wendy's, but losing in the stock market gives us plenty of company. Whatever else it is, it's not a lonely proposition. Why it is that losing your life savings should be less painful if you have lost it in the company of one million other losers, we don't know. But mankind is first of all a herd animal and fears nothing more than not being part of the herd.

We notice, for instance, that when Americans in Detroit lose jobs to other Americans in California, they might grumble a bit. But, by and large, they accept it as part of the nature of things. They move, or retrain, or change jobs. But when they lose their jobs to Japanese in Osaka or Indians in Bangalore, then a cry goes up. Unfair trade, howl the trade unions; race to the bottom, scold the social activists; yellow—or brown—peril, shriek the xenophobes and racists. And the same thing happens on the other side of the globe. Indian companies have been drying up and polluting their own rivers for the past 50 years without too much attention from the world press. But let a multinational do it, and it rouses the wrath of the political class—many of whom until recently were partners in crime with the old polluting companies. Thundering speeches, shaven heads, strikes, bandhs, and civil disobedience become the order of the day. We do not deny that oversized corporations and corrupt bureaucrats go together like wiener and schnitzel. But we notice that people tend to be selective about exploitation. They seem to prefer being ripped off by people of their own kind. You see, finally, it's all about the herd.

Unfair trade is yet another of the dodgy slogans festooning the spectacle of globalization like tinsel slithering around a pole dancer. How can different regulations and practices in different countries constitute unfairness? Isn't it the essence of trade that different countries have different things to offer—whether cheaper labor, or better technology, or more bountiful natural resources, or more welcoming business environments? Isn't it the reason trade takes place in the first place? If all countries had exactly the same things to offer each other, there would be no reason to trade at all. But what "fair" trade advocates are really advocating, of course, is unfair trade! They want to make sure that their foreign competitors divest themselves of the very advantages that they bring to trading. It is as though Joe Frazier were to find it unfair for Muhammad Ali to "float like a butterfly" or "sting like a bee"!

The whole point of such slogans is to get the limbic system to take over from the prefrontal lobe and trigger off a reaction. Just as the robin reacts to a clump of red feathers, you stampede into action along with the rest of the herd.

Race to the bottom! goes the cry. The idea behind this is that globalization allows corporations to seek out the countries with the weakest environmental regulations and lowest labor standards, thereby making other countries reduce or even undo their regulatory standards to keep up. The nightmare scenario is one in which an endless horde of starving third world slum dwellers drag first world wages down to their level; where polluted third world cities set the standard against which first world cities have to compete.

Quite a nightmare. But is it reality or simply something that haunts the delusions of the world improvers? Econometric studies have shown that environmental regulations do not actually deter industries from relocating wherever they think they have other important advantages. In fact, there are plenty of reasons why there may actually be a race to the *top*, sometimes. Firms often want to have standardized procedures across their different locations, so they will tend to adopt the highest standard they are subject to, across the board. And they will often anticipate a move to higher standards—which are usually also more productive—and they will want to stay ahead of the curve so as not to tie themselves to obsolete technology. And, finally and importantly, they will want to safeguard their reputation with the public for environmentally sound operations.

So argues Jagdish Bhagwati, professor of economics at Columbia University.

Dr. Bhagwati's is a reasoned and reasonable defense of globalization. It is exactly what we would expect from a famous economics professor and a member of the Council on Foreign Relations, which is why we admire it deeply . . . and suspect it thoroughly. Our fellow man can be reasoned and reasonable on many occasions, but on crucial ones he tends to be neither. And that is where it counts.

Dr. Bhagwati, for example, thinks the agreements on safety in agricultural trade contained in what's called the Uruguay round of the General Agreement on Trade and Tariffs (GATT) must be grounded in scientific evidence. He gives the example of the European Union initiative to ban the sale of hormone-fed beef. Since the EU couldn't muster enough scientific proof for the ban, the World Trade Organization was bound to find the EU in violation of World Trade Organization (WTO) rules, he argues in his book, *In Defense of Globalization*.

Dr. Bhagwati objects to the EU's moratorium on the sale of genetically modified seeds and foods for the same reason. There simply isn't enough scientific evidence to warrant it, he claims. The antiglobalization crew, however, thinks that scientific proof is not essential. They think the principle of precaution should be enough, whereas Dr. Bhagwati sides with "respectable scientists," who consider the ban fearmongering.[13]

We are pleased in this case to be on the opposite side of respectable science. We have nothing against it, of course, but we admit we vastly prefer disrespectful, unrespectable science. We thoroughly enjoy the kind of science that blows wind up the skirts of pompous blowhards. But respectable scientists, we fear, are consensus mongers and organization men—only with higher IQs. That only makes them more dangerous in our eyes. The tools with which they arrive at proofs sufficient to pass peer review are so fine we fear we can hardly see them. And, like the mills of God, they grind exceeding slow. It might take them 20 years to definitely prove that genetically modified beef plays Chinese checkers with your immune system or some other aspect of your body parts. By then, the beef might have set off a plague as widespread and deadly as AIDS. We will then have more proof than we want in the mortuaries. That is to say, when it comes to something as important as the health of the human race, averages, means, proofs, and evidence should not be captive solely to Dr. Bhagwati's standard of reasonableness. Why? Because when the worst-case scenario is as awful as an international plague, then the reasonable position actually becomes the most unreasonable. The unexpected, low-risk event may be just what should occupy center stage in people's minds.

BLACK SWANS AND FAT TAILS

What we are talking about is fat tails—events that lie so far outside the normal course of events that we tend to push them equally far away in our consciousness, events that are so devastating that when they do occur they cancel out every other consideration. There may be only a very slim chance that the human race will be wiped off the face of the earth, it is true. But it would probably pay us to take that slim chance very seriously.

Why? The reason lies in the deceptive nature of thought—in the way we think about risk. Our thinking has a huge blind spot; it seems to be skewed toward only *certain* sorts of risk—the risk involved in physical events, where what ends up happening depends on only a few, stable factors. Those events follow what statisticians call a normal distribution, which is a graph of the frequency of events that is curved like a bell. There is a big hump in the middle of the graph, where the average falls, and two tails on either side, where the less normal things happen. Physical phenomena like noise or the movement of photons can be modeled by a bell curve. In a bell curve, the normal event is the one you are likely to get most of the time, the one right in the middle of the hump. The abnormal event, the big outlier that you don't see coming, is out in the tapering ends of the curve. It's the event that happens so rarely that it isn't even reckoned with most of the time.

Now, the normal distribution (the Gaussian, it's called) is the most widely used family of distributions in statistics. A whole lot of statistical tests are based on the assumption of normality. As a result, we tend to think that it works everywhere and for all sorts of things. But in fact it doesn't, especially when you are talking about human society, where many activities, like stock trading, don't take place in a predictable, orderly fashion. Why? Because they are performed by human beings, who are unpredictable and *dis*orderly.

Human beings—no matter what economists tell us—*don't* maximize their advantage. They foul up. They change their minds in the middle of things. They get carried away by what the other fellow is doing. In the market, that means that a big jump from the normal doesn't happen once in thousands of years, which is what you'd expect from the bell curve, but every three or four years, instead. In fact, if the bell curve followed the way things really work in society, then the ends of the curve would be bumpy with fat tails.

Nassim Nicholas Taleb is someone who is obsessed with big, unpredictable events. He calls them Black Swans (or, more technically, "Type-2 randomness" or "large-impact events with small but incomputable probabilities").[14]

The crash of 1987, for instance, was a Black Swan. In the Gaussian world, it could only have occurred "every several billion lifetimes of the universe," or, in other words, *never*, because it was what statisticians call 20 standard deviations from the mean. But, in fact, Black Swans occur much more commonly than we think, since they are not the result of the *addition* of lots of small effects—as most normal distributions are—but the result of the *multiplication* of effects. Black Swans result from an *exponential* increase of small effects. This means that there is no inherent limit to how high—or low—a stock price can go. There is also no reason why a big jump shouldn't occur much more frequently than the bell curve lets us believe. Stock prices, in this regard, resemble sales of books. Both are examples of informational cascades, where each actor imitates those who have chosen previously and, all together, act like a herd. Since it is based on very little information, herding behavior is inherently fragile and can stop abruptly and head in the opposite direction very swiftly on the basis of even a small amount of additional information.

Human behavior, in other words, frequently conforms to what statisticians call a "power-law distribution," where instead of the bell shape of the Gaussian curve, you get most of the activity bunched up at one extreme.

Power-law distributions lie behind the well-known 80–20 rule, which predicts that 80 percent of productivity in a company will be done by 20 percent of employees, or, to take a more dismal example, that about 80 percent of crimes will be committed by 20 percent of criminals.[15]

Power laws explain why the rich get richer. The reason they do is that human beings are extremely imitative—money attracts more money; the spotlight follows the famous, not the obscure; we pick what everyone else picks. Unto those who have, more will be given, as even the Gospel tells us.

And what's really odd is that when people are confronted with more choices, they become even *more*—rather than less—imitative. It's as if having more choices makes it *harder*, not easier, to choose. Complexity overwhelms the brain, forcing it to revert to habit, instinct, or intuition.

But that is only part of the problem. Our reactions to risk are skewed in other ways, as well. And here, we turn once more to economist Steven Levitt. Levitt has argued that we tend to rate risks that strike us vividly as more dangerous than those that strike us less vividly. For example, we consider having a gun in the house far more dangerous to children than, say, a swimming pool, but in fact children die at the rate of 1 per 11,000 swimming pools, but only at the rate of 1 for more than a million guns. There is even a formula to express this emotional component of risk assessment: Risk Equals Hazard Plus Outrage (or dread). What it means is that people tend to exaggerate high-outrage risks like mad cow disease and terrorism, while tending to ignore low-outrage risks like kitchen infections, although these may in fact be far more dangerous.[16]

Risk assessment is also affected by the point in time at which we make the assessment. What people think they want, what they actually choose in the heat of the moment, and how they afterwards *think* they chose are quite different things. And none of them is easily measured.

According to psychologist Daniel Kahneman—who won the Nobel Prize in economics in 2002—given a choice of either getting a guaranteed $1,000 or a 50/50 chance of getting $2,500 (or no gain), people tend to prefer the safe $1,000. However, between either a certain loss of $1,000 or a 50/50 chance of a $2,500 loss (or no loss), the same people prefer taking the 50 percent chance. That is, they are risk-averse in seeking gains, but risk-seeking in reducing their losses.[17]

Let's put it this way: Most people aren't prepared to place a risky bet to make lots of money. But they are willing to take a risk of losing a lot of money if they think there is a chance they can keep from losing anything. In the market, that translates into a liking for small, steady gains, even though in making those gains, there may be a risk of losing everything in a crash.

What such distortions suggest is that we can never really get a handle on risk in a purely mathematical or statistical way. It simply doesn't work that way. We are fooled not just by the randomness of the universe, but equally by the unpredictability of our own emotional makeup.

Take legendary trader Victor Niederhoffer. In 1997, he bet on the very large chance of making small amounts of money on an options trade, if the market continued roughly as it was. As long as the market didn't do anything very abnormal, there was only a small chance of his losing a huge amount. But then came October 27, 1997, and the market fell 8 percent. Niederhoffer lost $130 million—and counting.

Several years later, after a painful and slow climb back from that loss, Niederhoffer, who had thought long and hard about his mistake, decided he was ready for a safe gamble again. After all, lightning doesn't strike twice in the same place, he reckoned. It was the fall of 2001 when he placed his new options trade. Everything seemed fine, at first. Then, one morning in September, two planes hurtled into the towers of the World Trade Center.[18]

ON THE CLEVERNESS OF CAULIFLOWER

Still, just because a fat-tail disaster might smack us in the face at any moment, does that mean we are in favor of more government regulations on food production?

Here, we are forced to hem and haw. Government regulation tends to be ineffective in many cases. And since regulators are frequently drawn from the same industries they are supposed to be regulating, we think they tend to be counterproductive in all the others.

So, we are neither prescribing policy nor proscribing it. We are merely grumbling in our curmudgeonly way that we liked the old

genetically unmodified world better. We have no desire to eat straw-
berries armed against frostbite with herring genes or cauliflower with
an IQ higher than ours. We like our food au naturel, unrefurbished,
unhedged, and in default drive. Unless it is communion wine, any
transformations of nature need to pass the smell test first. We need to
be protected from them, as surely as we need to be protected from
bad checks, assault, murder, and another Michael Jackson trial.

You see our problem, dear reader? We would like the state to
stop telling us what to do—whether it is in airports, in our schools,
or in our bedrooms—but we dig in our heels equally at efforts by
global corporations to improve our water, our potatoes, or our *boeuf
bourguignon* at the expense of our local culture and with subsidies from
our tax dollars.

This is unlikely to win us any popularity contests today when
there are only two acceptable positions on globalization: It is A Very
Good Thing. Or, it is A Very Bad Thing. But slogans don't always
do the trick. Each problem has to be thought through in its own
terms. Not only is globalization neither entirely good nor entirely
bad, it is not even one single thing. It is several. It is about free trade
and costly subsidies, about gourmet water and junk food, about hard
capital and soft drinks—all of which have their own reasons for being
and their own consequences, and all of which are mislabeled, poorly
understood, and constantly confused. In fact, the only thing you can
be sure of about globalization is that it provokes extremes of two
emotions in the mob—greed and fear. In other words, the only thing
that is certain about it is that it is a public spectacle.

DEVELOPMENTALLY DISABLED

Naturally, like all public spectacles, globalization is wrapped up in a
huge amount of cant. For instance, if you are a poor country, you
are supposed to take to the thing as eagerly as a diabetic to insulin.
Now, if it was just a matter of freeing up trade between countries,
we would nod our heads in agreement. The exchange of goods and

services between people is, and always has been, a good thing. It is, so far as we can see, a far better way of getting what you want than hitting your fellow man over the head. But for it to really work, trade—like driving—needs a set of rules everyone follows; otherwise you are liable to crash or be run over.

And this is where it gets complicated. Because it turns out that many of the rules of global trade are set by the very people who are weighing down the market with all sorts of subsidies, sweetheart deals, perks, pork, and privileges, in the first place.

Take the World Bank, which is in the business of telling countries what they need to do to play the global trade game. In the lumpen imagination, the World Bank is not too different from the local neighborhood savings and loan—a kind of multicultural version of the friendly bank in *It's a Wonderful Life*. But the real World Bank is headed up not by Jimmy Stewart but by people like Paul Wolfowitz, a man whom his best friend wouldn't call a soft touch. Confirmed as the bank's boss in 2005, Wolfowitz immediately proclaimed he was on a mission of mercy:

"Helping the poorest of the world to lift themselves out of poverty is a noble mission or, as former Secretary of State George Shultz said, 'a beautiful mission.' "[19]

But, the Sisters of Charity do not have to worry about the competition. Wolfowitz has been one of Washington's biggest hawks, ever since the days when he argued for the use of tactical nuclear weapons in Europe. To this day, he likes to praise Indonesia's Suharto, who in his 32-year reign looted $30 billion from the public treasury and turned his country into one of the most corrupt in the world. Of course, on second thought, that might be the perfect resume for the Bank.[20]

After all, the World Bank has a bit of a track record when it comes to getting and spending, not to mention laying waste.

We put before you two countries:

Both are Asian. One has little land, most of it eroded hillsides. Its population density, already the highest in the world, is exacerbated by heavy immigration. It has to import all its raw materials, water, and oil. It receives no foreign aid whatsoever and until recently was still a Western colony. It has an authoritarian government.

The other is also densely populated, but it has lots of arable land and natural resources. Free from colonial rule, it has also been the recipient of about $55 billion in aid over the past 40 years. It is a functioning democracy and the World Bank's pet project.[21]

Which do you bet would be better off? It seems to be a no-brainer—the second one, of course.

But wait—the country without resources is Hong Kong, today routinely at the top of lists of the best Asian cities in which to live and do business; and the well-endowed one is India, after 60 years of independence still one of the poorest countries in the world.

"The standard of living in Hong Kong had multiplied more than tenfold in forty years, while the standard of living in Calcutta has improved hardly at all," says John Templeton.[22]

After nearly half a century of centrally planned economic development, India's annual per capita income remains somewhere between $500 and $3,400 a year, depending on the type of calculation you use and whom you are talking to.[23]

A per capita income of around $750 puts India—the fourth largest economy in the world—in the company of sub-Saharan Africa. Meanwhile, Hong Kong has a per capita income of over $20,000 a year, on par with first world countries.[24]

What on earth is wrong here?

DO-GOODING DOO-DOO

We are not experts, dear reader, but when we study the matter, this is what we come up with: From 1960 to 1985 the United States, 13 other developed countries, and institutions like the World Bank accounted for 85 to 90 percent of total aid to India, the United States donating 50 percent of the total in 1961–1962 with a decline to 1 percent by 1988–1989, when the World Bank donated 65 percent of the total.[25]

What that tells us is that the World Bank has gradually taken over the role of the United States in sending aid to India. That alone should make anyone a trifle suspicious. Countries have no friends—they have only interests, goes the saying. What interest could the United States—a republic-turned-empire—have with the World Bank, the world's most notorious financial busybody? Oh what, indeed!

"I have never known much good done by those who affected to trade for the public good," was canny old Adam Smith's take on the matter.[26]

But the World Bank affects to do just that. It is one of the leading arbiters of the rules by which trade takes place in the world. And, making a sticky situation exponentially stickier, it is also in the business of making grants and loans to countries. Think of it like having an umpire at a baseball match who, in between calling outs, flings on his gear and rushes out to the field to bat. Even if he means to in good faith, he is unlikely to do either task very well. And all the rushing around is liable to trip up everyone else in sight.

But is it really in good faith? How does the World Bank set the trade rules? Not with the idea of protecting all the players equally—as traffic regulations protect drivers equally. Instead, the trade rules are written to suit all sorts of agendas that seem to have nothing to do with free trade. There are rules that let companies doing one sort of business get government subsidies; there are other rules that tell you what you can or cannot trade freely; there are agents to be paid off; bureaucrats to be bribed; taxes to be paid or passed along, or shucked off altogether. Free trade is anything but free. Instead it is mixed up with empire building, corporate subsidies, misguided humanitarian goals, *baksheesh*, and a hundred other irrelevant considerations. Whoever has the muscle can get the rules he wants.

So when we find that one of the major players in the global trade business is also in charge of the global *aid* business, we tend to look pop-eyed. We start wondering what sort of trade—or aid—is taking place.

And we get our answer:

Trade? Western import restrictions on third world products are not only unfair to Western consumers, they reduce third world national incomes by about twice as much as what those countries receive in direct foreign aid. What the right hand—foreign aid—giveth, the left hand—import barriers —taketh away.[27]

Aid? As one observer says, "Billions of dollars, collected from middle-class taxpayers of the West, have 'aided' Third World elites to possess grand estates, private zoos, classic car collections, and Swiss bank accounts."[28]

But, the free moola has also "aided" first world corporations, larding them with perks that have turned them into gigantic monopolies that crush competitors and consumers both abroad and at home. When the money goes as loans, it ends up grinding down taxpayers in the third world, who get to foot the bill even if they never see a dime in benefits.

And, when the aid goes as a grant, it is even worse, because it can be politicized more easily. The grant giver gets to pull the strings—he gets military bases, preferential treatment, votes in the UN, or even public assets on the cheap. It's an endless bonanza.

Even when it's not mixed up so directly with trade and credit, foreign aid often does not benefit countries, as its advocates claim. To begin with, how do you benefit a country, dear reader? We scratch our heads because we have no idea. We understand giving someone a few dollars. That would benefit them, we know, because they can now use the money to buy themselves a pair of trousers or a drink or whatever else they need at the moment. But does a whole country benefit when those same dollars are put into the till of useless hacks in various world capitals? As near as we can tell, the only ones who benefit are the lazy hacks. And the more money they get, they more power they have to squeeze the life out of everyone else in their countries.

Some of our goodest doers are knee-deep in this doo-doo.

Until 1950, Indian food production had been growing on track, with steady prices and limited importing. But India's rulers— steeped in the theories reigning in many American and British economic departments—were in love with Soviet planning. With its second five-year plan, the government began a program of heavy industrialization. As money in the public and even in the private sector was steered into industry, agriculture became starved of capital, say some scholars. Domestic food production fell, and farm laborers fled to the cities, looking for the jobs that were supposed to be created there by the new industrial plans. As food became short and the government turned to foreign governments for help, the United States sent food aid under P.L. 480. It was aid in the sense that the Indian government could pay for it either in rupees or in credit. And yes, it was critically needed. But what was the effect? The domestic price of wheat had to fall to match the lower-cost imported food. Farmers cutting back on wheat production went bankrupt. Because of the way the aid was structured, the shipments also led to deficit financing (the use of newly created money to finance budget disbursements) that accounted for around 35 percent of total deficit financing between 1962 and 1971. As a direct result, India's inflation rate shot up by 9.8 percent a year.[29] Meanwhile, the parthenium weed, which snuck into the country with the wheat shipments, morphed into an invasive species and took over millions of acres of productive land. This ended up making Indian agriculture dependent on foreign imports and credit until the late 1970s. Then, perhaps as a result of increases in productivity from the green revolution, food self-sufficiency was finally reached. But again, the picture is muddy. According to many, research into high-yielding crops actually accounted for less than 2 percent of the foreign aid India received in those years. The results were a vindication more of small investments in private agriculture than of foreign aid. In any case, since India signed up with the global trade game in the 1990s, it has again taken to foreign food imports and credits.[30]

What makes the World Bank an expert on aid or trade, with a record like this?

And what makes it an expert on the free market, when its stated goals are straight out of the Soviet Gosplan?

"The Bank would prefer to . . . base its financing on a national development program, provided that it is properly worked out in terms of projects by which the objectives of the program are to be attained," states the Bank's own annual report.[31]

That means the Bank is willing to hand out money to countries *only* if they pursue national development programs. You wouldn't be far wrong, then, if you said that the World Bank bribed most of the third world to stick with top-down central planning, with the sorry results we see today. The tender mercies of the wicked are cruel indeed.

In 1989–1990, after 40 years of foreign aid, Latin America ended up with a foreign debt of $430 billion and sub-Saharan Africa with per capita incomes lower than in the 1970s.

The World Bank pampered India's central planners and fed one of the world's biggest, most inefficient, and most corrupt public sectors. How inefficient? In 1988–1989, almost half of India's 222 biggest government companies sustained losses. The result was a central government deficit five times as big, in relative numbers, as the U.S. budget deficit.[32]

None of this is a revelation. It's public knowledge. So we wonder why those giant brains at the World Bank are such slow learners that they keep repeating their mistakes. Over the years, they've done so much damage, you could even be forgiven for wondering why they are still calling the shots on global free trade.

It boils down to one thing—global free trade as a theory preached by economists is a little different from how it actually plays out on the ground. And, when you have one part of the mob talking about theory and the other part arguing about practice, you get contradiction, cacophony, and claptrap.

Between do-gooding and doing good there is all the difference.

Between the global posturing of the World Bank, poverty programs, and humanitarian interventions on the one hand and the quiet goodness of human beings on the other yawns a Grand Canyon of self-delusion and bungling.

Between Dr. W at the World Bank and Dr. V at Aravind is more than an alphabet.

In the United States, it costs about $1,650 to perform a cataract operation. You wouldn't expect many such operations in a country such as India, where per capita income is less than $1,000. But in India today, there are five hospitals that perform more than 180,000 eye operations each year. Each operation costs only about $100. Most of the patients pay nothing. All this is thanks to Dr. Govindappa Venkataswamy, who set up his first 12-bed Aravind eye hospital in his brother's home in Madurai in 1976. At the time, he was already 57 years old.[33]

Dr. V set out to be an obstetrician, but he was crippled by rheumatoid arthritis at an early age. He spent two years recovering. Because he could no longer deliver babies he turned to the study of ophthalmology, designing special tools that suited his hands. He found that he could do eye operations faster and more simply and more cheaply than they had been done before.

The inspiration, he says, came from the way McDonald's operated its franchises. He first discovered the golden arches at the age of 55, and the discovery changed his life.

"In America, there are powerful marketing devices to sell products like Coca-Cola and hamburgers," he says. "All I want to sell is good eyesight, and there are millions of people who need it. . . . If Coca-Cola can sell billions of sodas and McDonald's can sell billions of burgers, why can't Aravind sell millions of sight-restoring operations . . . ? With sight, people could be freed from hunger, fear, and poverty."

"In the third world, a blind person is referred to as 'a mouth without hands,'" Dr. V says. "He is detrimental to his family and to the whole village. But all he needs is a 10-minute operation. One week the bandages go on, the next week they go off. High bang for the buck. But people don't realize that the surgery is available, or that they can afford it, because it's free. We have to sell them first on the need."

The hospital picks up the tab for those who can't pay. Paying customers are charged 50 rupees (about $1) for a consultation.

"A-class" rooms ($3 per day) are private; "B-class" rooms ($1.50 per day) have a shared toilet; "C-class" rooms ($1 per day) are a mat on the floor. Paying customers can have surgery with stitches ($110) or surgery without stitches ($120).

Since Dr. V began, his eye hospitals have restored sight in more than one million people in India. Even with such tiny revenues per patient, Aravind makes a profit, with a gross margin of 40 percent. One operation is completed; another is begun right away. A very efficient and productive enterprise, Aravind now does more eye surgeries than any other provider in the world, though it accepts no government grants. The hospitals are totally self-supporting. Nor does Dr. V even try to hustle a profit from the enterprise for himself. He lives on a pension, taking no money out of Aravind. In Tamil Nadu state, where his main hospital is located, the incidence of blindness is 20 percent below the rate in the rest of India.

"Consultants talk of 'the poor,'" he says. "No one at Aravind does. 'The poor' is a vulgar term. Would you call Christ a poor man?"

Part Five

The Bubble Kings

CHAPTER 12

FIN DE BUBBLE

Paper is poverty,...it is only the ghost of money, and not money itself.

—**Thomas Jefferson**

WHERE THE BUCK STARTS

In early 2006, in the *Daily Mail* in London, appeared the story of Mark McDonald, 43, of Norfolk, who suffered what the paper called "death by credit." Like your authors, the man was a writer. Like your authors, he was not particularly well paid. But unlike your authors, he had a great number of credit cards. His debt rose to about $120,000—on which he made minimum payments as long as he was able. But the burden of it got to be too great, and the father of two decided he would rather place himself on the rails in front of the 7:09 to London instead of remaining in the ranks of the indebted.

"Mr. McDonald's death was the fifth known suicide due to debt in the past two years," said the *Mail*. How can you account for such a bizarre action? How can you model it? How can you predict it?

McDonald's wife blasted the credit industry: "They are just interested in making money," said the woman. But who isn't? And five suicides in two years seems like a small price to pay for the benefits of unlimited consumer credit on which the whole grand tower of early twenty-first-century civilization was built.

The *Daily Mail* report had a certain fin de bubble tone to it. Twice as many people were calling for credit counseling that year as the year before, the paper noted. Twenty-five thousand picked up the phone in one month. What's more, for every decisive writer like McDonald there must be thousands of wishy-washy plumbers and doughy bakers who couldn't make up their minds. They muddle through, hoping that their debts will never catch up with them.

But these days, even muddling through is not predictable or reasonable, for wherever people stand, they are not far enough away to escape contagion from the great public spectacle of money.

The Buck Starts Here was a sign that sat on Alan Greenspan's desk when he was still head honcho at the Federal Reserve. It was the maestro's response to Harry S. Truman's famous quip, "The buck stops here." Truman's line acknowledged that he bore the ultimate responsibility for what happened on his watch.

But Greenspan's desktop motto has another sort of punch line hidden in it. As a young man, Alan Greenspan had written a celebrated essay explaining why paper dollars—unbacked by gold—were a swindle and a nuisance. Yet, more of these dollars started life while he was the nation's top banker than under all the other Fed chiefs combined. It was a remarkable feat. But he accepted no responsibility for it. Nor was anyone rubbing his nose in it. There was no "it" in which to rub. Yet.

So, to most of the world, the former Fed chairman's achievements still had a fair and fetching look to them in the early spring of 2006. The dollar still had street cred and Mr. Greenspan was still a genius.

We step forward now neither to praise the man nor to bury him but to marvel at one of the grandest public spectacles of all time—an epic of massive betrayal disguised as public-spirited action, of bullheaded absurdity masquerading as enlightened science—a tale as sweeping and panoramic as *Ben Hur* or *Gone with the Wind*, but with all the decent characters removed; a monumental farce, with a cast of fools and knaves as entertaining as those in *Family Guy*.

Every public spectacle, we have noted, begins with a lie, progresses into farce, and ends in disaster. The investment markets furnish countless examples; indeed, they are perfectly suited to them. We say that not in jest but in earnest admiration at how the markets, the financial industry, and the free press all work together in faultless harmony to deceive investors and bring them to do just the wrong thing at precisely the wrong moment.

So, let us begin at the end. Or at least at the end as it is today.

In 2007, life, as we have come to enjoy it, has been one long continuous boom. Stocks have been rising since before the Internet was invented. And the economy has enjoyed its longest continuous period of growth in nearly 40 years. Of course, this long boom—from the end of World War II to the present—has had its moments of crisis. But let us first focus on the period during which Mr. Alan Greenspan ruled the Fed—the 18-year period from 1987 to January 2006.

In the few instances—the Long Term Capital Management collapse, the Asian currency crisis, and the Y2K panic, for example—where prosperity seemed threatened, Mr. Greenspan stepped up to the plate and hit a grand slam. Investors came to expect it. Crisis equals Greenspan to the rescue. Investors regarded Mr. Greenspan's powers as godlike. *Fortune* magazine ran a cover story called "In Greenspan We Trust."[1]

Senator John McCain suggested appointing him to head the Fed not only for life, but for the afterlife, too. Greenspan may not have been able to walk on water, but it was widely believed that he could multiply the loaves and fishes.

THE TEMPTATIONS OF ST. ALAN

Alan Greenspan had been on the job only a few weeks when he was put to his first test. The crash of 1987 came as a shock to world stock markets and to Greenspan, too. The man had run an economic forecasting business—notoriously badly. If economic forecasting were driving an automobile, you would not have wanted to climb into the front seat with the maestro.[2] He drove blind and head-on—into financial potholes, stock crashes, bubbles, busts, and recessions.

On Monday, October 19, 1987, the Dow Jones Industrial Average fell 22.6 percent. A similar drop today would take off about 3,000 points, but back then, the drop began from a much lower level. The Dow was nearly 2,200 on Black Monday, when the crash took the stuffing out of the market and reduced stockholder wealth by about half a trillion dollars in a single day.

Markets all over the world skidded, too—even those without program trading or portfolio insurance. Australia dropped 41.8 percent. Hong Kong went down 45.8 percent by the end of the month. Some people became completely unhinged; at least one client came into his stockbroker's office and started shooting. Markets closed early, and surviving brokers locked their doors.

Alan Greenspan reacted quickly, nipping a couple of basis points off the federal funds rate. In retrospect, it was unnecessary. When the crash was over and the dust had settled, investors quickly recovered their nerve. Within five weeks, stock prices were in a new bull market, one that would, once again, take them up past 2,500 and then push on to the 12,000 mark 12 years later.

Those were happy times; the nation was at peace, more or less. The nation was prosperous. George Bush, the elder, was in the White House. (Note: This was the Bush whose biggest foreign policy blunder was throwing up on the prime minister of Japan.)

Greenspan did not understand that inflation was moderating and lending rates were in a long-term downtrend. Instead, the new chauffeur at the Fed put up the convertible roof, put his foot on the accelerator, and took off in the wrong direction. When he assumed the Fed's highest post, he began tightening interest rates, a process that was only interrupted, briefly, by his reaction to the 1987 crash. The fed funds rate went from 6.5 percent when he took office on August 11, 1987, to a high of 10.7 percent in 1989.[3] Higher borrowing costs probably produced the recession of 1990. The elder Bush believed Alan Greenspan had cost him the election. And Hillary Clinton seemed to think so, too. After the vote went to her husband, she chose to take a position next to Greenspan at the inauguration. The triumvirate ruled the nation for the next eight years. Greenspan had done a U-turn. He never looked back.

On almost the very same day Bill Clinton took office, the Tokyo stock market collapsed. In the 1990s, the poor Japanese, desperate to get the magic back, tried everything, including giving away money at zero interest. That created the carry trade, in which speculators borrowed from the land of Pokemon at very low interest rates and placed the money where it would produce a higher return. In the 1990s, the cash was often placed in the U.S. stock market. Since 2000, emerging markets and property have been favorite investments. More recently, U.S. Treasuries have been favored.

When Alan Greenspan came into the Fed, the Dow was just over 2,500 and a conventional 30-year mortgage rate was over 10 percent. When he left on January 31, 2006, the Dow was nearly 11,000 and 30-year mortgage rates were around 6 percent.[4]

Where exactly the trend toward lower rates will end is still not clear. But even if rates fall further, it is unlikely they will do so for the same pleasant reasons, or with the same beneficent results, that greeted Alan Greenspan. Investors who were worried and skittish in 1987 were complacent and confident 20 years later. Those who panicked when the Dow hit 2,500 were serene with it at 11,000. The global credit derivatives market barely existed in 1987; by the first half of 2006, it had risen to $370 trillion, a jump of 24 percent, compared to 5 percent in the second half of 2005—the largest since records started being kept.[5] And homeowners who wondered how they were going to pay off their $50,000 mortgages in the 1980s now borrow $200,000 with no intention of ever paying it off.

Why? It is simple. The central bank can make money either easier to get or harder to get. An increase in the fed funds rate, for example, makes it relatively harder to borrow money. Prevailing interest rates thus operate as a kind of speed governor on the economy.

At any given time, people contemplate all manner of spending. The significant calculation can be reduced to two questions—what will it cost, and what will it return?

Consumers focus mostly on the first question—how much will it cost?—and the corollary, can I afford it? Businesspeople, however, also look ahead at the return on borrowed money. If the return exceeds the cost of funds—with a margin for error—it makes sense to borrow and spend. Thus, the lower the rates, the more projects make sense, the faster the economy moves ahead, and the happier everyone is—for a while.

At the height of the dot-com bubble, venture capitalists and publicly traded businesses both found that they could borrow outrageous amounts of money—the telecoms, for example, took up 40 percent of all newly issued bonds between 1997 and 1999. Amazon.com alone borrowed $2.2 billion, without a tested business model. Growth and momentum were all anyone cared about, not credit quality or balance sheets. Even speculative junk—at the peak of the mania—was taken up with coupons as low as 7.5 percent. Said one telecom strategist later, "There were 14 companies that, [in] 1996, were worth about $100 billion. Four years later, during the bubble, they were worth about $1.4 trillion. Now they're back under $200 billion. So they went up a trillion, then down a trillion—in about four years."[6]

Greenspan's theory was that by carefully controlling the cost of credit and the money supply, he could avoid serious economic downturns. But, the Fed chief couldn't change anything that really mattered—he couldn't erase excess capacity or mortgage debt or Asian competition, nor raise U.S. wages. All he could do was to make money easier to get, and—as we will soon explain—he could do that only by resorting to a kind of fraud.

But investors gambled that Mr. Greenspan would turn the wheel or push on the brakes at the very moment it was most needed. Hadn't *Time* magazine put Greenspan on its cover, along with Robert Rubin and Larry Summers, with the headline, "Committee to Save the World"—with no trace of humor?[7]

In January 2000, when the NASDAQ cracked, the world lifted up its eyes unto the Potomac, where the great man sat.

WRECK OF THE TECH

Press reports said that the most powerful man on the face of the earth—indeed, more powerful than any asleep in its bowels, too—spent an hour in the tub every day.

Perhaps, were it not for its womblike comfort, he might have panicked, for he must have realized that over the first 13 years of his reign he had created the biggest debt bubble the world had ever seen. But a debt bubble lasts only as long as people are willing to spend more than they can afford. From 1982 to 1990, Japanese consumers spent like crazy. But then the group feel of the Japanese shifted inexplicably to thrift, and the Japanese markets did not recover their animal sprits for at least 16 years—and maybe not even then. What if the same thing happened in the United States? What if Americans turned into Japanese—working hard, saving their money, paying off their debts?[8]

If that were to happen, Alan Greenspan's aura would pop as fast as the bubble itself. Instead of enjoying the whole world's esteem in the final years of his career, he would be regarded as an old fool. And yet, if he could just pull off another save—as he had in 1998—his career would end on a note so high even the dogs wouldn't hear it. "This *is* a lot like 1998," he must have thought to himself, with a shiver. "And what did we do? We did what we always do," he reflected, perhaps running a little more hot water into the tub, "introduce more liquidity; it always works."

"We know where Alan Greenspan is headed," wrote Robert S. Salomon Jr. in *Forbes*, "down the rate-cutting path, potentially leading to a record number of mortgage refinancings and other benefits."

He was right.

As Jim Cramer put it:

"Now that Greenspan has taken his foot off the brake and begun to force interest rates down, you want exposure to the stock market. You have the Fed—and history—totally on your side."

He was right, too.

ALAN, THE TECHNICOLOR TURNCOAT

Unbelievably, our hero, Alan Greenspan, was once a bright young man facing a modest career as a jazz saxophonist and even more modest prospects as a gold bug and member of Ayn Rand's small, gabby circle of objectivists in New York.

In 1966, he even wrote:

> The financial policy of the welfare state requires that there be no way for the owners of wealth to protect themselves. This is the shabby secret of the welfare statists' tirades against gold.[9]

But neither clearheaded polemics nor saxophone riffs nor gold buggery pay very well. And so, our hero decided that rather than fight the statists, he would join them.

And thus did Alan Greenspan turn into one of the most powerful central planners in history since Joseph in the Old Testament became the Pharaoh's second in command.

Then, in 2001, after 18 fat years, the American economic Nile began to run dry and, unlike Joseph, Alan had not encouraged saving during the bountiful years. He had made that one remark about "irrational exuberance," true, but then he recanted. No need to worry, he said, and no need to save—future harvests would always be rich and full. Worse, he nurtured the myth that he, Alan Greenspan, could control the great river himself. Through the hocus-pocus of the central bankers' arts he would be able to restore the waters to their former level. He knew that this was not actually so, but he hoped the masses would keep believing it until the river recovered on its own.

Meanwhile, the drought began and the granaries emptied out. Those most exposed to the risk of drought—the dot-com investors—took the hugest losses. They were at the margins of the market, not down in the rich, fertile bottomlands of the Dow. And then came September 11, 2001; terrorists from desert lands afar struck the homeland of Pharaoh's great empire. Now the global capitalist system was in danger. This was no time to worry about moral hazards; this was the time for action!

MR. BUBBLES

It was perhaps because he had been dozing among slippery bubbles that the chief of the world's chief central bank had come to believe that the basic pattern of nature could be thus overturned or postponed. Mr. Greenspan decided that the solution to a bear market and recession caused by too much credit, was—even more credit!

He must have hardly waited to dry himself off that day in January 2001 when the Fed began cutting rates like a lumberjack at a chainsaw contest. Down they came ... faster than ever in history—a full 475 basis points over the next 12 months.

And it worked! Now, the Committee to Save the World was history—it was Greenspan who had saved the world single-handedly. He had defeated the business cycle.

That was the amazing thing about the recession of 2001–2002. A recession usually corrects the excesses of a boom—which is why it is sometimes called a correction. People tighten their belts, reduce spending, and rebuild their savings. But in 2001–2002 consumers just kept on borrowing and spending. If this was a correction, it corrected nothing.

Was this a new era, with perpetual booms never followed by recessions ... two steps forward and none back ... gain without pain ... Easter without Good Friday? Or was there another explanation?

The gaming tables of the pros were enticing the widows and orphans into the casino. Now, even the little guys could draw aces. They, too, could arbitrage interest rates—borrowing cheap money against their homes to pay off credit card bills. Lured by the lower lending rates, the poor mom-and-pop patsies, reached for the new credit like subway bums for free drinks. They sank further into debt but they still kept spending. And, since their houses were rising in price, they could borrow and spend even more—putting an army of real estate agents, kitchen installers, appraisers, and financiers to work, as well. Thus was the Great American Bubble reborn and sustained ... and thus, too, was the Great Bubble Maker's day of judgment deferred.

We do not know what accolade history will accord Mr. Greenspan. But Queen Elizabeth announced that she would grant him a knighthood; and even the French enrolled him in the *Legion d'Honneur*.[10]

NOTHING FAILS LIKE SUCCESS

Greenspan was a success, but a successful central banker can be truly dangerous, for his primary mission is to control the value of the currency. A casual reading of that sentence should not leave the unwary reader with a misapprehension. We repeat—a central banker must *control* the currency; but he mustn't *protect* it. That is to say, his primary mission is to control the rate of its destruction.

For, modern central banking, like bank robbing, is a nefarious métier. But while Bonnie and Clyde's crime was obvious and deplorable, a central banker is often confused with an honest man. He wears a respectable suit. He carries no handgun. He could be mistaken for a university professor or Supreme Court justice.

But in fact his trade is deception. He must deceive the world into believing that the nation's currency is stable ... all the while steadily undermining it. For the central banker is fundamentally a world improver hell-bent on making the world a better place, or at least on making it *look* better. And his tool is money.

What does almost everyone want? More money. And wouldn't the world be a better place if people had more money? Yes, most people think so. But a banker, even a central banker, cannot really give people more money—not more real money. If it were not so, all the world would already be rich. Richest of all in the year 2006 would be the Zimbabweans, whose central bank endeavored to give them more money at a breathtaking rate—over 1,000 percent. At the end of the year, Zimbabweans had 10 times as much money as they started out with.[11]

Clearly, the central bank of Zimbabwe has overdone it. But if the central bank of the United States has overdone it, few seem aware of it. The secret is to give people more money, but not *so* much more that they realize that all they're getting are pieces of paper. Paper money may be a fraud, but it still represents purchasing power. When more units of it appear, people assume they have more purchasing power. And when they spend more, the merchants think there is more demand and increase production—hiring workers and ordering machinery. Pretty soon, there is a boom.

This flimflam can go on over many years until people catch on that what they have is a rise in money supply and inflation, not an increase in wealth. Then, soon, prices are rising so fast that the government may even try price controls—as Emperor Diocletian did in 301 A.D. and Richard Nixon did in 1971–1972. In extreme cases, things may degenerate beyond farce, with prices rocketing 1,000 percent per month and people racing to the store to buy something—anything—before their money depreciates. In Weimar Germany in 1927, for example, someone might send a 1,000-mark note through the mail to pay a bill, and by the time it reached its destination, the 1,000 marks would be worth less than the stamp on the envelope. That is when the public spectacle turns into a disaster. Savings are wiped out. Industry collapses. Commerce halts, as inflation soars out of control. Ministers are sacked; governments fall. The currency is recalled, zeros are taken off, or a whole new currency is introduced. Then the cycle can start all over.

MONEY HEAVEN

Partial List of Defunct Currencies—Paper and Coin

Ancient World:

Drachma, Seleucid coinage, antoninianus, as, denarius, dupondius, Roman provincial coins, sesterce, solidus, Aksumite currency, Achaemenid currency.

Modern World:

Africa: dollar—Rhodesia; escudo—Mozambique, São Tomé, and Príncipe; ekwele (ekuele)—Equatorial Guinea; florin—Kenya, Somalia, Tanzania, and Uganda; franc—French Cameroon, Morocco, and Malagasy; metical—Mozambique; peseta—Equatorial Guinea; peso—Guinea Bissau; pound—Biafra, Cameroon, Gambia, Ghana, Libya, Malawi, Nigeria, Rhodesia, South Africa, Sierra Leone, and Zambia; rial—Morocco; rupee—Kenya, Somalia, Tanzania, and Uganda; shilling—Kenya, Somalia, Tanzania, and Uganda; syli—Guinea; zaire—Zaire.

Asia: customs gold unit—China; dollar—Mongolia; South Vietnamese đồng—South Vietnam; Elymais—Iran; Timor escudo—East Timor; hwan—Korea; mohar—Nepal; pound—Israel, Jordan, and Palestine; ruble—Tajikistan; rupee—Bahrain, Burma, Kuwait, Oman, Qatar, and U.A.E.; tael—China.

Australasia: pound—Australia, Fiji, New Zealand, Samoa, Solomon Islands, and Tonga.

Latin America: austral—Argentina; cruzeiro, cruzado—Brazil; escudo—Chile; inti—Peru; peso—Bolivia, Costa Rica, Guatemala, Honduras, Nicaragua, and Paraguay; scudo—Bolivia; sucre—Ecuador.

Caribbean: pound—Bahamas, Bermuda, and Jamaica.

Europe: 15 national currencies that were replaced by the euro in 2002 daler: rigsdaler—Denmark and Norway; rijkdaalder—Netherlands; riksdaler—Sweden; speciedaler—Norway; dinar—Bosnia and Herzegovina, Croatia, and Yugoslavia; drachma—Greece; escudo—Portugal; florin—Austria; franc—France, Luxembourg, and Belgium; gulden—Germany, Holland, and Austria; karbovanets—Ukraine; lira—Vatican, Italy, and Turkey; mark—German goldmark, German papiermark, German rentenmark, German reichsmark, East German mark, and German ostmark; marka—Poland; perper—Ragusa (Dubrovnik), Serbia, and Montenegro; perun—Montenegro; peseta—Andorra; peso—Spain; real—Spain, Portugal, and Gibraltar; pound—Ireland; rubļis—Latvia; shilling—Austria; scudo—Italy, Papal States, and Malta; talonas—Lithuania; thaler—Germany, Austria, and Hungary (conventionsthaler, reichsthaler, and vereinsthaler).

United States of America: Civil War token coin, compound interest Treasury note, Confederate States of America dollar, continental, demand note, Double Eagle, Draped Bust, Eagle Educational Note, Federal Reserve Bank note, fractional currency, gold certificate, gold dollar, Half Eagle, half cent, half dime, Indian Head cent, national bank note, national gold bank note, North Carolina 1861 five cents bank note, North Carolina Confederate currency, Quarter Eagle, refunding certificate, shinplaster, silver certificate, Southern States Confederate currency, stella, trade dollar.

And more: Allied military currency, assignat, cartone, Devil's Head, Japanese Invasion Money, military payment certificate, notgeld, patacone, pengö, Vampire Note, Victory Note...

Where has all this dead money gone? It represented the wealth of nations, the fruit of centuries of labor, the patrimony of great families ... but today a thousand Roman denarii would not satisfy the Internal Revenue Service. Yet, at least we can say this for gold and silver coins: If they cannot be redeemed at the bank or with the government, they still retain some value besides their historic value—you only have to melt them down. But paper money? There is nothing left of it at all at the end, except bits of paper in museums and collections. It has all gone to money heaven.

During Mr. Greenspan's tenure, more new dollars were brought to birth than under all previous Fed chairmen—thousands of them for every new ounce of gold from under the ground. Consumers used the dollars to overspend. The trade deficit soared as Americans spent roughly $1.07 on foreign goods for every dollar's worth of goods and services they exported.

The trade deficit and rising household debt had the curious effect of increasing U.S. business profits. Because consumers were still buying things (by borrowing against booming house prices), U.S. businesses could still increase their profits even though they were reducing their wage bills by sending jobs overseas. Usually, businesses can't do that, because taken as a whole, their wage cost is also their income. In a strange way, they can increase demand for their products only by increasing wages; otherwise consumers won't have the money to buy the things they make.

The endless American demand produced a smelly, noisy, dizzying construction boom overseas, driving up prices of energy and commodities all over the world. Foreigners pumped out their own currencies and, first in Japan in the 1980s and then in China in the 1990s and 2000s, they put up factories on a monumental scale, selling the products to Americans and reinvesting the proceeds in more capacity or in more dollar assets. One analyst half-seriously calculated that at that rate of foreign accumulation, the last U.S. Treasury bond held by an American would be purchased by the People's Bank of China on February 9, 2012.[12]

The supply of paper dollars, lent, relent, and used to back new and ever more complex lending, grew like kudzu.

MACROECONOMICS FOR DUMMIES

Gross Domestic Product: Between 2000 and 2006 GDP grew at only about 1 percent to 4 percent per year.[13] (See Table 12.1.)

Money Supply: From 1987 to 2005, M3 increased from around $3.5 trillion to over $10 trillion, growing after 1994 at nearly 8 percent—more than *twice* the rate of GDP growth.

At the end of January 2000, M3 was $6.6 trillion. By the end of January 2006, it was $10.2 trillion. Though M3 reporting ceased on March 23, 2006, it is estimated that another $1 trillion of new money will be added in 2007.[14] (See Figure 12.1.)

Assets: The supply of money goosed up the value of global stocks, bonds, and other assets to $140 trillion in 2005, *three* times the size of total output of good and services that year. In 1980, the ratio of financial assets to GDP stood at about 1.5 to 1. By 2007, it was

TABLE 12.1　Annual Percentage Change in GDP, 2000–2006

Year	Current $	Chained 2005 $
2000	5.9	3.7
2001	3.2	0.8
2002	3.4	1.6
2003	4.7	2.5
2004	6.9	3.9
2005	6.3	3.2
2006	6.3	3.3

Source: Bureau of Economic Analysis, U.S. Department of Commerce, http://www.bea.gov/national/xls/gdpchg.xls.

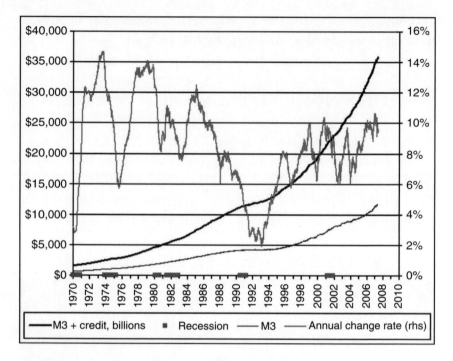

FIGURE 12.1   Growth in M3 plus Credit; 1970–2007.
Data Source: Federal Reserve.
Source: http://www.nowandfutures.comkey_stats.html.

about 4 to 1. By 2005, global cross-border capital flows topped $6 trillion, *more than double their level in 2002.* At the center, the United States took in about 85 percent of the capital exported from countries like Japan, China, and the Middle East, and bond issuance doubled.[15]

Housing: The ratio of house prices to rent recently hit all-time highs in the United States, Britain, Australia, New Zealand, France, Spain, the Netherlands, Ireland, and Belgium. In the United States, the ratio is actually 35 percent above its 1975–2000 average. In these countries, the total value of housing rose from 2000 to 2005 by over $30 trillion—to more than $70 trillion, which is about 100 percent of those countries' combined GDP. Compare this with the stock market bubbles in the late 1990s (an 80 percent rise in GDP over five years) or in the late 1920s (an increase of 55 percent in GDP).[16]

Incomes: The rich got richer at 6 percent or more a year—*double* the rate of growth of U.S. GDP. In 2004, the top 1 percent of taxpayers accounted for 16 percent of reported income, compared to 8 percent in 1980. Since 1927 the top 10 percent share in wage income has also increased strikingly.[17] (See Figure 12.2.)

In 2005, hourly wages of the average American worker were $23.10, up from 2004 ($23.03), but below 2001 ($23.77). Wages are actually lower today, adjusted for inflation, than there were in 1970. According to the Bureau of Labor Statistics, the average worker

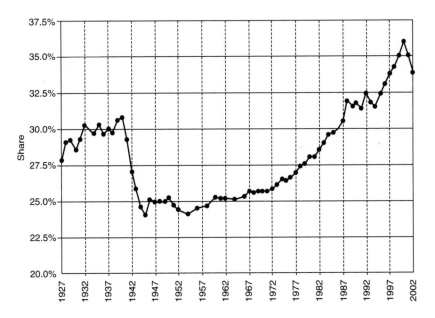

FIGURE 12.2 Top Decile Wage Income Share 1927–2002 (Including Bonuses and Profits from Exercised Stock Options).

Source: "Income Inequality in the United States, 1913–2002," Thomas Piketty, EHESS, Paris, and Emmanuel Saez, UC Berkeley and NBER, Table B2, column P90-100, p. 55 (updated version of Piketty and Saez, *Quarterly Journal of Economics* 118, no. 1, 2003, 1–39), http://elsa.berkeley.edu/~saez/piketty-saezOUP04US.pdf. Accessed June 23, 2007.

earned the equivalent of $334.60 a week in 1972. Now the figure is just $277.96. At the same time, medical costs have risen 73 percent in the past six years alone. Half of that increase comes from wage earners' pockets.[18] Consumer prices have been steadily eating into incomes. (See Figure 12.3.)

Debt: Between 1996 and 2006 householders added $5.9 trillion to their debts, most of it on their mortgages. From 1999 to 2006, household mortgage debt went from $4.4 trillion to $9.33 trillion.[19]

Mortgage equity withdrawal (MEW) by households (borrowing against the appreciated price of a home), was $156 billion in 2001; it had risen to a high of $540 billion by 2005.[20] According to the International Monetary Fund, MEW has risen from less

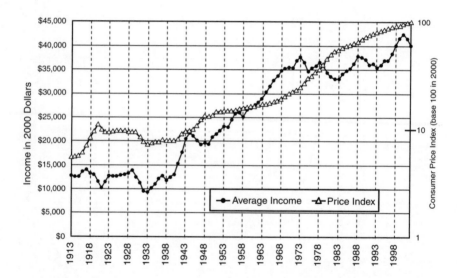

FIGURE 12.3   Average U.S. Real Income and Consumer Price Index, 1913–2002.

Source: "Income Inequality in the United States, 1913–2002," Thomas Piketty, EHESS, Paris, and Emmanuel Saez, UC Berkeley and NBER, Table A0, columns Average Income (in real 2000 dollars) and CPI (base 100 in 2000), p. 59 (updated version of Piketty and Saez, 2003, *Quarterly Journal of Economics* 118, no. 1, 2003, 1–39), http://elsa.berkeley.edu/~saez/piketty-saezOUP04US.pdf.

than 2 percent of household disposable income in the year 2000 to more than 9 percent in the third quarter of 2005.[21]

From 1999 to 2007, household debt went up more than all the debt that households had previously accumulated in the 220-year history of the United States. From 1999 to 2006 consumer credit outstanding, too, rose from $1.6 trillion to about $2.5 trillion.[22] Consumer credit went from less than 13 percent of GDP in the 1960s and 1970s to 18 percent now. Meanwhile, the personal savings rate collapsed from around 7.5 percent of income to below zero, and the aggregate national savings rate (which includes the public sector and corporations) went from 13 percent in the 1960s to just 0.8 percent in 2005.[23] (See Figure 12.4.)

Foreign Ownership: In 1989, the federal debt was around $2.7 trillion. Under George Bush, it has risen faster than under any other

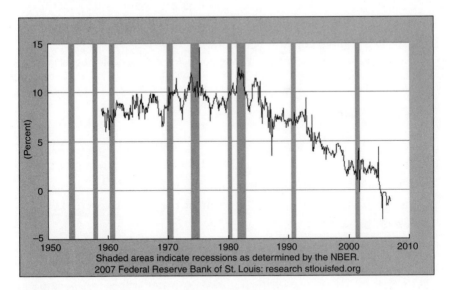

FIGURE 12.4   Personal Savings Rate, 1959–2006.
Source: U.S. Department of Commerce, Bureau of Economic Analysis, "Personal Income and Outlays, 1959-01-01 to 2006-11-01," cited in *Economic Research*, Federal Reserve Bank of St. Louis, 2007, http://research.stlouisfed.org/fred2/release?rid=54&soid=18.

	1820	1975	2004
G-8	29%	55%	44%
(U.S. only)	2	22	21
China	33	5	13
India	16	3	6
Latin America	2	7	6
Africa	5	3	3

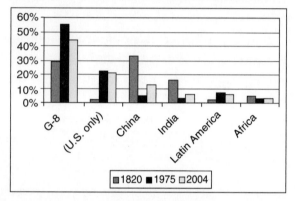

FIGURE 12.5   Shares of World GDP, 1820–2004.
Source: Progressive Policy Institute, www.globalpolicy.org/socecon/inequal/income/tables/history.htm.

president. By 2006, gross federal debt exceeded $8.3 trillion. In June 2004, foreigners owned more than half of the U.S. federal debt, and in 2006, about one out of three of corporate bonds was in foreign hands. In 2006, more than 13 percent of the U.S. stock market was in foreign hands.[24]

Redistributed Wealth: The inflation of the 2001–2007 period was as strange as the boom it produced. It was a new kind of inflation that never hit the masses with higher consumer prices but became a bonanza for the lucky 1 percent of the population with substantial assets (property, art, antiques, stocks) and the few hundred thousand who work in the financial industry.

As for middle-class workers, the American advantage, which had begun eroding in the mid-1970s, deteriorated even faster with

Greenspan's EZ Credit regime. Before the industrial revolution, laborers in China, India, or Massachusetts were paid roughly the same amount. Then, by 1950, an hour of a Yankee's time was worth 100 times more than that of an Indian, thanks to Western machinery. Now the trend has reversed; Asian earnings are growing much more rapidly than those in the United States. Greenspan intended to increase wages and productivity, and he did—in Asia. It is Asia's share of world GDP that has been steadily climbing. (See Figure 12.5.)

CHAPTER 13

THE MILLION-DOLLAR TRAILER

I can get no remedy against this consumption of the purse: borrowing only lingers and lingers it out, but the disease is incurable.
—**William Shakespeare, *King Henry the Fourth, Part II***

In the year of our Lord 2005, on the Pacific coast of North America, a two-bedroom trailer was offered for $1.4 million. This was hardly a first or even a most. Other mobile homes had sold for $1.3 million and $1.8 million.[1]

The $1.4 million trailer was in a gated community, on a triple-wide lot. Triple or even quadruple, why would people pay so much for a trailer? Location, location, location, you might say. And it was true—the views were spectacular. But the buyer of a trailer—even one costing a million dollars—does not buy location. The trailer owner only rents the location for a fee. "Space rent" for a $1.4 million mobile home would be $2,700 a month—not a fortune, but still a drain on your money. And mortgages are hard to get on trailers, because they might be pulled off the land, and then what would they be worth?

Meanwhile, in Miami, speculators would buy a group of five or ten condos—before a single shovelful of dirt had been displaced. The contracts would be flipped—sold to other speculators, none of whom had any intention of living in the object of their speculation, which in truth looked rather unloved. Many condos lay empty, awaiting the poor buyer who would actually live in them.

Two years later, we are still not sure that the great bull market in U.S. residential real estate is dead, but it definitely has a certain corpselike smell to it. The relatives are gathered in the parlor. The padre is already on the scene, administering last rites. And thus our funeral oration, which, like all good ones, begins with the memories of better days.

Or, at least, with the recollection of the comic high points, such as the house that Donald Trump bought in Palm Beach, Florida, for $41 million in 2004. For reasons unexplained, it was judged worth $125 million two years later. It looked just like the house you'd expect The Donald to live in. If he were to get his price, the profit would be a staggering $42 million for every year he held it. That is good work—earning $3.5 million per month, just for owning one of America's gaudiest beach houses.[2]

But pity the next poor owner, who has carrying costs of $6.25 million per year ($125 million at 5 percent interest), plus expenses. Instead of earning money, the new owner will probably be out of pocket more than a million dollars per month. And here, we let the fellow in on a little secret—houses don't go up in value every year, especially those that just rose $84 million.

We thought The Donald had set the pace for extravagantly priced houses, but, only a few weeks later, came news that Saudi Arabia's former ambassador to the United States, Prince Bandar bin Sultan, had put his ranch near Aspen, Colorado, on the market for $135 million—making it the most expensive private house ever offered for sale in the United States, and perhaps in the whole world.[3] All over the world, the rich went on a spending spree. They bought ranches in South America—even the Bush family bought one, a 98,000 acre estancia in Paraguay; they pulled out their fat wallets and snapped up apartments in Mayfair, on the Place Vendôme, and at the Puerto del Sol.

Meanwhile, the price of the average house rose approximately 60 percent during the same period. Next to the gains in Malibu and Manhattan, this was peanuts; but since nothing like it had happened in a hundred years, it was enough to make average folks giddy. In 2005, a survey of house buyers in Los Angeles showed that they expected average prices of houses to go up by a whopping 22 percent a year

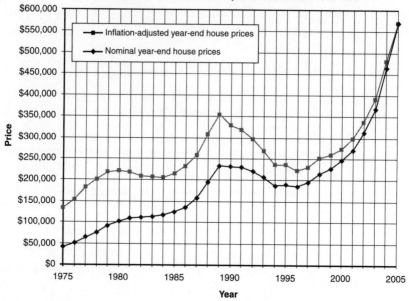

FIGURE 13.1 The Housing Bubble—Los Angeles Metropolitan Area House Prices.

Source: Q4 2006 median existing single-family home prices provided by the National Association of Realtors. Trailing house price index data provided by Standard & Poor's. Inflation data provided by the U.S. Department of Labor, Bureau of Labor Statistics. www.jparsons.net/housingbubble/.

over the next decade—that is, to *over $3 million.* It was an expectation common to most of the country. (See Figure 13.1.)

So it is. At the end of a bubble, the hallucinations become so extravagant that they blow up. The little cocktail reception turns into a wild party, with guests dancing on tables and throwing up outside. But, while the left sides of greedy brains were calculating their good fortune, the right sides couldn't seem to put two and two together. The average wage earner had an annual income of only $40,146.[4] How was he going to buy a $3 million house? Even with a 5 percent loan, it would still mean monthly payments of $12,500—almost four times his monthly income. Who would bet on it? And yet, it appears

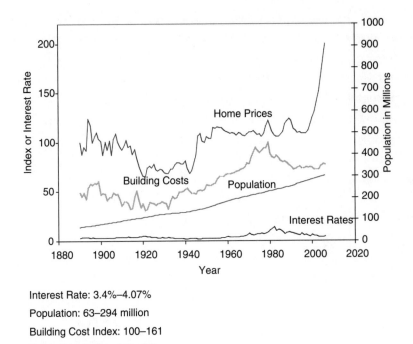

FIGURE 13.2   Growth in Home Prices Since 1890.
Source: Robert Shiller, *Irrational Exuberance*, 2nd ed. (Princeton, NJ: Princeton University Press, 2005). www.irrationalexuberance.com.

that thousands—maybe millions—of people not only betted on it, they staked their financial futures on it.

At the center of the swindle was the idea that houses go up in value perpetually. But for 100 years, from 1896 to 1996, houses merely kept up with GDP, inflation, and income growth. It was only in the following 10 years that they rose and rose remarkably. (See Figure 13.2.)

A homeowner might persuade himself that his pile of blocks, bricks, two-by-fours, and faded paint had somehow grown in worth—like a fine wine that had aged or a bond that had matured, but he knew that every individual item in the house was actually losing value as it aged. How was it possible then, that the house as a whole should go up?

Out came the experts and the salesmen. The homeowner's property value was rising, he was told, because there were so many new people coming into the area. But then how could it be that houses were rising *everywhere*—throughout the 50 states? Prices were rising, came the reply, because the country was running out of buildable land and building codes were more restrictive. New houses were actually becoming rare; that's why older houses were so sought after.

But here, too, the lump could have seen it wasn't so. There was clearly a house *building* boom, not merely a house *price* boom. Single-family homes were going up in old cow fields and auto lots. Single-family homes were being knocked down to make room for condominiums. Acres of previously empty land were being converted to housing. In many places, housing supply increased while population was actually decreasing:

Santa Clara County, 2000–2003: Housing Units per Person

Year	Units	÷	Population	=	Units per Person
2000	580,868	÷	1,686,474	=	0.344
2001	587,013	÷	1,692,299	=	0.346
2002	592,494	÷	1,677,426	=	0.353
2003	596,526	÷	1,678,421	=	0.355

Source: www.census.gov.

With all this new supply—how could prices nonetheless go *up*? The very idea of it should have contradicted the homeowner's intuition if not his instruction. A house, he should have told himself, is home sweet home, not a biotech stock.

Working on the problem like a gorilla trying to do long division, our plebe realized he'd got it all wrong. His house was not a dwelling at all, but an investment! And what an investment. Between 2002 and 2006, residential housing rose at 20 percent per year or more in many areas, better than most stocks. And what stock had granite countertops in the kitchen?

If he bought it for $200,000, with a prudent 20 percent down, he only had to pay $40,000 initially, and he got two forms of payoff:

a dividend in the form of a place to live or, say, $24,000 if he rented it out; plus, if the price went up 20 percent, a capital gain of $40,000. What a bonanza! The $40,000 investment was throwing off a $64,000 return every year.

The owner was now an investment genius. Just by living in his house, he was making more than the average wage. A more thoughtful person might have wondered how that was possible without either working or saving, but the plebe was now another Warren Buffett—only smarter. Buffett still lived in the same house he had bought 40 years ago. What a dolt! He should have traded up, flipped, and refinanced.

Then, another monstrous delusion developed—the homeowner came to believe he had an ATM machine in his bedroom. He could now regularly withdraw from the Bank of Four Walls and a Roof. A house appreciating $40,000 a year could easily provide $10,000 through refinancing or in mortgage equity withdrawal, he reckoned. And so he went out and borrowed—in 2004 and 2005, more than $1 trillion. Mortgage credit was cheap; better a home equity line than a credit card, the experts told him. Why not? With house prices seemingly hitched to a rocket launch at Cape Canaveral, how could he—or they—go wrong?

FLIMFLAM SPAM

By 2002, homeowners were ripe for even bigger absurdities.

Traditionally, mortgage lenders needed to first make sure that both the borrower and the market were solid, or they weren't prepared to lend money. They figured that if the borrower failed, the market would have to be strong enough for them to recover their loan. But the new mortgage lenders rarely met the borrower. And they had already judged the market foolproof.

Determined to prove it, they lent to the fools, and in so doing, turned into knaves.

There was no end to the number and variety of nontraditional mortgages flourishing—adjustable-rate mortgages (ARMs), of course (accounting for 40 to 50 percent of all mortgages between 2004 and 2006), but also zero-down payments, teaser rates, interest-only mortgages, flexible payments, and "stated income" applications—so-called liars' loans—which the borrowers used their imaginations to fill out. There was even a negative amortization (neg am) mortgage—a diabolical innovation wherein the principal actually grows, even while payments are being made on time. Many mortgages, thus, were not really purchases at all, but options that gave the borrower the right to buy the house sometime in the future—if things went well.

In 1999, only 5 percent of loans were subprime—that is, mortgages made to marginal borrowers. Five years later, 20 percent were.[5]

It is estimated that there are now $1.5 trillion in subprime loans in the market, a huge number of them with no money down at all. Now, the kicker is that in 2007 and 2008, the monthly payments on about $600 billion of these subprime mortgages will increase by as much as 50 percent, once the two-year teaser periods are up. Lured by ARM'd and dangerous loans, fewer and fewer people now own their homes at all. More and more are gamblers, betting that property values will rise fast enough for them to refinance again and again.[6]

Yes, the borrower could get some slack on the noose. With an optional payment plan, for example, he could skip a payment if he wished and let the principal of the loan rise, to a maximum of 115 percent of the original amount. Yes, he could wait out a month if he suffered some one-off calamity, and if he could make it up the next month, all would be well. But when he hit 115 percent, watch out! Then, no matter how many checks were in the mail, the rope would jerk tight and break his neck.

Renting had become a social faux pas, like dropping out of high school or eating spaghetti with a knife. The credit market was being democratized. Now, not only rich speculators could lose their cummerbunds. The common man could lose his sweaty T-shirt, too.

Still, we feel a little uneasy when we laugh, since the joke is on the people who can least afford it—the gullible borrowers of the subprime market. How we roar, though, at the gullibility of the subprime *lenders*! While the plebes received ARMs, the finance geniuses bought mortgage-backed securities (MBSs). More and more of these mortgages (29 percent in 2005, more than double the number in 2003) were not of the traditional kind—that is, backed by Fannie Mae or Freddie Mac. Instead, they were private-label, with no explicit or implicit guarantee, backed often by nothing more than imaginary incomes and fictitious appraisals.[7]

You see, before a public spectacle really lets loose, it needs a fellow to think he can get away with something. The great innovation of the lending industry was to make that possible—by breaking the link between lender and risk taker. The credit agencies rightly rated the home loans as poor, BBB–. But, in a miracle akin to the one at Cana, the bad credits were turned into triple A's by the PhDs at hedge funds.

Scientists often suggest that the Gospels lie. But as to the veracity of modern finance, they are mute. Asked to explain, the institutional salesmen sounded no smarter than the homeowner. The parts going into it might each be a little oily, they said, but put together, the sliced, diced, and processed mortgage packages were less risky than individual mortgages. It was as if you were less likely to get sick from eating a can of Spam than from eating any particular cut of meat in it. All Speculation Nation needed was to replace the stars on Old Glory with a roulette wheel; visitors would get the idea.

Cheap suits, expensive suits—when you got down to it, they all fell into the same trap. Just how bad some of it was became apparent only recently. Said *Fortune*:

> Since the housing market started to soar in 2001, mortgage fraud has become the fastest-growing white-collar crime, according to the FBI. Last year crooks skimmed at least $1 billion from the $3 trillion U.S. mortgage market.... As business dries up, there's increasing pressure on lenders, brokers, title companies, and appraisers to be profitable. That means loan and title documents aren't scrutinized as carefully as they might be, and courts—many of them so

low-tech they resemble Mayberry—can't keep up with the volume of paper. . . .

It's like a tasting menu for con artists and grifters, so tempting that in some cities drug dealers have turned to mortgage fraud, plaguing lower-income neighborhoods with crooked mortgages rather than crystal meth.[8]

Elsewhere, it was reported that lenders made millions in mortgage loans to inmates of the Colorado prison system. A whole group of miscreants issuing out of the Rocky Mountain state pen were able to buy 17 houses for inflated prices and take away $2.1 million in excess loan proceeds.[9]

And it was exactly at that moment—just *after* they had already cleared the runway—that regulators began begging the lending industry to be more careful. Thus it was that, in the autumn of 2006, a group of regulatory agencies looked up at the sky and had a fright; they had allowed too many marginal buyers to take off, they suddenly realized. The air was so dark with them, it looked like a scene from *The Birds*—and many were beginning to crash. Even Ben Bernanke, speaking in 2006, warned that borrowers ought to have some flying lessons, a little more "awareness" of lending practices.[10]

Then, the feds got on the case and people started going to jail.

But isn't that how these stories always end? In regret . . . in court . . . in Chapter 7 or Chapter 11 bankruptcy.

All public spectacles always end in correction of some sort—often, a house of correction. And if the force of the correction is equal and opposite to the deception that preceded it, this one ought to be a doozie.

Now, we realize that a genuine hard landing for U.S. housing will send up dust all over the world, which is why most people can't bear thinking about it. But, of course, we make it our business to think about precisely what most people can't bear thinking about, even if we don't know any more than anyone else.

And we come up with three good arguments for a long hard landing in the housing sector:

The first is demographic. The typical baby boomer has a total of $60,000 in net worth. For the past 10 years or so, a baby boomer hasn't had a reason to save. Why get 3 percent in the bank when you could get 12 percent from housing? Counting leverage, many people got at least twice that. The typical retirement plan was simple: buy a house in Florida, then sell the house in New Jersey. Naturally, the Sunshine State boomed. In the period from 2001 to 2005, employment growth averaged 2.2 percent per year—the third highest in the nation. But job growth in the property sector grew more than twice as fast, at 5.6 percent.

Now that the boom seems to be over, the baby boomers will most likely be net sellers—because they will need the money.

The second argument for a hard landing is technological. The invention of the modern automobile in the early twentieth century helped Americans who could afford them escape the city centers, which were noisy, dirty, bustling places of commerce.

Grant's Interest Rate Observer gives an example. In Boston, Mr. John C. Kiley, writing in 1941, observed that prices had been going down for 11 years. He noted that "in some of the older business and residential sections of the city of Boston have returned to levels below those of the pre-Civil War years."[11]

One hundred years of price appreciation—wiped out . . . by the depression and the automobile.

"When I was a young man in the early 1980s, I used to play in a rock and roll band in Minneapolis," writes another observer, alternative investment analyst George Paulos. "Like many bands of the era, we rented a 'band house' to live and rehearse in. Most of the band houses were located in southeast Minneapolis. There were many large homes in that area for rent and the price was cheap. . . . We often wondered about the original owners of these mansions. It was obviously a wealthy neighborhood at one time. Many of the homes in the area were huge and intricately designed. What happened to these people and why was the area now so downtrodden? It turns out that southeast Minneapolis was at the frontiers of development in the 1920s. Although within the city limits, they were essentially the suburbs at that time. Homes like our band house were the McMansions of the day. . . . The real estate bust of the 1930s had a permanent impact on many neighborhoods. The once wealthy neighborhood that surrounded our band house was still suffering 50 years later. . . . Even in the middle of a huge real estate boom, these neighborhoods are so blighted that they are still shunned."[12]

What technological innovation threatens U.S. suburbs today? The Internet. Just as the automobile meant you no longer had to live near your work, but only within commuting range, the Internet means that many people and businesses can put themselves anywhere and turn their backs on the suburbs.

Our third reason is the easiest to understand. Why will the bust in American housing be out of the ordinary? Because the boom that came before was.

House prices went nowhere for most of the 20th century. They rose only 0.4 percent per year from 1890 to 2004. And in many parts of the country, they went down. (The price of farmland in western Kansas, for example, hit a high in the commodities boom of the late 1880s and has still not recovered). Then, from 1997 to 2005 house prices soared, doubling in many areas, setting off a consumer boom.[13]

But, now falling prices in the housing sector mean that homeowners no longer have any equity to take out and spend. A 5 percent fall in house prices takes $1 trillion out of the net worth of American homeowners. A 40 percent drop—predicted by many experts—would probably set the economy back about as much as the Great Depression.

The International Monetary Fund analyzed home prices in a number of countries from 1970 to 2001 and found 20 busts—when real prices fell by almost 30 percent. All but one of those busts led to a recession.

What happened in the countries with busts?

House prices have fallen in nominal as well as in real terms in Germany and Japan over the past seven years. A house in Tokyo now costs less than half what it did in 1991, after a now legendary property-price bubble in the late 1980s. Yet the 36 percent real increase in average house prices in Japan in the seven years to 1991 was less than the increase over the past seven years in half of the countries we track in our index.

German houses used to be the most expensive in Europe: in 1975, they cost three times as much as French ones. Today the two have more or less evened up, largely because German house prices have been steadily declining in real terms. Germany is still suffering a hangover from a massive construction boom after unification, encouraged by government subsidies and tax breaks.[14]

"I recently visited my old band house," continues George Paulos. "It was just as I remembered it. The hedges were massively overgrown, the siding was still rotting, and the porch was still sagging. It was a bittersweet vision. . . . Seventy years after mass foreclosures and the place still hadn't recovered. How will it fare during the next real estate bust?"

WHAT GOES UP MUST COME DOWN

In September 2006, the median price of a new house dropped to $217,100—down 9.7 percent from a year before, erasing two years' worth of housing gains. Not since 1970 had a yearly decline been that sharp.[15]

Owners were cutting prices and throwing in appliances, automobiles, and other incentives. Sellers were willing to bargain. But buyers knew that they might be even more willing to bargain in a year or

278 THE BUBBLE KINGS

two, and inventories began sitting at near-record levels. And waiting in the future were still millions of ARMs that needed to be twisted and reset higher.

Billions of dollars of American housing wealth were going up in smoke. All we needed were marshmallows.

Default rates on subprime loans doubled in 2006—to 8 percent of the total, on track to be "the worst-performing loans ever."[16] In 2006, total foreclosure rates ran 42 percent greater than the year before, according to RealtyTrac's year-end report.

In November, some of the packaged securities backed by subprime mortgage loans were downgraded by Moody's an unheard-of six months after origination.[17]

"More homeowners going into default," said the *Los Angeles Times*. The number of Californians at risk of losing their homes to foreclosure more than doubled in the three months ending September 30, 2006.[18]

In the winter of 2007 came word that New Century Financial Corporation—the nation's second largest provider of subprime mortgages—was having a rough time of it. When its mortgages go bad, it is supposed to buy them back. Now it finds that it doesn't have the money. On February 8, investors marked down the stock by more than one-third. In April, it went broke.

It must have been a bad day for the insiders and large shareholders. They should have unloaded their shares on the unsuspecting public long before. Perhaps they did.

"Refinancing gets tougher," reported the *Wall Street Journal*. "Lenders battered by late payers," added the Associated Press.

Lending money to people who can't afford to pay it back turns out to be a bust. Who would have thought?

Cocktail conversation had turned from how much money people have made by selling their houses to how much money they might have made if they had sold a little earlier.

But while lips tell the stories, hearts still hope, and brains still want to believe. Homeowners are still borrowing and spending, and financiers are paying big money for mortgage derivatives and the companies that produce them. While the credits creak and wobble, the creditors haven't seen so many mergers and acquisitions (M&A) in 10 years. And judging by profits (Goldman's were up 16 percent in 2006), bonuses, and prices, the masters of the financial paper shuffling business never had it so good.

What is Goldman? Among people who sell debt in large volumes and at large prices, it is the leading brand. Debt comes in many varieties—especially after Goldman gets finished with it—but mortgage debt is especially educative and entertaining.

A mortgage-backed security is backed by a mortgage. But what backs the mortgage?

We put the question another way to a friend in Ireland. "Your houses are so expensive. How can people afford to buy them?"

"Ah ... it's debt, pure and simple. We had interest rates of 10 percent or more—until we joined the European Union and got the euro. Then, all of a sudden, you could borrow money for only 3 percent and the whole place went on a spending spree. The Irish love owning their own houses. I think it is something left over from British rule, when we weren't allowed to own property. Right now, lenders practically stop you on the street to give you money. That's the real source of our Irish renaissance.

"Here in Ireland, it was as if the pubs were giving away free pints 24 hours a day.

"So you see, we have everything you have in America: a property bubble even bigger than yours, with interest-only housing loans, new cars everywhere, new buildings ... everything."

And soon, we suspect, they will have a property bust, too.

That is when the liars default on their loans—and Goldman's bonus checks get smaller.

CHAPTER 14

CENTRAL BANK BAMBOOZLE

One may say that, apart from wars and revolutions, there is nothing in
our modern civilizations which compares in importance to it [inflation].
—Elias Canetti, *Crowds and Power*

A poll released in early 2006 told us that Americans opposed more
Federal Reserve rate increases by a margin of three to one. What was
amazing was not the particular opinion voiced but that voters should
have any opinion at all. The going rate for short-term credit—like that
of bread or of titanium bicycles—would not normally be a matter for
public debate. But now, voters expected to find it on the ballot along
with proposals to expand the number of daylight hours and round
off pi to the nearest whole number. The Fed's rates are no longer
seen as either interference in the free market or technical adjustments
best left to professionals, but as policy to be debated by plumbers and
deliverymen.

Those who believe in the perfection of man were greatly encouraged after 2002: Paul Volcker had already proved that the Fed
had mastered the art of taming inflation, and now the Greenspan
Fed had learned how to avoid deflation, too. The U.S. economy
was impregnable—a citadel of growth that would expand forever and
ever, amen.

As the skeptics pointed out, however, an increase in firepower
doesn't make war a thing of the past; it just makes it more costly.
The machinery of central banking may have become more sophisticated, but the engine drivers still have the same heaving, squeezing,

juice-pumping hearts. Like all humans, they are sometimes good, sometimes bad, and always subject to influence.

By year six of the twenty-first century, the housing market was in trouble . . . and so was the American consumer, the U.S. economy, and the whole world economy. But don't worry, said Mr. Greenspan: "It would take a large, and historically most unusual, fall in home prices to wipe out a significant part of home equity."[1]

But, if the rise in prices had been unusual, why wouldn't the fall be, too?

And we love this: "Improvements in lending practices driven by information technology have enabled lenders to reach out to households with previously unrecognized borrowing capacities."

Translation: Subprime borrowers can now get all the credit they want.

And this: "Short of a significant fall in overall household income or in home prices, debt servicing is unlikely to become destabilizing."

But just there was the big issue. With 70 percent of the economy now based on consumption and dependent on inflated house prices, if house prices didn't rise, there would be no more equity to take out. What would homeowners take out if they couldn't take out equity? Pizza?

Fixing prices in the private sector has always been a crime, like taking a dive in a prizefight; yet people accept it without a squawk when officials fix the single most important price of all—the price of money. They always have.

But, at least until the invention of paper money, this ancient fraud was restrained. Banks might mint more coins but only by making them smaller or putting less gold or silver in them—and people could readily see when their coins had been clipped or debased. But in the modern form of the deception, the precious metal content was taken out altogether. For convenience and profit, banks issued paper notes that circulated freely and were backed by gold and silver in their vaults. Throughout the nineteenth century, Europe's two largest and richest central banks—the Bank of England and the Bank of France—could be trusted to yield up an ounce of gold to whoever presented a valid note. Smaller banks all over the United States did likewise; if they couldn't make good on their promises, they went broke.

Eventually people forgot to worry about the collateral. And gradually the quantity of the notes increased, while the quality declined. In 1913, when the Fed opened for business, the gold-backed dollar bought as much as it had in 1813. But then, in World War I, all Europe's central banks were forced off the gold standard—they didn't have enough gold to back the paper money they'd issued or repay the loans they'd taken out. A longish period of peekaboo financial fidelity ensued, a bedroom farce, with doors swinging open and shut, lovers diving under beds, and jealous husbands storming into the room. In varying arrangements between central banks, sometimes a note could be redeemed for gold and silver, sometimes not. Then, in the Bretton Woods arrangement of July 1944 central banks agreed to honor their commitments to each other . . . but they all agreed to stiff their private citizens. Henceforth, only a sovereign central bank could exchange paper for gold.

On August 15, 1971, even that last door slammed shut at the U.S. Treasury. Thus began one of the bigger mass delusions of all time. The Nixon administration declared that it would no longer honor its notes. Not even foreign central banks could exchange their paper notes for actual gold or silver—the very situation that once galled the young Greenspan. Now, the Treasury, in cahoots with the Fed, could create as much money as it wanted. No one, nowhere, nohow, could do anything about it.

And so, the world went over to a faith-based currency. But faith in what? The foreigners stuffed their vaults with the alpha currency—dollars. They used it to buy oil or to settle accounts with other nations. Dollars were as good as gold—only better; they were flexible. In times of stress—financing a war, for example—gold was famously inflexible, entirely devoid of patriotism. But paper dollars, *oh la la!* They could be manufactured even on a whim.

Was there no outer limit where the supply of dollars would exceed the demand for them?

No one asked or cared. The Greenspan gases were heating up the entire financial world, putting it at risk of a runaway Greenspan effect, but global liquidity got less coverage than global warming. There were no celebrity campaigns against it. No candidates ran on a platform of Saving the Economy.

And thus was the economy spared the rod and spoiled by easy money.

George W. Bush was reelected, and the architect of the hothouse economy went down in history as a genius.

NOT YOUR FATHER'S BOOM

Every generation suffers its own follies.

The generation of the 1930s learned to save and hated debt. They paid dearly for this instruction after World War II, especially in the 1960s and 1970s, when their savings were wiped out by inflation. Meanwhile, the next generation had its lessons. In 1949, investors were so negative on the value of General Motors stock that they sold it down to five times earnings, where it produced a dividend yield of 11 percent. With the war over, they must have thought that GM might not be able to turn a profit. But, the United States boomed in the postwar period. The soldiers got to work, started families, and bought houses—and cars.

It was a classic boom. Output increased. Wages rose. Eisenhower's economy made it possible for ordinary people to buy out of increased earnings. The nation's manufacturing centers, especially, flourished—Dayton, Detroit, Fort Wayne. Our cousins lived in Donora, Pennsylvania, and worked in the steel mills. In the 1950s and 1960s they all earned high wages, drove new cars, and lived in nice houses with all the latest conveniences.

But drive through those neighborhoods now! They are ghost towns, with empty houses, boarded-up shops, abandoned cars, and rusty factories. Workers here have been left behind by economic history, earning in real terms the same as or less than they did 30 years ago. In the midst of the biggest boom of all time, they have fallen behind.

The boom is now in only a few places. Nowhere is this more evident than in central London, which record bonuses in 2006 have turned into Moola Metropole. One employee of Barclays Capital made history with a paycheck that was three times the total pay of the whole executive board. Roger Jenkins—nicknamed the Dodger—took home between $70 million and $140 million last year—not for having invented Velcro or written "White Christmas." What the Dodger dodges is taxes—noble work, to be sure, but not usually the stuff booms are made of. But it is the stuff that makes the new City players—dubbed the "have-and-have-yachts"—with their lavish Kensington residences, private jets, and expensive wives. London's highest-paid trader, Ben-Brahim, runs the highly lucrative Goldman Sachs proprietary trading desk, and his bonus is around 2,000 times the average British wage. America's answer to Roger Jenkins, Lloyd Blankfein, who became Goldman Sachs' CEO after Hank Paulson went on to greater glory at the Treasury Department, made $53.4 million in his first six months on the job. The 173,000 employees of New York's leading financial houses made more money last year than the entire population of Vietnam, some 84 million people, says financial writer Marc Faber. Never have so few done so little and made so much doing it. "Banker," once Cockney rhyming slang, is popular now as invective.[2]

Meanwhile, one of those firms—Morgan Stanley—says it bought CNL Hotels & Resorts for $6.6 billion. What does a New York investment house know about running a hospitality business? Nothing. But gone are the days when owners of a business knew their business.

All this bonus money has found its way into property, driving prices of London's priciest digs up 30 percent in a single year. And central London commercial property has reached record prices—with office space in the West End going for $212 per square foot per year, more than twice the cost of similar space in Paris.

London is now the official billionaires' playground, with 23 dollar billionaires—behind only New York, which has 34. Restaurants are full; Claridge's even offers a "chef's table" menu at 1,000 pounds per person. Shop counters sag with expensive merchandise. Last year, a single art auction at Christie's brought in $269 million—a new record. Fortunes have been created on a scale and in a time frame not witnessed for 100 years, if ever before.

But whence cometh the loot? And how come it doth not trickle down to more humble wage earners? A normal boom lifts up normal wage earners, but this one lifts up only luxury yachts. Why?

We will tell you why. The Great Boom is a fraud, because it is a Bush-age asset-price bubble, not an Eisenhower-era economic boom.

From the consumer price inflation of the 1960s and 1970s, the boomers learned a lesson: better to spend than to save. And those who live where house prices rose most rapidly—on both U.S. coasts, as well as in most of the United Kingdom—spent on a titanic scale.

We are witnesses to a massive transfer of wealth—the biggest ever. And the new wealth stays in assets, like London houses and Picassos, that are out of reach of most people, for whom purchasing power has declined, just as both debt and living costs—from health care to education—have risen sharply. The top 1 percent of Americans now have 190 times the wealth of the median Americans, a ratio that has shot up from 125 to 1 in the early 1960s.[3]

And when the boom ends, what lesson will the boomers learn next?

In the short story, *Disorder and Early Sorrow*, Thomas Mann describes how a German housewife coped with hyperinflation in the late 1920s:

> The floor is always swaying under her feet, and everything seems upside down. She speaks of what is uppermost in her mind: the eggs, they simply must be bought today. Six thousand marks a piece they are, and just so many are to be had on this one day of the week at one single shop fifteen minutes' journey away.

The inflation of the mark in Germany led to disorder ... and then sorrow. The inflation of the dollar leads in the same direction. Instead of feeding into consumer prices, the inflation of 1997–2007 drove up asset prices for the rich and housing prices for the middle class.

The real threat to the American middle class, circa 2007, is not a small band of Muslim fanatics. No, in the United States in the early twenty-first century, as in the Weimar Republic in the early twentieth, the saboteurs are the financiers and bank chiefs who enjoy their retirements like portly bishops, basking in a job done well.

All the middle and lower classes got out of the new inflation was an opportunity to ruin themselves—which they took up readily. When adjustable-rate mortgages wipe out the equity of millions of homeowners, where will they turn? The world they thought they understood will have given way beneath their feet. Like the citizens of the Weimar Republic, will they then trade one public spectacle for another?

I, GREENSPAN

I, Alan Aurifericus Nefarious Greenspan, chairman of the Federal Reserve Bank, holder of the Medal of Freedom, Knight of the British Empire, member of the French Legion of Honor, known to my peers as the "greatest central banker who ever lived" ... (I will not trouble you with all my titles. I will not mention, for example, that I was the winner of the prestigious Enron Prize for Distinguished Public Service—awarded on November 1, 2001.... That was a month before Enron filed the largest bankruptcy case in U.S. history ... and collapsed in a heap of corruption charges—and did I tell you that Ken Lay actually called me up? He wanted me to step in, like Long Term Capital Management, he said. Of course I didn't ... and of course I turned down the cash that went with it ... and that beastly little crystal trophy thing, too) ... yes ... where was I? Oh, yes. I, Greenspan, am about to give you the strange history of my later life.

For I will dispense with childhood and even with young adult-hood, and those dreary sessions with that very dreary woman, Ayn Rand, who couldn't write a compelling sentence if her life de-pended on it, and my own dreary years at the Council of Economic Advisers . . . and pass directly to the time I spent as the most powerful man in the world. For here are my real titles: emperor of the world's most powerful money, ruler of the world's largest and most dynamic economy, and architect of the most audacious financial system this sorry globe has ever seen.

Yes, I, Alan Greenspan, ruled the financial world. But who ruled Alan Greenspan? Ah—I will come to that . . . and tell you how, while presiding over the biggest boom ever, I became caught in what I call the "golden predicament," from which I have never since become disentangled.

I have written much over the years. True. But most readers fool-ishly saw only the cluttered mind of a dithering economist or the stuttering pen of a professional bureaucrat. Many, listening to my wandering speeches and twisting sentences, thought that English was not my first language. They thought they detected a faint accent, like that of Henry Kissinger or Michael Caine. They mocked me as in-comprehensible or indecipherable. They watched what they thought was an obsequious public servant squirm.

But they admired me, too, because they thought they saw in me a kind of genius—an Einstein of economics, whose mind worked at such a high pitch his thoughts were inaudible to most humans. They counted on me to keep the great empire's economy rolling forward. Little—actually *nothing*—did they know of my real thoughts and designs.

But now I have left my post. There is no further need for me to dissemble, to kowtow before congressional committees, or to hide the real facts from my employers and the American people. Now, I swear by the gods, what I write comes from my own hand and not from some highly paid anonymous flack.

Let me begin at the beginning. Some are born in crisis, some create crisis, and others just make a mess of things. Scarcely had I settled into the big chair at the Fed when a crisis was thrust upon me. There is a code of behavior for central bankers. Faced with a financial crisis, a central banker's first duty is to run to the monetary valves and open them. This I did in 1987. But I was new to the job and didn't open them enough. The U.S. economy lagged its rivals in Europe for several years. My old boss—George Bush, the elder—lost his bid for reelection in 1992 and blamed it on me. I resolved never to make that mistake again. Even thereafter, when faced with a slew of shocks, crises, and elections, I made sure that every valve, throttle, switch, and sluice gate was wide open.

But it was on December 5, 1996, that I had my first epiphany. That was when I made my celebrated remark about stock prices. I wondered if they did not reflect a kind of "irrational exuberance." Whether they did or did not, I do not know. But I came to realize two things: one, people, especially my bosses, actually *wanted* prices that were irrationally exuberant; and two, prices could become far more irrationally exuberant if we put our minds to it.

I was 70 years old at the time. I had weaseled (why not be honest about it?) my way to the top post by knowing the right people and by not saying anything anyone could disagree with. That was what the press first referred to as "Greenspanspeak." All the public and the politicians got was gobbledygook. But for good reason.

They would not have wanted to hear what I *really* thought. For I knew well and good what generally happened when politicians and central bankers got their hands on soft money and a compliant central banker. They used their control of the money to cheat people. It is as simple as that. (I explained this early in my career; fortunately, no one bothered to read it.) It was in 1966 in the *Objectivist*—that rag of the libertarians. They seem to sense—perhaps more clearly and subtly than other defenders of laissez-faire—that gold and economic freedom are inseparable:

> If men did not have some commodity of objective value which
> was generally acceptable as money, they would have to resort to
> primitive barter or be forced to live on self-sufficient farms and

forgo the inestimable advantages of specialization. If men had no means to store value, i.e., to save, neither long-range planning nor exchange would be possible.[4]

Then, after a long discussion of how money works, I gave the objectivists the conclusion they wanted to hear and one in which I myself then believed strongly, and still do:

> In the absence of the gold standard, there is no way to protect savings from confiscation through inflation . . . The financial policy of the welfare state requires that there be no way for the owners of wealth to protect themselves.[5]

I do not quote myself at such length to quarrel with me. *Au contraire*. I have never changed my opinion. But 10 years later, in 1974, I left New York for Washington—that is, I left its heart of commerce to take up residence in its gallbladder of politics. And naturally, I had to abandon the free-market, gold-standard currents of the East River for the malignant political eddies and festering statist swamps of the Potomac. I was no fool. That was where the real power and glory were.

I left New York to serve as the chairman of President Ford's Council of Economic Advisers. Ayn Rand told a reporter that I was "*her* man in Washington." I had to laugh. She expected *me* to change Washington!

And now I will let you in on a little secret. The problem with humankind is the same as the problem with the New Era itself. The New Era required a new, digital man to make it work—one who would respond logically and unemotionally to whatever came his way.

But we *Homo sapiens analogos* don't operate that way. Instead of ciphering new data, we try to make sense of it by comparing it to things we think we understand.

We don't say, "The stack of wood is 2.235 meters high." We say it is "as high as a pile of 15 tort lawyers." We don't know precisely how thick each tort lawyer is . . . but it doesn't matter. We know things only by analogy and metaphor and can imagine how much nicer things would be if tort lawyers were stacked like cordwood.

Human minds, except those of government economists, are flexible enough to absorb almost any new set of facts into known metaphors. But the trouble is that the metaphors are never perfect. In the popular imagination, I was the pilot at the controls of a vast airplane. I could lower the flaps or raise them—according to my wont. If the plane flew too high . . . or too low . . . it would be because of pilot error.

But the U.S. economy is not an airplane. It is far too complex. And in one critical respect, it is unlike any machine ever made: It anticipates the pilot's moves—and resists them.

"Tell me why—why do fools fall in love . . ." Well, that's the way markets work, too.

Waves of bullishness rise up between troughs of despair . . . and crash into the rocky shoreline. No matter how high the waves, nor how low the tide might ebb, sooner or later stock prices regress to sea level; the memory of man runneth not to the contrary. Competition holds profits down and directs investors' money so as to force all investment profits down to the same sea level of returns, adjusted for risk and other variables. Especially, after a long period of rising stock prices, what investors should expect is a long period of low or zero returns—as long as 10 to 15 years. And that's what they should have expected in 1999 or 2000. Instead, they wanted me to beat back the business cycle, as if I were King Canute. They expected me to ignore the tilt of the credit cycle and the lunatic phases of investor sentiment—that inconstant moon of irrational exuberance and unseasonable gloom.

Do you think I really failed to see the bubble in stock prices? You would have had to be blind, deaf, and dumb not to notice. Do you think I really believed in this New Era nonsense? Do you really think that I don't know what happens when I flood the world with cash? But what was I supposed to do? I couldn't exactly come out and say, "It's a bubble!" Investors would have panicked.

Once stock prices got to bubble levels, I had to think of a reason for why they might stay there—that was where that productivity razzamatazz came from. People wanted an explanation and I gave it to them. Do you think I learned nothing in all that time I spent with Ayn Rand?

That miserable, self-absorbed old tart! Reading her books was painful enough—but can you imagine those egocentric gabfests in those pitiful little apartments in lower Manhattan? I thought I would go mad. She was a minor cult figure, but what did it gain her? A following of marginalized nuts and kooks with bad taste, bad habits, and apartments cluttered with science fiction paperbacks. What I wanted was power, love, money—the same things we all want. And I could never have got them with the Randites.

If you want power, you have to go to where the power is. Hitler could have stuck with eating bratwurst in Austria. And Bill Clinton could have remained in Arkansas and starred in a grotesque Southern novel. But political power in the United States is in Washington, and financial power is in New York. And the real power is where the two come together—in the Federal Reserve System. Of course, the purpose of the Fed—as with any cartel—is to make sure the member banks make money. But the Fed only gets its clout from Washington—and it has to pay for this privilege somehow.

The Fed may have been chartered to protect the currency, but its job now is to get the politicians reelected and keep the money flowing to Washington. Why? Because give people the impression that they are better off, and they won't fuss about taxes.

When the Fed was founded in 1913, Washington took only about 5 percent of the nation's income and the dollar was solid. Since then, Washington's percentage of GDP has increased by nearly 600 percent, and the dollar has fallen 95 percent. Do you really think that was an accident? Inflation pushes people into higher and higher tax brackets and makes them think they are getting richer—just what Washington wants. Of course, if the inflation rate goes too high, people begin to complain and then you have to take action. Thank God it was Volcker on watch back in the late 1970s and not me.

But here's the important thing. A central bank can control the quantity of money or, indirectly, the quality of money. What it can't do is increase the quantity while still protecting the quality. And now let me tell you another secret—how I became the most successful central banker ever. Keynes' idea was for the government to spend like crazy when the economy was weak—to stimulate it. The government would run deficits during the down cycles, and then make up for them by running surpluses in good times.

But guess what? The politicians forgot to run surpluses in the good times. Why? Because they really don't care about the long term or about fiscal responsibility. So, the debts mounted up, but people felt like they were getting something for nothing and so it worked for a long time.

Well, what I figured out was that you could use monetary policy in roughly the same way. You always favor rates that are lower than they ought to be, because you want to encourage more business expansion—and a greater illusion of prosperity—than would otherwise be justified. And who knows or cares that the dollar today is worth only five cents in 1913 terms?

The goal here—as with all government programs—is to produce the desired benefits while pushing the costs onto someone else. That's how politics works. You promise something . . . and you force someone else to pay for it. You rob one Peter voter . . . and spread the loot among the Pauls.

Sooner or later, people will catch on. They will try to switch from one currency to another, but by then, all the paper currencies will be weak and untrustworthy. Most likely, people will turn to gold. It's the only thing that we can't manipulate. But that may be years ahead. And it's a problem for someone else.

You see, if central banking were an honest métier, there would be no reason to have it at all. Private banks could do the job better. But people are ready to believe anything. Somehow, they think that rich financiers and power-mad politicians get together to run a central bank for the benefit of the people! Well, I've got news: It doesn't work that way.

An honest banker cannot dilute the depositors' money. But that is exactly what central bankers do. They issue a certain quantity of currency. Then, they issue more and more of it. So, the people who got it and saved it lose a little bit of the value each year. In effect, the value is lost by the savers and captured by the people who control the currency. It is really a very simple swindle.

And an old one. In 64 A.D., Nero decreed that the number of aureus coins minted from a pound of gold would increase from 41 to 45 (each coin would be about 10 percent less valuable). The silver denarius, meanwhile, lost 99.98 percent in the five centuries before the sacking of Rome. Paper sheds value even faster. Single-handedly, I cut the value of the dollar in half while I was at the Fed.

A successful central banker in the age of compliant paper money is one who is able to control the rate of ruin so that the rubes don't catch on. Everybody is happy. Everyone feels richer. It's almost a perfect crime, because no one objects as long as it is done right.

I return to my narrative. After I made my remark about "irrational exuberance," I was called into Congress. The politicians who confronted me were the usual oafs and know-nothings. They made it clear that if I wanted to keep my job, I would have to stop worrying about whether asset prices were too high; instead, I would have to goose them up even higher! It was on that very day—I recall it well—that what I had previously seen only in foggy theory came out into the clear, bright daylight of applied central banking.

No one wants honest money. *No* one. The politicians, bankers, investors, voters, and householders—anyone with a voice in the matter wants easy money. It is just too delicious to resist. Debtors want a little inflation to lighten their step. Creditors want inflation to swell their asset values. Politicians want to be reelected. Businesspeople want customers with money to throw around. Is there anyone who doesn't like the stuff?

And yet, of course, easy come; easy go. The magic fades. What can a central banker do? He can "take the punch bowl away," as my predecessors used to say. But, take away the punch bowl, and they begin punching you! I recall they burned Paul Volcker in effigy on the Capitol steps. They would have burned him alive if they could have gotten their hands on him.

Why should I, Greenspan, suffer such a fate? This was the "golden predicament" I faced. Yes, I knew well that the nation would be better off if the punch bowl were removed, but I knew that I would be removed, too, if I did it. And I knew, also, that people would never resist the temptation to make the money easier and easier—until it got so wobbly and woozy it fell on its face. Better that it fell sooner rather than later? Better that the lesson was taught now, not 10 years from now? No! Better the lean times on the next man's watch, not on mine! I owe that also to old Ayn; she taught me who rules Greenspan—Greenspan! Ayn taught me the number one rule: Look out for numero uno.

I remember it so clearly. I was sitting in a House committee hearing room. My tormentors kept asking questions. I kept giving the kind of answers for which I later became famous—answers that didn't say anything. And I thought to myself—if these lard heads want easy money, I'll give them easy money. I'll give them the easiest money the planet has ever seen! I'll give it to them good and hard!

And so, I did.

On my watch, outstanding home-mortgage debt jumped from $1.8 trillion to over $8 trillion. Total consumer debt went from $2.7 trillion to over $11 trillion. And government debt, too, exploded. The feds owed less than $2 trillion in the second Reagan administration, as it had for the previous 40 years. But under my direction, the red ink overflowed like the Nile again—to over $7 trillion.[6]

The trade deficit, too, has more than quintupled since I've been at the Fed, from $150.7 to $756.8 billion, and will reach $830 billion in 2006. When I came to power, the United States was still a creditor. Now it is a debtor. When I left, out of all Federal government debt owed to the public as Treasury bonds and T-bills, around $2 trillion was owned by foreigners, up about 10 times from $0.2 trillion in 1987.[7]

Who can argue with such a record? Who can compete with it? Who would want to?

But that is the smooth, perverse pleasure a cynical old man takes in his achievements. I have practically ruined the nation, and I know it. If you distributed the cost of the federal government's programs, promises, and pledges to the voters, along with the nation's private debt, the typical household, and the nation itself, would be broke. And yet, almost everywhere I go, I am still revered as a maestro and saluted as if I were a war hero. It is as if I had won World War II all by myself. The same numskulls who wanted easy money 10 years ago now praise me for causing what they call "The Great Moderation"— as if there were anything moderate about this borrowing binge. Others say that my real legacy is that I finally "made central banking work." Yes, I made it work—just like it's supposed to work. I gave the people enough rope to hang themselves. And that's what they've done.

And poor Ben Bernanke will get the blame for it. He and his stupid helicopters . . . he almost deserves it.

CHAPTER 15

THE MOTHER OF
THE MOTHER OF
ALL BUBBLES

Prophesy as much as you like, but always hedge.
—Oliver Wendell Holmes, 1861

Mr. Greenspan blew up the Grand Coolee Dam and sent a wall of cash and credit flooding around the world like a rogue wave. But he was not the inventor of monetary dynamite, nor the only one with access to it. The Japanese set off their own deluge in the late 1980s, and then again in the mid-1990s, dropping interest rates to zero. The combination of Nipponese desperation with American ingenuity is what we have to thank for today's bubbles.

After the Japanese stock market imploded in 1990, the U.S. tech stocks took off—up 900 percent between 1995 and 2000. Then the Kuwait stock market ballooned, up 471 percent in the next five years. Bombay stocks took off in 2003 and rose 340 percent. Meanwhile, U.S. housing prices doubled between 1995 and 2005. In England, the increase was even greater. Average house prices rose 220 percent in those 10 years.

Twenty years ago, the total notional sum of derivatives in the entire world was close to zero. At least that is the impression you get from looking at a chart showing the growth of derivatives in the years since. Since then, from nothing, the global supply of derivatives has risen faster than the NASDAQ, faster than oil, faster even than prices of Mayfair apartments. The twitty quants at big investment

296

firms invent complex derivative contracts, give them a jolt of juice, and millions—no, billions or trillions—of these abominations spring to life.

Other market bubbles are soap bubbles compared to the *Hindenburg* of derivatives. The volume of outstanding interest rate and currency derivatives has grown from zero to $865 billion during the 15 years from 1972 to 1987, according to the International Swaps and Derivatives Association. During the next 15 years, from 1987 to 2002, the derivative market grew to $100 trillion, *or more than a hundredfold*, trebling on average every four years. In 2007, this haunt of the hedges had reached a total face value of around $500 trillion. That is roughly 30 times the size of the U.S. economy and 10 times the size of the old global economy itself. What a jolly time to be alive! There, in front of us, is the fattest, juiciest balloon that has ever existed. If only we had a long sharp pin in our hand![1] (See Figure 15.1.)

Meanwhile, trading in derivatives is now the mother of a whole tribe of bubbles throughout the financial sector. Google (GOOG) was the big tech hit of 2006; by the end of the year, the stock was trading at around $500. At that price, it was worth more than the entire Thai stock market. But buyers of the Chicago Mercantile Exchange (CME) paid an even higher price. The CME is where futures and derivatives are traded. The stock came out at the end of 2002 at just over $40. Three years later, it had gone up 14 times, to more than $550. Meanwhile, the New York Stock Exchange (NYSE) gets half its daily volume from hedge fund trading, and its stock, too, has been on a roll.

But what are all these bubbled-up derivatives, really?

Simple. Packages of debt. Bundles of debt. Piles of debt. Rocky Mountains of debt. Debt that is stuffed into hedge fund portfolios as an investment. Debt that is laid away at insurance companies and pension funds as an asset. Debt that is traded, extended, extruded, pressed, bolted, wrung out, and wadded up. It is debt for all seasons, all people, all times, and all places. It is *urbi et orbi* debt. There. We have given you the technical description of it.

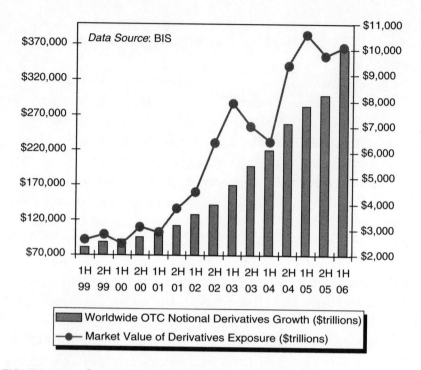

FIGURE 15.1   Growth of Credit Derivatives Market.
Source: Brian Pretti, ContraryInvestor.com (www.financialsense.com/market/pretti/2007/0216.html).

Now we will tell you what it means to you—it means, for one thing, that trillions of dollars' worth of securities are bound up with the U.S. housing market. Fast-talking lenders wrote mortgages for slow-witted homeowners. Then the lenders sold the contracts, which were packaged with thousands of others into a mortgage-backed security (MBS). The MBS is backed by a mortgage. But who backs the mortgage? That would be those sad-sack homeowners we mentioned, who stretched too far to buy too much house with an ARM far too long. (See Figure 15.2.)

Most of the time, and especially during the long bull market in housing—which is roughly equal to the bull market in credit derivatives—the payers are ready and able to pay. Sometimes they are not. When they are not, the security of securities disappears.

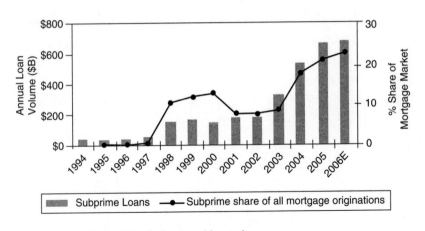

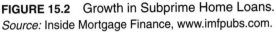

FIGURE 15.2 Growth in Subprime Home Loans.
Source: Inside Mortgage Finance, www.imfpubs.com.

The crux of the matter is that derivatives are not a zero-sum game. Instead, they are a game in which the actual odds themselves follow long patterns of boom and bust. During the boom, people become upwardly mobile by proxy, piggybacking on the shiny surfaces of the bubbles . . . in credit . . . in debt . . . and in housing. But then comes the day when the bubbles take a bath. When the poor homeowners must find another source of funds—another money tree—or miss their mortgage payment. And when they miss, what a hit they will take! That will be the day—perhaps soon—when the mother of all bubbles will finally pop, and the other bubbles will follow. Five thousand hedge fund managers will be on the streets looking for the next big thing. Our guess is that when the history of the early twenty-first-century economy is finally written, derivatives will get a special "tipping point'" place—like the *Hindenburg* in the history of the Zeppelin business—or the Little Big Horn in the life of George Armstrong Custer. . . .

A HEDGE TOO FAR

Hardly had we finished mopping up the dot-com mess before the hedge funds began blowing up. Take poor Bernie Ebbers. His number was up only in 2006, on September 27. That was when the man drove up to the Oakdale Correctional Complex in Louisiana in his Mercedes and joined the former governor of the state, Edwin Edwards, in the federal pen. Hizonner faces 10 years in the hoosegow for extorting money out of riverboat casinos. Ebbers got 25 years for his role in a telecom scandal. Accountants under him took some whole numbers out of the operational columns, they say, and slipped them into the capital budget. Both men were naughty, we don't deny it. But putting poor Bernie behind bars for a quarter of a century for some financial hanky-panky seems excessive.

But excess is what it's all about these days. And now the hedge hogs are already putting the telecom scandals in the shade. "Somebody was not monitoring this correctly," said one pro, referring to the extraordinary bet that energy trader Brian Hunter placed on gas prices, a bet so large that at one time he held about 10 percent of the global market in natural gas futures.

As far as we can tell, these are the numbers in a nutshell: Hunter was long, and investors were short—as much as $6 billion. "It appears we have had a major malfunction," he might have said. But that famous understatement has already been taken when the space shuttle *Challenger* broke up and physicist Richard Feynman charged that NASA's standards had been perverted by bureaucrats.[2]

In the financial world, standards are perverted so easily they must have a twisted gene to start with. Like Ebbers, Hunter came from nothing to make a fortune. But the 32-year-old math star had barely gotten used to being extraordinarily rich and extraordinarily talented when a very ordinary slipup with numbers derailed him. We will return to him, but meanwhile, what is behind the fascination with derivatives?

The professionals may explain that derivatives help globalized, information-drenched markets disperse risk, but this is wishful thinking. They don't really disperse risk at all; they aggregate it. Fund managers all learn the same theories. They all read the same papers and attend the same conferences. And now they all trade the same things, using more or less the same strategies and formulas.

Every hedge fund manager's head pulsates with the same delusions and prejudices. They pretend they are disinterested scientists, but they are actually more like hairstylists, ready to coif their portfolios to suit the latest fashion. And they make their customers into clowns when their returns get trimmed.

Old tricks are reinvented. The Constant Proportion Debt Obligation (CPDO) was launched in 2006. Meant to protect investors against credit defaults, it is the reincarnation of the constant proportion portfolio insurance (CPPI) of 20 years back. The CPPI, too, was supposed to protect investors from a crash—only nobody quite understood how. Then, in 1987, a year after it was introduced, the market crashed and investors finally figured it out. CPPI's fancy programs had actually magnified the losses. We don't know how the CPDO will hold up, but whenever the higher math and the greater greed come together, there are bound to be thrills.

The truth is that no risk-control gimmick, however complex, can protect a whole market for the simple reason that the whole market cannot outperform itself. The more people climb onto an investment platform—whether it is derivatives, dot-coms, dollars . . . or dirigibles—the more it creaks and cracks.

Indeed, in 2006 you could have actually done better by accident than in the average hedge fund, which was up only about 13 percent.[3] This was at a time when the FTSE index had risen 11 percent[4] and the Dow by 19 percent, including dividends.[5] Still, that has only made investors more desperate to get into the tiny group of funds doing well, and top-performing funds are often closed. Smart managers know that when too much money chases too few good investment ideas, returns will only regress to the mean, so they aren't accepting new money.

In fact, on November 27, a story appeared in the press telling readers that rich investors were having to resort to "underhanded" means and special favors in order to get into the best hedge funds. Somewhere in the dark mush of our own brain came a flicker of light and the ringing of a bell. We recalled the initial public offerings (IPOs) of the late 1990s. Since managers found it convenient for the shares to rise quickly following the release of IPOs, they were normally priced at a level from which they were bound to go up, even though they might already be selling for far more than they were worth. Getting in early on an IPO was, thus, guaranteed money in the bank, which is why Barbra Streisand would send IPO managers tickets to her shows, hoping for more than a round of applause.

Of course, the dot-coms blew up in January 2000, and since then, the free tickets have started going to hedge fund managers, not investment bankers.

Then, by the fall of 2006, at least two hedge fund companies had gone public on the London Stock Exchange. What sense does it make for exclusive hedge funds to sell their shares to complete strangers? Plenty. With returns falling and customers beginning to ask questions, hedge fund impresarios are getting out while the getting is good, selling to investors who don't know any better.

But now the gumshoes are taking a look at the swindle. Timothy Geithner, chief of the Federal Reserve Bank of New York, says hedge funds are a "major risk." Neither hedge funds nor derivatives cure markets of manias, he says. Instead they might even amplify them.[6]

And even J. Edgar Hoover's team is worried that hedge funds may be "luring small savers into risky investments." Chip Burrus speaks for the lawmen: "People that aren't expecting to have this type of risky investment in their portfolio end up taking a bath. . . . [They] just get fleeced left and right."[7]

Investors taking losses was never before on the G-men's beat. But hedge fund managers must be getting nervous; soon the Department of Homeland Security will be rounding them up and sending them to Syria for waterboarding. And not a moment too soon, in our opinion.

HEDGE, I WIN; FAILS, YOU LOSE

Am·a·ranth: Pronunciation: 'a-ma-"ran(t)th

Function: *noun*

Etymology: Latin *amarantus*, a flower, from neuter of *amarantos* unfading, from *a-* + *marainein* to waste away

1. any of a large genus (*Amaranthus* of the family Amaranthaceae, the amaranth family) of coarse annual herbs. Also called pigweed.

2. An imaginary flower that never fades.

Recently, investors found to their chagrin that the Greenwich, Connecticut, genus of the pigweed is not only not imaginary, it can fade out at lightning speed. Hedge fund Amaranth Advisors managed to lose $4.6 billion—about half its entire value—in a matter of just a few days, through a miscalculation of the price of natural gas futures in the spring of 2007.

The figure soon grew to over $6 billion. It seems that Amaranth's star trader, the aforementioned Brian Hunter, bet the farm on the idea that the gap between the March 2007 price of natural gas and the April 2007 price would widen. Instead, it narrowed from about $2.00 per 1,000 cubic feet to about 63 cents, transforming Amaranth's 20-plus percent yearly returns, in one fell swoop, to a 35 percent loss.[8]

Hunter, a Canadian, had made millions for the firm after natural gas prices exploded in the wake of Hurricane Katrina. He was thought to be so savvy about gas futures that his bosses at Amaranth let him work out of his home in Calgary, where he drove a Ferrari in the summer and a Bentley in the winter. The jazzy wheels matched the snazzy wheeling and dealing at the American energy fund, where 1.4 percent of net assets went for "bonus compensation to designated traders" and another 2.3 percent was doled out for "operating expenses." When an account made a net profit, the manager took care to cut himself up to 1.5 percent of the account balance per year, in addition to a 20 percent cut of its net profits—less the traders' bonuses and operating expenses. But when the account lost money, the manager suffered no penalty, though the investors still remained on the hook for the operating expenses and possibly for trader bonuses as well.

What kind of a gig is that, where investors have to pay to play and then pay to lose, as well? What can investors be thinking when they see their accounts shrivel, while their managers grow sleek and prosperous in their Greenwich pads?

The hedge fund world is famously populated by math whizzes, each one claiming to have solved Poincaré's Conjecture. But the important math of hedge funds is very simple—it's heads I win, tails you lose. The typical fund charges 2 percent of capital, plus 20 percent of the gains above a benchmark, often the risk-free rate of return—say, around 5 percent today. So, a fund with a 10 percent return charges its clients 2 percent of capital plus another 2 percent (20 percent of 10 percent) for the performance. Even a fund that is able to do twice as well as the benchmark—a difficult feat—leaves the investor with only a 6 percent return, net. Suppose that for four years in a row, the fund gets twice the return as the risk-free rate, and every fifth year it suffers a 10 percent loss. When this happens, do you think the fund managers send out a letter offering to share 20 percent of the loss? No, they are happy to take a percentage of the profits, but not the losses. So, in the four fat years, the fund builds up—with the managers taking their cut. But in the fifth year, investors take all of the loss, effectively magnifying it, and making a dollar of loss equal to $1.25 of gain.

The math is not only easy, it is perverse. For fund managers, there is every incentive to take wild gambles. If the gamble pays off, they become rich and famous. If it does not, they are still the same prodigies they were before. But for clients, hedge fund investing is like playing strip poker with a beautiful woman—by her rules: When you lose a hand, you take off your shirt; but when *she* loses, she puts on a leather coat!

Why do investors think they can get anywhere in such a game? The quick answer is that in the late stages of a public spectacle, thinking becomes a vestigial function—about as useful as an appendix ... and as liable to be cut out in a crisis. Instead, investors rationalize and theorize to justify the excesses. Why buy a hedge fund? Better returns, they tell themselves—though hedge fund returns have been so abysmally low that their money would have slept sounder tucked up in a cozy money market account. Different market, they argue—claiming that the new conditions demand trading rather than buying and holding. Don't marry your stocks. Just shack up for a few months and unload them when the next hottie comes along; that's what the celebrity hedgies do. But, is filling your portfolio with fast-moving floozies any way to make money? They've all been on the street too long already; they're overpriced and overworked. And when the market goes down, they go down faster and further.

The hedge funds have smarter managers, claim investors. And here, finally, they might have a point. Who but a real sharpie could have come up with such a scheme? Hedge fund clients might be dripping in red the past few years, but the fund managers themselves are in clover.

In this respect, Amaranth is only following the hedge fund play-book. Deals for hedge bosses are so sweet that Warren Buffett claims the funds aren't really investment vehicles at all but compensation strategies—ways to keep star managers in their multimillion-dollar digs while the funds themselves turn in lower and lower returns—sub-10 percent on average, and in some cases, pushing below 5 percent, according to the Hedge Fund Index. In fact, in 2005, some 848 hedge funds closed down their business, says one hedge fund consultancy firm.[9]

Is it just a case of too much of a good thing diluting the returns? Could be. When Alfred Winslow Jones coined the term in 1949, hedge funds operated on the margins of the investment world. "Hedge fund" then simply meant a portfolio of stocks with long and short positions, the shorts acting as a hedge against losses in the longs.

Today, the term better describes the legal structure of the groups—private, and limited to a specific number of investors with a minimum of $1 million in assets. The actual strategies employed vary dramatically, from commodity trading to distressed investing.

And today, hedge funds have spread like a tropical parasite. There are now 8,000 or so of them, infesting even institutional investors and pension funds, and sucking in total assets of about $1.2 trillion.

Meanwhile, hedge funds specifically engaged in energy trading—like Amaranth—have proliferated, soaring from about $5 billion to a stratospheric $100 billion.[10]

You'd think this would give at least the pros in the business some pause. Yet, Morgan Stanley, for example, pumped 6 percent of its $2.3 billion fund of hedge funds into Amaranth. And, Goldman Sachs' fund of hedge funds also admitted that an anonymous energy-related investment—guess which one?—had wiped off a chunky 3 percent off its monthly return.[11]

Hubris and excessive risk run through the entire sorry story. Hunter himself was borrowing $8 for every $1 of Amaranth's own funds, while taking positions 10 times larger than a veteran energy trader like Goldman. Hunter also expanded Amaranth's natural gas holdings from 7 percent to half of the firm's entire exposure.

Like Long Term Capital Management (LTCM), the hedge fund that blew up in 1998, Amaranth held such large positions in the market that it could not unravel its positions. Like LTCM, also, Amaranth boasted on its web site that it would never fail.

But, unlike LTCM, the financial community is reacting with odd indifference to Amaranth's fiasco. Peter Fusaro, co-founder of the Energy Hedge Fund Center, which tracks 520 energy hedge funds, shrugs that Amaranth is "a hiccup." Amaranth's blowup doesn't affect as many institutional investors and banks and other financial VIPs as LTCM's did. Only its rich clients have to endure the pangs of portfolios sliced neatly in half.[12]

Maybe so. Maybe not.

If vanity were gravity, Greenwich, Connecticut, the home of the hedge fund stars, would be a black hole. It sucks in money from all over the financial world and turns it into—nothing. We think of the typical hedge fund manager: not yet 30, no experience of a real bear market, let alone a credit contraction. The man thinks only of the mansion he will build in Greenwich if his bets pay off. He imagines that he will take his place alongside George Soros and the Quantum Fund. More likely, he will join Nicholas Maounis in the pigweed.

LOW IN THE WATER

While Amaranth was registering the largest single loss in history, housing registered the first nationwide decline in 11 years, and for the first time in 90 years, the United States turned into a debtor nation. The whole world rocked, too. In Mexico, millions protested the presidential elections and teachers in Oaxaca threatened revolution. Thailand's elected government was replaced in a military coup. In Hungary, citizens rioted. Hugo Chavez told the UN that the United States of America was run by the "devil." This same US of A is now widely thought to be preparing a military strike against Iran. Yet these remarkable events have been greeted by the market with such a comalike indifference that we feel like holding a mirror under its nose and taking its pulse.

Venezuela may be run by a fox or a fool, but what kind of investor buys its bonds at only 2.3 percent over U.S. Treasuries? And Thailand may have nice beaches, but investors who lend money to the Thai government for barely a single percentage point more than to the U.S. government may have had too much sun. It is as if someone has put lithium into the Manhattan water supply. And now, the Zen-like calm threatens the entire world financial system. Even institutional analysts are enjoying a tranquility normally available only to the brain-dead: "The results suggest that the important drivers of volatility reduction seem to be structural, and may therefore have a permanent effect on volatility ..." said a study sponsored by the Bank for International Settlements.[13]

The lack of panic is not limited to sovereign debt. On the 14th of September, the Ford Motor Company announced that it would lose $9 billion making automobiles in 2006,[14] a loss that would once have caused investors to race for the exits. But on the 15th of September, trading in Ford debt continued as normal. Nor do investors seem to care that value-at-risk, the measure by which the security industry calculates its exposure, has gone up 48 percent since 2001, while it is up 136 percent for Goldman Sachs, ranked the biggest "hedge fund" in the world, in *Alpha* magazine's annual list,[15] or that the assets-to-equity ratio rose 29 percent for the industry, while it went up 49 percent for Goldman. Yet, in mid-September, Goldman lenders stood willing and able to front the company $1.5 billion, at a rate only one percentage point greater than a 10-year loan to the U.S. Treasury.

There is a difference between lending to Thailand or to Goldman Sachs, and lending to the U.S. Treasury. And it is not merely a difference of degree. Thailand may squeeze its citizens. Goldman may swindle its customers. But only the U.S. Treasury has the power to do both. That is why U.S. Treasuries are regarded as such safe credits. In a storm, it is Treasuries you will probably want to own, not Goldman or baht bonds. In what circumstances, then, should you run after the meager extra yield? Only when you think storms are a long way away.

The complacency is endemic. The Dow was at a high in the last few weeks of 2006. And in December of that same year, the VIX hit a new all-time record low. The VIX is an index of activity in the options market. People buy options when they are afraid that prices might get away from them. A put option, for example, gives them the right to sell shares in the future at a predetermined price. The record low VIX reading meant that investors weren't worried. They expected the going to be good forever. Also at a near-record low in 2006 was the spread between junk bonds and better credits. When the going gets rough, or people expect it to get rough, they insist on high-grade bonds and lend only to so-called junk borrowers at much higher rates of interest. When the spread between the junk and the high-grade bonds narrows, it means investors see little risk.

So confident and complacent were investors that they lent money for a 30-year period to the U.S. government—the world's biggest single debtor—at an annual interest rate of only 4.51 percent. On that very same day, December 1, 2006, they could have lent for just 91 days and gotten an even higher rate of interest—4.91 percent.

One absurdity leads to another one. It made no logical sense for investors to lend short-term at higher rates than they would lend long-term. Every loan is a race against the future. Revolutions, market crashes, defaults, inflation—a loan will go bad sooner or later if it is left to go on long enough, so long-term loans are almost always at higher rates than short-term ones. The future is the best long-distance runner, and when it wins, it will wipe out your loan.

In 2006, lenders were lending not simply illogically, but downright suicidally. The inflation rate was over 2 percent. And the tax rate, too, represented about 2 percentage points of a 5 percent return. Reduce the remainder by fees and accidents and there was nothing left; investors were making a bet that they couldn't win. Investment firms sold credit default swaps by the boatload, so sure were they that the boat would never run aground. This is not a Goldilocks scenario, said Ed Yardeni, speaking for the securities industry and the terminally delusional. This is "better than Goldilocks."[16]

And the *London Times* cited an International Monetary Fund (IMF) paper:

> Moreover, when the IMF's researchers consider the familiar long-term risks to the global outlook—the trade deficits in America (and to a lesser extent in Britain), the risks of a boom-bust cycle in house prices and mortgage borrowing, the danger from soaring energy prices, the threats to financial stability from speculators and hedge funds—they now conclude that all these trends are far less troubling than they seemed even a year ago.[17]

Markets make opinions. After a long period of serenity, investors begin to forget that the winds can howl and the seas can suddenly well up and knock down whole cities.

But opinions make markets, too. Seeing no menace, investors reach for yield on tippy toes . . . stretching . . . grasping . . . hastening toward danger. As they do, storm insurance becomes a greater and greater bargain.

Of course, we don't get to see tomorrow's weather any sooner than anyone else. Perhaps the IMF is right. Maybe, in the next 12 months, the seas will be as placid and quiet as a strangled nun. The world economy is on course to grow another 5 percent or so in the year ahead, claims the IMF. The passengers are so cocksure, they have traded their life vests for rubber ducks from Asia.

As to the new technology and globalization, this crew thinks they invented it. But they are mistaken in that, too. Back in the 1920s, there came a burst of new technology even bigger and more powerful than the information revolution. Automobiles, electric fans, refrigerators, radios, telephones, and mechanized agriculture—the new technology was breathtaking. And globalization? Back then, too, ships plied the seven seas, laden with pineapples and bananas from plantations in Latin America, tea from India, rubber from Malaysia, tobacco from Virginia, and automobiles from Detroit.

Even today, Trenton, New Jersey, hangs on to its old motto—now rusty and fraudulent—"Trenton Makes, the World Takes." In the 1920s, it was burnished and true. Globalized commerce created a boom in Trenton back then. Products from the town and its hinterland were loaded onto transport and shipped all over the world. Prices for Trenton's properties and Trenton's companies soared. Trenton became famous as a major manufacturing center for steel, rubber, wire, rope, linoleum, and ceramics.

But then came what was supposed never to come. The Great Depression hit. By 1933, one-tenth of the population of the entire state had become dependent on the government for its living and New Jersey was giving out begging licenses to the poor, after state funds ran out. In 1937, even the local gravediggers went on strike. The landscape had turned so bleak that during the radio broadcast of "The War of the Worlds," when Orson Welles announced that a "huge, flaming object" had fallen on a farm 22 miles from Trenton and extraterrestrials were on their way, there was widespread panic as people clogged the highways fleeing the state, and others blockaded their homes against the Martians.

Actually, in a strange coincidence, a huge flaming object *did* descend on New Jersey in 1937. The German zeppelin *Hindenburg*—flying loaded with hydrogen—caught fire while approaching a mooring mast in Manchester. It took only half a minute for the blaze to devour the vessel and kill 36 of the 97 people on board. It might have been an omen; two years later, World War II broke out.

But, there was a bright side to things. While almost 10 percent of New Jersey's population was carted off to the war front, the employment situation in the state did finally get better. Soon New Jersey shipyards were bustling once again—this time, with the construction of battle ships, aircraft carriers, cruisers, and destroyers. All told, the state received 9 percent of all Allied war-related contracts during the war years. At the height of its boom in the 1920s, New Jersey could never have known that it was on the edge of the worst depression in U.S. history. And it could never have guessed that the bust ahead of it would run so deep and last so long that it would take a world war to fix.

All of America rode low in the water in the 1920s, and got swamped in the storms that blew up later. In the middle of 2007, with only 100 basis points between the gunwale of the world's safest credit and the water line of one of its riskiest, marine insurance looks like a good buy.

THE HIGHWAYMEN

"A fool and his money are soon parted," goes the old saying. What has always puzzled us is how the two of them got together in the first place. Markets are supposed to sort such things out. In their free give-and-take, human strengths and weaknesses are rewarded or punished, as the case may be. And if the results seem unfair, who are we to argue with them? Do unto others—and they will do unto you. And the more you do for others, the more you can expect them to do for you. People bake bread not to put bread on others' tables, but to put it on their own. Thank God. Otherwise, we'd all go hungry. Nor does the busboy bus for the benefit of mankind. Instead, everyone schleps, humps, sweats, and toils for reasons of his own.

This insight is the central insight of all modern economists who aren't idiots. The symmetry is of it is elegant. The morality of it is appealing.

That is why a properly functioning economy does seem to deliver something close to rough justice. Henry Ford brought the benefits of automobile transportation to the masses. He deserved to make a lot of money. Andrew Carnegie provided the nation with steel. John D. Rockefeller rolled up and rationalized an early market in oil. Who can say these tycoons of yesteryear did not deserve what they got?

But, today, give-and-take is replaced by assault and battery. The market is a public spectacle, where nothing quite works as promised and almost no one gets what he deserves. Mountebanks are adulated, while honest citizens are robbed, bossed around, and even killed.

And here, it is only fair to give warning: Karl Marx would be pleased with us. For we will argue that today's winners make their gains perversely, unlike the winners of the past. You can tell a boom by its fattest cats, and today's fat cats got rich at the expense of the poor.

"Them that has, gits" is the general drift of things. In countries like France, the gittin' of those who have is detested by those who haven't. "Behind great fortune lies a crime," observed the great novelist Balzac. Sensible people in France try to look poorer than they are to avoid being detested.

But in the Anglo-Saxon countries, people try to appear richer than they are, because the lower classes tend to admire the rich; they have no desire to cut their heads off. In the United States, those who want others to think highly of them just have to announce that they have swindled the Department of Homeland Security or won the lottery, and they rise in stature overnight. People begin to care what they think and will ask their opinion on politics or even wine. The poor genuinely believe the rich are better than they are. They are smarter and better educated. The poor even support low tax rates for the rich, as long as they have a lurking chance of joining them.

Thanks to *Vanity Fair*, we were recently able to press our noses to the glass and look in on the lives—or at least the architectural follies—of the superrich.[18]

Backed by speculators from Goldman Sachs, builders are putting up a mammoth 19,000-square-foot house on Zaccheus Meade Lane in Greenwich, Connecticut. The builders will spend $5 million to build the house and plan to sell it to "the hedge fund guys" for $12 million. In Greenwich, there are enough of them to make that assumption.

Known as the "richest town per capita in the world," Greenwich attracts hedge quants like a soccer match draws hooligans. The average house sold in the city last year brought $2.5 million, up 40 percent in the past two years. Five times as many sold for $10 million or more than two years ago. Clifford Asness, of AQR Capital Management, bought a 12,500-square-foot place on North Street for $9.6 million. Steven Braverman, of Braverman Asset Management, paid $9.5 million for his pile. And David Ganek, of Level Global Investors, has a nine-bedroom, 15,710-square-foot English manor house not far away. *Trader Monthly* reports that Ganek made between $75 million and $100 million last year. We also learn that he hired Los Angeles artist Ed Ruscha, famous for doing paintings of words, to paint the word LEVEL on canvas for the Ganek house.

A house that might not be built, however, is one proposed by Joseph Jacobs of Wexford Capital—with 32,114 square feet and an additional 1,165-square-foot pool house. *Vanity Fair* says it is reminiscent of Venice's Ducal Palace and has everything a deluxe hotel should have—wine cellars, exercise rooms, panic rooms, hockey rink, massage rooms with waterfalls, and even a yoga room. "Enough is enough," said the local authorities. It was too big, too gaudy, too over-the-top, even for Greenwich. They denied him a building permit.

Still, the Christmas season, 2006, managed to bring out a spectacular light show at the waterfront home of Paul Tudor Jones, manager of a $15 billion hedge fund. There were tens of thousands of lights rigged up and around his house, which resembles Tara in *Gone with the Wind*. Further up the Connecticut Turnpike, another little town favored by the new moneyed classes, Norwalk, has fallen into the hands of the bubble kings. Here, steamship magnate (later head of U.S. Steel) James Augustus Farrell built a granite mansion on Long Island Sound, and here, in the 1940s, Remington Rand developed the first commercial computer. But now it is the home of Graham Capital Management, a hedge fund with $5 billion in assets and 150 employees. After a $10 million renovation, it now has a gym, a cafeteria, a game room, and a bar. Graham's founder, Kenneth Tropin, lives nearby in a mansion once owned by a former chairman of IBM. And Graham's chief financial officer lives on the other side of the Sound and commutes to work by boat.[19] What a shock. This late in the credit cycle, we—along with everyone else—were convinced that bubble kings needed no boats; they walked on water!

Greenwich, of course, has always been a haven for titans of industry. In the 1920s, Zalmon Gilbert Simmons, who made his fortune in mattresses, spent part of his fortune there; the monumental house he constructed later housed the Skakels, one of whom, Ethel, married Robert Kennedy.[20] The heir to the Phelps Dodge fortune had a sixteenth-century Tudor house taken apart in England so that it could be reassembled in Greenwich. Then there were men like Jeremiah Milbank of Borden's condensed milk, the Rockefellers, and the Carnegies—the old captains of industry.

Still, who could begrudge the tycoons of the past their wealth? They made the nation rich, too. Families who lived in stinking tenements with hardly enough to eat at the beginning of the twentieth century ended it in air-conditioned houses with wall-to-wall carpeting and plenty on their plates. But what advances have the new winners brought the common folk who admire them so? We have no answer, for these new rich are titans not of industry but of speculation. In the new "financialized" economy, their profits are made from lending money, not from manufacturing.

No wonder mommas now only want their babies to grow up to be hedge fund managers. There's no money in religion—unless you're a TV evangelist; and even a politician, however slick, can skim off only a certain amount without getting caught. It is nothing compared to the kind of loot hedge fund managers can take in and take in when they are still young enough to enjoy it.

In 2006, James Simon of Renaissance Technologies set the pace with $1.7 billion in compensation. Compared to him, George Soros must have felt like a charity case, with only about $950 million in pay for looking after Soros Fund Management. But he still did better than Paul Tudor Jones of Tudor Investment, who earned $690 million and Carl Icahn of Icahn Partners, who made $600 million.[21] Meanwhile, Google CEO Eric Schmidt and co-founders Larry Page and Sergey Brin took home a mere $1 annual salary, again, in 2007. Yahoo chairman and CEO Terry Semel did the same, as did Steve Jobs, CEO of Apple Computer.[22]

The hedge fund industry is transforming the social geography of Britain, says one commentator.

"Fortunes have been created on a scale and in a time-frame that we have not witnessed for 100 years, if ever. The average age of buyers of Old Rectories [the quaint country houses, once the home of Anglican priests, now favored by the new-moneyed classes] in Britain has fallen by ten years to people in their early 30s."[23]

We do not report these facts out of jealousy, but from simple puzzlement. Every penny the hedge kings earn has to come from some client's pockets; and their clients must be among the richest, savviest people in the world. Still, with no gun to their heads, they parted with billions of dollars' worth of earnings to overpaid promoters—and felt smarter for doing so.

Never have so few done so little and made so much doing it.

Nor spent so much. A survey of 294 hedge fund managers, with an average net worth of $61.7 million, says they spent the following quantities of money last year:

$3.99 million on fine art
$429,700 on yacht charters
$376,400 on jewelery
$204,200 on clothes and accessories[24]

"When you got it, flaunt it" is the 11th Commandment of the Age of Mammon.

In London, the hedge fund managers are conducting "champagne battles," according to the *Sunday Times*. They don't just drink champagne. They shake up the bottles and spray each other. According to one club director, a single night battle for "effervescent supremacy" set the sharpies back £89,000 (about $150,000).[25]

Come the revolution . . .

But wait, you might say, while no one likes the highwayman who robs the poor, who can fail to appreciate these polished society burglars who, after all, charm the rich only to relieve them of their riches? On the *Forbes* list of rich people, you will find hedge fund managers in droves, but no one who made his money as a hedge fund *client*. The 26 top hedge kings—many of them with houses in Greenwich—earned an average of $363 million in 2005, up 45 percent from the year before.[26] Goldman paid out $16.5 billion in compensations, with employees taking an average of $622,000 last year and top 11 executives accounting for $150 million. Where did all this money come from? From people with too much money and too little sense. Two percent, before any performance fees, on a fund of say, $2 billion, is $40 million in management fees alone. Steven Cohen keeps as much as 50 percent of the returns on other people's money—and all without a bullet being fired! Why, it's almost respectable![27]

But, while the hedge funds are run for the rich, a good bit of the securities they hold are tied to housing debt. That means that, ultimately, the princes of finance monger *debt* to the middle class. Meanwhile, they themselves pay *cash* for their palaces in Greenwich. When the bubbles finally pop, you can be sure it won't be these money men who lose their homes.

Who will? Here we point to some statistics: From 1992 to 2004, the percentage of households 55 and older with debt grew faster than the rate of the population. The 75-plus group's debt load shot up 160 percent to $20,234 (says the Employee Benefit Research Institute); credit card debt for the 65-plus group more than doubled to $4,907, according to Demos, a New York think tank; the 65-plus group was the fastest growing group in bankruptcy.[28]

One observer notes:

The [United States] and world economic system [have] been distorted in these people's favor for more than a decade, to the excessive benefit of their net worth. . . . the Goldman Sachs participation in the Initial Public Offering for the Industrial and Commercial Bank of China, in which the firm and its partners, mostly the latter individually, made a $6 billion profit due entirely to its insider position in the world financial markets, might have landed them in jail for insider trading in a more stringent environment but in this market only further fattened their bonus pool.[29]

Financiers—like bank robbers—do not create wealth. They merely redistribute it. While the mob may idolize holdup men in good times, in the bad times it lynches them. What they will do to the new money men when their blood is up, we wait eagerly to find out.

Part Six

Far from the Madding Mob

CHAPTER 16

HOW NOT TO BE CHUMPED BY WALL STREET

> You gotta ask yourself one question . . . do you feel lucky? Well, do ya, punk?
>
> **—Clint Eastwood as Dirty Harry**

The hardest thing for a man to do is simply get through life with his grace and dignity intact. He is always imagining that his wife is having an affair with the plumber, that the Muslims want to cut his throat, and that he can get rich without working. The next thing you know, he is making a fool of himself. Fortunately, since it is only his private life, he merely makes his friends embarrassed for him.

A young man may be a fool by definition, but at least no one takes him seriously enough to care. But a middle-aged man lives on the verge of disaster. Most of the time, he goes about his business without too many problems. But at any moment, he may feel an irresistible urge to step out of this routine—to buy a sports car or dye his hair. He will be lucky if he gets through it and returns to his senses. If not, people will laugh at him behind his back and tell their daughters to stay away.

Even if he is a sober and sensible man, he is always in danger of glancing at the headlines. Soon thereafter, you may find him at the local hardware store, buying duct tape and plastic to seal off his house against terrorists' chemical weapons attacks. Or maybe you will see him walking around town with a plastic water bottle, convinced he must hydrate himself every hour of the day. Then there are the financial markets, where he is susceptible to not only embarrassment, but impoverishment.

Money may make the world go round, but in matters of money, as in other things, the whirl of the public spectacle tends to make a man's head spin just as fast. Whether he is getting money or getting rid of it, he is rarely far from mass sentiments, and never far from calamity. In getting money, he is lured toward destruction by the markets, by commentators and economists, by the headlines, and by the financial industry itself. In spending, he has a whole world of entrepreneurs and businessmen ready to help separate him from it. They spend billions to make *him* spend ever more conspicuously and to transform what used to be extravagant luxuries into everyday necessities.

The Pew Research Center released a study of consumer attitudes among Americans in December 2006 that showed that 91 percent of Americans surveyed considered an automobile a necessity. Four out of five thought you couldn't get by without a clothes dryer. Even air-conditioning was thought to be a necessity by 70 percent of respondents, while 64 percent thought television was an essential. Cell phones were considered necessary by only one in two respondents; three out of a hundred thought an iPod was a must-have device.[1]

As to TV, air-conditioning, and automobiles . . . if they were really necessary for a person to be happy, everyone who lived prior to the mid-1900s would have been out of luck.

The benefits of central heating and painless dentistry, for example, are obvious. But why would a man work so hard for so long to buy a bottle of Cheval Blanc?

And, one man's necessity is often another man's bugaboo. Television is clearly one of the most successful inventions of the twentieth century; there is hardly a single family in all America without one, and a solid majority believes it indispensable. But what makes it so necessary? What makes it even desirable? For every life improved by television there are probably 20 that are made more pathetic. People spend hours . . . days . . . weeks . . . years in front of the TV; they neglect their work, their families, their friends; their bodies and brains go soft; worse, they watch the shows and begin to take them seriously. They begin to care what people wear on the screen, what the newscasters say, and what the financial pundits tell them. Television, perhaps even more than the newspapers, amplifies the public spectacle, exaggerating whatever fads and fashions are popular.

"Man is an expectant, thinking being," says recent Nobel laureate Edmund Phelps. He should have inserted an *or* in that sentence. Man tends to expect . . . *or* think. Rarely does he do both at once. If he wants a TV set, he will buy one. What it really does for him he can't be bothered to think about. He buys a TV set, and then he buys what he sees on TV or is told to buy on it. On one end of the money spectrum, his expectations lead him to invest stupidly, and on the other, his expectations lead him to spend wantonly. And all through the middle, he is tempted, prodded, pulled, lulled, and gulled into one mug's game after another.

You have probably already figured out the central message in this book: how to avoid getting caught up in the public spectacle of money. In this section, we take a shot at telling you how to avoid losing what money you have, and maybe even how to make some.

Here, we look at the bright side. While the story of public thinking in statecraft is nothing but a long list of battles, massacres, revolutions, famines, evil deeds by evil persons, and bungled opportunities by incompetents and carpetbaggers, at least when we turn to the markets we find no trail of corpses heaped up—financial manias are farces, not tragedies.

The naive scientist looks at the stock market and figures it must follow some pattern. Prices go up, and then they go down. When? How? Why? He studies the situation and proposes a trading hypothesis: "I will only buy stocks that have gone up for the last three months" or "I will follow the stochastics." And so, he sets out to invest rationally and logically . . . often until all his money is gone.

Experts say that 90 percent of traders eventually lose their money. We are amazed; we thought the number was closer to 100 percent.

But aren't markets fundamentally logical? Isn't it all a matter of numbers? Doesn't a rational approach to investing pay off?

Where have you been, dear reader?

As far as anyone knows, markets are unpredictable. And if anyone knows anything to the contrary, he is keeping quiet about it, because as soon as other investors caught on, the secret would be rendered useless. He might just as well give out the address of a bar that serves free drinks; the place would soon be mobbed and useless to him.

Ms. Market, we have found, is like a woman: coy, changeable, and contemptuous of our efforts to understand her. Will she be perky and charming today? Or will she be sulky and distant? Oh my, my, she seems frisky today, doesn't she? We will never fathom what moves her; we might as well be a golden retriever trying to decipher the Tokyo train schedules.

But market commentary is another thing altogether. It is more masculine, which is to say, it is more logical, more understandable, and lamely predictable. Just read the papers. You will find analyses there that even a 10-year-old could grasp. Are they correct? No more correct than a man trying to dope out his mistress's moods. Are they reliable? Yes, of course—mainly because they are almost always wrong.

Markets are infinitely complex systems. The parts of a clock or a hamburger are identifiable and limited. But an infinite number of factors influence the stock market. Each stock has its own universe of influences; the cosmic dust surrounding even a single small company is mind-boggling. That's why even the insiders—top management and main shareholders—are often wrong about how well the company will do in any given period of time. That is why a strategy of blindly following the insiders is not likely to work much better than simply buying the index.

Markets are chaotic systems, say the mathematicians, subject to feedback loops from their constituent parts. Imagine the cuckoo clock that ran slower because the cuckoo was feeling tired! Well, that's what markets do—to the constant amusement of those who are hip to it. After prices have been pushed up by too much investor interest—investors seem to get worn out and prices fall.

Chaotic systems are also subject to inputs that are largely invisible and have impacts that are wholly unforeseeable—a butterfly flapping its wings in China could set off a chain reaction that leads to a hurricane in the Gulf of Mexico.

Jules Henri Poincaré described the butterfly effect in 1908:

> A very small cause which escapes our notice determines a considerable effect that we cannot fail to see, and then we say that the effect is due to chance. . . . it may happen that small differences in the initial conditions produce very great ones in the final phenomena. A small error in the former will produce an enormous error in the latter. Prediction becomes impossible.[2]

Poincaré proved that even if the initial measurements were refined a million times, the differences in results remained huge, as if the predictions had been randomly made.

So, even if you were somehow able to see the parts of the market system clearly, and even if your logic about how they interacted were impeccable, you still wouldn't know what was going to happen next, because you could never foresee the impact of every little winged insect in the financial world. It was the collapse of an unknown and unimportant Viennese bank—CreditAnstalt—that triggered the Great Depression in the United States. Right at this very moment, there is surely some butterfly of a hedge fund manager sweating some multibillion-dollar trade and praying it doesn't go against him. Who knows what the consequences for the whole system would be if it does?

We've been around the investment markets long enough to know that they defy our best-thought-out theories; like God, they can do whatever they want. Thus, we approach the subject cautiously, as a man approaches a woman in the early morning or the rim of an active volcano in the late evening. He can't know for sure what will be waiting for him.

SO YOU REALLY WANT TO BE RICH?

The first question to ask yourself is: What do you really want? "More money," comes the typical answer. It is a reasonable one, but we are suspicious of it. As we will see, people's relationships with money are formed not by what they *say* they want, but what they actually *do* want—or what they actually deserve. When fat people are asked if they want to lose weight, they say yes. Rarely is one impolite enough to follow up with the obvious question: Then why haven't you done so already? Contrary to popular opinion, losing weight is easy. It involves no self-discipline, willpower, planning, or action. What it requires is the opposite—inaction, lethargy, and indifference. In order to eat too much, people must work at it. They must or-ganize meals, take the time to eat them, and find the money to pay for them. Not only must they take a positive interest in their nour-ishment, they must take an inordinate and exaggerated one. Those who wish to lose weight, though, can relax. They don't have to do a thing.

Watching a fat man with the keen eye of a zoologist observing a species of dumb animal, you would come to the conclusion that losing weight is not his primary concern. He also desires other things—such as Krispy Kreme donuts and Aunt Jemima's pancakes. The two desires, he knows as well as you do, are incompatible. It is his preferences you see in his waist size, not his desire for weight loss.

So is it with matters of money. Assuming you are employed, on welfare, or make your living picking pockets, you too could easily have more money, simply by inaction. Do nothing and let your earnings accumulate. Do not spend them. Instead, let your money go forth and multiply. God commanded Adam to do it. Money and rabbits do it naturally.

The vast majority of wealth—both individual and national—is made the old-fashioned way, by accumulation. Thrift used to be a virtue. Now it is a mystery. We had to check the dictionary to see if the word was still there. We thought it might have been tossed out for lack of use. But no. There it is.

"Wise economy in the management of resources; frugality," says the American Heritage Dictionary.

Traditionally, the way to get rich was the same as the way to get a good night's sleep—you looked at two numbers. One was revenue. The other was expense. If the former was larger than the latter, you slept well at night. Nor was getting rich any great mystery. It was just a matter of degree; the larger the spread between the former and the latter, the richer you became. People typically tried to spend less than they made. The difference became "retained earnings" for a corporation or "savings" for a family. The greater the savings, generally, the richer the family, the business, or the nation.

But the housing boom of the early twenty-first century, following as it did the great stock market boom of the preceding century, changed everything. It was a new era, in that people got so lucky they began to think that luck was the only way to get rich. Suddenly, the difference between income and outgo seemed irrelevant.

People have gotten so lucky they think they'll never need to save again. Even supposedly sophisticated investors have given up on the tried-and-true method of building wealth; now, they only need to buy and hold stocks—or houses. They all must feel very lucky.

But let us go back to the beginning. Before you invest at all, you need to ask yourself a key question: Why are you doing it?

Most people respond automatically, "To make money." But most people do not really invest to make money. Many invest their money because they don't know what else to do with it, or they invest to achieve other goals, like status, respectability, and security. They do not care about making money primarily, or even secondarily. Instead, they invest to feel good. They invest in what is trendy ... or popular ... or socially acceptable. That way, at least no one can fault them for doing something reckless with the family fortune; they put it in mutual funds, just like everyone else!

A doctor's wife may open up an art gallery, for example, to make herself feel stylish and arty. A young mortgage broker may put his own money into an ethical fund, because he feels guilty about selling neg-am, subprime mortgages.

No one has "more money" as his only goal. Few have it even as a primary goal, for who but a fool would want money above all else? Literature, religion, and even mythology are full of alarums against it. Ebenezer Scrooge was miserable until he learned to put money in its proper place. And King Midas—of ancient Lydia—desired wealth so much that he asked the gods to grant him an extraordinary wish—that everything he touched would turn to gold. It took him only a few minutes to realize that he couldn't eat or drink the yellow metal.

People invest for all sorts of reasons; earning more money is just one of them.

Even investments that seem to be purely return-driven have other angles to them. If you step into one of the world's prestigious hedge funds—say Medallion or Lone Pine—you grow taller immediately. Your friends admire you. Your wife thinks better of you. For you are not only rich, but smart and well-connected. By comparison, a man who tells his family and friends that he is invested in a pig farm, slum apartments, or a down-market retailer almost shrinks. "He must not have very much money," say his friends. "He must not have very good friends," says his money.

But what you gain in stature today may be lost in both inches and dollars tomorrow, for there is likely to come a time when you will have to do some explaining. That is an important consideration for many people. Some crave their returns—in whatever form—right now, rather than in the future. If an investment would pay off—even handsomely—in 5, 10, or 20 years, they wouldn't be interested. Others worry about what they will tell the grandchildren when they ask: "What happened to the family fortune, granddad?" Granddad will want to have a ready answer.

"It disappeared in the great crash of 2008," you might be able to say—as if it had vanished by magic. "A hedge fund manager leveraged it and put it into leveraged derivatives," perhaps you could say, dazzling the children while putting the blame squarely on someone else. "When the housing market collapsed, we lost everything," might be a good way of describing it; the little tykes couldn't expect you to beat that one.

HOW MUCH IS RICH?

There is another economic principle worth thinking about when it comes to money: the law of marginal utility. Put simply, an extra dollar of income means less to Bill Gates than it does to you. The more you have, the less more is worth to you. Additions to your wealth won't be as valuable, dollar for dollar, as what you already have. Logically, this suggests that most people would rather not lose a dollar than make one, since incremental income is worth less than existing wealth. It also suggests that if the odds of any gamble are only 50/50, no reasonable investor would take it.

Being rich is easier than you think. You just have to get away from Miami or Los Angeles. If you were to live in India or Burkina Faso, even an income of $5,000 a year would make you feel rich. In fact, a new study by the UN says that a net wealth of $2,200 will put you in the richer half of the world's people. If you can scrape together $61,000 in net assets, you are in the top 10 percent. What does it take to be in the top 1 percent? Just $500,000.[3]

The study found that the three richest people in the world—Bill Gates, Warren Buffett, and Carlos Slim Helú, the Mexican who owns his country's telephone system—have a combined net worth higher than the total assets of the 48 poorest countries on earth.

On the other hand, London publisher Felix Dennis recently estimated what he thought it took in total assets to be rich today:

Translating his terms into dollars, $2 million to $4 million make you only one of the comfortable poor, he says. To be comfortably off, you need $4 million to $10 million, and to be comfortably wealthy you need $10 million to $30 million. The lesser rich, he maintains, begin around $30 million and extend to $80 million; then come the comfortably rich, with $80 million to $150 million; $150 million to $200 million and we are talking money. You have serious money once you get to $200 million to $400 million. Past that, you are truly wealthy at $400 million to $800 million, filthy rich at $800 million to $2 billion, and superrich if you have more than $2 billion. So you see, it's all relative, even to multimillionaires.[4]

From another point of view, millions of Americans are actually poorer, in terms of their net wealth, than the people who sleep on India's filthy streets. The poor in India have nothing. But many of America's poor have less than nothing. They are in debt, often by thousands of dollars. India's poor people, in contrast, have no credit cards. They have no access to credit. They are not rich enough to be that poor.

Another interesting item: a McKinsey study puts total U.S. financial assets at about $48 trillion in 2005.[5] We don't know where this figure came from. But we will guess that it doesn't include the U.S. government's so-called fiscal gap of about *minus* $65.9 trillion. Summing up those numbers, the entire country is poorer than the most miserable beggar in Calcutta.[6]

Still, most people believe they need about twice as much money as they presently have—no matter how much they have. A tramp with five bucks thinks another five bucks would make him happy. A millionaire estimates the price of happiness at another million.

But getting more money, like losing weight, involves complex trade-offs and contradictory desires and emotions. Even without spending less, a person could have more money simply by working more, but he would again be giving up something—free time.

In popular usage, being rich refers to not only how much money you have, but how much you can spend without going broke. In that sense, almost all people in the Western world are rich. They might not have any money, but they have high salaries, high welfare subsidies, and credit cards. Even the poor in the developed countries can buy more stuff than an average person in the poor countries. But people who buy too much stuff soon have little money. Every effort to enjoy their riches has, from a balance-sheet perspective, impoverished them.

Ah, there's the rub. For most people, the choice is to be rich one way or the other . . . but not both. They can be the "millionaire next door" by spending less than they earn and letting their wealth accumulate. Or, they can spend as much as they earn—and even more—and live as richly as their creditors permit.

Most people would say that it is stored-up, balance-sheet wealth that counts. But in this sense, too, money is perverse and strange. What is the point of stockpiling money? You might as well keep your kisses to yourself. The only value of money—especially in its electronic form—is that it gives you purchasing power. The more you have of it, the more stuff you can buy. And if you do not use your money to buy the stuff you want, then what is the point of having it at all?

Modern man is, thus, bamboozled by money any way he goes. If he saves all his life, he goes to his grave without enjoying it. If he spends it, he has less to spend later. Even if he saves it only so he can spend it later, when he finally does spend it, he is practically guaranteed to make a public spectacle of himself.

Once people have all the stuff they can reasonably want, the marginal utility of additional money not only collapses, it sometimes goes negative. There is no human gene that makes people want Ralph Lauren written on their clothes. It is simply a way those with a few bucks can distinguish themselves from those who have less money or more taste. Pretty soon, their spending backfires, and they become rich buffoons, building gaudy palaces, throwing wild parties, and buying status and admirers at enormous cost.

But what can you expect? The typical person spends his life trying to make money. When he finally gets some, he is completely unprepared for the next step—getting rid of it. So he looks to media and advertising for inspiration. And in spending, as in earning, it makes a chump of him.

CONFESSIONS OF A NEWSLETTER MAN

Both of your authors have worked in the financial newsletter industry, one for nearly 30 years. Was ever there a fairer métier, we wonder? The poor carpenter risks cutting his fingers or banging his knee. The used car salesman's hearing goes bad as soon as he takes up his job:

"No, I don't hear any rattle," says he. The foot soldier gets sent to a godforsaken hole like Iraq, where the women are covered up and the liquor stashed away.

But in our trade, hardly a newspaper or a day passes without a good laugh. Our only occupational hazard is a rupture of the midriff.

Perhaps we should explain whence cometh this heightened sense of humor. Most people, after all, read the news pages for information. They lack the proper training and perspective to fully enjoy the jolly news. As a result, they are always in danger of taking its humbug seriously and finding the people in the headlines important. If you really want to appreciate the media, though, you have to get close enough to see how things work—like a prairie dog peering into a hay bailer—but not so close that you get caught up in it yourself. The newsletter business is perfect; it is a part of the media, but no one would mistake it for the most respectable part.

Back in the 1970s, the investment newsletter business was even more fun than it is today. Since then, years of television, heavy-handed regulation, and airport security have taken much of the lightheartedness out of American life. In its place, a kind of earnest timidity has settled over the 50 states. You can barely talk about an honest investment without some ambitious prosecutor wanting to make a federal case out of it.

But back in the 1970s, the folks you met in the newsletter trade were wilder and more disreputable. We remember attending an investment conference with an investment adviser from East Germany who had escaped the Soviets by stealing a small plane and flying to the West. This alone made him a bit of a hero back in the 1970s. But his talk to the investors endeared him further:

"Take a look at zis chart," he would begin, pointing to the bottom of what appeared to be a wave pattern. "Investing is *reeelly verry* simple. You just buy at zee bottom. Heere! Zen, ven ze stock goes up, vat do ve do? Ve sell. Heere! [Pointing to the top of the wave pattern.] It is reeelly verrry simple."

"Well, what if the stock doesn't go up?" asked an investor, not prepared for patterns or people that weren't perfectly straight.

"Ah, ve just keep our eyes on ze chart. If it doesn't go up, ve don't buy it."

We don't recall the man's name. It was something like Dr. Friederich Hasselbauer. We were always a bit suspicious of financial advisers who used the "Dr." title, though many did. We imagined they had been run out of the medical profession. Perhaps they were administering cyanide to elderly patients in nursing homes before they turned their attention to our portfolios.

And then there was the Quack man. His name was "Red" Robin. As near as we could figure, he liked ducks so he called his financial analysis "The Quack Report." Apparently, he had made his money paving airport runways. Then, in his 50s or 60s, he decided to devote himself to financial analysis and saving the world from a small group of criminal conspirators known as the Bilderburgers, rumored to be in cahoots with the English government. Once, flying on the Concorde across the Atlantic, old Red saw the UK chancellor of the exchequer (it must have been Lord Barber) on the same flight. He told us that he decided to confront his lordship right there and then, when he had the chance.

"I just went up to him and I said, 'I'm onto you, ol' buddy.'"

It must have been quite a scene. Red Robin was a funny-looking fellow with a paunchy stomach who always dressed in orange coveralls—which made him look a little like a red-breasted sapsucker. Why he wore orange overalls, we don't know; perhaps they were a holdover from his days working on airport runways when he didn't want the cement trucks to run him down.

Red had funny ideas about investment advice, too. He offered readers a lifetime guarantee—they could have their money back anytime. But then he added a caveat: "My life, not yours."

As it turned out, the guarantee was less valuable than readers imagined or Red himself had hoped. He was gunned down on a beach in Costa Rica, where he happened to be on business with his partners—a shady pair who made their livings selling business franchises to unwary investors. After he was shot, they put him in their car and drove to the hospital—a long, slow drive, according to industry legend. Poor Red didn't make it. The two had taken out a large insurance policy on him.

One of the partners, called, let us say, "Professor Smith," was so fat he could barely walk without the help of two canes. How he could have been ambling along on a tropical beach with the Quack man we don't know. But equally implausibly, he was having an affair with a young woman. When his wife found out, she demanded a divorce. The Professor calculated the cost of the divorce settlement and reached a conclusion. With the help of his partner, the poor old lady was soon history. Then it was Red Robin's turn to go, and then, not too much later, the Professor, too, feared for his life. He sent out a desperate letter saying that he was next in line, but the fellows in the newsletter business were not especially moved. Whether he had it coming or not, they figured, he would probably get it soon enough. He did. He was dead a week later.

But that was the strange milieu in which we decided to make our career—nuts and kooks, charlatans and dreamers, brazen hucksters and earnest geniuses. Here were thinkers whose thoughts were untainted by any rudimentary training—let alone advanced doctrine—of any sort. Here were mountebanks and scalawags galore, along with a few saints, dispensing market wisdom, stock recommendations, and macroeconomic analysis so far-reaching you needed a Hubble telescope to see where it came from. And here, too, were the sort of men whom rich widows were warned about and the sort of theorists who made you wonder about human reason itself.

"There's old A.J.," a friend remarked recently about a colleague. "He never stops thinking. Too bad. He should stop. Really."

Thought leads to action, which frequently leads to reconsideration and regret—or maybe not. One friend of ours, Gary North, began studying the possible consequences of the Y2K computer problem in the late 1990s. The more closely he looked, the more alarmed he became. He began writing about the subject. And the more he thought about it, the more convinced he became that it would lead to a complete meltdown of modern society. He looked and he saw commerce coming to a stop. He saw trains that couldn't run without electronic instruction. He saw cash machines frozen up. He saw power plants idled by their computer brains. And what would happen to all that electronic information—bank accounts, trading records, inventories—on which the whole financial world depended? He saw millions of people with no money, and then no food. He saw riots in the street—and worse.

Then, he looked around and saw that he and his family were as exposed to the menace as everyone else. He decided to take precautions—moving his family to an isolated rural area where they would be safe from the apocalypse he saw coming.

Maybe he would be wrong, he reasoned. But what if he were right? The cost of being right and failing to protect himself and his family could be catastrophic. He moved to a mountain hollow, buried provisions, and began the countdown to the year 2000.

Of course, when the big day came, nothing happened. The clocks worked. The trains ran. The power was still on. Apparently, not a single cash machine failed.

People pointed and laughed. But was he wrong? What if the odds of a meltdown had been only 1 in 100 or 1 in a 1,000? Was he not right to give a warning in the strongest possible terms? And wasn't it partly because of him and others like him that billions were spent to correct the problem before January 2000?

Colorful eccentrics, careful analysts, cheerful con men, self-assured delusionals, and honest *penseurs* trying to figure out how things are put together—this is the world of investment gurus.

But guess what? The gurus are often right. True, some financial gurus have gone broke following their own advice. But many have gotten rich.

In the late 1970s, we undertook a study—with Mark Hulbert, who is still at it—of how well these financial gurus actually performed. We wouldn't presume to summarize Mark Hulbert's nearly 30 years of work; we will just tell you what we took from it:

There is no right way to invest.

There are a lot of different ways, almost any of which can make money. On the one hand, a method that works spectacularly in one period may collapse completely when the market changes course. On the other hand, one that works poorly under certain conditions may also work poorly in others.

But generally, an investment adviser who works hard to develop and refine a system, and who sticks with it, can do reasonably well. He can be a technical analyst, a chartist, a Graham and Dodd follower, even an astrologer. Almost any disciplined approach, pursued intelligently and steadily, can pay off.

Why is this so? Investing is, when you get down to the gritty basement of it, a competitive undertaking. If you do what everyone else does, you will get the same returns as everyone else. In order to get better returns, you have to do things differently. Investment gurus seem to be favored, in this regard, by their own originality and quirky self-reliance. "Sometimes right, sometimes wrong," they say. "But never in doubt." Taken together, they are probably the most independent and contrary professional class in the world. And this contrariness, alone, seems to put them at odds with the great mass of lumpen investors, allowing them to make more—or, sometimes, less—than the common results.

By contrast, what dooms the average investor is the same mushy quality that seems to be ruining the whole country. He will wait in line—without a word of protest—while guards frisk Girl Scouts and old ladies for dangerous weapons. He cheers on the troops as though they were a football team. And he will believe any line of guff—no matter how fantastic—as long as everyone else falls for it, too. Dow 36,000? House prices always go up? Interest-only neg-am mortgage?

Investors who follow newsletter gurus have no guarantee of making money; but those who follow the crowd are practically guaranteed that they will not.

STEERING CLEAR OF THE MOB

So, what should you do to make money?

It immediately occurs to us that we are not asking the right question. The proper question is: What should you *not* do?

In war, politics, and every other form of the public spectacle, the critical protection comes in the form of a prohibition, not a command. Because it is the commission you have to worry about, not so much the omissions. Action, not inaction, is what normally ruins you.

Thou shalt not kill—if only Mao or Che or George W. had bothered to listen. Thou shalt not bear false witness—if only witch hunters, child social workers, and dot-com analysts would think of that! Thou shalt not covet thy neighbor's wife, nor his ass. Think of all the embarrassment that could be avoided if people remembered that one.

Well, there are interdictions in investing, too, that can help you avoid being swept along by the manias of the market.

If an investor merely recognizes the way mob sentiment works, he is far ahead of most punters. Most people put their faith in experts and their money in mutual funds, and they get their opinions from the headlines. But if he can tune out the noise of the public spectacle altogether, an investor has a chance of at least keeping his dignity . . . and maybe even his money.

Don't Go Looking for Trouble

Here we are reminded of a recent letter from a reader. We paraphrase:

> I know you do not give advice, but I was just curious what you think about my financial position and/or what you would do in it.
>
> I own a 14-unit apartment building in Huntington Beach, California. I bought it a couple of years ago. There has been about

$1 million in appreciation. My wife wants to sell, but I always considered it as my retirement after paying for 30 years.

The problem with selling would be:

1. Capital gains taxes.

2. What to do with the money.

3. We live in the front owner's home of the same property.

I feel stuck because my property taxes are relatively low, as I purchased the building from my father, and I was able to benefit from a California tax law that basically lets me keep his tax rate.

But I have a feeling that the bottom is going to fall out of our real estate market. Would you rather be the owner of an apartment building that has historically always been at 100 percent, or cash out the building and buy a home, or sell and just rent?

In response, we posed an equally absurd question: I am a happily married man. I love my wife; she's beautiful and smart and she loves me. But here's the problem. She is an actress. I've always heard that actresses make bad wives. So I'm thinking about divorcing her. Am I being an idiot?

Answer: Yes, you are an idiot. We don't see what your wife sees in you. You'll be lucky if she doesn't leave *you*.

In both cases, the real and the hypothetical, you have someone caught between a rock and a soft place, between the private world he can understand and master and the public spectacle with its frauds, conceits, and wild guesses.

Our reader is wondering whether he should stick with a good investment or speculate on the housing market. The husband is wondering if he should divorce his wife, because he hears that actresses—she is one—make bad wives. Statistically, it could be true. But statistics do not make a person happy or rich. Actresses typically may be a vain and fickle lot; but he seems to have found a good one. The fact that other actresses may be more trouble than they are worth should be irrelevant to him.

Our dear reader, meanwhile, believes property prices will fall. Though we've said so many times ourselves, at least we haven't taken the idea seriously enough to ditch a good situation just to test our theories out.

"Statistically, the average man may die at 73; but if we were you, we wouldn't drop dead until we were good and ready," we volunteered.

Never Expect the Market to Give a Sucker an Even Break

We are as suspicious of public markets as we are of public toilets. But the average investor believes he can buy a stock in the public markets at the market price and get a fair deal. It isn't so.

Traditionally, most people were smart enough to know that the stock market was no place for an honest working man. The proles and plebes put their money in banks; earned a fixed, reliable rate of return; and left the speculation in equities to the pros. Even today, in much of the rest of the world, people know better. Ordinary people are not fool enough to think they can beat the insiders at their own game.

"Here in Argentina," an economist explained to us, "most people put their money in the bank or buy property with it, because it is something they understand."

Argentina has been through inflation rates as high as 1,000 percent, major depression, debt default, a currency crisis, bank closings, and a stock market crash—all in the past 10 years. What the Argentines don't know about financial risks, in other words, isn't worth knowing.

But in the United States, the lumpeninvestoriat has not faced such challenges in more than 70 years. It sees almost no risks at all. It thinks it can invest—and invest like the pros.

Some things, we all recognize immediately, are simply too amazing for words: Shakespeare. Mozart. Sex. Air transportation. And the attitude of amateur investors in the United States, circa 2007. They leave us in shock and awe. Ordinary people turn over billions of dollars' worth of their hard-earned money—immediate, tangible, *personal* money—believing that strangers will give them back even more. A plumber is supposed to have about as much chance of winning at stock speculation as a corporate insider, they believe.

Of course, it is a monumental fraud—almost equal to "every vote counts" or the "divine right of kings." The market is supposed to be a level playing field, with all the players having an equal chance to kick the ball. The little guy is supposed to be as likely to make money as the big guy.

In theory it works perfectly; in practice, the little guys lose consistently. They lose in two ways: First, they pay out too much to the financial industry in fees, commissions, and spreads. And second, they lose money because they become patsies of the public spectacle. They read the newspapers. They watch TV. They listen to the experts, the commentators, the pundits. As a consequence, they are buyers to whom the elite sells. They are the sellers from whom the elite buys. Without the amateurs, investing wouldn't be nearly as rewarding for the pros . . . or nearly as amusing to the spectator.

What's more, this con is aided and abetted by the U.S. Supreme Court itself, which held in *Basic Inc. v. Levinson*, in 1988, that manipulating a share price constituted a "fraud on the market" that could be measured by movements in the share price itself. In other words, the market really does know best. The market's judgment is "perfect,'" declared the Supremes.

They were convinced by the academic theory we mentioned earlier, the Efficient Market Hypothesis (EMH), according to which prices set by the market are so perfect you're wasting your time trying to outsmart them.

But prices are not perfect at all. They are constantly in motion—subject to influence, sometimes too expensive, sometimes too cheap—always correcting and overcorrecting. Still, if you believe the Supreme Court, the Securities and Exchange Commission (SEC), and the academics, you'd think that unless there is some illegal manipulation, the little guy can pay whatever price the market dictates and still get a fair deal.

Yet, at the same time, the market is also famously fickle and indecisive. A stock can be perfectly priced at $50 one day and then at $10 the next. Which price is correct? Both, says the theory. The market can do no wrong!

The whole idea is preposterous. But every public spectacle needs its myths. And the myth of an efficient market keeps the chumps at the investing tables. They think they have as much chance of making money as Goldman traders, they believe, because—no matter how much they pay—it can't be too much.

Then in 2006, along came a hot new trend suggesting not only that markets are far from perfect, but that the little mom-and-pop investors haven't a chance. Private equity it's called, and it works on the opposite principle of the EMH. It supposes that markets are *not* efficient and *not* fair and that a few rich, smart, well-connected people can outsmart the many ignorant middle-class investors. In fact, it *counts* on it.

For example, private equity firms bought the Hertz rental car business from Ford, a public company, in December 2005. Eleven months later, they sold it back to the public in an initial public offering. Michael Lewis assesses the damage to the public:

> In buying the company they put up $2.3 billion in equity capital. By the time they sold it, they had gotten $1.3 billion of their money back, and held shares—which they no doubt plan to get rid of as soon as they can—valued at another $3.5 billion or so. In less than a year they had netted a fairly clean $2.5 billion profit.[7]

Where did the profit come from? Not from other private equity firms, nor from shrewd private investors such as Warren Buffett. It came from the investors in the public market.

The lesson: Don't be a public market investor. Invest like a private investor.

And what do private investors buy? They buy private businesses. They buy the business next door. They buy the businesses they know better than anyone else.

Don't Be a Patsy

There are investment markets, and there are markets of investments.

In the markets of investments, buyers and sellers apply their individual judgments to the value of an investment, and the market price is established.

In the investment markets, on the other hand, both buyers and sellers read the papers in order to try to figure out what "the market" is doing. That is to say, an investor leaves behind the things he knows and understands for things he knows very little about and will never understand. The neighborhood bank stock is dumped like an old girlfriend; the man is ready for big-time action on Wall Street. He listens to Jim Cramer and forgets to smirk. He looks for the consensus view on next year's earnings and the likely direction of the market in the months ahead. He is no longer an intelligent, independent investor, but a mass market speculator.

Actually, calling him a speculator is pure flattery. A real speculator has a realistic view of the odds and almost always operates on a simple premise—that the crowd usually underestimates the odds of discontinuity.

Take the case of the market that goes up every year for 10 straight years. What are the odds that it will go up again? There is no way to know. But mankind is a credulous beast. If he smites his firstborn and it rains the next day, he will be smiting his firstborn every time there is a drought for centuries to come. And if the market has gone up for 10 years straight, a kind of sentimental momentum tells him it will keep going up. He is loath to accept pure chance as an explanation. He knows there's a reason for it. Low inflation, record profits, favorable Fed policies: He reads the papers; he knows what's up.

The real speculator may know no more about tomorrow than the common man. But he has an advantage—he knows the common man. And he knows you don't win by predicting the future; you win by getting the odds right. You can be right about the future and *still* not make any money. At the racetrack, for example, the favorite horse may be the one most likely to win, but since everyone wants to bet on the favorite, how likely is it that betting on the favorite will make you money? The horse to bet on is the one *more likely to win than most people expect.* That's the one that gives you the best odds. That's the bet that pays off over time.

Unlike the lump, the speculator *knows* he is guessing. So, if he has his wits about him, he will insist that the odds be wildly in his favor. He will buy a stock trading at half its usual price, for example, on the hunch that it will soon revert to its mean. Or he will take a position in a risky gold exploration company or an improbable new technology—betting that if it doesn't blow up in his face, it will produce a 10 for 1 bonanza. He might even take a flier on the supposed next Microsoft, hoping that if it doesn't bankrupt him, it will make him rich.

When you make an investment, the last thing you want is a level playing field. If, as the SEC assumes, everyone actually has the same information to go on, investors' results would be completely random. They'd win sometimes and lose sometime, just as they would at a slot machine at Las Vegas where everyone faces the same odds. And since it costs money to play—the house has to make money somehow—over time they'd lose money. Of course, that is exactly what happens to most investors. But not to everyone.

The mark of the real speculator is that he looks for bets that are not fair; he looks for opportunities to play where the field is tilted in his favor. In this sense, the public market investor who believes the market will go up next year because it went up last year and because Abby Joseph Cohen said so is not even a real speculator. He is merely a patsy. He is the person you want to keep in your sights, the way a hunter targets a deer. If you want to speculate, you need to know what he is doing—and do the opposite.

Better yet, be a real investor.

How can you be a real investor? Buy a real investment, the kind of investment chumps don't buy. What kind of investment is that?

A low price is generally an outward sign of inward grace. And one sector that looks cheap now is commodities—especially soft commodities, such as grains and foodstuffs.

"Here's the only trade you have to make in the next 25 years," says our friend Steve Sjuggerud. "Buy commodities now. Sell them in 2016." Steve points out that when stocks zig, commodities zag. Bull markets in commodities last about 16 years. This one began about 6 years ago and has about 10 left to run. By contrast, the bull market in stocks began in 1982 and must be near its end. Buy into a bull market after it has gotten under way, says Steve, but before it has gotten very far. Stick with it until it reaches an end. And then, sell the thing that is most popular at its peak and buy what is least popular.

While more and more farmland is taken out of production by encroaching suburbs and highways, the demand for food is soaring. Forty percent of the world's population—mostly in Asia—is generating the financial means to buy food on the world market. The Chinese, for example, consume about 2,500 calories per day—the same as the Taiwanese. But on the island of Taiwan, more of the calories tend to be of the animal variety; the average Taiwanese person consumes nine times as much meat as his cousin on the mainland. The Chinese are trying to catch up—with meat consumption rising at a 20 percent annual rate. What this means to the grain market is obvious, too. It takes about nine units of grain to produce one unit of meat. This is why China and India, both of whom used to be self-sufficient in grains, now need to import the stuff. But from where?

Everywhere you look, the entire agricultural sector is short of water. Just as the planet seems ready to reach peak oil production—the point at which future production is likely to be lower than past production—so too, does it appear to be reaching a kind of peak water limit. India and China both have their well-known problems with water, but so does the United States. The great lake under the American prairie—the Ogallala Aquifer—is the world's fastest disappearing water supply. The water under the Klamath Basin in Northern California is also dropping fast—down 20 feet in the past three years.

Energy companies, hustlers, and hallucinators are trying to replace oil with grain. But it takes huge amounts of land, water, and energy to produce enough grain to make a significant impact. Switching from oil to ethanol will merely suck the earth dry of water faster—and send food prices soaring.

Never Get Too Far from the Facts

Investments go up ... and down. The secret is to buy them when they are down and sell them when they are up. The lumpenpatsies do the opposite. If every public spectacle has its victims, here they are. The lumps get excited about an investment when everyone else is excited about it—which is precisely the time *not* to buy. Buying low and selling high seem simple enough, but you do have to know which way is up.

Donald Rumsfeld tells us, pithily, that there are known unknowns, there are unknown unknowns, and there are things about which we don't have a clue. Of course, that didn't stop the Bush administration from launching the most ill-advised war in U.S. history, nor does it stop us from having opinions and ideas about things we know nothing about. In fact, as we get older, the less we seem to know about anything. But the less you know for sure, the more important it is to have rules and principles you can follow. So, as we become more ignorant about what is actually going on, we become more stubborn in our opinions about what should be.

Now, imagine that there were no *Financial Times*, no *Barron's*, no commentators, and no one writing books predicting the future performance of the Dow. You'd have to rely only on your own eyes and ears, and your own wits. Investing would become a private matter. And it would be better for it.

Why? Because useful intelligence decreases, like gravity, by the square of the distance from the facts. A private investor is closer to the facts. It's how he knows which way is up. Besides, his brain is better equipped for the scale of private investing. He can get to know the key people personally. And he can see how the business operates, up close, where it counts. By really knowing the industry and the business he is able to eliminate some of the unknowns and make a better decision. Generally, that means he pays less for his investments and works harder to get them.

A town meeting in New England is a long way from the U.S. Congress. Both are, broadly speaking, forms of democracy. But the folks voting on where to put the new town dump are acting on information that is very close to hand. They don't want to put the dump in the wrong place, because they are the ones who will have to live with it.

The U.S. Congress, by contrast, routinely votes on legislation it hasn't even read. It spends money that hasn't even been earned by taxpayers who haven't yet been born. And recently, members of Congress went along with Bush's war in a country they'd never been to, for reasons they didn't understand, paid for with money they didn't have, and fought by soldiers who weren't their own sons and daughters.

In ancient Rome, engineers were forced to stand under the arches they had designed when the scaffolding was removed. And in ancient Greece not only did the sons of the assemblymen go out to fight, so did the leaders themselves. Not only that; the oldest veterans were put in the front lines! And during the period of the Athenian democracy, if a delegate proposed a scheme to improve the future and it was not approved, he would be put to death. If Americans want to make their government more responsible, it can be easily done. They can force members of Congress to put all their wealth in U.S. dollar bonds, serve in every war they start, and pay the ultimate price when they propose some absurd new program.

In the same vein, the further you get from your investments and the less you suffer the consequences, the worse your investments will be. That's why collective investments like index-linked funds, mutual funds, hedge funds, insurance funds, and pension funds are usually so bad. The investor is too far from the facts—and the managers are too far from the consequences. Since the rates of return are always reduced by the managers' fees, you'll—over time and on average—get less than the market itself. And getting the market return minus fees, inflation, taxes, and commissions often results in a negative real rate of return.

In this regard, real estate is the perfect investment—most of the time—for the simple reason that it is easy to get close to and to understand. And there are still many places in the United States where property is still a good buy, like Texas. In El Paso, for example, you can buy some of the cheapest houses in the country. There are towns in West Virginia that are practically deserted, where you can buy a house for as little as $30,000. If you are trying to save money you could sell your million-dollar place in San Francisco, buy the place in West Virginia, and end up with $970,000. The surplus would provide you with an annual income—invested at 5 percent— of $48,500.

And there may be even better property deals to be found abroad, both from a quality of life perspective and from a financial one. The *Economist Intelligence Unit* says the world's most livable city is Vancouver, Canada. Mercer Consulting rates Geneva and Zurich as the cities with the highest quality of life and puts Vancouver in the third spot.[8] They are nice cities, but the values seem fully priced. Where are the bargains? According to the *Economist*, the world's cheapest major city is Asunción in Paraguay. In Europe, Germany and Eastern Europe are relatively cheap. Still, there are plenty of bargains, in our opinion, even in the 50 states.

Never Buy Tuna Unless It's on Sale

A friend of ours likes to tell this story: A man and his wife go shopping and the woman goes into the grocery store. Noticing that cans of tuna fish have been marked down by 50 percent, she decides to take advantage of the low prices and stock up. Her husband, meanwhile, wanders over to his stockbroker, who tells him about some stock that he says is a good investment. The man buys it. A week later, when the two go shopping again, the woman sees the tuna fish selling for twice what she paid the previous time, so instead she buys chicken. The man, on the other hand, goes into his broker's office, finds to his joy that the stock has doubled because "everyone is buying it," and buys twice as much as he bought the week before.

Which of these two people is doing the right thing? The woman, of course. She is buying value based on her own private lights. The man is speculating, but without the real speculator's keen insight into human nature and actual odds. He is not buying a business; in fact, he may not even know what business the company is in. He is buying to be in the market, to be in that great, modern brotherhood of money-savvy alphas, up there with George Soros and Peter Lynch.

A real investor buys a stock as though it were a can of tuna fish. He knows what it is worth to him and buys it when it is a bargain. But how do you know what a business is worth? How do you know when the perfect market has slipped up?

Traditionally and sensibly, the investment value of a business is measured by how much money it will return to the investor. This seems only self-evident, but few investors actually figure it out and invest accordingly. The calculation—at least in theory—is very simple: an investment is worth the present value of the money it will give you back, reduced by the risk that it won't ($V = PV \times MIWGYB \times R$, where R and PV are less than 1).

You may wonder: Why, then, do prices for investments go up and down? (Even if the question doesn't occur to you, we will answer it; it is important.)

In a properly functioning stock market, prices move all the time because investors keep changing their minds about *PV*, *MIWGYB*, and *R*. If they think inflation rates are going up, present value gets discounted. *PV* goes down. Why is that? Because at higher inflation rates, a given future stream of income is worth less money in the present. If you expect consumer price inflation to increase from 5 percent to 6 percent, for example, you'll discount next year's income by an additional percentage point, because you expect the money you receive will have lower purchasing power.

And if you think interest rates are going up, you'll probably want to discount the *MIWGYB*, too. When interest rates rise, consumer credit is more expensive. Consumers then have less money to spend, which is likely to depress sales in your target business. (Besides, why buy a stream of earnings equal to 5 percent of the capital you put up, when you can get 6 percent lending to the U.S. government?)

Of course, a lot of other things can affect *MIWGYB*. Each business and each industry has its own rhythms and cycles. A business that has increased sales greatly may be ready for them to fall. A sector that has attracted a lot of investment interest may have overbuilt its capacity. And consumers' tastes change all the time. These are the things you have to figure out when you try to calculate how much money your investment is likely to give you back.

This is, of course, just another illustration of the general point: that you must study your stock market investments as though you owned companies in their entirety. You need to understand the trends, weaknesses, and opportunities. Only then can you make a reasonable assessment of the *MIWGYB*. And even then you'll probably be more wrong than right.

Then there is *R*—risk. Many are the risks a business faces, and virtually all businesses sooner or later succumb to them. The oldest company in the Dow is General Electric, and it's the only one that has been there for more than 100 years. All the rest of the original 12 have sold off, been taken over, declined in importance, or gone out of business. Most companies are out of business within 10 years. And all stocks quoted today on the New York Stock Exchange (NYSE) will eventually be worthless due to inflation, war, chicanery, bad judgment, bad luck, defaults, competition, or technological change.

How do you calculate the risk? You have to get to know the business, its managers, the industry, the competition—everything you possibly can. And then, of course, you still have the macroeconomic risk—the danger that the whole economy might go down the tubes. There is no sure way to figure it. All you can do is to do your homework and take your chances.

Most people don't even try. They do not bother to figure out the likely return on investments or the real risk. They just go along with the crowd of yahoos—with some cockamamie notion in their heads, such as "stocks for the long run."

What they don't realize is that there is a life cycle to all things—institutions, insects, and insurrections. They begin small, they grow, they mature, they get taken over by parasites, and they die. Just so, in the stock market there is a life cycle of from 30 to 40 years from one peak to the next. In the twentieth century, the big peak in 1929 was followed by another peak in 1966 to 1968, almost 40 years later. The most recent peak is still in question.

We believe it came in January 2000. The Dow was higher at the end of 2006, but only in nominal terms. Adjusted for inflation, it was actually about 20 percent lower. Adjusted to euros, the Dow was still a bit lower. But it is in terms of gold that the Dow has really been hacked down. Since 2000, it was been cut in half. In that year, it took more than 40 ounces of gold to buy the Dow stocks. In 2007, it took only 20 ounces. And if we're right about these cyclical patterns, the next major bull market in stocks may not come until the year 2040.

One little insight into how these cycles work: In the 1970s you could buy a seat on the NYSE for about the same price as you could buy a New York taxi medallion. You needed a seat on the NYSE if you wanted to sell shares. You needed a taxi medallion if you wanted to operate a cab. Investor sentiment was so negative on equities at the time, the authorities seemed to think you'd make as much from driving a cab as selling stocks.

But in the bullish trend that began in 1982, shares—and seats on the NYSE—sprouted wings. Now, they're flying. You could buy a taxi medallion for about $400,000 at the end of 2006. But if you wanted a seat on the stock exchange it would cost you 18 times as much—$5 million. We have no way of knowing, but if the patterns of the past repeat themselves, seats on the NYSE—and shares generally—are now a bad bet. If the bear market trend really did begin in January 2000, it will probably take another 10 or 15 years for shares to hit the ground! "Markets always do what they're supposed to do," say the old-timers, "but never when they're supposed to do it."

We turn to Jeremy Grantham for another hint about where we might be in the cycle:

Grantham divides stock market history according to how cheap or expensive stocks were at the time and looks to see what happened next. Since 1929, had you bought stocks at times when they were among the cheapest 20 percent in terms of P/E ratios, you would have earned an average return of 10.6 percent over the 10 years that followed. If you had bought them when they were at their most expensive—the top 20 percent in terms of P/E ratios—you would have earned only 0.6 percent per year during the following 10 years.[9]

Where are stocks now? In the most expensive quintile. What can investors reasonably expect? If history and theory are any guide, less than 1 percent annual rate of return. Why would any thinking investor buy stocks under those conditions? Of course, one wouldn't.

Steve Leuthold conducted a similar study and came to the same conclusion:

When stocks are selling below a 9.9 P/E ratio, the average return over 10 years is 16.9 percent.

P/Es of 10.9 to 12.1 and the average return over 10 years is 15.3 percent.

P/Es of 13.7 to 15.1 and the average return over 10 years is 11.0 percent.

P/Es of 16.8 to 17.9 and the average return over 10 years is 8.2 percent.

P/Es of 17.9 to 19.3 and the average return over 10 years is 5 percent. P/Es of 20.9 and above and the average return over 10 years is 4.8 percent.[10]

Currently, stocks are at the very top of the range. Investors should expect low returns from equities over the next 10 years.

But while the Dow, U.S. bonds, and U.S. housing are probably going down, some things are probably going up. Japan was in a slump for 16 years; it now looks like it has changed direction.

And gold suffered a bear market that lasted for the last two decades of the twentieth century. Since George W. Bush entered the Oval Office, gold has more than doubled. It seems to be in a long-term bull market, and your authors think its price will go to $1,000 an ounce. But we are not fools enough to say when.

Another thing we believe to be on the way up is Argentina. Both property and investments are still cheap south of the Rio Plata. A house that would cost $3 million in Paris or $5 million or more in London or New York is only about $800,000 in Buenos Aires. Prices may never reach Miami heights, but the difference could easily narrow.

In U.S. dollar terms, the Argentine economy was more than cut in half from 1998 to 2002, but since 2003 it has had one of the fastest growing economies in the world—with growth rates around 9 percent annually. The country produces trade surpluses—led by the agricultural sector and aided by a cheaper peso. The Argentine index is one of the best performers in the world.

There are three ways to invest in Argentina. The first is property. The second is electrical utilities. Argentina's power companies produce no more juice now than they did before the financial crisis, while electricity consumption has increased 24 percent. As demand increases, the government will be forced to allow prices to rise to draw in additional investment.

Steve Sjuggerud recommends an Argentine real estate conglomerate, publicly traded on New York's NASDAQ. It is the largest rural landowner in Argentina and has little debt. He believes it will rise in price along with the food it produces—fitting in with our general view that soft commodities are going to go up for years to come. Argentina is the world's second-largest corn exporter after the United States, and the third-largest soybean exporter. Currently, the world produces less wheat, corn, and other agricultural commodities than people want to eat. The supply of wheat, for example, is expected to come in at about 605 million metric tons in 2006–2007. The demand for it is supposed to be roughly 615 million metric tons. Inventories are now at historically low levels—close to the lows set more than 30 years ago, just before the last major bull market in soft commodities.[11]

Argentina's big advantages are that it has a huge underground water supply—the Guarani Aquifer—and that the land on top of it is cheap. In terms of productive capacity, an acre in Argentina costs only about one-sixth as much as an acre in the United States. Over the long pull, investors in Argentine farmland will probably do well.

Poor people typically get most of their calories from grains. As they get richer, they begin feeding the grain to animals and eat the animals. But increasing food production is not as easy as increasing the output of derivative contracts. China, for example, lacks the resources—land and water, principally—to produce a lot more grain or animals. In fact, it is rapidly losing agricultural capacity—at least for grains—because land is being urbanized or dried up. Much of China is naturally very dry. Water is in short supply. What water there is is being directed toward more high-value output, such as factories, homes, and nongrain crops. The Gobi Desert is expanding, partly because irrigation systems are not being properly maintained or supplied. And on what land is left for agricultural production, farmers are switching to more expensive crops like apples, which are exported and generate higher profits than cheap crops like wheat, which are sold internally. In the 1980s, the United States was the world's largest producer of apples. China now grows four times as many as the United States, while its grain production is down 10 percent over the past decade.

That is why the world's low-cost producers tend to be in areas where labor costs are low, but also where land and water are abundant, like Latin America. Both Mexico and Brazil have extremely efficient chicken producers, for example. Because of concerns over bird flu, shares of these companies sell at very reasonable prices, even though they have strong balance sheets and good growth potential.

Never Buy What Someone Else Really Wants to Sell

Our next prohibition is this: The more someone wants to sell you an investment, the more you don't want to buy it.

This applies to the expensive suits on Wall Street, who specialize in selling U.S. Treasuries to their rich clients, as well as to the cheap suits in brokers' boiler rooms in Boca Raton, who specialize in calling poor clients on the phone to sell them small-cap stocks. Both the cheap suits and the expensive suits have to earn a living. On Wall Street, the average salary is $300,000—and that includes the janitors. As for Boca Raton salaries, we don't know, but Florida is no longer cheap.

But there's more to it than just the cost of the inter-mediaries—what Warren Buffett calls the "friction" in the system. The owner of an investment usually knows the asset better than the buyer does. If it were such a good business, why would the owner want to sell it to complete strangers? If it could earn a decent return on equity, why share it?

You could expect to buy a good used car, for example, simply because the previous owner needed a bigger one or wanted a snappy convertible. So, too, might you get a good deal on a watermelon if the farmer had an especially bountiful crop. A nice house might be offered to you if the previous owners' children had grown up and moved away. They might feel it was time to downsize.

But no sensible investor downsizes a portfolio on a whim or sells an investment just because he has too many of them. Serious investors hold good investments until they believe they are no longer so good.

There are many possible reasons to sell, you will reply. You are right; but a buyer should be on guard. Unless the seller is either desperate or dead, he has figured out that he can get a better return on his money elsewhere.

The other reason you don't want to buy the investments that others are eager to sell to you is that selling costs money. Every investment that is packaged and sold requires lawyers, accountants, secretaries, not to mention advertising costs and sales commissions. Just look in the financial press. What do you see advertised? Mutual funds. Insurance programs. Managed accounts. Private banking. All the things that have such wide margins that they can afford to advertise. You will find ads for funds, funds of funds, and maybe even funds of funds of funds. Each layer requires an extra little bit of grease. The investor who buys a fund of funds of funds is practically walking down a dark street in a bad neighborhood with a sign on his back—I'm Carrying $500 in Cash!

"But the professional gets a better rate of return," you might protest. "So it's worth paying a little bit in commissions."

Is that so? A recent Bloomberg study of 350 of the top brokerage houses—companies that had the brightest employees, with the plummiest salaries, the nattiest suits, and the slickest educations—found something extraordinary. The very best of them, Merrill Lynch, got it right only 34 percent of the time. Merrill picked 200 stocks, of which only 68 turned out to be winners.[12] These are full-time professional analysts, earning an average of about $600,000 per year. And behind Merrill Lynch were dozens of other firms with even worse performance. If the pros do so badly, imagine how the average investor is likely to do, unless he works very hard.

It's probably true, however, that the professional will not do anything patently absurd or foolish and has usually learned enough about investing to avoid the obvious mistakes. In this sense, the rank amateur—if he is too lazy to read a book or think about it for a few hours—is indeed better off paying the commission. But serious investors are better off figuring it out for themselves and avoiding unnecessary friction.

The best investments are those no one wants to sell. They are the investments that pay no commissions or fees, that have no managers, that give no press conferences, that issue no quarterly reports. They are the ones you have to work hard to find. These are the kind of investments private investors look for and often wait years to buy at a good price.[13]

A friend of ours made a fortune in this way. He simply found a business that he liked. It was not a public business. It was not for sale. It was not advertised, written up in a magazine, or even discussed in business circles. It was not even a business he wanted to own or control. But he met the people running it. He liked their business model. So he simply made them an offer. He wanted to buy a piece of it.

The owners didn't need the money. They weren't looking for partners. Still, they were flattered that anyone would want to invest in it. So they took $25,000 for a 5 percent interest. Twenty years later, that 5 percent interest had an estimated market value of $16 million.

Never Buy What Everyone Else Is Rushing to Buy

Yogi Berra once remarked of a restaurant—"Oh, nobody goes there anymore; it's too crowded." In the restaurant world, good eateries soon become overcrowded; service deteriorates and prices rise. In the investment world, too much capital quickly ends up chasing too few good opportunities. A good deal is a good deal only so long as too many people don't try to take advantage of it.

That's why initial investors in a new trend often do well. They are able to choose the best opportunities at the most reasonable prices. Those who come along later have progressively less and less choice at progressively higher and higher prices. As prices rise, so do expectations. But as expectations rise, thinking declines. Logically, as the amount of money flowing into a market increases, prices should rise and the attractiveness of the opportunities should recede. But investors are not merely thinking beings—and not even primarily thinking beings. That they think at all is open to argument. That they let themselves be driven by emotions is beyond question.

But we have to admire the symmetry of it. A market that is a public spectacle needs most investors to do the wrong thing at the wrong time. If investors knew what was coming, the trend would not climax and you would get a kind of sterile spectacle interruptus, with no fruit, no boom, no bust, no laughs. The future would be discounted, marked to market, and condensed down to a single moment, now. Time would stand still.

For in investing, as in everything else, you don't get something for nothing. The investors who succeed are generally those who work hard at it and avoid getting caught up in manias. In fact, only lazy investors are ever "in the market." The more serious they are, the more they are out of the market and into specific companies that they know quite well.

That insiders generally do better than outsiders should come as a surprise to no one. The insider is the person who has eliminated the most unknowns. He is the most private investor, whose knowledge is closest to the facts. But even if ordinary investors cannot be insiders in the stocks they buy, they can come very close, by shunning popular stocks in favor of those no one wants. Then, they must work hard at studying the businesses and getting to know, in detail, both the numbers and the management. If they do their work well, they will choose those they like and understand and stick with them long enough to come to know the businesses better than the real insiders. That's what Warren Buffett tries to do. It's also why he is the most successful investor who ever lived.

What kind of investments do others *not* want? Cheapness is usually a sign of a lack of interest. But some types of investments are so disreputable and unappealing that they are almost always cheap. Hog-rendering plants are an example. No one wants one in his backyard. Almost no one wants a hog-rendering business in his investment portfolio, either. Slum rentals are usually cheap, too . . . for the same reason. Another category is vice businesses.

Our interest in vice is, needless to say, purely professional. We simply observe that when economies go soft, investors tend to switch to defensive positions, and vice stocks are a favorite. When times get tough, people turn to drinking, smoking, gambling, and sex, say the experts.

But good men, we think, are loyal to their vices. They don't give up on them when times get tough, but neither do they favor them when they are in the chips. People need a well-developed vice they can stick with through thick or thin. Otherwise, they are prey for every new fad. A man can't, for example, be a womanizer and a drunk at the same time. Nor is heavy gambling compatible with heavy drinking. No, a man has to find a vice that suits him and stick with it.

So, when the economy goes sour, a smoker doesn't give up smoking. A real drinker doesn't give up the bottle. Instead, he gives up fair-weather spending, to which he has no attachment, and sunny-day stocks to which he owes no fidelity. By comparison, the vice stocks do pretty well.

Is this the time to buy vice stocks? Well, no. It is a comment on our era that prices of tobacco, liquor, sex, and gambling companies are already high. Usually, they can be counted on to be low, because in normal times, the vice investor is a little timid to mention it.

You see, people want more than money from money. They want status. And who feels his chest expand when he admits that his money is invested in companies that sell booze, 24 hours, on-off?

But today, a man announces buying an online pornography company with the same pride as announcing his daughter's first birthday, which means that the prices for vice stocks are not as low as you might think. Wait for a downdraft in the stock market—or an updraft in hypocrisy. Then it will be time to buy.

Don't Do Anything

Nothing. Nada. Zilch. The null category gets no respect. The hollowness of it is repulsive. The emptiness of it is unbearable. Even nature is said to abhor a vacuum. The poor man who has nothing to say is a pariah. He is like the investment adviser with nothing to recommend, save cash. He will get no work as a hedge fund manager; he will not drive a fancy car, nor live in a beach palace in the Hamptons.

And zero? For centuries the number couldn't even be found. Mathematicians didn't know what to make of a number that was not a number at all but an absence of numbers, a graphic display of nothing, a round, empty hole.

Few things are as damnable as inaction. In politics, it is cause for recrimination. In marriage, even the Catholics allow for annulment in cases of nonconsummation. In finance, it is cause for regrets. In war, it is cause for firing squads. In conversation, an absence of words is embarrassing. When a man stares you in the face and says nothing, you assume he is thinking something dreadful. Unless he smiles; then you think he has lost his mind.

The other problem with inaction is that there is never any excuse for it. Stalin's generals, charged with inaction during the early days of the German assault on Moscow, might have explained that they were busy with their mistresses or attending a child's birthday party. Either excuse would be perfectly satisfactory to a civilized man, for both were better than killing people in order to defend the Soviet Union. But Stalin was scarcely civilized.

No, dear reader, inactivity is almost always unpardonable. But here, nevertheless, we say a kind word for it, maybe two. First, we point out that doing nothing is usually the best course of action, especially in public affairs and investments. Second, we deny the possibility of really doing nothing.

Since the entire world nurses a prejudice against inaction, the burden of proof is clearly on us. So, let us bend to our work like a field hand, knowing that our labors will be many, our rewards few.

In public affairs, as in private ones, there is a powerful compulsion to do something. Think about what Hitler's desire to do something got him into. After the Battle of Britain, he found time hanging heavy on his hands. Western Europe was buttoned up, from Poland to Spain. He was master of all and everyone. Only Britain held out.

But he had not the means to invade Britain, so his eyes wandered across the map—as Napoleon's had done many years before—and saw Russia.

He would have been much better off staying home. Then, Stalin's generals could have continued to bounce their mistresses on their knees and hand out candy at birthday parties. Inaction would have begotten more inaction, in other words. And the world might have been a better place.

But our beat in this chapter is money. So we ask—are you ever better off doing nothing with your money? The answer falls into our lap like a ripe cocktail waitress:

Of course.

Warren Buffett holds billions in cash. He is probably the best investor who has ever lived. If he cannot find anything better to do with his money than to leave it in cash—effectively doing nothing with it—how can the average lumpeninvestor expect to do better?

Is this the time to buy stocks? Probably not. The idea is to buy low and sell high later. When stocks are high already, there is no alternative; you must do nothing.

Is it time to buy bonds? Again, probably not. Bonds are expensive, too; yields are low. Will they become even more expensive? Will yields go even lower? Maybe. But we cannot predict the future. All we can do is look at the present and the past. The past tells us that bonds have become more expensive almost every year for the last quarter of a century. At today's prices, you are not likely to make money in bonds, especially corporate and junk bonds. It is better to do nothing.

But there is always real estate, isn't there? Since 2001, investors have made such rapid advances in the property market they would have made Guderian or Rommel envious. In the late summer of 1941, Guderian, the leading proponent of panzer-led blitzkrieg warfare, was racing toward Moscow. The man could not bear inaction; he took to the offensive even against his Führer's orders. On the other side, the Russians were full of action themselves. Guderian faced Zhukov, who was beginning to understand how to beat the panzers. You know what happened next: Action produced reaction. Finally, the whole campaign ended in a bloody mess.

Should you buy property? Not unless you're feeling lucky. So, what should you do? Do nothing is our advice. Most houses are too expensive. You will get more for your money as a renter. Most likely, you will be able to buy later at better prices.

But don't worry; doing nothing quickly turns into doing something—whether you like it or not.

"You are either long or short," said our old friend Mark Hulbert 20 years ago. "There is no such thing as a hold."

You might like to wait and see what happens, but the trouble is—you can't only wait and see. You can't stop breathing. You can't stop eating. And you can't stop investing. There is no such thing as suspended animation when it comes to your money and no such place as nowhere in the financial world. Every minute of every day, for every asset class, either you are long or you are short. Either you own it or you don't own it. Of course, you can be leveraged or unleveraged, too, but that is merely a measure of how bad the damage will be if you are wrong. If you don't own shares in Google, for example, you will lose potential gains, if it goes up. And if it goes down relative to the rest of the world—which includes Google holders—you will be ahead of the game.

You may say to yourself, "Oh, I'm staying out. I'm in cash." But when you are in cash, you are short stocks and long the currency. If stocks go down, your cash goes up relative to the stocks. If stocks go up, your cash—measured in stocks—becomes less valuable.

No, dear reader, there's no way to stay out of the game. There's no refuge. There's no place where history stands still and prices stop moving. No matter where you are, you're in it whether you like it or not.

When all major asset classes are expensive, the sensible thing to do is nothing. But the trouble with cash is that it is much more something than nothing. For most Americans, being in cash means being in the cash watched over by the central bank of Ben Bernanke. But dollars are a gamble. They are IOUs issued by the world's biggest

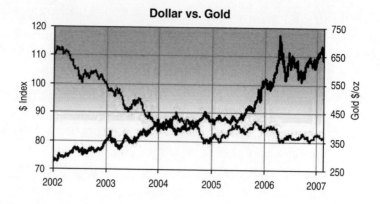

FIGURE 16.1   The Fall of the Dollar versus The Rise of Gold.
Source: St. Louis Federal Reserve Bank.
Chart by Adrian Ash, BullionVault.com.

debtor. Despite a hundred years of decline, they are still expensive, in our view. In 2006 alone, they went down 10 percent against the cash of the European Central Bank.

A more perfect "nothing" is gold. It is a sort of an anti-asset. It pays no interest, issues no press releases, and offers no guidance on quarterly earnings. It has no earnings. It does no mergers and no acquisitions and it never restructures. It hires no celebrity CEOs. It makes no excuses. It charges neither commissions nor management fees. But it is the thing that goes up when other assets go down. In 2006, it went up 20 percent against the dollar. (See Figure 16.1.)

Gold is as close to "nothing" as you can ever get.

Will you make money by buying gold now? We don't know. Besides, even calling gold an investment stretches the truth. Gold produces no profits and doesn't even pay interest. But while it may go up or down in price, it won't go away.

If you want gold, but you don't want to pay storage fees, have the responsibility of physical ownership, or go through the trouble of digging a hole in your backyard to store it, try the EverBank 5-Year MarketSafe Gold Bullion CD.

For those who want to own actual physical gold, another idea might be gold coins. Steve Sjuggerud recommends St. Gaudens gold coins. The premium you will pay for the coin over the price of the metal itself is at an all-time low, he says.

Of course, there are other more indirect ways to profit from the ongoing boom in gold. One is to buy gold producers, like mining and exploration companies. While the price of gold has significantly increased in the past year, mining stocks have not. We are not making a recommendation, but readers could look at a major gold producer, like Newmont, with a market capitalization of $20.1 billion and 93.2 million ounces of proven and probable reserves. Then there are junior mining companies, like IAMGOLD (market cap of $1.5 billion), with 4.6 million ounces of proven and probable gold reserves. Another idea might be Bema Gold, a midtier producer with 11.4 million proven and probable ounces of gold in the ground.

Another popular way to own gold is through the exchange-traded funds (ETFs), like the popular GLD, which allows you to buy and sell gold as you would a stock. You can do that with other precious metals like silver, as well.

CHAPTER 17

THE DUPE OF HEARTS

Thinking in its lower grades is comparable to paper money, and in its
higher forms it is a kind of poetry.

—Havelock Ellis

ONE AND ONE MAKE ELEVEN

We have already described our encounter with James Surowiecki's
opus, *The Wisdom of Crowds*,[1] in our previous book. We not only
expected to be appalled by it; we counted on it—it is much easier
to write a review of a man's errors than it is to praise his merits.
Besides, having come to believe that crowds are full of dumbbells
and psychopaths, it would be a nuisance to alter our strongly held
opinions at this stage in life.

"Large groups of people are smarter than an elite few, no matter
how brilliant," says the jacket cover.

But we have observed exactly the opposite. When they are thrown
into the company of legions of their fellow men, some chemistry
turns humans who are individually of irreproachable integrity and
unimpeachable prudence into stark, raving blockheads. That this is
sometimes called democracy does not improve matters. And that
popular business columnists announce the very opposite practically
seals the matter for us.

Did a large group of people write Shakespeare's sonnets?, we
wonder. Did a large group of people invent the beret or crispy duck?
However, it was a large group of people who wanted Adolf Hitler in
the chancellor's office in Berlin.

Nevertheless, Surowiecki's book is not bad. In fact, it is delightful in its deceptiveness. Its idea is the old one: "Two heads are better than one."

Here, we don't disagree. Putting people together with different points of view, different tastes, different brains, and different incentives *can* actually work a kind of magic—multiplying the talents of the people involved. Surowiecki provides many examples. We have our own: Laurel and Hardy. Rogers and Hammerstein. Antony and Cleopatra. Brad and Jennifer. Dow and Jones. Jagger and Richards. Scrooge and Marley. Jack and Daniels.

Alone, a person cannot really do much. We are only in our present state of comfort as a result of centuries of tugging by millions of different people. Someone had to realize that you could burn oil; someone else had to discover iron; someone, somehow, sometime had to put the pieces together—and millions of others—to manufacture the modern automobile. A man on his own could never manufacture even a single automobile; there are just too many component parts involving too much detailed knowledge. On his own, a man would be lucky to fashion a go-kart out of soft wood.

And, the more elevated people's situation, the more they rely not only on past generations, but on their neighbors—and many people they have never met. *Ek aur ek gyarah*, says a Hindi proverb—one plus one equals eleven.

Even—or perhaps *especially*—the world's greatest and loneliest geniuses realize that their contributions rest largely on the work of others. Science is cumulative and universal. Isaac Newton mentioned that he could only rise so high because he was "standing on ye shoulders of Giants." But he used his famous phrase in a letter to a rival, Robert Hooke . . . who was a dwarf. Science may have marched forward, but Newton's heart was as mischievous—or perhaps as cruel—as any since the Flood.[2]

But, Surowiecki seems only dimly aware of what goes on in the human heart. Crowds are wise, he says. Two heads are better than one. The genius of the few stands on the shoulders of the many who have gone before. At this point, we begin to guess that he does not mean "crowds" at all—he means independent individuals voluntarily getting together.

What is amusing is that Surowiecki describes what Hayek called the "spontaneous order" as if he had just discovered it himself. He seems astonished—and perhaps disappointed—that people go about their daily lives and get things done without anyone telling them what to do. It is as if he had never heard of culture, or trust, or fairness, or convention, or tradition—or any of the millions and millions of small acts of cooperation that make civilization possible. It makes the book fun to read—it's like taking a Baptist teenager to a whorehouse; "So this is what it's all about," he asks, his face lit up and his pulse racing.

"Yep," you feel like replying. "What did you think?"

Surowiecki has managed to write something wise and moronic about crowds: wise to notice that two heads are sometimes better than one, moronic to fail to notice why. Like the Bolsheviks and syndicalists, he is right to claim that collectives work. But it is only *voluntary* collectives—families, markets, communities, religious groups, enterprises (the very things that the coercive collectivists want to destroy)—that work.

What Surowiecki doesn't seem to get is that every time you get a couple of knuckleheads together they're not going to write good music or build an atomic bomb; nor will even a hundred of the smartest people on the planet do a better job of telling us what we want for breakfast than we can do for ourselves. You do not get any extra benefit from having a group of yes-men sitting around the table—they merely reinforce the harebrained ideas of the leader. And even in decent groups, people tend to get bullied or bamboozled, setting off a cascade of ideas and opinions that tumbles toward outcomes—randomly benign or malevolent.

The extermination of the Polish Jews, for instance, was something that no one man could have accomplished on his own. It took the cooperation of thousands—no, probably millions—to make it work, people who had to stand on the shoulders of many generations of engineers before them so they could push a few generations of Jews into open trenches or burn them in open-air furnaces.

Where was the wisdom of the crowd in that? Surowiecki doesn't bother to raise the question. Perhaps there was not enough "diversity" in the Nazi ranks, he might suggest. The Nazis were not "independent" enough, he might add; nor were they allowed to express their "private judgment."

All of which may be true. But who was going to stop a top SS meeting and suggest that they bring in a gay gypsy or Bantu democrat to give an alternative point of view? Who among them doubted that they did not already have all the judgment, opinions, and information they needed? Likewise, at the peak of the bubble market in tech stocks at the end of the 1990s, which investors who had made fortunes on Microsoft and Amazon wondered if they needed more diversity in their portfolios?

Surowiecki's book has missed the whole point.

What he is describing as "wise crowds" are really the fluid, unfettered interactions between individuals in a civilized society. In many cities, for example, people drive around with hardly a traffic light or traffic cop anywhere, yet most get where they are going without accident. That is also how primitive groups hunted animals larger and fiercer than any one of the hunters. This kind of cooperation is the foundation of civilization, of the division of labor, and of the accumulation of expertise and knowledge.

But cooperation does not make a crowd. It makes a group.

What is the difference between a group and a crowd? Just this—a group never reduces itself to one. A crowd, in contrast, always acts as one—and soon makes a public spectacle of itself. An army, for example, acts with one mind, one emotion, for one purpose. Deserters are shot. You wouldn't want to go into battle with a free-spirited intellectual at your back; you want a knucklehead with a single-minded goal—to kill the enemy and protect you.

When the crowd takes up a corrupt wish—to get something for nothing or to make the world a better place by killing people—the last thing it wants is another point of view. The few people who are able to think clearly can only try to get out of the way. If they are in a bubble market, they can easily sell. If they are in a country that has lost its head, they can try to leave. If they are in an army, it is probably too late.

Democracy, says Surowiecki, demonstrates the wisdom of the crowd. Does it? To our way of thinking, voters seem quintessentially a crowd, swayed by demagogues, pundits, and the false signals of central bankers. They pass judgment on people they have never met and ideas they can't understand, eventually taking money that doesn't belong to them and spending it on things that are usually disastrous for them. Democracy of this sort replaces reasoned cooperation with high-handed fraud, the wise congregation of independent citizens with a mob with silly slogans on their bumpers and mischief in their hearts; it goes from building consensus to building concentration camps.

EMPIRE OF EXPERTS

The problem is that modern society forces human beings to inter-act in groups far larger than their brains can handle effectively. In the public spectacles of modern governments and armies, people are asked to decide on issues that affect the lives of tens and hundreds of thousands of people. They have to understand budgets that jug-gle with dollar figures of millions, billions, and even trillions. They grope in the bilge for something to hang onto and finding nothing that they remotely understand, they turn—like the social creatures they are—to others for guidance. In the old days, they would have consulted the headman of the tribe or an elder, the witch doctor, or a wise woman. Lacking these today, people do their best. They thumb through Thomas Friedman's columns. If they are investors, they scan the ratings given by the analysts. They even listen to Jim Cramer.

How do they know whether what experts know is any more useful ultimately than what they know? They don't. And, in many cases, it isn't.

In his book, *Expert Political Judgment—How Good Is It? How Can We Know?*, political psychologist Philip Tetlock reports on his 20-year study of some 287 political experts whom he asked a range of questions: Would there be a nonviolent end to apartheid in South Africa? Would the United States go to war in the Persian Gulf? Would Canada disintegrate? At the end of the study, he had collected 82,361 forecasts. Tetlock then wanted to find out how his subjects had made their judgments—what did they think about information that didn't support their conclusions, for instance, and how did they look at other people's predictions? He also wanted to find out how they would react if they were proved wrong.

The result? Blindfolded lab rats would have done better. Indeed, blindfolded lab rats *have*.[3]

And they would probably have been more honest about where they went wrong. The experts not only turned out to be bad at predicting, they were also huffy when they were shown up. Nor did specializing in a field improve their answers; it tended to make them worse. Knowing too much about too little seemed to bring experts "diminishing marginal predictive returns." In other words, journalists and alert laymen did about as well as specialists when it came to predicting the future.

Fame didn't help, either. Famous experts tended to go wrong far more than their obscure colleagues. The loudmouths in the limelight tripped up because of overconfidence, but also for other reasons—if they were on TV talk shows, they were under pressure to be entertaining; as experts, they couldn't just say the most obvious thing; they felt compelled to come up with ingenious, or at least counterintuitive, predictions that would justify their status. The trouble is, often, obvious conclusions are also the right ones.

It seems that knowing a lot is simply not as helpful in making predictions about human behavior as people tend to assume. Too much knowledge can actually trip you up, because it gets enlisted on behalf of your favorite hunches—or fears—instead of being evaluated objectively. Having more facts at their disposal, experts are able to support their theories more ingeniously; they are more reluctant to change their minds, even when proved wrong. And finally, experts—no different from laymen—tend to grab onto facts that support their views and pass on those that don't.

The result is that in finance and politics, especially, not only are experts no better than smart amateurs, they are sometimes worse than them; and they are *invariably* worse than quite simple mathematical models—a fact that is now well established from 50 years of research in over a hundred fields of expertise. Events that experts rate as impossible or near-impossible happen as often as 15 percent of the time, and certainties or near-certainties fail to happen 27 percent of the time.[4]

Yet, despite this abysmal record, pundits keep pontificating, and people keep listening. Why? Because man's greatest need is not to be right; it is to have the approval of his fellow men. He would rather be wrong following the leader than right on his own. The newsman Edward R. Murrow recognized this. A nation of sheep, he said, will beget a government of wolves.

Yet, there are a thousand ways in which people can be held together without being browbeaten or bullied. There are a hundred voluntary associations, none of which have to do with governments or armies. There are churches, charities, reading groups, stamp clubs, sports leagues, sewing circles, scout troops, and firefighting brigades where people cooperate, exchange, learn, debate, and act—and all without a gun being fired, a law being passed, or a single cop being hired.

This type of spontaneous order—unlike the *zugzwang* of central planning—is the result of natural processes. Not the result of physical nature, it is true, but of something related to it—but far more elusive and changeable—human nature.

LAW AND DISORDER

Unlike the order of physical nature, the spontaneous order of human nature is not geometrical—as statists like Hobbes thought. It is not so much a system of pulleys and levers as a whorl of snowflakes. We like to think this means chaos, but for a long time now, science has come to see chaos as not the absence of order, but a more complex kind of order.

There is a pattern even in what we call chaos, just as there is a pattern in the formation of clouds, the shape of mountain ranges, or even the movement of waves. Why would we expect human society to be any less organic in its functioning? Why would we not expect it to exhibit the same complex self-organization that snowflakes show? And, on the other hand, isn't it likely that a society that is ordered too mechanically will not function as it should? A dynamic living society needs to have the organization that corresponds to the real sentiments and wills of its members. But a bureaucracy handing down regulations substitutes a rigid, destructive order for the living fabric of human interactions.

Looked at like that, the hurly-burly of a free market seems to be closer to the patterns of nature than the simple-minded schemes of pundits. In a free market—in theory at least—each actor acts from his own needs and goals and from his perception of the needs and goals of a handful of others. He expresses this through the mechanism of pricing. The price feeds back to everyone whatever he needs to know about the needs and wishes of everyone else. Pricing is a way of communicating that allows people to cooperate and produce spontaneously in a way that would otherwise require the omniscience of a god. A command economy, on the other hand, fails because it doesn't have a network of information as extensive and complex. In a command economy, clueless government hacks are free to impose any fatheaded scheme they can come up with on their hapless subjects. Where nature produces unpredictable order, the hacks create thoroughly predictable chaos.

You can pass all the orders, laws, and policies you want; you can employ stables full of pedigreed lawyers. But, if there is nothing to back the laws and policies, you are in trouble. Businesses aren't going to want to do business with you. Investors are going to want their investments back. Likewise, you can print all the money you want, but if there is nothing to back it up, then you are in a bit of trouble. Your creditors are unlikely to put much store in you as a credit risk. After some time, they start fretting, just as investors are now wringing their hands over the dollar.

Gold does not have the same problem, because unlike paper money there is a limited supply of it. It has to occur in nature. It has to be found somewhere underground and then mined and refined. It's an expensive business that takes risk, time, and money. There are costs attached to it that someone has to pay. Paper money, by contrast, can be printed anytime you want. Just ask Ben Bernanke. He plans to drop it by the helicopter load from the clouds.

Customs, conventions, and traditions resemble gold, rather than paper—because they can't be manufactured out of nothing. They can only be found in the soil in which they live. They reflect the way people really think and act at any given time, unlike policies and laws so far ahead of—or behind—the times that people resist them or are indifferent to them.

Like gold, traditions reflect real value. They contain more information from the past—from the history of the people among whom they are practiced. And, like the pricing mechanism, traditions are a communication system that lets people signal their desires and expectations faster and better to each other. Government policies reflect only the demands and desires of one generation—the living. Even if they are passed by a democracy, they are not fully democratic at all, or at least, not democratic enough. They consult only living citizens. They forget the dead.

That is why lamebrained policies and programs are ultimately as much a part of the public spectacle as wars and market manias. They are the creations of the human brain when it stands apart from the facts of history and experience, as the Cartesian *cogito, ergo sum* (I think, therefore I am) of reason operating on its own. And Cartesian reason, while good at technical and physical problems, is not very good when it is turned on itself or on human life. Instead, we are much more likely to understand who and what we are by looking at things we ourselves have done in the past—history—or things we ourselves have made—culture.

Man is, first of all, *Homo faber* (man the creator), and we understand him best by looking at his creations.

Customs and traditions, in other words, work because they constitute *verum factum* (truth as an act)—as the Italian philosopher Giambattista Vico wrote in 1710.[5]

"The criterion and rule of the true is to have made it. Accordingly, our clear and distinct idea of the mind cannot be a criterion of the mind itself, still less of other truths. For while the mind perceives itself, it does not make itself," wrote Vico.

When man ceases to be *Homo faber*—fashioning the world around him with his own hands and wits—he ends up just another factory hand, a clerk in a counting house, anonymous and nameless. He becomes alienated both from his own nature and from the natural world around him—a change mourned by both radicals and conservatives.

The son of one of your authors, given a chance to work in his father's business this summer, showed signs of alienation.

"I don't know how people do it," he complained. "This is brain numbing and soul destroying, sitting all day in front of a computer terminal, working on things you don't really care about. If I had to do this for the rest of my life, I'd slash my wrists."

Of course, most people don't slash their wrists; they pick up their tools day after day and get to work. The suicide rate has not noticeably soared with advances in living standards and the division of labor. As long as people feel they are making progress toward a better life, their wrists seem to be tolerably safe.

Still, we cannot deny that there *has* been a definite change in the way man sees himself and his place in the group. In earlier times, a man drew his sense of worth and his place in the community from his trade. The baker baked. The blacksmith hammered. And there, for all the world to see, was what he did and what he was. But in modern industrial society, things are no longer valued for their use, but for the quantity of cash for which they can be exchanged. Karl Marx called this "commodity fetishism." Marx was more than a trifle unhinged on a number of things, but on this, we think he had a point.

We can remember how, as late as the 1970s, we still felt master of our tools and the world around us. We had no idea how a particle accelerator worked, but we could still take apart a carburetor and tinker with it. Now, we can barely find it. As more and more of our world is no longer made by us, we understand it less and less. We are forced to fall back on theory and speculation, on isolated reasoning.

But thinking, as Vico pointed out, is hopeless when it is unassisted by either wisdom or emotion. In fact, Vico argued that the rise of pure rationality in history signaled a declining phase of human culture—the *barbarie della reflessione* (the barbarism of reflection). It was characteristic, he claimed, of the Age of Man, which was the last phase of the cycle of civilizations, as he saw it. In the Age of Man, popular democracy would run amok and lead to tyranny and empires, which would finally end in chaos.[6]

Then, of course, the whole cycle would start up all over again, with the age of the gods.

NOBLE ROT

And so it goes on from eon to eon, these inevitable cycles, said Vico. Man learns to use his reason to master the world around him, only to turn it on himself. He strives to discover truth and instead concocts the delusory spectacles with which he destroys himself. From a modest republic of the self-reliant, he converts his nation into a boastful empire of debtors that eventually collapses of its own weight. He rises, only to fall.

Vico's is the classical view of history, the tragic view, and it tells us that history does not pull in at the doorstep of progress, democracy, and liberalism like the 5:15 from Paddington. Instead, history rises and falls ... like waves emerging from the ocean spume and disappearing back into it.

In modern Western culture, time is linear. We see it going forward, in a kind of eternal march of progress toward the future. But in pagan cultures, it is circular. For instance, the Hindi word for tomorrow, *kal*, is the same as the word for yesterday, because yesterday is in the future, too: *kal* (yesterday)—*aaj* (today)—*kal* (tomorrow).

Yesterday, today, tomorrow, and yesterday, again. Rise and decline. It makes one wonder.

Over time, everything breaks down and dies. Even granite eventually is worn down to a fine sand. No tree ever grows to the sky, they say on Wall Street.

Does anything ever escape decay, ultimately?

We have no answer, but we notice one thing—like beautiful women, fine wines, or graceful buildings, civilizations too are never more alluring than when there is a hint of decay about them. Age gives them grace and mystery . . . before destroying them completely.

And it is with nations as it is with human beings. What man is any good until he has been tempered by age and hammered at the forge of mortality? As a young man, he walked upward, climbing the mountain every day, but it is the downhill walk that puts him to the test. Like an army in retreat, he tries to hold himself together and meet his fate without making a fool of himself.

It seems like progress to us, even if it isn't always uphill.

Decay, degeneration, death—and then, renaissance. Unstoppable. Irremediable.

Civilizations rise, and then decline—and then rise again. Markets arise, soar, collapse, and begin rising again. History records the whole thing as a pack of lies and misunderstandings involving hairy people with tails, doing foolish things for absurd reasons. But there are moments of glory, too, when men occasionally stand on two feet.

Sometimes, nature seems to draw out its best from the dregs of corruption.

We saw that recently when we visited the vineyards on our Argentine estate. There, too, the process of corruption brings the grapes to a majestic and honorable conclusion. As they mature, they store up sugar, an oenologist explained to us. They also collect what they call a "noble rot"—a type of decay that begins the process of fermentation and turns grape juice into wine.

Noble rot is a specific fungus—*Botrytis cinerea*—a grayish mold that looks like ash on the grapes and is found on certain grapes. It is famous at the Chateau Yquem, which produces some of the finest sauternes in the world. When the winegrowers see the fungus forming, they carefully watch the grapes and pick them at just the moment when there is enough rot to produce a fine wine, but not enough to destroy it.

The fungus is, of course, a parasite—like a leech on a dog or a lobbyist in Congress. But the rot it engenders does not make the grape go bad; instead, it concentrates the sweetness.

The world and everything in it seems set up for disappointment. The green buds come out in spring, unaware that they are all doomed. But when the crisp weather comes, they do not simply droop and die. Instead, the stress of approaching death brings out the best in them. Like Sidney Carton, in *A Tale of Two Cities*, they seem to rise in grace and dignity as they mount the scaffold. They are at their moment of glory when the hangman slips the noose around their necks. And, as the ship's officer remarked when the *Titanic* took on water, the orchestra never sounded better.

MOMENTS OF GLORY

Rot has its own rationale.

Without death and decay, there would be no redemption, no hope of heaven, no fear of hell, and no chance of everlasting life. Without them, life everlasting would have no meaning; all movement would cease, because the earth would be frozen into a meaningless past and an equally meaningless future.

Even our religious beliefs regress to the mean. They get cheapened. They go through cycles—saints and sinners, bulls and bears, never wholly good nor wholly bad, but always subject to influence. And one measure of it is how they lose their own meanings to the slogans of a public spectacle.

Take our own Episcopal Church: First, they rewrote the prayer book. "Follow me and I will make you fishers of men," said Jesus. They were so eager to make this politically fashionable—by taking out the reference to "men"—that they rewrote it as, "Follow me and I will make you fish for people."

What that means is a matter of emphasis and diction. "I will make you *fish* for people" is one thing, in which "fish" is meant as a noun—as in, we will all become catfish. Or, if "make you fish" is taken as a verb—we are forced to fish, as though we were slaves. Or you could put the emphasis on "the people," in which case we will have to imagine a hook through our jaws.

To be a fisher of men, on the other hand, is to undergo a personal transformation. That is the Christian vision of renewal—not the socialist. A renewal that calls for changing the way *we* are, first. A renewal that transcends the public spectacle.

There was a hymn we used to sing at school:

And one was a soldier, and one was a priest,

And one was slain by a fierce wild beast. . . .

They were all of them saints of God;

And I mean, God helping, to be one too.

But life is not school. In real life you never know when the tests will come or what form they will take. You don't even know when you are being tested. If life were like school, George W. Bush would have known that Iraq would test him and he might have prepared by boning up on the history of the greatest empire ever—Rome. He could have read about Emperor Trajan's attack on Ctesiphon, near present-day Baghdad. At least Trajan had a plan. He captured 100,000 prisoners, whom he sold into slavery. Back then, empire was not only a source of glory, but of profits.

But glory is our subject here, not profits. We wonder who gets it and who deserves it. Generally, we note, they are different people. And here, for once, we do not pause in sorrow over the depths of darkness in mankind; no, we rejoice in those rare moments of dignity and courage in which people rise above the cycle of life and decay. In which they become heroes.

Our first hero was asked to serve his country in Vietnam, but he famously said no. The media branded Muhammad Ali a coward, although he actually faced no threat in going into the army in 1967. It had already offered him a cushy job teaching boxing and acting as a PR man for the Pentagon. The war in Vietnam was already very unpopular. Ali could have served his time in relative safety and luxury, making appearances for the cameras and the clowns, talking up the war effort.

However, if he didn't go into the army, the punishment would be severe. He would be stripped of his boxing title. He wouldn't be able to box; he would have a hard time earning a living, let alone paying the legal fees that would be needed to keep him out of jail. Plus, he would be called a traitor.

But Ali still said no. It was against his Black Muslim religion. And he added: "I ain't got nothin' against them Vietcong" and "No Vietcong ever called me a nigger."

No medals were pinned on Muhammad Ali. They give you medals for helping the politicians with their public spectacles. They don't give you medals for standing in their way.

But many are the heroes made far from the rivers of history, on the hidden banks where private lives unfold quietly year after year.

On January 13, 1982, at 3:59 in the afternoon, Air Florida Flight 90 took off in heavy snow from Washington's National Airport. The plane's wings had been deiced. But there was a long line waiting to take off from the airport that day, and the pilots decided not to return to the gate for more deicing. Instead, they took off. A few minutes later, the black box recorded this brief conversation in the cockpit:

"Larry, we're going down, Larry."

"Yeah . . ."

Where they were going down was right onto Washington's busiest highway, U.S. 395, and just at the 14th Street bridge. The plane crashed into the bridge and then into the Potomac River. Most of the crew and passengers were killed immediately, but six survived and were thrown into the icy river. They wouldn't last long, a fact that was obvious to Roger Olian, who jumped from his truck and dove into the water to try to save them. He had almost stopped breathing and was turning blue by the time a helicopter came to his rescue.

It was a bad day in Washington. The snowstorm had caused a train wreck, and traffic was gridlocked, too. But finally a helicopter arrived and began to drop a line to pluck the passengers out of the water. Most were barely alert. Bert Hamilton was the first passenger to be rescued.

Then, when the line came to Arland D. Williams Jr., instead of taking the line himself he gave it to flight attendant Kelly Duncan. On the next trip, he passed it to Joe Stiley, who was severely injured ... and then to Priscilla Tirado ... and Patricia Felch. But, Ms. Tirado, whose husband and baby had just been killed in the crash, was hysterical and fell back into the water, too weak to hold on to the line. And here, another hero appeared. Lenny Skutnik took off his coat and boots and swam out to help her. The two were rescued.

That left the "sixth passenger," Arland D. Williams Jr., still in the river. The helicopter rushed back to get him. But he had been in the freezing water too long. When the helicopter got there, he had slipped into the river's icy embrace forever.

Arland D. Williams Jr., R.I.P.

PILATE ERROR

"To this end was I born, and for this cause came I into the world, that I should bear witness unto the world."

On Good Friday our office is always silent because of something that happened under imperial Rome. A Jew was brought before the

Roman governor of Judaea, accused of disturbing the peace. Upon looking into the matter, the governor concluded that the accusers erred. Hadn't the accused admitted in public that he was the King of the Jews?

But, so what? The Roman, Pontius Pilate, saw nothing in what Jesus was saying that posed a threat to the empire, or even to Roman rule in Judaea.

"I find no fault in him at all," he concluded.

That wasn't good enough for the local authorities. Jesus may have been no menace to Rome, but he was a troublemaker in the Levant. The elders wanted to get rid of him. The mob wanted his blood.

"Crucify him! Crucify him!" they yelled.

So be it, said Pilate, but the blood won't be on my hands. "Take ye him and crucify him, for I find no fault in him."

We began our book with this story, and we come back to it at the end. It is a history that has been retold every year for the last two millennia, and like any history, we have no way of knowing what part of it is humbug and what part is true. Still, like the jesting Pilate—whom Francis Bacon invented—when the question is posed, we don't wait for an answer. Whether history or not, the story itself is a masterpiece.

We pay attention to it, as we pay attention to all masterpieces—to all art, tradition, and culture. Indeed, we pay attention to everything that comes to us bearing the mysterious freight of the past. We fear that if we do not, we might miss learning something, even if we are not quite sure what.

"I have but one lamp by which my feet are guided, and that is the lamp of experience. I know no way of judging of the future but by the past," wrote Edward Gibbon.

As a member of Parliament, Gibbon was an ignominious failure, but as a historian of the Roman Empire, he told the story so vividly that generations of readers have taken his history for gospel, even though it was full of the author's prejudices, half-truths, and misapprehensions. What history isn't? It is the great, bloody river on which all the public spectacles sail.

But, if history rises and falls as chaotically as the waves, how can it have anything to teach us?

If grace and glory are to be found only in the acts of isolated individuals, why do we bother to turn to the past at all? If the story of mankind is not marching inexorably toward a better world, what could it possibly teach us?

The financial authorities in England and America have a somewhat similar idea. "Past performance is no guide to future performance," they say.

You can argue about the meaning, relevance, or accuracy of this pronouncement. On both sides of the Atlantic, it is a statement required by law and it is usually affixed to an ad for a mutual fund, partnership, or—in England—even for an investment analysis. What you can't do is argue with those who pronounce it—the financial regulators themselves. The regulators won't give an inch; the past is not indicative of the future, they say, no matter what.

Here, we pose the question again to ourselves. Is history indeed useful? Does it bear on the present? Or is it simply a legal dead letter that says nothing about future performance? We want to know. You, however, may want to know if this perambulation has been worth reading. Where does it lead? We will tell you right now—it tells us that regulators are usually Pharisees.

Of course, the bureaucrats, regulators, world improvers, and Pilates think they are doing the public a favor. They are delivering us from evil. The Securities and Exchange Commission (SEC), for example, believes investors need reminding that the future is a chancy and perfidious thing. Even though a mutual fund registered 20 solid years of above-market gains, this doesn't mean it will do it in the 21st year. Maybe it just got lucky.

And of course, they are right; it might all be luck. And it is certainly true that history can be deceptive, misleading, and coy. So can life. But the average investor—like the average voter—is much more likely to be deceived by too *little* history than by too *much*.

History may not fly in a straight arrow toward goodness, truth, and beauty. It may not unfold inexorably like a five-act play from exposition to denouement.

But the fact that the patterns of history are not obvious and regular does not mean there are no patterns at all. Although the lessons are opaque, even contradictory, it does not follow that there no lessons at all. Instead, the patterns of history follow their own chaotic laws, like the beating of the heart, or the structure of genes, or the shapes of clouds and mountains. History moves to its own fractured rhythms.

And what does it shows us? It shows us that things don't stand still. They go up and down, back and forth. It shows us that what goes around comes around, and that there are short cycles and long ones—circadian and imperial. Rome rose for 500 years and fell for another 500.

The British Empire took a couple of hundred years getting there and only a few decades to unravel.

As near as we can guess, property prices rose in central Baltimore from its founding in the eighteenth century until 1929. Then, they went down, at least until the end of the century. They seem to be rising now, but we won't know until later if this is a genuine interruption of the trend. Farmland in western Kansas experienced a real bubble in the 1880s. Today, 125 years later, it is still not as expensive as it was then. But who looks that far back?

Major cycles in the stock market seem to last about 30 to 40 years, peak to peak or trough to trough. As we said earlier, stocks hit a high point in 1929 and then collapsed—bouncing around for a while but not recovering until the 1950s, in nominal terms. Stocks hit a new high in the late 1960s; then it was down for another spell, until 1975 or 1982, depending on how you look at it, until a new bull market took over—bringing prices to another cyclical high in 2000, more than 30 years after the last one.

If history is not helpful, then we are completely lost, for the only events we have any knowledge of are those in the past. Those in the future are as unfamiliar, unknowable, and unsavory to us as local cheese.

"Those who do not study history are doomed to repeat it," say earnest history teachers and terminal optimists. But it's not that easy. Studying history is a little like learning a foreign language; until you really get the hang of it, there are likely to be some misunderstandings. They come, as you might expect, in the compound tenses and subtle, subjunctive moods. The casual reader understands the major verbs, but misses the veiled meaning. He is like a Hudson River hustler trying to do business in Hyderabad—or a man trying to reason with his wife. The words will be deceptively familiar; but he'll miss the sense of the conversation completely.

However, if he is cut off entirely from history, the lumpen investor is encouraged to not even try. He's led to believe that every new day is as detached from the last as Mars is from Jupiter. He is not supposed to notice that they both revolve around the same star and repeat the same cycles over and over until the crack of doom. Taking the regulators at their word, he sees the planets in the heavens and sees no reason to think they will ever be anywhere other than where they are right now.

The lumpen investor looks at the prices on Wall Street or those of houses in his neighborhood. Those, too, must be permanent, he reckons. He has no frame of reference, no theory to tell him otherwise, and no way to make a reasonable guess about where they will be tomorrow—he is as misled as a voter. And yet, surely he is not the complete imbecile the authorities make him out to be. And surely also, warning him not to trust history is like warning a sailor not to go near brothels when he is on shore leave. He will end up there anyway.

Today, the stock market investor feels as old as Methuselah, even if he only entered the market in the mid-1990s. He has seen but a decade, but he thinks he's seen it all. The market went up and then went down, didn't it? It should be ready to go up again. He can't help but notice that stock prices have gone up in the past five years, but he's discouraged by the regulators from looking any further. It's not worth the trouble, they tell him. Past performance is no indication of future performance. The past doesn't count. Forget it.

And so the little bit of recent history he picks up cheats him. It is as though he had noticed Mars zipping through space, without realizing it is merely retracing its steps from millions of years ago. He hasn't enough history. He has never heard of Copernicus. He thinks Pontius Pilate led a peasant revolt in Mexico. And so, he draws conclusions that are both erroneous and preposterous. Whatever he sees, he can only imagine that nothing like it has ever happened before. History has come to a dead stop. This really is a New Era on Wall Street. He sees Mars heading out into space and he imagines himself going where no man has ever gone before . . . when, actually, he never left home.

OMNES GENTES ALLELUIA

Without history, the investor is lost. Even with it, you have to be suspicious of what people say to you, even when they call them facts. More important, you have to be suspicious of what you say to yourself! As we said, the older we get, the less we know about anything; the more facts, opinions, and ideas we collect, the less sure we are of any of them.

Besides, we get more and more experience with facts that turn out not to be so.

A woman says she will be ready in five minutes. A teenager believes he has done his homework. And George W. Bush and Tony Blair may have actually believed that there were weapons of mass destruction in Iraq. Reason is slave to our wishes. Our minds work for our desires, not the other way around. "The brain is merely the heart's dupe," said French writer and philosopher La Rochefoucauld.

But there are different kinds of facts. The little white lies we tell ourselves and each other to get through life gracefully are not the big, mass illusions of the public spectacle.

Global freezing—who can forget that? It was widely believed in the 1960s and 1970s that the planet was getting colder. When the oil shock of 1973 came along, "We will all shiver in the dark," said the pundits. Then the oil price was supposed to go to $100 a barrel. Of course, it collapsed down to $10 a barrel and stayed there for the next 20 years. And then Dow 36,000 was just around the corner in the late 1990s. And, oh, yes, remember "The Great Crash of 2004"? This was one of our own mistakes. It seemed like a decent guess at the time. But that day didn't come in 2004. Or in 2005. Or in 2006. Will it come in 2008? We don't know. We're too modest to know. It is not given to man to know his fate. At least it isn't given to us.

We discovered our modesty during the bear market in gold from 1980 until 1999. There is nothing like a 20-year bear market to hone a man's sense of humility. But life is full of gives and takes and yins and yangs. The value of our gold coins might have gone down, but our stock of humility rose. Dollar by dollar, year after year, we became poorer but wiser. It is a form of tuition, like paying college fees for your children. Each year you pay $20,000, $30,000, $40,000, in order to make your children wiser. And each year, you get wiser—you realize that your children have been going to beer parties and that your money is largely wasted.

You pay, you suffer, you sweat and strain; but you become wiser.

Frankly, we would rather have the money. But a man who has just lived through a 20-year bear market sees humility as a vital asset; it is all he has left. Since we were flush with humility at the end of the period, we had to make the most of it. A handsome man looks for mirrors. A well-bred man thinks that it is class that counts, while a rich one measures himself in dollars or pounds. A humble one comes to think that the meek will really inherit the world; they just have to wait for the other arrogant SOBs to drop dead.

Wisdom costs.

Except a grain of wheat fall into the ground and die, it abideth alone: but if it die, it bringeth forth much fruit, said Jesus.

This sort of give-and-take goes all the way down to the deepest, darkest roots of our situation here on earth. When you are born, you are full of life. It is all ahead of you: years of energy and excitement. But you use them up; you trade them off for experience, wisdom, money. Little by little, day by day, year by year, your life gets used up, until you are all experience, all wisdom, all memories, and no life left. That is when your life is all behind you ... and nothing is left in front. We are, as Sophocles put it, nothing but a "deathward going tribe," after all.

This is just a way of describing how the world really works. You can't get something for nothing. Instead, you have to give something up; you have to invest time and money. There's no other way.

The only exception is the grace of God. God can do what He wants.

What we are describing is a world governed by moral rules as well as physical equations. Water boils at 212 degrees Fahrenheit, but so, too, when you sow the wind, you reap the whirlwind. The yield on the long Treasury bond may be 4.74 percent, but there are times when it is better to "neither a borrower nor a lender be." You may be able to get away with cheating a client, but "Do to others as you would have them do to you" is a better business practice. And it may be true that stocks will go up this year, but generally, you want to "buy low, sell high," not buy high and hope to sell even higher.

"Everything is moral," said Emerson. He meant that there are principles that we ignore at our peril. And, the critical element of public spectacles is that people forget this. They begin to think that they can get something for nothing, or do something to someone else that they wouldn't want done to them—and not have to answer for it. It is a New Era, they say; the old rules no longer apply. Then, the spectacle progresses to farce, when the lies begin to catch up. Finally, it ends in disaster. You see this pattern playing itself out in Iraq today, or in World War II. Hitler's lies—racial superiority, the need for lebensraum (living room) in the east—were soon followed by absurd programs and torchlight spectacles, before they ended in the disasters at Stalingrad and Berlin.

And, looked at with a particularly wide-angle lens, even the type of spectacle changes over time, as Vico noted. Societies go through small fads and big ones, cute little peccadilloes and major public spectacles. There are cycles within cycles and, of course, countertrends within trends: from religion to politics to money, from God to Caesar to Mammon, and back again. All this turning, churning, and recycling is what makes the world go round.

First there were the heresies and persecutions of the age of religion. Then came the world's great love affair with politics. We recall life as a student in Paris in the 1960s. It must have been like being a student in Constantinople 16 centuries earlier. We sat around in cafes arguing the most obscure and preposterous points of doctrine. But they were political doctrines, not religious doctrines. Which was better—Marxism, communism, Trotskyism, radical syndicalism, Maoism? How could the proletariat be radicalized in preindustrial societies? Who set up Che in Bolivia, the CIA or bourgeois counteragents in his own movement?

The twentieth century was clearly the bubble phase of politics. The death toll was staggering—more than 100 million. In the United States, the Kennedy administration probably marked the high-water mark. Then came the Vietnam War, the war on poverty, and the war on drugs—all disasters—and the youthful eagerness for politics waned and was soon over. People looked around sheepishly, embarrassed. They prosecuted a few war criminals but generally wanted to think about other things. And then they moved on. To Mammon!

And now China says it is a communist country, but neither it nor anyone else cares what the Chinese call themselves. The only thing anyone cares about is that China is open for business. They could eat the entrails of sheep or tear the beating hearts out of their enemies—as long as their economy grew at 10 percent per year, no one would care. And we have a war on terror, which no thinking person mentions without an ironic smirk—for it is only a campaign designed to protect the flanks of the great financial empire. If it were discovered to have diminished consumer spending, for example, it would be stopped tomorrow. Politics has yielded to money.

Now, money may not seem to have the hold over people that power and faith do, but from time to time it does flare up as the main thing. If it is true that it is easier for a camel to pass through the eye of the needle than for a rich man to get into heaven, in the early twenty-first century there were plenty of men willing to take a chance.

In New York, for instance, young hedge fund managers and investment bankers go out to celebrate ripping off some poor pension fund by ordering $1,000 martinis. And, of course, here in London, prices are so high that most people in the City would consider a $1,000 martini a bargain. In Paris a fashionable and very expensive place to frequent is an ice bar—which is literally covered in ice, like the inside of a giant freezer. Everyone seems to want to show off, to splurge, to celebrate the one thing that matters most to them—making money—by spending it.

Every bubble era, too, has its winners and losers, its kings and queens as well as its cannon fodder and concentration camp victims. The bubble royalty of this era works in London in the City or in New York on Wall Street, making their fortunes from the huge gush of liquidity flooding the world. The *Economist* estimates liquidity to have risen at 18 percent per year for the past four years—"probably the fastest pace ever."[7] Liquidity lifts up almost all financial boats. So, the captains of industry and finance have never had it so good. Too bad the galley slaves aren't doing better, too.

Someone has to row the boat in a public spectacle—and that makes the ordinary voter, the patriot, the soldier, and the saver the chumps! They have to go fight and die—in wars that mean nothing to them personally. They have to be set up and then wiped out by inflation and stock market crashes. Every excess has to be dealt with and every bubble pricked. Imperial armies are eventually defeated; paper currencies eventually disappear; religious heresies are stamped out or exterminate themselves with doctrines so pure they do not even permit procreation—think of the Albigensians or the Cathars.

The press gives us two ways to look at this phenomenon. On the one hand, the plebes and finger-pointers are outraged. Something should be done, they say, to cap executive salaries. Apparently they think executive salaries should be determined by politicians rather than by businessmen.

Of course, there's another way to look at it. Capitalism is the finest system ever devised, say true believers. If it gives huge incentives to corporate managers to increase shareholder value, well, that's just what makes it work so well. Besides, every mother's son in the United States, 2007, hopes he might someday be able to get that kind of money for himself. He's not worried about heaven; he figures he'll be able to grease his way in somehow.

Will he? We don't know, of course. But in the here and now, is there anything out there that supports Emerson? Have not all these people gotten away with something?

From one point of view—the point of the view of the people who get them—enormous bonuses are something to celebrate. From another—from the point of view of those who don't get them—they are terrible examples of waste and extravagance. Since the people who don't get enormous bonuses clearly outweigh those who do, we can imagine a time of rebellion among the unbonused masses. But then again, we are not sure we think that bonuses make such a big difference either way. After all, they will ultimately be spent, and usually in as inexplicable a way as they were earned.

Waitstaff at ice bars, Rolls-Royce salesmen, condominium boards—a host of workers and middlemen stands ready to relieve the rich of their riches. It is not simply that in the long run we are all dead, as John Maynard Keynes said. It is that in the short run we all have to live, and there is nothing to say that a Goldman bonus is necessary to do that well.

But that, of course, is the delusion of the current public spectacle ... and who are we to stand in its way?

NOTES

CHAPTER 1: DO-GOODERS GONE BAD

1. Roger Boyes, "Cannibal Reveals Man-Eater Network," *Times of London*, January 7, 2004.
2. "Mitford Girl Dies," *Sydney Morning Herald*, August 13, 2003.
3. James Lees-Milne, quoted in "Mitford Girl Dies," *Sydney Morning Herald*, August 13, 2003.
4. "1962: Violence Flares at Right Wing Rally—In Context," On This Day (31 July), BBC.co.uk, http://news.bbc.co.uk/onthisday/hi/dates/stories/july/31/newsid_2776000/2776295.stm. See also Security Services Records Release, November 25–26, 2002, www.nationalarchives.gov.uk/documents/nov2002.pdf.
5. Mary S. Lovell, *The Mitford Girls: The Biography of an Extraordinary Family* (London: Abacus, 2002).
6. Riccardo Orizio, *Talk of the Devil: Encounters with Seven Dictators*, trans. Avril Bardoni (London: Secker & Warburg, 2003).
7. "Mitford Girl Dies," *Sydney Morning Herald*, August 13, 2003.
8. "A Proposal to End Poverty," Editorial, *New York Times*, January 22, 2005.
9. "Bush Vows to Rid the World of Evil-Doers," CNN, September 16, 2001.
10. David Brooks, "Ideals and Reality," *New York Times*, January 22, 2005.
11. Thomas L. Friedman, "America's Failure of Imagination," *New York Times*, May 20, 2002.
12. Ibid.
13. Thomas L. Friedman, "Our War with France," *New York Times*, September 18, 2003.
14. Thomas L. Friedman, "The Chant Not Heard," *New York Times*, November 30, 2003.
15. Thomas L. Friedman, "No Mullah Left Behind," *New York Times*, February 13, 2005.
16. Amin Maalouf, *The Crusades through Arab Eyes*, trans. Jon Rothschild (New York: Schocken Books, 1984), 51.
17. Ibid., 50.
18. Ibid., 51.

19. Ibid., 156–157.
20. Ibid., 192–193.

CHAPTER 2: LOVE IN THE TIME OF VIAGRA

1. John Locke, *An Essay Concerning Human Understanding*, Book II, edited Roger Woolhouse (London: Penguin, 1997), Chapter XXI, 50–51, 244.
2. Nassim Nicholas Taleb, "Scaring Us Senseless," *New York Times*, July 24, 2005.
3. Stephanie Coontz, *Marriage, a History: From Obedience to Intimacy* (New York: Viking, 2005).
4. Samuel Butler, *Notebooks, 1912*, Chapter 1, para. xvi.
5. Ben White and Carrie Johnson, "Executives Cash In Regardless of Performance," *Washington Post*, March 22, 2005, E01.
6. Loren Steffy, "Oh, to Be a Failed CEO and Reap the Big Bucks," *Houston Chronicle*, March 30, 2005. See also *Executive Excess 2006—13th Annual CEO Compensation Survey*, Sarah Anderson, John Cavanagh—Institute for Policy Studies; Chuck Collins, Eric Benjamin—*United for a Fair Economy*, ed. Sam Pizzigati, August 30, 2006, p. 30, www.faireconomy.org/reports/2006/ExecutiveExcess2006.pdf. See also *Executive Excess 2005—12th Annual CEO Compensation Survey*, Sarah Anderson, John Cavanagh—Institute for Policy Studies; Scott Klinger, Liz Stanton—*United for Peace and Justice*, August 30, 2005, p. 1, http://www.faireconomy.org/press/2005/EE2005.pdf. In 2004 the CEO-to-worker pay ratio reached 431:1.
7. *Executive Excess—12th Annual Survey*, ibid., 20.
8. *Executive Excess—13th Annual Survey*, op. cit, 5–6, 10–11. Defense contractors enjoyed average pay levels that are double the amounts they received during the four years leading up to 9/11. Their average compensation jumped from $3.6 million during the pre-9/11 period of 1998–2001 to $7.2 million during the post-9/11 period of 2002–2005.
9. Catherine Elsworth, "Artist Wins Battle over Nude Barbie," *Telegraph*, June 28, 2004.
10. The original quote is said to be from Act 1, Scene 1 of Hanns Johst's play, *Schlageter*, which was performed in 1933 for Adolf Hitler's birthday. The original line was: "Wenn ich Kultur höre...entsichere ich meinen Browning!" ("When I hear 'culture,' I release the safety catch on my Browning!")
11. Contemporary Art Evening Auction, Sotheby's, May 10, 2006, www.thecityreview.com/s06con1.html. See also " Sotheby's Sale of Contemporary Art Brings $128,752,000," ArtKnowledgeNews.com.
12. Matthew J. Salganik, Peter Sheridan Dodds, and Duncan J. Watts, "Experimental Study of Inequality and Unpredictability in an Artificial

Cultural Market," *Science* 311, no. 5762, February 10, 2006, 854–856, www.sciencemag.org/cgi/content/short/311/5762/854.

13. "Sensation," David Cohen, artnet.com, October 24, 1997, http://www .artcritical.com/dc'sdozen/sensation.htm.

14. "The Picture of Health?" *Times Online*, November 27, 2005, http://www .entertainment.timesonline.co.uk/tol/arts_and_entertainment/article596620 .ece.

15. Brian Appel, "New York Auctions, Spring 2006," ArtCritical.com, July 2006, http://www.artcritical.com/appel/BASpring2006.htm.

16. David Barboza, "The Emperor Is Butt Naked," *New York Times* News Service, Shanghai, China, May 11, 2006.

17. Ibid.

18. Andrew Fabricant, cited in "The Art Market—Going, Going Up," *Economist*, January 11, 2007. See also Deborah Brewster, "Moving to Embrace the Modern," *Financial Times*, May 16, 2005; Deepak Gopinath, "Fund Plays Percentages in Buying Works of Art," *International Herald Tribune*, January 27, 2006, and *Opalesque Research*, Issue 01, January 16, 2007, http://www .opalesque.com/ASQUARE/ASQUARE16Jan2007.pdf. In the bubble period of 1985–1989, the contemporary index rose even faster, by 41 percent a year, only to fall by 60 percent over the next five years when the bubble collapsed. The price of Renoirs and Monets fell by 35 percent after 1990.

19. Art Market Watch, November 3, 2006, artnet.com.

20. Desmond Morris, *The Naked Ape* (New York: Bantam, 1967), Introduction, 9. "There are one hundred and ninety-three living species of monkeys and apes. One hundred and ninety-two of them are covered with hair. The exception is a naked ape self-named Homo sapiens. This unusual and highly successful species spends a great deal of time examining his higher motives and an equal amount of time studiously ignoring his fundamental ones. He is proud that he has the biggest brain of all the primates, but attempts to conceal the fact that he also has the biggest penis, preferring to accord this honor falsely to the mighty gorilla."

21. Malcolm Gladwell, *Blink* (New York: Little, Brown, 2005), 86, 88.

22. Johann H. G. van der Dennen, "Ritualized 'Primitive' Warfare and Rituals in War: Phenocopy, Homology, or . . . ?," University of Groningen Faculty of Law, April 4, 2005, http://irs.ub.rug.nl/ppn/280499396.

CHAPTER 3: THE TRANSIT OF VENUS

1. Footage obtained by a team from the American NBC network, November 16, 2004.

2. H. D. S. Greenway, "Hostility Grows over U.S. Stance," *Boston Globe*, January 30, 2004.

3. Jim Garamone, "JCS Chairman: U.S. Troops Fight for American Ideas, Ideals" *AFPS*, August 24, 2005. See also President Bush's Address to the Nation, September 11, 2006.

4. Michael Sivak and Michael Flannagan, "Flying and Driving after the September 11 Attacks," *American Scientist* 91, no. 1 (January–February 2003), 6–9.

5. John McCain and Marshall Salter, *Why Courage Matters: The Way to a Braver Life* (New York: Random House, 2004).

6. Leif Wenar, cited in John Mueller, "Simplicity and Spook: Terrorism and the Dynamics of Threat Exaggeration," *International Studies Perspectives* 6, no. 2 (2005), 221.

7. Interview with General Richard Myers, CNN, aired November 11, 2000.

8. "CEOs More Likely to Rely on Intuition Than Metrics When Making Business Decisions," *Business Wire*, November 6, 2006.

9. Dani Rodrik and Romain Wacziarg, "Do Democratic Transitions Produce Bad Economic Outcomes?," *American Economic Review Papers and Proceedings* 95, no. 2 (May 2005): 50–55. Table at p. 53, www.stanford.edu/~wacziarg/downloads/democratictransitions.pdf. Cited in Daniel Altman, "Politics as Growth Stimulant," *International Herald Tribune*, January 8, 2005.

10. James Bartholomew, *The Welfare State We're In* (London: Methuen, 2006).

11. "Sleep on It, Decision-Makers Told," *BBC News*, February 17, 2006.

12. Jonathan Haidt, "The Emotional Dog and Its Rational Tail: A Social Intuitionist Approach to Moral Judgment," University of Virginia, October 31, 2000.

CHAPTER 4: THE DEVIL MADE THEM DO IT

1. Karen McVeigh, "Chef to Stars Unmasked as a Sex-Obsessed Bully," *Times*, March 30, 2006, http://business.timesonline.co.uk/tol/business/law/public/article699091.ece.

2. *Le Monde Diplomatique*, January 10, 2002.

3. See Ronald Hutton, *Triumph of the Moon: A History of Modern Pagan Witchcraft* (Oxford: Oxford University Press, 1999). Scholars seem to have come to the opinion that the worst of the witch hunts began around 1450 and continued until the mid-eighteenth century. See Lila Rajiva, "Satan and Sex Manias," Peace and Earth Justice web site, January 24, 2007, from which this section draws.

4. Norman Cohn, *Europe's Inner Demons: The Demonization of Christians in Medieval Christianity* (Chicago: University of Chicago Press, 2001).

5. Elaine Pagels, *The Origin of Satan* (New York: Vintage, 1996).

6. Ben-Yehuda, "The European Witch Craze of the 14th to 17th Centuries: A Sociologist's Perspective," *American Journal of Sociology* 86, no. 1 (July 1980): 15, 23.

7. Robin Briggs, *Witches and Neighbours: The Social and Cultural Context of European Witchcraft* (New York: Viking, 1996). Briggs shows that accusations of witchcraft drew on familial tensions, exacerbated by war and food shortages, as well as the presence in communities of single older women living on their own.

8. This was argued by writers like Pennethorne Hughes in her *Witchcraft* (London: Penguin, 1970). See also Ronald Hutton, *Triumph of the Moon*, chapter 18, 340–368, for his account of feminist histories of witchcraft. She uses the frequently cited figure—now considered erroneous—of a genocide of nine million women.

9. Charles Mackay, *Extraordinary Popular Delusions and the Madness of Crowds*, vol. 2, (Hertfordshire: Wordsworth Editions Ltd., 1995), 536–538.

10. Jenny Gibbons, "Recent Developments in the Study of the Great European Witch Hunt," *Virtual Pomegranate*, issue 5, Lammas, 1998.

11. Quoted in Steven Katz, *The Holocaust in Historical Context*, vol. 1, *The Holocaust and Mass Death before the Modern Age* (New York: Oxford University Press, 1994), 438–439.

12. For a description of how misogyny really played into the trials, see Katz, *Holocaust*, 435.

13. Carlo Ginzburg, *Ecstasies: Deciphering the Witches' Sabbat* (New York: Random House, 1993).

14. Robert B. Cialdini, *Influence: The Psychology of Persuasion* (New York: William Morrow, 1984), 2.

15. Ibid., 3.

16. Details about the case are taken in large part from Debbie Nathan, "The Ritual Sex Abuse Hoax," *Village Voice*, January 12, 1990.

17. Kyle Zirpolo, as told to Debbie Nathan, "'I'm Sorry': A Long-Delayed Apology from One of the Accusers in the Notorious McMartin Pre-School Molestation Case," *Los Angeles Times*, October 30, 2005.

18. Alexander Cockburn, "Out of the Mouths of Babes: Child Abuse and the Abuse of Adults," *Nation* 250, no. 6, February 12, 1990, 190.

19. Paul Craig Roberts, "How a Mantra Ate Justice," *Washington Times*, November 7, 2002.

20. Cockburn, "Out of the Mouths of Babes."

21. Ibid.

22. Rael Jean Isaac, "Janet Reno and Her Record as a So-Called Champion of Children," *Manchester Union Leader*, April 27, 2000.

23. See Alexander Cockburn, "Janet Reno's Coerced Confession," *Nation*, March 8, 1993.

24. Dr. Shawn Carlson et al., *Satanism in America: Final Report for the Committee for Scientific Examination of Religion (CSER)*, December 1989. Between 1983 and 1988 there were one million violent crimes committed in the United States. The three-year 200-page report principally written by Berkeley physicist Carlson states that, according to police, only about 60 of these have involved satanism.

25. David Alexander, "Giving the Devil More Than His Due," *Humanist*, March–April 1990.

26. Richard N. Ostling, "No Sympathy for the Devil: A Cardinal Decries Satanic Influence," *Time*, March 19, 1990. See also Anson Shupe, "Pitchmen of the Satan Scare," *Wall Street Journal*, March 9, 1990.

27. Alexander, "Giving the Devil."

CHAPTER 5: WORDS OF WAR

1. "Atlanta Named Top Asthma Capital for 2007," *Medical News Today*, April 27, 2007.

2. Michael Schrage, "Use Every Article in the Arsenal," *Washington Post*, January 15, 2006. See Lila Rajiva, "Riding the Tale of the Elephant," *Dissident Voice*, January 24, 2006, on which this chapter is based.

3. "*WSJ* Reporter Fassihi's Email to Friends," *Poynter Online*, September 29, 2004.

4. Howard Kurtz, "Jeff Gannon Admits Past 'Mistakes,' Berates Critics," *Washington Post*, February 19, 2005, C01.

5. James Bamford, "The Man Who Sold the War," *Rolling Stone*, November 17, 2005.

6. Ibid.

7. Ibid.

8. Kevin Zeese, "The Best War Ever—Interview with Sheldon Rampton," *Counterpunch*, September 1, 2006.

9. Thomas Fleming, *The Illusion of Victory: America in World War I* (New York: Basic Books, 2003), 45.

10. Ibid., 43–48. This story was taken up eagerly by the Belgians themselves, since it seemed to excuse them for having done this very thing to thousands of natives in the Congo.

11. Fleming, *Illusion of Victory*, 52.

CHAPTER 6: WAR AND REMEMBRANCE

1. Statistics cited from Colin Nicholson, *The Longman Companion to the First World War* (Saddle River, NJ: Longman, 2001), 248. See also www.english .emory.edu/LostPoets/Casualties.html.
2. Cecil Woodham-Smith, *The Reason Why* (New York: McGraw-Hill, 1953), 224–226.
3. Theodore Ropp, *War in the Modern World*, rev. ed. (New York: Collier Books, 1962), 222, cited in Stephen Van Evera, "Militarism," MIT, July 2001.
4. *The CIA: World Fact Book*, https://www.cia.gov/library/publications/the-world-factbook/rankorder/2001rank.html (updated June 19, 2007). See also Dr. Marc Faber, "Asia the Place to Invest after a U.S. Financial Crash," *Gloom, Boom and Doom Report*, October 1, 2003, www.ameinfo.com/28859 .html.
5. Willcock, M. M. *The* Iliad *of Homer* (London: Macmillan, 1978), xiii, cited in J. Christoph Amberger, *The Secret History of the Sword: Adventures in Ancient Martial Arts*, (Burbank, CA: Multimedia Books, 1998), 70–71.
6. Marshall, S. L. A., *Men Against Fire* (New York: William Morrow, 1927), as quoted in John Kegan, *The Face of Battle: A Study of Agincourt, Waterloo, and the Somme* (London: Jonathan Cape, 1976; Penguin, 1978), 71.
7. Robert Cialdini, *Influence: The Psychology of Persuasion* (New York: William Morrow, 1984), 18, citing the research of R. E. Leakey and R. Lewin in 1978.
8. Catherine Merridale, *Ivan's War: Life and Death in the Red Army, 1939–1945* (London: Faber & Faber, 2005), 3.
9. Ibid., 4–5.
10. Ibid., 5.
11. Thucydides (ca. 460/455–ca. 399 BCE): *Peloponnesian War*, Book 2.34–46, *Internet Ancient History Sourcebook*, www.fordham.edu/Halsall/ancient/pericles-funeralspeech.html.

CHAPTER 7: EMPIRE OF DELUSION

1. William Shakespeare, *Julius Caesar*, act II, scene ii, lines 23–28 (Oxford Shakespeare, 1914).
2. Deepak Lal, *In Praise of Empires: Globalization and Order* (London: Palgrave Macmillan, 2004), 79.

3. Paul Kennedy, "The Greatest Superpower Ever," *New Perspectives Quarterly* 19, Winter 2002.

4. Thomas L. Friedman, "Sinbad vs. the Mermaids," *New York Times*, October 5, 2005, A27.

5. Ibid.

6. Peter Beaumont, "Abuse Worse Than Under Saddam Says Iraqi Leader," *Observer*, November 27, 2005.

7. Dana Priest, "The CIA Holds Terror Suspects in Secret Prisons," *Washington Post*, November 2, 2005. See also Lila Rajiva, "Hiding Offshore Assets, *Dissident Voice*, November 7, 2006.

8. "Coalition Partners Accused of Abuse," MSNBC, May 28, 2004.

9. Lawrence Korb, "U.S. Military in Europe," *New York Times*, August 2, 2003.

10. "CIA Suffering James Bond Envy," *Reuters*, September 29, 1999. In[intelligence]-Q-It[information technology took its name from the enigmatic "Q" who supplied Ian Fleming's James Bond with lethal gadgets. Using $28 million in funds appropriated by Congress, it was set up as a nonprofit, yet "as in a normal private sector business model" was expected to create "spin-off value" for those working with In-Q-It, who could then take products back to market. CEO Gilman Louie made his name in computer video games; the board of trustees included the chairman of Lockheed Martin and William Perry, former secretary of defense.

11. Ted Gup, "'The Company' Goes Corporate: The CIA's New Business Model Is the World of Commerce," *Slate*, November 4, 2003.

12. Security Affairs Support Association (SASA) Online, officers and board. Contractors like CACI and Titan hire retired intelligence employees, lobby government, and shower key members of Congress with contributions—Tim Shorrock, "The Spy Who Billed Me," *Mother Jones*, January–February 2005.

13. "Buzzy" Krongard, until December 2004 the CIA's third-ranked executive, claims that Osama should be seen "not as a chief executive but more like a venture capitalist"—Tony Allen-Mills, "Let Bin Laden Stay Free, Says CIA Man," *Times Online* (U.K.), January 9, 2005. Krongard was once vice chairman of one of the 20 largest banks in the United States. See also Fran Shorr, "Follow the Money: Bush, 9/11, and Deep Threat," *Common Dreams*, May 22, 2002, and Tim Shorrock, "The Spy Who Billed Me," *Mother Jones*, January–February 2005.

14. Zbigniew Brzezinski, "George W. Bush's Suicidal State-Craft," *International Herald Tribune*, October 13, 2005.

15. Patrick Cockburn, "Iraq: The State We're In," *Independent*, October 14, 2005.

CHAPTER 8: HEROES OF THE REVOLUTION

1. David Howden, "In the Footsteps of Che Guevara: Democracy in South America," *The Independent*, December 16, 2005.
2. Humberto Fontova, "Che at the Oscars," *LewRockwell.com*, April 2, 2005. Also, Fontova, "Che Guevara: Assassin and Bumbler," *News Max*, February 23, 2004.
3. Jon Lee Anderson, *Che Guevara: A Revolutionary Life* (New York: Grove Press, 1998), 773.
4. Cited in Fontova, "Che Guevara: Assassin and Bumbler."
5. Ibid.
6. Humberto Fontova, *Fidel: Hollywood's Favorite Tyrant* (New York: Regnery Publishing, 2005), 84. See also Humberto Fontova, "Castro Is Still Dead," *LewRockwell.com*, August 16, 2006.
7. Fontova, "Castro Is Still Dead."
8. "The North Korean Refugee Crisis: Human Rights and International Response," edited by Stephen Haggard and Marcus Noland, U.S. Committee for Human Rights in North Korea, 2006. Admittedly, this is a U.S. government report.
9. The socialist scholar Samuel Farber in "The Resurrection of Che Guevara," *New Politics*, Summer 1998: "Clearly, Che Guevara played a key role in inaugurating a tradition of arbitrary, non-judicial detentions, and later used the UMAP (Military Units to Aid Production) camps for the confinement of dissidents and social 'deviants': homosexuals, Jehovah's Witnesses, practitioners of secret Afro-Cuban religions such as Abakua, and non-political rebels. In the 1980s and 1990s this non-judicial forced confinement was also applied to AIDS victims." See also Alvaro Vargas Llosa, "The Killing Machine: Che Guevara, from Communist Firebrand to Capitalist Brand," *New Republic*, July 11, 2005.
10. Fontova, "Che Guevara: Assassin and Bumbler."
11. According to Philip Gavi's biography of Che, cited in Vargas Llosa, "The Killing Machine."
12. Peter Canby, "Poster Boy for the Revolution," *New York Times*, May 18, 1997.
13. Vargas Llosa, "The Killing Machine."
14. Victoria B. Bekiempis, "The Che Paradox," *Capitalism*, October 29, 2006.
15. Vargas Llosa, "The Killing Machine."
16. Joseph R. Stromberg, "Man, Economy, and Che," *LewRockwell.com*, March 13, 2000.
17. Vargas Llosa, "The Killing Machine."

18. Ibid.

19. This is only one of several accounts of their meeting. Another, more colorful, has them meeting at a benefit gala for the earthquake that destroyed the city of San Juan in January 1944. Eva supposedly grabbed the seat next to Perón from a well-known film actress and remained next to him through the night and into the following days.

20. See, for instance, Timothy Geithner, "Lessons from the Crisis in Argentina," International Monetary Fund, October 8, 2003.

21. "Crisis in Argentina: Share Your Experiences," *BBC*, April 30, 2002.

22. Juan Domingo Perón, *Perónist Doctrine*, ed. Perónist Party, Buenos Aires, 1952, cited in *Internet Modern History Sourcebook*, www.fordham.edu/halsall/mod/1950peronism2.html. Further details about Perónism are taken from here.

23. "More Thunder than Blood," *Time*, September 12, 1955.

24. Uki Goni, "Perón Gets a Grand and Final Resting Place," *Guardian*, October 16, 2006.

25. Grant M. Nülle, "Argentina's Paper-Money Mire," *The Mises Institute*, March 16, 2004.

26. Georg Hodel, "Evita, the Swiss & the Nazis," *Consortium News*, January 7, 1999.

27. Alicia Dujovne Ortiz, *Eva Perón: A Biography*, trans. Shawn Fields (New York: St. Martin's Press, 1996), 150.

28. Eugene Robinson, "Eva: A Figure Who Refuses to Die," *Washington Post Foreign Service*, January 1, 1997.

29. Jung Chang and Jon Halliday, *Mao: The Unknown Story* (London: Vintage, 2006).

30. Li Zhi-sui, *The Private Life of Chairman Mao* (New York: Random House, 1996), 107, 133, 221, 642n. Zhi-sui's account of his relationship with Mao has been widely questioned.

31. The demographer Judith Banister in *China's Changing Population* (Stanford University Press, 1987) claims a death toll of about 30 million. See also Joseph Ball, "Did Mao Really Kill Millions in the Great Leap Forward?," *Monthly Review*, September 2006, for an extended criticism of the numbers used by Chang and Halliday.

32. "Marginal notes to Friedrich Paulsen, A System of Ethics," Mao Zedong zaoqi wengao (Early manuscripts of Mao Zedong), CCP Archive Study Office and CCP Hunan Committee, eds. (Changsha: Hunan chubanshe, 1990), 116–275, cited in Steven W. Mosher, "Left-Wing Monster: Mao Zedong," *Front Page*, December 6, 2005.

33. Chang and Halliday, *Mao*, 544.

34. Ibid., 13.

35. Ibid., 494.

36. Ibid., 454.

37. Jasper Becker, *Hungry Ghosts: Mao's Secret Famine* (New York: Henry Holt, 1996).

38. In the introduction to Michele Manceaux, *Les Maos en France* (Paris: Gallimard, 1972).

39. Roderick MacFarquhar and Michael Schoenhals, *Mao's Last Revolution* (Cambridge, MA: Belknap Press of Harvard University Press, 2006).

40. For example, see Li Zhi-sui, *Private Life of Chairman Mao*, 6.

41. Ibid., 99–103, 504–507.

CHAPTER 9: THE NUMBER GAME

1. Robin Dunbar, cited in Malcolm Gladwell, *The Tipping Point* (New York: Little, Brown, 2000), 178–181. See also Lila Rajiva, "Minding the Crowd," *Dissident Voice*, December 30, 2006.

2. Robin Dunbar, "Co-Evolution of Neo-Cortex Size, Group Size and Language in Humans," *Behavioral and Brain Sciences*, 16 (4): 681–735.

3. Steven D. Levitt and Stephen J. Dubner, *Freakonomics: A Rogue Economist Explores the Hidden Side of Everything* (New York: HarperCollins, 2005), 11–12.

4. Gustave Le Bon, *The Crowd: A Study of the Popular Mind* (New York: Dover, 2002).

5. Jeremy Bentham, *The Works of Jeremy Bentham*, vol. 2, *Anarchical Fallacies*, ed. John Bowring (Edinburgh: Simpkin, Marshal Co., 1843), 493.

CHAPTER 10: THE FLAT EARTH SOCIETY

1. Thomas L. Friedman, *The World Is Flat* (New York: Anchor, 2000).

2. Stephen Roach, "Globalization's New Underclass," *Asia Times*, April 26, 2006. See also Roach, "Back to the Drawing Board," *Japan Focus*, July 8, 2005, www.japanfocus.org.

3. As to the ratio of CEO to worker pay, it is around 61:1 and 23:1 in America's neighbors, Mexico and Canada; 36:1 in rival China; 20:1 in Germany; and a mere 11:1 in Japan. But in the United States it is 411:1—Towers Perrin and the Institute for Policy Studies, Rich Clabaugh, cited in Mark Trumbull, "America's CEO Pay May Soon Face Squeeze," *Christian Science Monitor*, January 4, 2007.

4. David H. Autor and Mark G. Duggan, "The Growth in the Social Security Disability Rolls: A Fiscal Crisis Unfolding," *Journal of Economic Perspectives* 20, no. 3, (Summer 2006): 79, http://econ-www.mit.edu/faculty/download_pdf.php?id=1461.

5. David Streitfeld, "The Jobless Count Skips Millions: The Rate Hits 9.7% When the Underemployed and Those Who Have Given Up the Hunt Are Added," *Los Angeles Times*, December 29, 2003.

6. Ibid.

7. Nell Henderson, "Payroll Growth Slows Dramatically in July," *Washington Post*, August 6, 2004. See also "U.S. Unemployment Rate Tops E.U.," www.thinkandask.com/news/jobs.html.

8. Nell Henderson, "Unemployment Rate Falls to 5.7%," *Washington Post*, January 9, 2004.

9. "Augmented Employment Rate," http://bigpicture.typepad.com/ comments/2004/01/augmented_unemp.html. See also Paul Krugman, "So-Called Boom," *New York Times*, December 30, 2003.

10. Thomas L. Friedman, *The Lexus and the Olive Tree* (New York: Anchor, 2000), 102–111. See also Lila Rajiva, "The Incredible Shrinking Lexus," *Dissident Voice*, October 4, 2006.

11. Friedman, *The Lexus and the Olive Tree*, 112–142.

12. K. M. Panikkar, *Asia and Western Dominance: A Survey of the Vasco Da Gama Epoch of Asian History* (London: George Allen & Unwin, 1953), 78–79.

13. Mike Davis, *Late Victorian Holocausts: El Nino, Famines, and the Making of the Third World* (New York: Verso, 2001), 6–7. See also Romesh Dutt, *The Economic History of India in the Victorian Age* (London: Kegan Paul, Trench, and Truber Ltd, 1906).

14. Ibid., 46, 47, 51.

15. Geoffrey Regan, *The Brassey's Book of Military Blunders* (Washington, DC: Brassey's, 2000), 31–34.

16. David McWilliams, *The Pope's Children* (Dublin: Gill & Macmillan, 2005).

17. Ibid.

18. Martin de Vlieghere and Paul Vreymans, "Europe's Ailing Social Model: Facts and Fairy-Tales," *Work for All*, March 23, 2006.

CHAPTER 11: WHAT THE YONGHY-BONGHY-BO DIDN'T KNOW

1. Eileen Maybin and Kevan Bundell, "After the Prawn Rush: The Human and Environmental Costs of Commercial Prawn Farming," Christian Aid, May, 1996, www.christian-aid.org.uk/indepth/9605praw/prawn.htm.

2. Alexander Cockburn, "Message in a Bottle," *The Nation*, April 14, 2005.

3. "Asian Cities and Regions of the Future 2005–06," *fDi*, December 12, 2005, www.fdimagazine.com/news/fullstory.php/aid/1489/ASIAN_CITIES_REGIONS_OF_THE_FUTURE_2005_06.html.

4. "Tamil Nadu Most Preferred Destination for Foreign Investors, Says Jayalalithaa," *Hindu*, February 18, 2006.

5. Methil Renuka with Stephen David and Amarnath K. Menon, "Surging South," *India Today*, May 29, 2000.

6. G. H. Hardy, cited in Gina Kolata, "Remembering a 'Magical Genius,'" *Science* 236 (1987): 1,519.

7. Sebastian Mallaby, "Detroit's Next Big Threat," *Washington Post*, December 15, 2005, A21. Tamil Nadu has won the Deming Prize, awarded for manufacturing excellence by a Japanese committee. Reports say that Chennai's business leaders use Japanese management lingo extensively.

8. P. Sainath, "The Anatomy of a Tiger: India High and Low," *Hindu*, November 12, 2006.

9. Robert Zoellick, "Globalization, Trade and Economic Security," Remarks at the National Press Club, October 1, 2002, www.state.gov/e/eb/rls/rm/2002/14014.htm.

10. Eyal Press, "Rebel with a Cause," *Nation*, May 23, 2002. Of course, Chinese growth has not been without its own problems.

11. According to Richard Blackhurst and Kym Anderson, *GATT Annual Report* (Geneva: GATT, 1991), cited in Jagdish Bhagwati, *In Defense of Globalization* (New York: Oxford University Press, 2004), 138.

12. Bhagwati, *In Defense of Globalization*, 139.

13. Ibid., 153.

14. See Nassim Nicholas Taleb, *Fooled by Randomness: The Hidden Role of Chance in the Markets and in Life* (New York: Thomson Texere, 2001). Taleb's Black Swans are related to but of course not precisely the same as the birds made famous by Scottish philosopher David Hume. "No amount of observations of white swans can allow the inference that all swans are white, but the observation of a single black swan is sufficient to refute that conclusion," wrote Hume in *The Problem of Induction*. The black swan he was talking about was the problem with drawing general conclusions from specific instances of things—what is termed the logical problem of induction. There is also the psychological problem—why do we tend to think (irrationally, in Hume's belief) that the occurrence of repeated instances of a thing means that that pattern will continue? Hume's explanation—seen as unsatisfactory by many—was that we think so simply from habit or custom.

15. Vilfredo Pareto, the economist, was among the first to observe that about 80 percent of the wealth was held by 20 percent of people. Pareto's law of

income distribution is described in his lecture notes, *Cours d'économie politique* (1896, 1897), where he also criticizes the concept of "utility," and argues that human beings do not choose what is rationally best for them, but what they *think* is desirable. That is, they choose their preferences, not their best interests.

16. Steven D. Levitt and Stephen J. Dubner, *Freakonomics: A Rogue Economist Explores the Hidden Side of Everything* (New York: HarperCollins, 2005), 150–152.

17. Daniel Kahneman and Amos Tversky, "Prospect Theory: An Analysis of Decision under Risk," *Econometrica* 47, no. 2 (March 1979): 263–291. See also Peter Bernstein, *Against the Gods: The Remarkable Story of Risk* (New York: John Wiley & Sons, 1996).

18. Malcolm Gladwell, "Blowing Up: How Nassim Taleb Turned the Inevitability of Disaster into an Investment Strategy," *New Yorker*, April 22 & 29, 2002.

19. "Wolfowitz Confirmed at World Bank," *BBC*, March 31, 2005.

20. Joseph Nevins, "Wolfowitz Visited Indonesia for Closer Military Ties, Not Tsunami Relief," *Pacific News Service*, January 19, 2005.

21. Shyam Kamath, "Foreign Aid and India: Financing the Leviathan State," Cato Institute, Policy Analysis no. 170, May 6, 1992, www.cato.org/pubs/pas/pa-170.html.

22. John Templeton, cited in William Proctor, *The Templeton Prizes* (New York: Doubleday, 1983), 72.

23. "What Is India's Per Capita Income?," *Rediff*, October 13, 2005.

24. "World Bank Development Indicators, 2006—The World by Income," http://devdata.worldbank.org/wdi2006/contents/income.htm.

25. Kamath, "Foreign Aid and India."

26. Adam Smith, *An Inquiry into the Nature and Causes of the Wealth of Nations*, 1776, London: Methuen and Co., 1904. Fifth Edition.

27. Kamath, "Foreign Aid and India."

28. Book Review: *Perpetuating Poverty: The World Bank, the IMF, and the Developing World*, ed. Doug Bandow and Ian Vasquez (Cato Institute, 1994), reviewed by Ken S. Ewart, *Freeman* 45, no. 4 (April 1995).

29. B. R. Shenoy, *P.L. 480 Aid and India's Food Problem* (New Delhi: Affiliated East-West Press, 1974), especially Chapter 3, cited in Kamath, "Foreign Aid and India."

30. Amitava Kumar, "On Reading 'Paper,'" *Kenyon Review*, Summer 2002. See also Vandana Shiva, "The Great Grain Robbery," *Znet*, June 21, 2006.

31. World Bank, *Fifth Annual Report (1949–50)* (Washington, DC: World Bank, 1950), 8.

32. Steve Coll, "Budget Axe Endangers India's Socialist Icons: Massive Bureaucracy under Attack," *Washington Post*, February 26, 1991, A-16, cited in Kamath, "Foreign Aid and India."

33. Harriet Rubin, "The Perfect Vision of Dr. V," *FastCompany.com*, issue 43, January 2001, 146. The comments from Dr. V are taken from her article.

CHAPTER 12: FIN DE BUBBLE

1. "In Greenspan We Trust," *Fortune*, March 18, 1996, cover.

2. It was Bob Woodward who called him the "Maestro." See Bob Woodward, *Maestro: Greenspan's Fed and the American Boom* (New York: Simon & Schuster, 2000).

3. Federal Funds Effective Rate, http://www.federalreserve.gov/releases/h15/data/Daily/H15_FF_O.txt.

4. 30-Year Conventional Mortgage Rates, http://www.federalreserve.gov/releases/h15/data/Monthly/H15_MORTG_NA.txt.

5. Hamish Risk, "Derivative Trading Soars to $370 Trillion, BIS Says," *Bloomberg.com*, November 17, 2006, citing the Bank for International Settlements.

6. Interview with Scott Cleland conducted by Hedrick Smith, "The Wall Street Fix," *PBS Frontline*, January 21, 2003.

7. Joshua Cooper Ramo, "The Three Musketeers," *Time*, February 15, 1999.

8. In Japan, credit jumped 130 percent, while disposable income rose just 27 percent. See William Bonner with Addison Wiggin, *Financial Reckoning Day* (Hoboken, NJ: John Wiley & Sons, 2003), 104–105.

9. Alan Greenspan, "Gold and Economic Freedom," in *Capitalism: The Unknown Ideal*, Ayn Rand, ed. (New York: Signet, 1967), 96–101 (reprinted from *The Objectivist*, 1966).

10. "Greenspan Joins a Distinguished Club," *CNN*, August 7, 2002. See also Alan Greenspan, Source Watch, Project of the Center for Media and Democracy, www.sourcewatch.org/ index.php?title=Alan_Greenspan.

11. "Zimbabwe's Inflation Tops 1200%," *BBC*, September 15, 2006.

12. Niall Ferguson, " Debt Nation: Reason to Worry," *New York Times Magazine*, June 11, 2006.

13. Gross Domestic Product, Bureau of Economic Analysis, http://www.bea.gov/national/xls/gdpchg.xls.

14. http://www.federalreserve.gov/releases/h6/hist. From 1970 to 1981 M3 increased from $685 billion to $2.2 trillion. See also N. Shanmughanathan,

"The US Inflation Game," *Hindu Online*, July 21, 2006. The estimate of M3 in 2007 is by financial newsletter writer Adrian Van Eck.

15. McKinsey Global Institute, "Mapping the Global Capital Markets," cited in Joanna Slater, "World Assets Hit Record Value of $140 Trillion," *Wall Street Journal*, January 10, 2007, C8. McKinsey extrapolates to reach a number of $213 trillion by 2010. Between 1993 and 2003, the total value of world financial assets moved up from $53 trillion to $118 trillion, growing annually at 8.3 percent.

16. "The Global Housing Boom," *Economist*, June 16, 2005.

17. Jim Webb, "Class Struggle—American Workers Have a Chance to Be Heard," *Opinion Journal*, November 15, 2006, and Alan Reynolds, "The Top 1% ... of What?" *Opinion Journal*, December 17, 2006. See also Paul Krugman, "The Great Wealth Transfer," *Rolling Stone*, November 30, 2006. In 2003 CEOs made 185 times as much as their workers; in 2005, more than 300 times as much as their workers.

18. Elise Gould, "Young College Grads Face Weak Labor Market," *Counterpunch*, May 25, 2006 (uses figures from the Bureau of Labor Statistics) and Webb, "Class Struggle."

19. Max Fraad Wolff, "Hard US Lessons, Harder Landings," *Asia Times*, November 21, 2006.

20. Based on figures supplied by the *Federal Reserve Flow of Funds Report*, December 7, 2006, 102–106, www.federalreserve.gov/releases/z1/current/z1r-5.pdf, and calculations by blogger Calculated Risk, November 4, 2006, http://calculatedrisk.blogspot.com/2006_11_01_archive.html, in response to incorrect numbers used in Damon Darlin, "Mortgage Lesson No. 1: Home Is Not a Piggy Bank," *New York Times*, November 4, 2006, C1. MEW hit a record high annualized rate of $732 billion (8.1 percent of disposable personal income) in the third quarter of 2005. As of the second quarter of 2006, the annualized rate of MEW had slipped to $327 billion (about $156 billion for the first half of 2006). See Paul Kasriel, "Near a Bottom in Housing," *Northern Trust Global Economic Research*, November 3, 2006, http://www.investorinsight.com/otb_va_print.aspx?EditionID=416, and John H. Makin, "The Fed: Pulling on a Rubber Band," *American Enterprise Institute Online*, April 1, 2006.

21. Ferguson, "Debt Nation," 1.

22. Wolff, "Hard US Lessons, Harder Landings."

23. Ferguson, "Debt Nation," 2.

24. Ibid., 3. See also "Report on Foreign Portfolio Holdings of U.S. Securities," Dept. of Treasury, Federal Reserve Bank of New York, May 2007.

CHAPTER 13: THE MILLION-DOLLAR TRAILER

1. Matt Krantz, "Mobile Home Madness: Prices Top $1 Million," *USA Today*, July 5, 2005. One even sold for $2.7 million. Meanwhile, in Malibu in 2005, the average house sold for $4.4 million.
2. "Home for Sale: Over $100 Million," *AP, International Herald Tribune*, October 3, 2006.
3. Chad Abraham, "For Sale: Nation's Most Expensive Home," *Aspen Times*, July 12, 2006.
4. Bureau of Economic Analysis, Average Wage per Job, http://bea.gov/bea/regional/reis/drill.cfm., CA34.
5. Kirsten Downey, "Mortgage-Trapped," *Washington Post*, January 14, 2007, F01. From 2000 through the third quarter of 2006, the share of nontraditional loans rose from 2 percent to more than a third. See also "Breaking New Ground in U.S. Mortgage Lending," *FDIC Summer Outlook, 2006*. In 2001, only 25 percent of all subprimes were of the "stated income" variety. By 2006, loans with limited documentation numbered 40 percent. By 2005, the number of no-money-down mortgages was 32.6 percent. See Lon Witter, "The No Money Down Disaster," *Barron's*, August 21, 2006.
6. Niall Ferguson, "Debt Nation: Reason to Worry," *New York Times Magazine*, June 11, 2006. Numbers cited range from around $1 trillion worth of ARMs readjusting for 2007 to a high figure of $3 trillion worth for the period 2006–2008.
7. *FDIC Summer Outlook, 2006*.
8. Marcia Vickers, "The Bonnie and Clyde of Mortgage Fraud," *Fortune*, November 14, 2006, told the story of the Bonnie and Clyde of mortgage fraud, who did very naughty things—pretending to be who they weren't, borrowing to buy houses at inflated prices, forging documents, stealing identities, and defrauding sellers and lenders alike before making off finally with millions of dollars.
9. David Olinger, "Steal of a Deal," *Denver Post*, October 29, 2006. According to the report, hundreds of houses were sold in what were called "price puffs"—at prices above real market value. The price puffs began modestly—with buyers taking out $6,000 to $12,000 at the time of settlement. But amounts grew, until they were walking away with 30 percent of the purchase price, or amounts over $100,000. By the autumn of 2006 these houses were going into foreclosure at the rate of 1 out of every 13.
10. Bernanke's comments followed the draft of a new set of industry standards in a report entitled "Interagency Guidance on Nontraditional Mortgage Product Risks."

11. John C. Kiley, "Changes in Realty Values in the Nineteenth and Twentieth Centuries," Bulletin of the Business Historical Society 15, no. 3, June 1941, 33–41, cited in *Grant's Interest Rate Observer*, August 11, 2006.

12. George Paulos, "There Goes the Neighborhood," Freebuck.com, May 5, 2004, http://www.freebuck.com/articles/gpaulos/040505gpaulos.htm.

13. Robert J. Shiller, *Irrational Exuberance*, 2nd ed. (Princeton, NJ: Princeton University Press, 2005), cited in "Irrational Exuberance—Again," *CNN Money*, January 25, 2005. Shiller, a Yale professor of economics who won fame for his perfectly timed book on the bubble in the stock market, has been in the forefront in warning about the impact of a housing market crash.

14. "House of Cards," *Economist*, May 29, 2003: "In real terms, price declines of one-third or more are nothing unusual, examples being Australia, Italy, and Spain in the early 1980s. Falls in nominal prices are much more common in big cities. Not only London but Boston, New York, and San Francisco, too, saw prices drop steeply in the early 1990s."

15. "New Home Prices Fall by Largest Amount in More Than 35 Years," *Associated Press*, October 26, 2006.

16. "UBS: 2006 Subprime Loans Doing Badly," *AP*, November 21, 2006, cited in "Big Surge in U.S. Mortgage Delinquencies—Wall Street Journal," *Finfacts Team*, Finfacts Ireland, December 5, 2006. Not only have delinquencies risen faster in 2006 than in earlier years, but 2006 loans have entered the foreclosure process faster.

17. "Fitch, Moody's Change Ratings," *National Mortgage News*, November 11, 2006. In 2006, $437 billion worth of mortgage securities had been issued in the United States. See Saskia Scholtes, Michael Mackenzie, and David Wighton, "U.S. Subprime Loans Face Trouble," *Financial Times*, December 7, 2006.

18. David Streitfeld and Martin Zimmerman, "More Home Owners Going into Default," *Los Angeles Times*, October 19, 2006. Lenders sent out 26,705 default notices, the first step toward a foreclosure, more than twice the number sent out in the same quarter in 2005.

CHAPTER 14: CENTRAL BANK BAMBOOZLE

1. Remarks by Chairman Alan Greenspan, "The Mortgage Market and Consumer Debt," at America's Community Bankers Annual Convention, Washington, DC, October 19, 2004, www.federalreserve.gov/boardDocs/Speeches/2004/20041019.

2. The top five Wall Street firms gave away $36 billion in bonuses in 2006, up by 30 percent, while Goldman Sachs provided its employees with average bonuses of about $400,000. In London, one employee got a bonus of almost $100 million. Guy Adams and Sarah Harris, "The Super Rich: Britain's Billionaires," *Independent*, December 17, 2006. Roger Jenkins is referenced in Helen Dunne, "The P40m Banker," *Business*, January 17, 2007.
3. Andrew Bary, "Rich Man, Poor Man," *Barron's*, February 2007. See also Jeanne Sahadi, "Wealth Gap Widens," *CNN Money*, August 29, 2006.
4. Alan Greenspan, "Gold and Economic Freedom," in *Capitalism: The Unknown Ideal*, Ayn Rand, ed. (New York: Signet, 1967), 96–101 (reprinted from *The Objectivist*, 1966).
5. Ibid.
6. Flow of Funds Accounts of the U.S., Federal Reserve Board, http://www.federalreserve.gov/releases/Z1/current/data.htm.
7. Bill Bonner, "Eat, Drink and Buy Merrily," *American Conservative*, February 13, 2006. See also Arnaud de Borchgrave, "Our Disappearing Dollar," *Pittsburgh Tribune-Review*, December 18, 2004, and Michael Hodges, "Grandfather Economic Report," December 2006.

CHAPTER 15: THE MOTHER OF THE MOTHER OF ALL BUBBLES

1. Hedge funds hold a large part of other types of loan insurance. They account for 32 percent of credit default swap sellers and 28 percent of buyers, up from 15 percent and 16 percent in 2004, according to a British Bankers' Association report, September 2006, cited in Shannon Harrington and John Glover, "Potential for Abuse of Credit-Default Swaps May Lead to Regulation," *Bloomberg News*, October 11, 2006. See also "Looking for Options," *The Economist*, April 15, 2007.
2. Joshua Roebke, "Mr. Feynman Goes to Washington," *seedmagazine.com*, January 27, 2006.
3. Alistair Barr, "Hedge Funds Have Biggest Gains since 2003," *MarketWatch*, January 10, 2007.
4. Sitaraman Shankar, "European Shares Gain 16 Percent in 2006," *Scotsman*, December 29, 2006.
5. Elizabeth Kelleher, "Dow Jones Stock Index Hits Record High, Again," *USINFO*, January 12, 2007.

6. Timothy F. Geithner, "Risk Management Challenges in the U.S. Financial System," Federal Reserve Bank of New York, February 28, 2006, http://www.ny.frb.org/newsevents/speeches/2006/gei060228.html.

7. Robert Schmidt, "FBI Promises Crackdown as Stock Option Cases Increase," *Bloomberg*, September 26, 2006.

8. Katherine Burton and Jenny Strasburg, "Amaranth's $6.6 Billion Slide Began With Trader's Bid to Quit," *Bloomberg*, December 6, 2006. See also "A Fee Frenzy at Hedge Funds," *BusinessWeek*, June 6, 2006.

9. Amanda Cantrell, "Hedge Funds Launch, Close in Record Numbers," *CNN Money*, March 1, 2006. See also Amy Borrus, "Is the Hedge-Fund Party Over?" *BusinessWeek*, August 8, 2005.

10. In January 2006 there were 450 hedge funds focused on energy with a value of $60 billion, according to Alexei Barrionuevo and Simon Romero, "Energy Trading, Without a Certain 'E,'" *New York Times*, January 15, 2006.

11. Patrick Hosking, "Goldman Admits Loss from Amaranth," *Times Online*, September 20, 2006, http://business. timesonline.co.uk/article/0,9063-2366370,00.html. See also Bill Bonner and Lila Rajiva, "Hedge I Win, Fails You Lose," *Daily Reckoning*, September 22, 2006.

12. Steven Mufson, "Hedge-Fund's Collapse Met with a Shrug," *Washington Post*, September 20, 2006, D01.

13. "The Recent Behavior of Financial Market Volatility," BIS Papers, No. 29, Bank for International Settlements, August 2006, p. 2. http://www.bis.org/publ/bppdf/bispap29.pdf.

14. "Ford May Lose Up to $9 Billion This Year," *International Business Times*, September 14, 2006.

15. Cited in "Goldman Sachs Runs Largest Hedge Fund," *Financial Advisor*, June 21, 2006. See Lila Rajiva, "Why It's Time to Sell Goldman," *Money Week*, June 30, 2006. See also Naked Shorts blog, September 25, 2006, http://nakedshorts.typepad.com.

16. "Soft Landing? Many See a Goldilocks Market, While Others See Stagflation Lite," August 18, 2006. Ed Yardeni in an interview with Mark Gongloff, *Wall Street Journal Online*.

17. Anatole Kaletsky, "If You See World Economists Beaming Brightly, No, You're Not Hallucinating," *Times Online*, September 21, 2006.

18. Nina Munk, "Greenwich's Outrageous Fortunes," *Vanity Fair*, July 1, 2006.

19. Ianthe Jeanne Dugan and Anita Raghavan, "The Atlas of New Money," *Wall Street Journal*, December 16, 2006, A1.

20. Prescott Bush, grandfather of George W. Bush and father of George H.W. Bush, also lived there.

21. Dane Hamilton, "Top Hedge-Fund Managers Salaries Ballooned in '06," *Reuters*, April 24, 2007.

22. Paul R. La Monica, "Google CEO, Co-founder Stick with $1 Salary," *CNN Money*, March 5, 2007.
23. Simon Nixon, "Can the New Breed of Hedge Fund Managers Be Trusted," *Money Week*, November 24, 2006.
24. Russ Alan Prince (Prince & Associates), "Fortune's Fortress: A Primer on Wealth Preservation for Hedge Fund Professionals," cited in "The Spending Habit of Hedgies," *New York Times*, November 9, 2006.
25. Simon Mills, "Blowing the Bonus," *Sunday Times*, January 7, 2007.
26. Adam Shell, "$363M Is Average Pay for Top Hedge Fund Managers," *USA Today*, May 26, 2006.
27. Landon Thomas Jr., "For $500 Million Payday, Forget Wall St.," *New York Times*, February 2, 2006. See also Robert Gavin, "Good Deal: Average Goldman Sachs Employee Makes $622,000," *Boston Globe*, December 12, 2006.
28. Kathy Chu, "Retirees Up Against Debt," *USA Today*, January 22, 2007.
29. Martin Hutchinson, "Lady Bountiful's Ill-Gotten Gains," The Bear's Lair, *PrudentBear.com*, January 21, 2007.

CHAPTER 16: HOW NOT TO BE CHUMPED BY WALL STREET

1. "Luxury or Necessity," Pew Research Center, December 14, 2006.
2. Jules Henri Poincaré, *Science et Methode*, 1908.
3. "Got $2,200? In This World, You're Rich," *MarketWatch*, December 13, 2006, citing a UN study by the World Institute for Development Economics Research.
4. Felix Dennis, "If You Want to Be Rich, First Stop Being So Frightened," *Sunday Times*, July 30, 2006.
5. Joanna Slater, "World's Assets Hit Record Value of $140 Trillion," *Wall Street Journal*, January 10, 2007, C8.
6. Laurence J. Kotlikoff, "Is the United States Bankrupt?" *Federal Reserve Bank of St. Louis Review* 88, no. 4 (July/August 2006), 235–249.
7. Michael Lewis, "Stocks: Coach Class of Capitalism," *Bloomberg*, December 11, 2006.
8. "Zurich, Geneva Have Highest Quality of Living," *Bloomberg*, April 10, 2006. See also 2007 Worldwide Cost of Living Survey (WCOL) of the Economist Intelligence Unit.
9. Jeremy Grantham, 1st Quarter letter to investors, GMO, April 2007.

10. Leuthold Group, "The Market's Average Total Return over 10 Year Periods," *Money*, November 1999, 108, www.secinfo.com/dstVy.54b.htm.

11. Food Outlook—No. 2, December 2006, Economic and Social Department, Food and Agriculture Organization of the United Nations, http://www.fao.org/docrep/009/j8126e/j8126e02.htm.

12. Richard Teitelbaum, "Merrill Lynch Leads as Hedge Funds Drive a Resurgence in Wall Street Research," *Bloomberg Markets*, November 2006.

13. We are not providing the names for these companies, because circumstances are likely to change significantly between the writing of this book and your reading it. For up-to-date investment ideas, please feel free to go to our web site at DailyReckoning.com.

CHAPTER 17: THE DUPE OF HEARTS

1. James Surowiecki, *The Wisdom of Crowds* (New York: Doubleday, 2004).

2. "What Des-Cartes did was a good step. You have added much several ways, & especially in taking ye colours of thin plates into philosophical consideration. If I have seen further it is by *standing on ye shoulders of Giants*," Isaac Newton, February 5, 1676. He used his famous phrase in a letter to a rival, Robert Hooke, who was a dwarf.

3. Philip Tetlock, *Expert Political Judgment: How Good Is It? How Can We Know?* (Princeton, NJ: Princeton University Press, 2005). See also the review of the book (Louis Menand, "Everybody's an Expert," *New Yorker*, December 5, 2005): Rats were put in a T-shaped maze, with food placed in either the left or the right transept of the T in a random sequence. Over the long run, the food was in the left transept more often. Neither the students nor (needless to say) the rats were told these frequencies. The students were asked to predict on which side of the T the food would appear each time. The rats ended up doing better than the students—who were at Yale.

4. Tetlock, *Expert Political Judgment.*

5. Giambattista Vico, *On the Most Ancient Wisdom of the Italians*, translated, L. M. Palmer (Ithaca and London: Cornell University Press, 1988), Chapter One, II, 52. See also Lila Rajiva, "Minding the Crowd," *Dissident Voice*, December 30, 2006.

6. Thomas Goddard Bergin and Max Harold Fisch, *The New Science of Giambattista Vico*, translation of the third edition (Ithaca and London: Cornell University Press, 1948), Conclusion of the Work, 1106, 424.

7. "The Global Gusher," *Economist*, January 4, 2007.

INDEX